ReFocus: The Literary Films of Richard Brooks

ReFocus: The American Directors Series

Series Editors: Gary D. Rhodes, Robert Singer, and Frances Smith

Editorial Board: Kelly Basilio, Donna Campbell, Claire Perkins, Christopher Sharrett, and Yannis Tzioumakis

*ReFocus* is a series of contemporary methodological and theoretical approaches to the interdisciplinary analyses and interpretations of neglected American directors, from the once-famous to the ignored, in direct relationship to American culture—its myths, values, and historical precepts.

Titles in the series include:

*Preston Sturges* Edited by Jeff Jaeckle and Sarah Kozloff

*Delmer Daves* Edited by Matthew Carter and Andrew Nelson

*Amy Heckerling* Edited by Frances Smith and Timothy Shary

*Budd Boetticher* Edited by Gary D. Rhodes and Robert Singer

*Kelly Reichardt* By E. Dawn Hall

*William Castle* Edited by Murray Leeder

*Barbara Kopple* Edited by Jeff Jaeckle and Susan Ryan

*Elaine May* Edited by Alexandra Heller-Nicholas and Dean Brandum

*Spike Jonze* Edited by Kim Wilkins and Wyatt Moss-Wellington

*Paul Schrader* Edited by Michelle E. Moore and Brian Brems

*John Hughes* Edited by Timothy Shary and Frances Smith

*Doris Wishman* Edited by Alicia Kozma and Finley Freibert

*Albert Brooks* Edited by Christian B. Long

*William Friedkin* By Steve Choe

*Robert Altman* Edited by Lisa Dombrowski and Justin Wyatt

*Mary Harron* Edited by Kyle Barrett

*Wallace Fox* Edited by Gary D. Rhodes and Joanna Hearne

*Richard Linklater* Edited by Kim Wilkins and Timotheus Vermeulen

*Roberta Findlay* Edited by Peter Alilunas and Whitney Strub

*Richard Brooks* Edited by R. Barton Palmer and Homer B. Pettey

edinburghuniversitypress.com/series/refoc

# ReFocus:
# The Literary Films of Richard Brooks

Edited by R. Barton Palmer and Homer B. Pettey

University Press

Edinburgh University Press is one of the leading university presses in the UK. We publish academic books and journals in our selected subject areas across the humanities and social sciences, combining cutting-edge scholarship with high editorial and production values to produce academic works of lasting importance. For more information visit our website: edinburghuniversitypress.com

© editorial matter and organization Barton Palmer and Homer B. Pettey, 2023, 2024
© the chapters their several authors, 2023, 2024

Edinburgh University Press Ltd
13 Infirmary Street
Edinburgh EH1 1LT

First published in hardback by Edinburgh University Press 2023

Typeset in 11/13 Ehrhardt MT by
IDSUK (DataConnection) Ltd

A CIP record for this book is available from the British Library

ISBN 978 1 4744 9657 5 (hardback)
ISBN 978 1 4744 9658 2 (paperback)
ISBN 978 1 4744 9659 9 (webready PDF)
ISBN 978 1 4744 9660 5 (epub)

The right of Barton Palmer and Homer B. Pettey to be identified as editors of his work has been asserted in accordance with the Copyright, Designs and Patent Act 1988, and the Copyright and Related Rights Regulations 2003 (SI No. 2498).

# Contents

| | | |
|---|---|---|
| List of Figures | | vii |
| Notes on Contributors | | ix |
| Acknowledgments | | xii |
| 1 | Introduction | 1 |
| | R. Barton Palmer and Homer B. Pettey | |
| 2 | *The Brick Foxhole* (1945): Richard Brooks's American Vision | 14 |
| | Matthew H. Bernstein | |
| 3 | The Muted Voices of Conscience and Responsibility in *Crisis* (1950) | 31 |
| | Alan Woolfolk | |
| 4 | *Deadline—U.S.A.* (1952): A Fox Film of Fact | 44 |
| | R. Barton Palmer | |
| 5 | "Man Against the Times": Conformity, Anti-Statism, and the "Unknown" Korean War in *Battle Circus* (1953) | 63 |
| | Ian Scott | |
| 6 | Captured Interiors: Female Performances in *The Last Time I Saw Paris* (1954) and *The Happy Ending* (1969) | 75 |
| | Daniel Varndell | |
| 7 | *Blackboard Jungle* (1955): A Cinematic Education | 90 |
| | Steven Rybin | |
| 8 | Hunting and the Economics of Adaptation: *The Last Hunt* (1956) and *The Professionals* (1966) | 107 |
| | Homer B. Pettey | |
| 9 | The Curse of Money: Negotiating Marriage in *The Catered Affair* (1956) | 123 |
| | Elisabeth Bronfen | |

| | |
|---|---|
| 10  Adapting Modernism: Richard Brooks and<br>*The Brothers Karamazov* (1958)<br>*Douglas McFarland* | 138 |
| 11  Haunted: *Cat on a Hot Tin Roof* (1958)<br>*David Sterritt* | 152 |
| 12  A Bite of Salvation<br>*Murray Pomerance* | 166 |
| 13  "Monstrous Cinemascope": Richard Brooks Adapts<br>*Sweet Bird of Youth* (1962)<br>*William H. Epstein* | 183 |
| 14  Adapting the Unadaptables: *Lord Jim* (1965)<br>*Thomas Leitch* | 200 |
| 15  Adaptation as Mutation: *In Cold Blood* (1967)<br>*Jennifer L. Jenkins* | 215 |
| 16  Looking for Mr. Good Guy: Anatomizing '70s Fracture and<br>Fragmentation<br>*Julie Grossman* | 231 |
| 17  Failing to Locate *Wrong is Right* (1982) and What that Reveals<br>about Cinematic Reality<br>*Allen H. Redmon* | 246 |
| Bibliography | 261 |
| Index | 272 |

# Figures

| | | |
|---|---|---|
| 1.1 | First appearance of self-satisfied, self-indulgent deviant gangster Johnny Rocco | 8 |
| 2.1 | Robert Mitchum fully embodies Brooks's concept of the worldly-wise, sarcastic, but compassionate Sergeant Peter Keeley | 22 |
| 2.2 | Leroy does not want to be involved in the Samuels murder case | 23 |
| 3.1 | Neurosurgeon Eugene Ferguson meets dictator Raoul Farrago | 34 |
| 3.2 | The death of Gonzales | 40 |
| 4.1 | Frank Costello and Martin Gabel as Tomas Rienzi | 50 |
| 4.2 | Brooks emphasizes the editor's passionate control of the production of the newspaper | 55 |
| 4.3 | Hutchens passionately defends the freedom of the press in court | 57 |
| 5.1 | Major Webbe carries Ruth McCara to safety during an air attack | 67 |
| 6.1 | Wistfully, Charles Wills stares at a mural of a woman standing in a fountain | 80 |
| 7.1 | Dadier framed from behind as he tries to control the class | 96 |
| 7.2 | Dadier projecting an animated "Jack and the Beanstalk" to his class | 100 |
| 7.3 | Dadier confronts Miller on the staircase | 104 |
| 8.1 | The professionals ride off at the end | 111 |
| 8.2 | Charlie frozen to death within the newly killed buffalo's hide | 112 |
| 9.1 | Aggie's quiet desperation | 126 |
| 9.2 | Aggie's laughter of reconciliation | 136 |
| 10.1 | Opening credits image of Rouault-like stained glass of the Karamazovs | 141 |
| 11.1 | Brick confronting Big Daddy among the capitalistic and athletic trophies of their pasts | 155 |

| | | |
|---|---|---|
| 11.2 | Elizabeth Taylor, seductive and voluptuous as Maggie | 160 |
| 12.1 | Elmer Gantry amuses Sister Sharon Falconer at their first meeting on a train | 167 |
| 13.1 | Alexandra Del Lago's monstrous close-up | 185 |
| 13.2 | Boss Finley in Miss Lucy's room before a television playing a scene of violence | 189 |
| 14.1 | Jim agonizes over the decision that will haunt him for the rest of his life | 201 |
| 14.2 | At the most suspenseful moment in the attack on the General's stockade, Dain Waris and The Girl find Jim looking away from them into the distance | 206 |
| 15.1 | Dick Hickock being led by up the courthouse steps | 225 |
| 15.2 | Rain shadows from the cell window produce tear images on Perry's face moments before he is removed to face execution | 227 |
| 16.1 | Diane Keaton, luminously shot while Brooks also opts for a documentary style in the film's opening sequence | 232 |
| 16.2 | Diane Keaton and Richard Gere playfully discuss Mario Puzo's *The Godfather* and Coppola's film adaptation | 237 |
| 16.3 | Laura Parker and Theresa Dunn, radiant embodiments of traumatized female characters | 240 |
| 17.1 | Mallory on the phone congratulating the newly re-elected President Lockwood | 249 |
| 17.2 | Vice President Ford responding to the political dilemma with her party face | 257 |

# Notes on Contributors

**Matthew H. Bernstein** is Goodrich C. White Professor of Film and Media Studies at Emory University. He wrote *Walter Wanger, Hollywood Independent* (2000) and *Screening A Lynching: The Leo Frank Case on Film and TV* (2009), many articles, and is editor or co-editor of four anthologies on Hollywood history.

**Elisabeth Bronfen** is full professor at the English Department, University of Zürich and Global Distinguished Professor at New York University. She has published widely in the area of visual culture, film, and television: *Home in Hollywood. The Imaginary Geography of Cinema* (2004), *Specters of War. Hollywood's Engagement with Military Conflict* (2012), *Mad Men, Death and the American Dream* (2016). She is also the author of *Obsessed. The Cultural Critic's Life in the Kitchen* (2019).

**William H. Epstein**, Professor Emeritus of English, University of Arizona, has published four books and numerous articles on British and American literature, literary theory, the study of biography, and film criticism, most recently (with R. Barton Palmer) *Invented Lives, Imagined Communities: The Biopic and American National Identity* (2016).

**Julie Grossman**, professor of English and Communication and Film Studies at Le Moyne College, U.S.A., is author of *Rethinking the Femme Fatale in Film Noir: Ready for Her Close-Up* (2009), *Literature, Film, and Their Hideous Progeny: Adaptation and ElasTEXTity* (2015), and *The Femme Fatale* (2020). She is co-author (with Therese Grisham) of *Ida Lupino, Director: Her Art and Resilience in Times of Transition* (2017) and co-author (with Will Scheibel) of *Twin Peaks* (2020). She is founding co-editor (with R. Barton Palmer) of the book series *Adaptation and Visual Culture* and, with R. Barton Palmer, co-editor of the essay collection *Adaptation in Visual Culture: Images, Texts, and Their Multiple Worlds* (2017).

**Jennifer L. Jenkins** is Professor of Literature, Film, and Archival Studies at the University of Arizona. Her recent work focuses on the history of nontheatrical film and archiving the ephemeral in the U.S. Southwest and northern Mexico. She directs the NEH-funded Tribesourcingfilm.com project for cultural reclamation of midcentury educational films about Native Americans.

**Thomas Leitch** is Professor of English at the University of Delaware. His most recent books are *The Oxford Handbook of Adaptation Studies* (2017) and *The History of American Literature on Film* (2019).

**Douglas McFarland** is a retired Professor of English and Classical Studies at Flagler College, St. Augustine, Florida, where he taught Renaissance literature, Latin, and Greek. He has published on sixteenth-century English and French literature, as well as numerous articles and chapters on film. He is the co-editor of *John Huston as Adaptor* (2017) and *Patricia Highsmith on Screen* (2018).

**R. Barton Palmer** is Calhoun Lemon Professor of Literature Emeritus at Clemson University. He is the author or editor of more than fifty scholarly volumes and has published widely in the fields of film studies and adaptation studies.

**Homer B. Pettey** is Professor Emeritus of Film and Comparative Literature at the University of Arizona. With R. Barton Palmer, he co-edited *Film Noir* and *International Noir* (both Edinburgh University Press, 2014), and *Hitchcock's Moral Gaze* (2017), *Britannia! The Biopics and British National Identity* (2018), and *French Literature on Screen* (2019). He has also edited a collection on *Cold War Film Genres* (Edinburgh University Press, 2018) and a collection on *The Films of Costa-Gavras—New Perspectives*, and has written *Mind Reeling—Psychopathology on Film* (2020).

**Murray Pomerance** is an independent scholar living in Toronto, and Adjunct Professor in the School of Media and Communication at RMIT University, Melbourne. He is the author of *Uncanny Cinema: Agonies of the Viewing Experience* (forthcoming 2022), *A Voyage with Hitchcock* (2021), *The Film Cheat: Screen Artifice and Viewing Pleasure* (2020), *Grammatical Dreams* (2020), *Virtuoso: Film Performance and the Actor's Magic* (2019), *A Dream of Hitchcock* (2019), and *Cinema, If You Please: The Memory of Taste, the Taste of Memory* (Edinburgh University Press, 2018), among other books. *A Silence from Hitchcock* is forthcoming early in 2023. He edits the "Horizons of Cinema" series and the "Techniques of the Moving Image" series, and with Lester D. Friedman and Adrienne L. McLean respectively, the "Screen Decades" and "Star Decades" series.

**Allen H. Redmon** is Professor of English and Film Studies in the Department of Humanities at Texas A&M University-Central Texas. He is the author of *Rewatching on the Point of the Cinematic Index* (2022) and *Constructing the Coens: from* Blood Simple *to* Inside Llewyn Davis (2015) and editor of *Next Generation Adaptation: Spectatorship and Process* (2021) with the University Press of Mississippi. He currently serves as the President of the Literature/Film Association and on the Executive Committee for the Adaptation Forum at the Modern Language Association.

**Steven Rybin** is associate professor of film studies and co-director of the Film and Media Studies program at Minnesota State University, Mankato. He is the author of *Geraldine Chaplin: The Gift of Film Performance* (Edinburgh University Press, 2020) and *Gestures of Love: Romancing Performance in Classical Hollywood Cinema* (2017), among other books and edited volumes.

**Ian Scott** is Professor of American Film and History at the University of Manchester. He is the author of several books on American political and historical movies including *American Politics in Hollywood Film* (2nd edn, 2011) and *Robert Riskin: The Life and Times of a Hollywood Screenwriter* (2021) as well as numerous articles and reviews. He also works in TV and radio documentary having collaborated on the 2015 ARTE/PBS film, *Projections of America* which won numerous awards. His BBC Radio 4 series, *The Californian Century*, narrated by Stanley Tucci, was nominated for the Broadcasting Press Guild Radio Programme of the Year award in 2021. He is currently working on a new book about director James Mangold and he contributes regularly to the longstanding American film magazine, *Cineaste*, as well as featuring in *BBC World Histories* magazine and the *Daily Beast* online.

**David Sterritt** is editor of *Quarterly Review of Film and Video*, film professor at the Maryland Institute College of Art, and author/editor of fifteen books. As film critic of *The Christian Science Monitor* he chaired both the New York Film Critics Circle and the National Society of Film Critics.

**Daniel Varndell** is a senior lecturer in English Literature at the University of Winchester, U.K. He is the author of *Hollywood Remakes, Deleuze and the Grandfather Paradox* (Edinburgh University Press, 2014), as well as publications on subjects including *Shane*, and nostalgia and autism. His new monograph looks at etiquette and torture in film performance.

**Alan Woolfolk** is Vice President of Academic Affairs and Dean of the Faculty at Flagler College in St. Augustine, Florida. He is a social and political theorist who has published extensively on contemporary culture, public intellectuals, film, and religion. He has twice been a National Endowment for the Humanities Fellow and is currently completing a book entitled *Dark Charisma: Agency, Authenticity, and the Alien Cosmos in Noir*.

# Acknowledgments

Homer B. Pettey would like to thank this collection's contributors for their profound and clear insights into the literary cinema of Richard Brooks. He would also like to acknowledge long-term friendships with industry professionals Carter Burwell and Chip Johannessen, sharing with him perpetual membership in the *Harvard Lampoon*, that fine American institution. As always, he remains so very grateful for having Jennifer's intimate love, care, and kindness and Anastasia's warmth in his life, since they make him better each day.

CHAPTER I

# Introduction

R. Barton Palmer and Homer B. Pettey

A committed intellectual with a strong streak of independence, Richard Brooks acceded to the director's chair after spending a number of years as a screenwriter, first at Universal and Warners, then at M-G-M, where he became acquainted with producer Arthur Freed during the making of *Any Number Can Play* (1949, Mervyn Leroy), for which he wrote the adapted screenplay. Brooks would eventually sign a long-term contract with Metro. Impressed by Brooks, Freed encouraged him to make the move to directing, promoting the idea with head of studio Louis B. Mayer. Mayer eventually agreed, even though he reportedly discouraged Brooks from taking a position that he disingenuously dismissed as less important than that of screenwriter: "Anyone can direct, but not everyone can write."[1] A friendship with actor Cary Grant, then signed to star in the M-G-M project that Brooks eventually wrote and directed as *Crisis* (1950), helped with this "promotion."

The erstwhile screenwriter was also encouraged to refocus his career by Freed, who convinced Mayer that Brooks was well qualified by experience and temperament to take charge of projects rather than simply writing the scripts for them. This path to the director's chair was thoroughly traditional: a fortunate mix of unexpected opportunities, considerable talent, and a forceful personality. It also did not hurt that Brooks was not shy about having something to say, as he proved by writing *The Brick Foxhole* (1945), one of the best ex-serviceman WWII novels. The book is an acerbic and wide-ranging indictment of the destructive tensions in American society uncovered by the forced togetherness of military life. Though it deals only with the experiences of men stationed stateside, it is otherwise very much in the tradition of the better-known works by James Jones (*From Here to Eternity*), Irwin Shaw (*The Young Lions*), Leon Uris (*Battle Cry*), and Norman Mailer (*The Naked and the Dead*).[2]

In addition to writing scripts for some forgettable productions (such as *Swell Guy* [1946], based on a Gilbert Emery play), Brooks learned much about the craft of directing by working closely with hands-on producer Mark Hellinger on *The Killers* (1946, uncredited) and *Brute Force* (1947), for which he received a screen credit. He collaborated with John Huston on the script for *Key Largo* (1948), adapting the Maxwell Anderson play, and as a result spent a good deal of time on set. During the production he struck up a close friendship with Humphrey Bogart, an experience that taught him a good deal about screen acting and the director's role in shaping performance.

Unlike many who would begin their directorial careers in the postwar era as the studio system waned, Brooks served an apprenticeship of sorts that substantially shaped his artistic interests, his flair for writing succinct and engaging dialogue, and his feel for visual composition. Like Huston and, to a lesser extent, Hellinger, he was attracted to the several then-current varieties of what for want of a better label might be termed "serious" Hollywood filmmaking. These were films that explored the darker sides of modern, especially national, experience. An important part of this seriousness, and one that will receive a good deal of attention in this volume, was an interest that Brooks shared with his mentor Huston in the adaptation of literary classics, including those that might seem unfilmable or, at least, resistant to screen reversioning.[3]

Huston adapted/directed for the screen works by James Joyce, Flannery O'Connor, Stephen Crane, Arthur Miller, Herman Melville, and Rudyard Kipling, and even the Old Testament, while Brooks reversioned classic works by Fyodor Dostoevsky, Joseph Conrad, F. Scott Fitzgerald, and Sinclair Lewis. In terms of adaptation, especially the vexed protocol of "authenticity," all these projects raised considerable difficulties. The two filmmakers shared an enthusiasm for the drama of Tennessee Williams, with Huston writing/directing a version of *Night of the Iguana* (1964) and Brooks doing the same for both *Cat on a Hot Tin Roof* (1958) and *Sweet Bird of Youth* (1962). Huston and Brooks were also interested in sub-classic writers who were important voices of the era and contributed to public debate: for Huston these were B. Traven, C. S. Forester, Ellen Glasgow, Romain Gary, Alan Le May, Malcolm Lowry, Leonard Gardner, Claude Cockburn, Pierre Le Mure, Maxwell Anderson, W. R. Burnett, Richard Condon, and Dashiell Hammett; for Brooks, Truman Capote, Evan Hunter, Robert Ruark, Paddy Chayefsky, and Frank O'Rourke. There have been other, perhaps more prominent, Hollywood practitioners of a literary cinema, most notably William Wyler, whose career similarly included works by "classic" writers like Theodore Dreiser, Sinclair Lewis, and Emily Brontë and more popular figures such as Lillian Hellman, Lew Wallace, and John Fowles.

However, in the postwar era this kind of filmmaking, defined by the complexities and compromises involved in the respectful adaptation of fiction familiar to and valued by many in the audience, was most clearly dominated by

John Huston, and his erstwhile protégé, Richard Brooks.[4] To be sure, Brooks, like Huston, sustained his career in the industry with occasional genre projects in which his approach was not to highlight the vision of a favored author but rather to exploit the entertainment and (often) intellectual value that could be extracted from a property. In *The Kremlin Letter* (1973) and *Macintosh Man* (1973), Huston assayed with varying success the adventure/thriller that in the era was perhaps Hollywood's dominant genre. Brooks did much the same in *The Light Touch* (1951) and *Wrong is Right* (1982). Neither director, however, aspired to become Alfred Hitchcock. Their métier was elsewhere. They pursued a form of seriousness within the parameters of genre quite different from what Hitchcock so spectacularly achieved in the course of the postwar era. Neither did they aspire, like Ford and Peckinpah, to make their mark on the Western. If Huston (*The Life and Times of Judge Roy Bean* [1972]) and Brooks (*Bite the Bullet* [1975]) explored in quite different ways the expressive possibilities of the adult Western, neither developed a deep interest in the genre itself. Brooks's *The Last Hunt* (1956) and *The Professionals* (1966), like Huston's *The Treasure of the Sierra Madre* (1948), are serious films, first and foremost; they are only secondarily Westerns.

In his discussion of serious filmmaking in the period, Chris Cagle usefully observes that such films "thrived in the nexus of middle-class and middlebrow culture, between a broad audience and the logic of aesthetic differentiation." The most interesting releases in this production trend offered a "self-critical commentary on middle-class life," though they also ventured into other forms of sociological critique, falling into the category of social problem films. To be sure, responding to the time-honored Hollywood business model, postwar serious films were "mass culture geared toward a mass audience," even as, paradoxically, they were "speaking to a class ethos of certain audience factions."[5] Huston and Brooks both assayed noir narratives that spoke to values, experiences, and what for want of a better term we might call modes of thinking associated with middlebrow culture. Huston's *The Asphalt Jungle* (1950), *The Maltese Falcon* (1941), and *Fat City* (1972) all offer poignant critiques of the so-called American dream, which is also, broadly speaking, the subject of Brooks's *The Blackboard Jungle* (1955), *Deadline—U.S.A.* (1952), *$* (1971), and *Fever Pitch* (1986).

As a literary director, Brooks was among the most prominent newcomers in a postwar Hollywood that was roiled by institutional uncertainty and an America undergoing radical cultural shifts. With a career interestingly split between contract assignments and independent projects, Brooks, in his successes and failures, reflects both the usable past of a profoundly stressed studio system, as well as the difficulties involved in exercising more creative freedom as an independent. In this, his career arc resembles that of fellow Americans Elia Kazan, Martin Ritt, John Frankenheimer, Sidney Lumet, Robert Rossen, and Robert Wise, all of whom pursued careers that can be claimed for a literary cinema.

It was as an (more or less) independent director, writer, and producer that Brooks was responsible for some of the finest films of the first two decades or so after the war: *Deadline—U.S.A.* (1952), *Elmer Gantry* (1960), *The Professionals* (1966), and *In Cold Blood* (1967). Of this group, only *Deadline* is based on an original script, penned by Brooks for an on-approval deal as a loan-out to 20th Century Fox. Working later in his career as semi-independent, and perhaps overreaching, Brooks was the creative center of projects that can only be called, at least in terms of critical approval, magnificent failures: *The Brothers Karamazov* (1958) and *Lord Jim* 1965). As a contract director he endured a rough beginning, eventually proving capable of excellence with material that needed a more conventional handling, as exemplified by releases such as *The Last Time I Saw Paris* (1954), *The Blackboard Jungle* (1955), *The Catered Affair* (1965), and *Cat on a Hot Tin Roof* (1958), which can be seen in part as variations of the studio-era melodrama, a flexible form that could accommodate a wide range of material.

Brooks's interest in something beyond "entertainment" has long been noticed, if only to be maligned in the early days of academic film study as "the mortal sin of pretentiousness" by Andrew Sarris, who was then the spokesman for critics (including his erstwhile foe Pauline Kael) who were hostile to Hollywood directors with something to say and an interest in adapting for the cinema literary texts that would inevitably be changed by such popularization.[6] There was something of a chic anti-intellectualism in Sarris's easy dismissal not only of Brooks, but also of Lumet, Huston, Billy Wilder, William Wyler, and Fred Zinnemann, among a good many other directors who now hold honored places in histories of the American cinema. It would be much fairer to the Brooks oeuvre to say that it is uniformly middlebrow in the sense defined by John Guillory as the "ambivalent mediation of high culture within the field of the mass cultural," a wave of filmmaking that gained strength and breadth during the postwar era.[7] Much of Sarris's cutie-pie taxonomy of American directors might strike contemporary film scholars as laughably effete. In an interesting move, however, he reveals a larger historical truth, grouping Brooks with the core group of realist directors who are now celebrated as the British New Wave: Jack Clayton, Bryan Forbes, Richard Lester, Karel Reisz, Tony Richardson, and John Schlesinger. Like them, Brooks succeeded in furthering a literary cinema based on respectful and ingenious adaptation that would produce films of intellectual substance, as entertaining as they were engaged with issues that commanded widespread interest. This was a production trend of important intellectual and sociocultural reach, and Richard Brooks was among its most notable practitioners.

\*

Love posed a practical question. "Do you think you can write a short story every day?"

"You talking about originals?" Richard asked. "If I steal, sure."[8]

Brooks's honest response to NBC Radio network executive A. C. Love in 1941 characterizes the tricks and traits of a fiction writer now turned scenario writer. In the Introduction to his collection on the place of scriptwriting in cinematic adaptation, Jack Boozer early on sums up the distinction between the literary and the scriptive, to coin a term:

> The expressive language of fiction in paragraph and chapter form describes circumstances, attitudes, and feeling that readers are left to invoke ("imagine") directly for themselves, while the screenplay is structured to work in the service of narrative that is read in the moving scenic terms of imaging for the cinema.[9]

Key here are the concepts of the ability to "imagine" as a reader of fiction and the product of "imaging" in cinema, but what is not considered is that elusive but fundamental ability of the scriptwriter's imagination. Boozer pragmatically constrains the scriptwriter to his function within industry production, thereby aligning the adapted screenplay not so much with the scriptwriter's imagination but within the real world of the film industry: "not only under the shadow of myriad narrative expectations but in a complex environment of business, industrial, and artistic considerations."[10] Again, the imaginative craft of the scriptwriter remains shifted to other concerns, often addressed by adaptation scholars as fidelity to the original text, transmediation, or intertextual processes from one medium to another, or as a product of the collaboration between scriptwriter and director. As first a short-story writer, then radio scenario writer, and sometime later a novelist, Brooks came to scriptwriting as an imaginative writer, much like the way Raymond Chandler relied on his own artistic abilities to alter essential elements of texts, to reconfigure genre and narrative structures, particularly endings, to accentuate new character development, and most evidently, to invent memorable dialogue, particularly for *Double Indemnity* (1944). The result of such inventiveness usually takes the form of a hybrid screenplay, one in which the scriptwriter exercises his innovative changes in order to reduce the genre, thematic, and character elements of a text to fit the temporal restrictions of a feature film's length. For his first major screen adaptation, Brooks's script for transforming Maxwell Anderson's play *Key Largo* to the screen reveals these same imaginative sensibilities of a fiction writer.[11]

To understand the relationship of the screenwriter to the adapted text requires not simply a one-to-one mapping of inclusions and differences, but rather a more detailed examination of the art of screenwriting as its own imaginative product. To some extent, the concept of a ready-made à la Marcel Duchamp describes the transformative, subjective imagination that creates a new work of art from an existing, recognizable text. To dismiss this hybrid text for a lack of fidelity to the original novel would be similar to discounting Marcel Duchamp's artistry in *L.H.O.O.Q.* as mere graffiti.

Raymond Chandler's transformation of James M. Cain's novel, *Double Indemnity*, reflects his own creation of Philip Marlowe's first-person narration, especially giving a hard-boiled edge to the film's dialogue. In later years, Chandler claimed that he alone was responsible for the script adaptation of the film: "Without question, *Double Indemnity*, which I wrote for an odd little director with a touch of genius, Billy Wilder."[12] One very memorable scene from the film of *Double Indemnity* occurs during the flirtation between Walter Neff (Fred MacMurray) and Phyllis Dietrichson (Barbara Stanwyck). The sexual banter, taking the sarcastic form of a speeding driver (Neff) impeded by a patrol officer (Dietrichson), moves from a request for a ticket, countered with a warning, to a violent "whack you over your knuckles," to bringing in her husband again to end the back-and-forth. As Neff leaves, he and Phyllis exchange pure Chandler dialogue, when Neff offers yet another sexual innuendo about meeting for an insurance discussion the next night:

> NEFF: Same chair, same perfume, same anklet.
>     (Opening the door)
> PHYLLIS: I wonder if I know what you mean.
> NEFF: I wonder if you wonder.[13]

Chandler also radically altered the novel's ending. He has Neff and Phyllis shooting one another, then dissolves to Neff completing his Dictaphone confession to Keyes (Edward G. Robinson); the novel concludes with an implied ending about Huff (Neff in the film) awaiting the lamia figure of Phyllis arriving in a scene of literal and literary lunacy:

> She looks like what came aboard the ship to shoot dice for souls in the Rime of the Ancient Mariner.
>     I didn't hear the stateroom door open, but she's beside me now while I'm writing. I can feel her.
>     The moon.[14]

Clearly, Chandler imposed his hard-boiled worldview of the mean streets upon Cain's novel with its *faux naïf* style, a type Chandler disliked as much as the comparisons drawn between Cain and him.[15] Chandler transformed Cain's ready-made text into a new hybrid by reorienting the novel's genre, narrative, and closure.

Similarly to Chandler's screenwork of Cain's novel, Brooks reconfigured the overly poetic dialogue and antifascist plot of Anderson's *Key Largo*, although keeping the general political allegory intact, whereby European fascism, as in Brooks's novel *The Brick Foxhole*, finds its counterpart within American society. Unlike the play, *Key Largo* refocuses attention away from the returning war veteran, Frank McCloud (Humphrey Bogart), and gives center stage to the rapacious, tyrannical gangster, Johnny Rocco (Edward G. Robinson). Murillo, in Anderson's play, serves as a personification of evil that King must destroy in order to regain his sense of masculinity and to rescue his soul. Rocco in Brooks's script, however, is a paper tiger from the bygone days of Prohibition, who still seeks to satisfy his deviant appetites for lust and money through violence and intimidation. Rocco and his gang await the arrival of Ziggy, another mobster, who will take their merchandise of counterfeit money and allow them safe passage back to Cuba.

For most of the film, McCloud remains cynically indifferent to Rocco's plans. As a WWII veteran, he has witnessed far too much loss of life, including that of the valorous George, son of wheelchair-bound Mr. Temple (Lionel Barrymore) and husband to Nora (Lauren Bacall). When confronted with Mr. Brown (an apt allegorical color for brown-shirted fascists), Rocco's alias at the Temple Hotel, McCloud pessimistically recognizes the futility of that World War that has still left home-grown thugs waiting to regain their murderous power. While maintaining that sociopolitical allegory from Anderson's play, Brooks redirected this political parable to create a tense, hybrid *film noir* and gangster tale, with Rocco's sadism, perversion, and paranoia propelling the plot. As Rocco, Robinson teases the wheelchair-bound Mr. Temple, whispers sexual vulgarities into Nora's ear, and, as the hurricane rages, paces in abject fear and paranoia about the rising natural forces of winds and tides that he cannot control.

*Variety* understood the sociopolitical message of *Key Largo*, but also saw the artistry of the genre created on screen:

> There are overtones of soapboxing on a better world but this is never permitted to interfere with basic plot, resulting in sturdy film fare for the meller fan. The Anderson play has been brought up to the postwar period by scripters Richard Brooks and John Huston, making a disillusioned veteran and a vice lord represent present-day problems in winning the peace. As noted, that particular theme doesn't interfere with the essential aim of telling a gangster yarn.[16]

*The Hollywood Reporter* also found considerably high merit in this adaptation of Anderson's play, which had "shorn it of the poet-playwright's indulgent verbosity and cloudy imagery":

The film's reflections are pithy and directly related to the action at hand. Never are they allowed to create lull in the picture's brisk pace or tension. Huston and his screenplay collaborator, Richard Brooks, have turned a mediocre play into a brilliant, penetrating and exciting scenario.[17]

In Los Angeles, the lobby advertisement for the film took on a very odd twist, although one that understood Rocco's prominence in *Key Largo*. Reg Streeter, who headed the studio's campaign, took the first scene of Rocco in a bathtub and made it public:

> Streeter obtained an 8X10 of Edward G. Robinson taking a bath. A life-sized blow-up was made from this, and Robinson's figure cut out. A bathtub was then promoted from a local plumber, filled with water, and the cutout placed in it, achieving a realistic effect. Dry ice was put in the tub periodically, causing steam and bubbles to erupt. According to Streeter, hundreds of people came into the theatre just to see the display.[18]

Few film moments of gangster decadence, before Al Pacino's extremes in *Scarface* (1983), captured that overt materialism and self-satisfaction as much as Rocco smoking a cigar, reading the paper, submerged in a bathtub, electric fan whirling, and an ironic Cuba Libre resting on the tub railing.

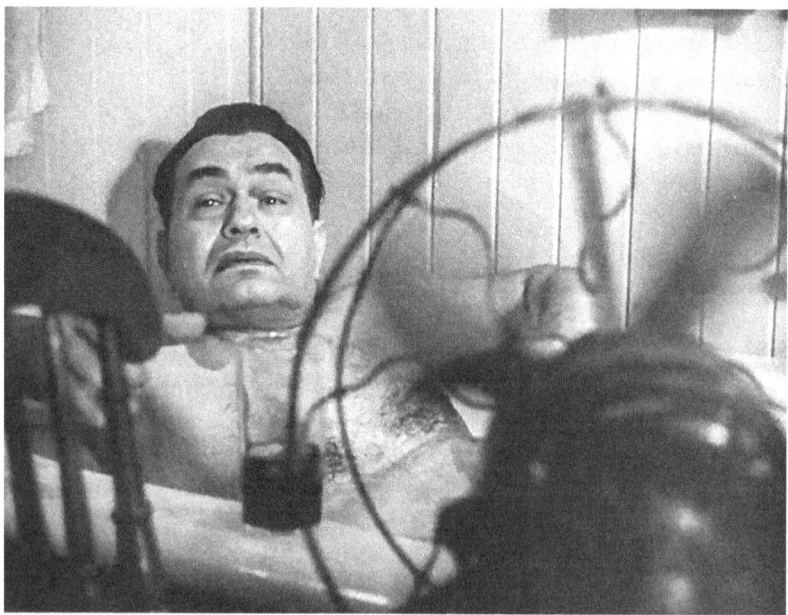

Figure 1.1 First appearance in *Key Largo* of self-satisfied, self-indulgent deviant gangster Johnny Rocco (Edward G. Robinson) in his element.

To understand Brooks's imaginative approach to adaptive scriptwriting, it is necessary to work through the substantial changes he made to the play. Anderson's play consists of a prologue set in northern Spain during the resistance fighting against Franco's fascist forces, and two acts set at the d'Alcala's place in Key Largo, Florida. Anderson's prologue consists of poetic, philosophic dialogue among a group of expat American volunteers in the fight against fascism, with King McCloud representing the voice of almost nihilistic realism:

> Was there ever a crusade without an ignominious end? Before we came to Spain we should have thought of that. The knights in rusty armor crippling home with an increment of blood and bone diseases from Palestine—leaving the infidels in charge as usual. Or the A.E.F overseas for democracy, and winning—along with other diseases—this Mussolini and Hitler. Yes, and Franco, very likely.[19]

The futility of fighting to the death for a cause, explains King to Victor, d'Alcala's son, just how empty a dream their struggle has been for an already dead cause:

> We should know by this time—we've looked at Europe long enough to know there's nothing to fight for here—that nothing you win means freedom or equality or justice—that all the formulas are false—and known to be false—democracy, communism, socialism, naziism—dead religions nobody believes in—[20]

For the 1948 film, Brooks jettisons the Spanish leftist backdrop of the 1930s for retrospective dialogue about the Italian campaign of early December 1943 during the Battle of San Pietro. Pragmatically, the shift from an ultra-leftist to an American veteran returning from WWII would enlist audience support, as well as grounding McCloud's native morality. The allegorical names of King and Victor Brooks replaced with the commonplace Americana of Frank and George. The political diatribes of Anderson's prologue have been replaced with nostalgia for hearth and home, with lone, frontline troop observer George talking over the wire to stay awake with McCloud for three days:

> . . . Most of his talk was about you.
> [His glance covers both Temple and Nora.]
>  You'd never guess the things I know about you both. Like the inscription, Nora, in your wedding ring. It says: "Evermore."[21]

While ambivalent at times about the war's promise "to cleanse the world of ancient evils, ancient ills," Frank reserves his most devastating sociopolitical commentary for attacks on Rocco:

> McCLOUD (to Temple): Sir: Johnny Rocco was more than a king—he was an emperor. His rule extended over beer, slot machines, the numbers racket and a dozen other forbidden enterprises. He was a master of them all. Whom he couldn't corrupt he terrified. Whom he couldn't terrify he murdered.[22]

McCloud's confrontations with Rocco remain primarily verbal, with Frank retreating often from the oppressive gangster, to the dismay of Nora. Unlike King in Anderson's play, who is willing to sacrifice his life to save the Seminoles, Osceolas, from death row, McCloud remains powerless against Rocco's lies that force the Sheriff to shoot and kill the Osceolas. McCloud's impotence before the malicious, violent Rocco subsides by degrees, again revealing how much Rocco dominates, like the hurricane itself, the theme, plot, and characters of Brooks's script.

As Brooks knew well, the gangster and *film noir* genres rely upon the feminine as both sexual distraction and deadly intrigue. Brooks's creation of Gaye Dawn (Claire Trevor), the erstwhile moll for Rocco, has no counterpart in Anderson's play. Gaye serves as the ubiquitous chanteuse of early *film noir*, as well as a type of *femme fatale*; in this case, she aids McCloud (and the plot) by stealing Rocco's gun during a fake fit of hysteria and handing it over to McCloud, hoping he will do more than simply protect himself against Rocco. Gaye's number in *Key Largo* reinforces Rocco's sadism, since he will not indulge his gal's alcoholism unless she does her old act, singing *Moanin' Low*, a 1930s blues song made popular in 1937 by Billie Holiday. Her performance, one of the most memorable *femme* numbers in all of *film noir*, remains difficult to watch, as Gaye spirals down into an unsustainable voice overmatched by time and immoderation, as Robert Miklitsch notes:

> Drawing like an aging athlete on her past experience as a performer, Gaye starts out strong, her voice momentarily invigorated by the challenge. Then all the years and all the drinks finally take their toll: "Don't know any reason why he treats me so poorly,/What have I gone and done?" At the end of the verse, Gaye's voice breaks and the camera cuts away to Curley who, shaking his head, looks over to Rocco who mirrors his disapproval.[23]

Gaye finishes the blues number, obviously exhausted and disgraced, as Brooks's script indicates:

There is no longer any question now of applause. The dreadful silence is broken by Toots' giggle repeating itself. However, even that infuriating sound serves to relieve the situation. Gaye's knees buckle. She slips down onto a chair, holding her hands, trying to keep them from trembling.[24]

To further humiliate Gaye, Rocco refuses her the promised drink after her number. During the performance McCloud and Nora both lower their heads and avert their eyes, feeling Gaye's shame and embarrassment. McCloud defies Rocco and goes behind the bar to pour Gaye her deserved shot. Just prior to this scene, revealing the Western roots of *film noir*, Rocco challenges McCloud to a gunfight, but McCloud declines, an act viewed as cowardice by Nora. Here, though, Nora feels new-found admiration for McCloud's heroism and chivalry in this minor yet potentially dangerous act.

Unlike the fatal shoot-out between King and Murillo that concludes Anderson's play, Brooks extends that gunplay, having Rocco face McCloud aboard the boat headed for Cuba. Having shot and killed two of Rocco's henchmen, McCloud takes control of the vessel and Rocco. Brooks brilliantly has McCloud remain silent throughout this final siege, with Rocco fighting the unknown presence of death very much as he faced the storm at the Temple Hotel:

**132. CLOSE ROCCO**
Desperation seizes him. The same sort of fear that gripped him during the hurricane.[25]

McCloud's silent victory over Rocco replays the European campaign against fascism. With Rocco's death, McCloud regains his masculinity and valor, as Nora awaits word of his survival at the Temple Hotel. When she answers Frank's shipboard call, she realizes that a new day dawns, which Brooks accounts for symbolically with Nora crossing the lobby to open the large storm shutters as the fog lifts and sunlight fills the room. From *film noir* to gangster tale to political allegory to romantic ending, Brooks's hybrid script fulfilled his imaginative requirement for converting Anderson's stage play into a successful feature film.

Brooks's impressive, imaginative adaptation of Anderson's play reveals signs of his future screenwriting. While sustaining elements of theme and general plot, Brooks often played with established genres to create hybrid forms that allowed for the variety of shifts of mood, realism, and theme needed to move literary texts to the screen. The chapters in this collection address the variety of adaptation techniques employed by Brooks the screenwriter and director. The contributors' insights concerning plot, theme, imagery, and technical filmmaking also address pertinent issues of the adaptation process. Brooks tackles a number of challenging script and directorial adaptations, including bringing classic, popular, and controversial novels, stage plays, and nonfiction works to the screen. An overarching characteristic of Brooks's inventive approach remains the hybrid quality of his genre interrelationships within his screenplays. Imaginatively, Brooks seeks the pleasure of genres for not only the audience but also for himself as filmmaker. In doing so, Brooks's creative act of scriptwriting allows for romance and melodrama to meld, documentary style and fictional narrative to converge, social problem ideology and cinematic realism to coalesce, and gender politics to unite with elements of the thriller. As an industry maverick, at times Brooks allowed himself to engage in imaginative experimentations to reconfigure seemingly unadaptable classic works for the screen, usually with little commercial success. We have arranged this collection chronologically in the hope that readers will be afforded the opportunity to observe the complex and astonishing career of one of America's truly great, imaginative filmmakers.

## NOTES

1. Qtd. in Douglass K. Daniel, *Tough as Nails: The Life and Films of Richard Brooks* (Madison: University of Wisconsin Press, 2011), p. 7.
2. For detailed discussion, see Bernstein in this volume.
3. See Kamilla Elliott, "Unfilmable Books," *South Atlantic Review* 80 No. 3–4 (2015): pp. 79–95.
4. See the discussion of this aspect of Huston's career in Douglas McFarland and Wesley King (eds.), *John Huston as Adaptor* (Albany: SUNY Press, 2018).
5. Chris Cagle, *Sociology on Film: Postwar Hollywood's Prestige Commodity* (New Brunswick, NJ: Rutgers University Press, 2017), p. 15.
6. Andrew Sarris, *The American Cinema: Directors and Directions, 1929–1968* (New York: Da Capo, 1996), p. 189.
7. "The Ordeal of Middlebrow Culture," *Transition* 67 (1995): p. 87.
8. Daniel, *Tough as Nails*, p. 22.
9. Jack Boozer (ed.), "Introduction," *Authorship and Film Adaptation* (Austin: University of Texas Press, 2008), p. 5.
10. Ibid.
11. The concept of the artistic imagination, confined to romanticism or to modernist psychosexual dream-like states for surrealism, has had little to no analysis in adaptation studies. Very fine foundational works on adaptation do not even list imagination as an index category, such as: Thomas Leitch (ed.), *The Oxford Handbook of Adaptation Studies* (Oxford: Oxford University Press, 2017).
12. As quoted in Jeffrey Meyers, "Introduction," *Double Indemnity: The complete screenplay* (Berkeley: University of California Press, 2000), p. xi.
13. Ibid. p. 18.
14. James M. Cain, *Double Indemnity* (1936; New York: Vintage Crime, 1992), pp. 114–15.
15. Tom Hiney and Frank MacShane (eds.), *The Raymond Chandler Papers: Selected Letters and Nonfiction, 1909–1959* (New York: Grove Press, 2000), p. 38.

16. "Key Largo," *Variety*, Wednesday, July 7, 1948: p. 6.
17. Irving Hoffman, "'Key Largo' Greeted With Good Reviews in Gotham", *The Hollywood Reporter*, July 20, 1948: p. 6
18. "Robinson Is No Bathing Beauty But He Draws in Lobby Bathtub Scene," *Boxoffice*, September 25, 1948: p. 46.
19. Maxwell Anderson, *Key Largo: A Play In a Prologue and Two Acts* (Washington, D.C.: Anderson House, 1939), p. 15.
20. Ibid. p. 22.
21. *Key Largo (1948): SHOOTING SCRIPT, Screenplay by Richard Brooks and John Huston*: p. 21.
22. Ibid. pp. 39, 37.
23. Robert Miklitsch, *Siren City: Sound and Source Music in Classic American Noir* (New Brunswick, NJ: Rutgers University Press, 2011), p. 168.
24. *Key Largo (1948) SHOOTING SCRIPT*: p. 72.
25. Ibid. p. 113.

CHAPTER 2

# *The Brick Foxhole* (1945): Richard Brooks's American Vision

*Matthew H. Bernstein*

Richard Brooks's 1945 debut novel *The Brick Foxhole* made only a slight impression on the literary establishment, but it definitely provided him with the entrée into Hollywood that in a few years led to his assuming the director's chair at M-G-M. The novel would quickly be adapted for the screen as *Crossfire* (1947), and it would find considerable popular and critical success. Playwright Clifford Odets, who hoped that a version of *The Brick Foxhole* might find its way to the stage, introduced Brooks to Adrian Scott at RKO. Scott already knew of the novel; impressed, he optioned the rights and produced the film from a script by John Paxton with Edward Dmytryk directing. Before that deal was finalized, however, Humphrey Bogart read *The Brick Foxhole* and recommended it to reporter-turned-producer Mark Hellinger. Hellinger passed on the project, but he was impressed enough with Brooks's abilities to hire him to work (if uncredited) on the script for *The Killers* (1946); soon thereafter, this time for screen credit, Brooks wrote the screenplay for Hellinger's production of *Brute Force* (1947), directed by Jules Dassin.[1] That next year, Bogart and Brooks would work together on John Huston's *Key Largo* (1948). Brooks profited from the tutelage of the director and screenwriter in completing the script. After he was promoted to directing, his friendship with Bogart led to two other collaborations: on *Deadline—U.S.A.* (1952) and *Battle Circus* (1953).

Doubtless, because of this networking, *The Brick Foxhole* was crucial in furthering Brooks's film career. *Crossfire* is a landmark social problem film/detective noir. The film dramatizes the murder of a Jewish civilian by a bigoted soldier and the resulting investigation of the crime. In so doing, it explores the uncertainties that challenged returning soldiers, offering a denunciation of divisive social prejudice. The novel also exposes the degrading and alienating conditions endured by soldiers posted stateside in wartime. Throughout the novel Brooks dramatizes the existence of racism, anti-Semitism, and nascent fascism among civilians and soldiers alike. He also demonstrates how military training makes men susceptible to pervasive racism, one of the strands of a nascent fascism in the national culture. Published just weeks after Germany's surrender but before the end of the war, *The Brick Foxhole* appealed to Scott because he and his creative team, Paxton and Dmytryk, agreed with Brooks's warning about the threat of a home-grown fascism and racial hatred now that its overseas version had been defeated.[2] The studio's noiresque publicity material paraphrases a major observation from police Captain Finlay (Robert Young) as "Hate is like a loaded gun."[3]

RKO's liberal head of production, Dore Schary, hurried *Crossfire* into production so that it could be released before Fox's *Gentleman's Agreement*, whose theme was also anti-Semitism. The film was greeted with industry, critical, and box office approval, despite anxious debates within the Jewish community about whether the film was helpful or harmful in combatting anti-Semitism. *Crossfire* was RKO's most profitable film of the 1947–8 season. The Academy nominated it for five awards: Best Picture, Supporting Actor (Robert Ryan as Sergeant Montgomery), Supporting Actress (Gloria Graham as the bar-gal Ginny), Director, and Screenplay. Though they added and subtracted characters and created new scenes, Scott and Paxton retained and amplified Brooks's central ideas and the novel's hard-boiled sensibility, which they translated into *Crossfire*'s celebrated *film noir* tone and style.

*The Brick Foxhole* constitutes the first full-blown articulation of Brooks's career-long fascination with masculinity under siege, here situated within a hard-boiled/*film noir* vision of an America gone very wrong. As in his subsequent work—whether he originated the scripts or adapted them from existing works—Brooks's male protagonists are compelled to make ethical choices in a pressure-cooker setting.

Apparently in disgust with his early Hollywood experiences, and possibly to escape his marriage, Brooks joined the Marines in the summer of 1943. He did not serve overseas, but was assigned to the School Detachment barracks in Quantico, Virginia, where he worked in the film-producing unit. In his spare time he wrote the novel that would document what he saw as the miserable situation of servicemen destined for service in the "brick foxhole" of stateside barracks, the strange world depicted in the first third of the novel which he defined and described in his preface to it:[4]

> Among the millions of men in brick foxholes there are thousands whose lot is the least enviable in the armed services. These are the warriors who will never fight in this war. And theirs is the task of the damned . . . These men see others trained and shipped off to ports of embarkation,

but they themselves are always left behind . . . the disillusioned soldier who finds himself trapped in a brick foxhole is a victim of another kind of fear . . . bedeviled by frustration, loss of dignity, and all the most fantastic shapes that rumor can breed.[5]

Omitting this depiction of stateside duty, *Crossfire* is set in D.C. at the end of the war, where the soldiers, now demobilized, are attempting their reintegration into postwar society, thematic territory first explored the year before in both the melodrama *The Best Years of Our Lives* (1946) and the noir *The Blue Dahlia* (1946).

Brooks reminds the reader that the barracks are dirty, disgusting, and claustrophobic; at one point, protagonist Corporal Jeff Mitchell thinks "he was tied down. Trapped. Buried in a military base. A prison. A brick casket filled with living corpses."[6] Military training fosters intense bigotry and hatred. Nearly every white male character, except Mitchell and his buddy Sgt. Peter Keeley, freely uses racial slurs, as Brooks acidly records. That he was a Jewish outsider in this military milieu perhaps explains in part Brooks's revulsion at the intense racism of both enlisted men and civilians.[7] According to *The New York Times* critic Orville Prescott, Brooks "may wear the uniform, but at heart he is still a civilian, a sensitive and outraged liberal, and a writer . . . and he has poured out all his rage and disgust and lacerated emotion in a blistering novel."[8] His *New York Times* obituary emphasizes this intense reformism, observing that Brooks "frequently made films exposing social and moral conditions he deplored . . ."[9]

The racial hatred of both Montgomery and Bowers problematizes the image of the American armed forces promoted by wartime film as fighting units made up of a cross-section of American men, in terms of regions, classes, and faiths, who work together to defeat fascism, as in Howard Hawks's 1943 *Air Force*. In *The Brick Foxhole*, stateside soldiers have not shared a unifying life-and-death experience and wind up hating one another. Mitchell, Montgomery, and Bowers register most keenly this degradation of spirit. A Disney animator, Mitchell creates animated maps for military films. Resting on his bunk, he imagines his imminent, happy furlough reunion with his wife Mary in southern California. Nearby, card-playing soldiers repeat the boasts of Red Appleton, a soldier who claims that he slept with another soldier's wife named Mary in southern California. Mitchell becomes convinced this is *his* Mary. He imagines coming home to find Mary in bed with Red and killing them both, while his anger extends to the rumor-mongers, whom he envisions attacking:

> . . . Fighting was the answer. The only answer. Even if beaten and bloodied he would feel better . . . He would begin with the man who had told the story and then continue and take them on one at a time. Until they all were lying on the floor bloodied and apologetic . . . He had been

trained to fight . . . To get up and destroy the enemy, the hateful voices which sifted into his ears and dropped with a crash into his belly.[10]

Yet, after all this self-righteous rumination, Mitchell just remains in his bunk, stewing in his mix of jealousy, rage, and the desire for action, until he has to leave the barracks. Keeley, the only person Mitchell trusts, cannot persuade him simply to return home as planned to see his wife and "get in bed."[11] By the time Mitchell leaves the post for D.C., determined to get smashed and forget Mary's imagined betrayal, he is convinced the only philosophy that should guide his conduct is "Kill or be killed," either in combat or stateside.[12]

Brooks's narrative method depends on indirect free discourse, sharing with the reader in the most vivid way the interior thoughts/monologues of several characters, not just Mitchell, but Montgomery, Keeley, Ginny the prostitute, Mary, and Finlay. In chapter V, the narration alternates among the thoughts of Mitchell, Keeley, and Monty as they watch the overmatched Jewish soldier Max Brockey fight the experienced barrel-chested mid-western boxer "Whitey": Monty wants Brockey to be killed in the ring so he can't prove Jews are as good fighters as everyone else; Keeley wants Brockey to go as many rounds as possible to prove that they are; and Mitchell, oblivious to Brockey's motivations, wants him to give up so he won't get pummeled in the ring. Indirect free discourse also gives us access to Keeley's rumination on the nature of the American soldier and the larger stakes of WWII.

*Crossfire* reproduces this kind of character subjectivity most overtly in the justly celebrated two conflicting flashbacks related by Montgomery and Mitchell (George Cooper). Mitchell's hazy drunkenness and confusion is visually conveyed by blurred shots, doubled images, and various transitions, as when he leaves Samuels's (Sam Levene) apartment, walks the streets, meets Ginny suddenly, and wakes up in her apartment. As Homer B. Pettey has noted, the two flashbacks also differ in more subtle ways: Monty is both lit and behaves pleasantly in his own flashback, while he is lit more harshly and acts more angry and intoxicated in Mitchell's.[13] At the same time, the film's dark and foreboding lighting and mise en scène in so many scenes, including the first, in which Samuels is beaten to death, reinforce its nightmarish sensibility.[14]

*The Brick Foxhole* limns a more venal, violent world, rife with bitter hatred, and poisoned by bigotry and desperate behavior, than *Crossfire* or any other studio film in 1947 could have been permitted to recreate on screen. (The adaptation of James Jones's *From Here to Eternity* would encounter similar challenges in the early 1950s.) Beyond the Production Code Administration (PCA), which was generally hostile to critiques of national institutions, the filmmakers had to gain the military's approval of *Crossfire*. Brooks had nearly faced a court martial for not submitting the book to the military authorities prior to publication.

In critical accounts of the film, the most notable change that the filmmakers made during the adaptation process involved the murder victim: the novel's gay interior decorator Mr. Edwards makes way for Mr. Samuels (Sam Levene), whom Montgomery suspects is a "typical" Jewish coward; the film reveals that Samuels, ironically, was honorably discharged after being wounded on Okinawa. Scott and his team anticipated that a Jewish victim rendered the story more acceptable to the Breen Office, reluctant to have issues of "sex perversion" raised that were prohibited by the Code.[15] Indeed, *Crossfire* is more concerned with racism and anti-Semitism than homophobia. As James Naremore notes, the change resulted in "the colossal irony of a Jew being murdered by a U.S. soldier during the immediate aftermath of World War II."[16]

Brooks gave the filmmakers his blessing for this change: "They all got the same problems," he recalled telling them in an early 1990s interview; "Everybody does."[17] In a 1952 essay, Brooks justified the choice even more forcefully: "while it switched the symbol of the victim from a homosexual to a Jew, *it did not in any way alter the basic story* (emphasis Brooks's):

> The basic story was the violence, not the victim. *The Brick Foxhole* was not a novel about a homosexual, and *Crossfire* was not a picture about a Jew. Both were the story of unthinking passion, of vicious, hysterical, violent compulsion toward brutality, which is sometimes engendered by the militarization of civilians.[18]

In the novel, the bigoted Montgomery and the southern racist Floyd Bowers (whom Montgomery eventually also kills) embody these unthinking passions. Monty is a brutal former cop who has worked in the south (Black) side of Chicago. He boasts of being acquitted on three charges of manslaughter after he killed three criminal suspects, two Black and one Jewish, by shooting them in the stomach to see who is tougher. He is disgusted to find the Jewish man died right away rather than writhe in agony for minutes like his Black victims. By contrast, *Crossfire*'s Montgomery reveals his anti-Semitism through few but direct comments: "I don't like Jews. And I don't like nobody who likes Jews," he says as he knocks out Bowers before strangling him with his tie. (Robert Ryan's intense, tough performance as Monty aptly captures the character's brutal, bigoted nature.) The depiction of domestic anti-Semitism in the film was groundbreaking. Still, nothing Montgomery says in *Crossfire* is as base and repulsive as his comments in the novel. Montgomery's fascism is also apparent in his preference for military hierarchies, believing the U.S. would be better off if generals ran it: "Then everything would be shipshape. No trouble with unions. No trouble with traitors. No trouble of any kind."[19] Montgomery is exhibit A in Brooks's argument that, as Judith E. Smith puts it, "it is sadistic militarism and racist brutality that threaten the extension of democracy after the war."[20]

The southerner Bowers is also an appalling racist; in the novel he revoltingly boasts to Mitchell of raping a Black woman and enjoying it. He later drunkenly claims he killed a Black soldier who earned a Purple Heart for not giving up his train seat. As with Montgomery's police murders, there were no consequences; Bowers says the community understood the soldier had committed suicide. Riled up by Montgomery, Bowers promises to lynch the returning Black soldiers who in his view threaten to rape white women: "I hate niggers more'n I hate anythin' else in the world worl'. I kill everyone of 'em."[21] For *Crossfire*, presumably determined to avoid offending the southern audience and to avoid the issue of race relations entirely, the filmmakers portrayed Bowers (Steve Brodie) as Montgomery's money-obsessed sidekick rather than as a southerner. That position falls to the naïve Leroy (William Phipps), whom Monty constantly calls stupid, but Leroy displays no prejudice at all and is ultimately persuaded to help entrap Monty by police Captain Finlay.

The most grotesque, hate-filled element of the novel is the killing of Mr. Edwards, who gives the soldiers a lift from the base into D.C. for the weekend. While Montgomery and Bowers sarcastically flatter Edwards's work as a designer, Mitchell concludes from his delicate looks that he is "a fairy."[22] Mitchell and Bowers complain to Edwards about how difficult it is to be a poor soldier and even more difficult to get women to sleep with them even if they buy them drinks and dinner. Montgomery comments, "But a man's got to have *some* fun," suggesting his openness to a gay sexual encounter.[23] Edwards responds by licking his lips and inviting them to his apartment for quality liquor and sandwiches. In the back seat, Bowers whispers to Mitchell, "We're set, buddy. Set. I ain't beaten up a queer in I don't know how long."[24] At this crucial moment, Mitchell knows what's about to happen. Though he openly expresses appreciation for Edwards's creativity as a fellow artist, Mitchell, too obsessed with his own feelings of emasculation, goes along with Monty and Bowers. As Jennifer Langdon notes:

> In this context, being a soldier *requires* Mitchell to participate in the brutalization of Mr. Edwards. "Beating up a queer" becomes a rite of passage, an initiation into the fascist band of brothers . . . Mitchell's failure to do the right thing—to warn Mr. Edwards, to protect him or at least stick by him in the face of the fascist threat posed by Monty and Floyd—results in his own implication in the murder.[25]

*Crossfire*, Langdon points out, gives Mitchell an out because he is too drunk, sick, and confused to stay. In the novel, there is a kind of poetic justice for Mitchell's passivity.

Brooks's novel innovated by making the gay character a victim. That said, as Langdon notes, Brooks shows little interest in, even contempt for,

Mr. Edwards, his life history and subjectivity—and by extension that of gay men in or out of the military.[26] Edwards is dramatically different from *Crossfire*'s Samuels, who is older, dignified, and overtly heterosexual (he has a girlfriend). Even so, as Naremore has commented, because of staging and casting, the scenes between Samuels and Mitchell, and others in the film, connote a homoerotic connection and "oneiric" atmosphere too elusive for PCA scrutiny to detect and reject.[27]

In the novel, Edwards is found naked and dead in his bathroom, his skull crushed "like a cantaloupe" by a porcelain toilet tank top.[28] Montgomery claims he was naked because he was coming on to Mitchell; more likely, Montgomery raped him before killing him.[29] Regardless, Montgomery's brutal beating of Samuels, darkly filmed in *Crossfire*'s famous opening scene, creatively reimagines the novel's most violent act. In *The Brick Foxhole*, Montgomery insists to Finlay in front of Keeley that Mitchell is innocent but nonetheless frames him. Even if Mitchell did kill Edwards, he was justified in doing so: "They oughta kill every one of them fairies."[30]

Anticipating questions of plausibility readers might have about such shocking details in the novel as these, Brooks in his preface insisted that they came from his own experiences: ". . . the men whose story is presented here are neither fictitious, nor are they symbolic. They are real . . . This is not an autobiographical novel. That I should make altogether clear. But I know what I know, and what I know I have written."[31] Decades later, Brooks explained the origin of Edwards's murder: "Servicemen used to pick up homosexuals and take their money from them and beat the shit out of them on their way into Washington."[32]

The murder of Edwards represents the lowest depths of human brutality Brooks plumbs in the novel, yet he also portrays Washington, D.C. as a kind of Goethean Walpurgisnacht of drunken sexual revelry. Mitchell has an awkward, ultimately tender time in bed with the prostitute Ginny, but before and after these chapters, Brooks provides numerous incidents of sexual encounters desired or realized by soldiers and civilians. Sexual license, profound bigotry, and fascistic impulses go hand in hand in this fallen D.C. Two small-town businessmen, both pompous, married, and irredeemably racist, proudly extol a plan to hire returning soldiers to guard property, exact revenge on striking unions, and guard against "all those niggers [who] will be coming home with big ideas. They're going to think they own the good old U.S.A."[33] Mitchell notices that their ideas sound a lot like Montgomery's, but they express them in a much more friendly way. They talk to Mitchell about the "Bedrock of America, the good wife," then go off with a woman they intend to sleep with before the evening ends.[34]

In his review of the novel, Prescott comments: "The lurid glare he throws on Washington in wartime is enough to make that city seem more like Sodom and Gomorrah than like a great capital from which a victorious war has been directed."[35] Similarly, Richard Wright praised the novel's depiction of the "frenzy of wartime America on a moral holiday . . . the apartments of men who like to pick up lonely soldiers, the bars where men who have made their pile of profits out of war contracts spew hate against the world, especially against Jews, Negroes, and organized labor."[36] Sinclair Lewis himself commended Brooks for precisely this quality: "He courageously faces every seaminess in a soldier's holiday, sexual or social."[37]

Some reviewers noted that *Foxhole* was a work of sensational realism adhering to the practices of hard-boiled detective fiction typified by Dashiell Hammett. Prescott was typical in observing that this "account of military life in barracks and on leave in Washington is shocking and revolting. Drunkenness and brutality seem healthy and natural compared with the sadism, perversion, murder and abject and crawling weakness of character that make [the novel] so ghastly an indictment . . . Sergeant Brooks seems to have read carefully in the works of James M. Cain, Dashiell Hammett and Ernest Hemingway."[38] Niven Busch thought the "Dashiell Hammett-style manhunt for Jeff" distracted from the novel's main themes, not recognizing the ways that precise style facilitated those themes' expression.[39] Dan Norton in *The New York Times* accused Brooks of creating flat types: "He tries to tell a story of frustration and spiritual decay in terms of the hardboiled action story. Most of the characters are straight from the tough fiction factory: a lone wolf, full of irony and pity [Keeley]; a true wife; an imitation Circe [Lucy, the woman the businessmen pick up at the bar]; a prostitute with an undersized but genuine heart of gold; a sly sadistic villain; a homosexual."[40] If formulaic, the characters establish that Brooks's vision in this novel and his later work is dialectical, featuring a clash of viewpoints and experiences.

As Langdon notes, the novel counters its "intolerance, homophobia, racism, and particularly anti-Semitism" with a promotion of American liberal values—"tolerance, individualism, universalism—[that] still represent the best defense against the threat of fascism, both at home and abroad."[41] Like Brooks, the novel's Keeley is both an ardent believer in democratic values and liberal internationalism. He is also an eloquent and wry commentator on American delusions of grandeur (including those fed by the movies). Having seen combat in the Pacific and earned medals for valor, Keeley, now an army reporter, has the novel's wisest opinions and the broadest perspective on Mitchell's plight, the brick foxhole, and the conflict they are engaged in. The casting of the quintessentially laconic but confident Robert Mitchum in the role of Keeley translates Brooks's conception of the character marvelously. As in the novel, the film's Keeley is charismatic, self-contained, loyal, and capable of on-the-spot leadership. He organizes fellow ex-soldier poker players into a search mission for Mitchell before the cops can arrest him.[42]

Figure 2.1 Robert Mitchum fully embodies Brooks's concept of the worldly-wise, sarcastic, but compassionate Sergeant Peter Keeley, seen here with his bewildered buddy Mitchell (George Cooper) in a movie theater balcony: "You ought be kept in a cage."

In the book's penultimate chapter, the antagonism between Keeley and Montgomery prompts hand-to-hand combat. Now revealed as an enemy of American ideals, Montgomery arms himself with a Japanese sword, while Keeley defends himself with an antique American bayonet. After being fatally stabbed, Montgomery still manages to finish off Keeley because he is a blind killing machine fueled by hate, constantly calling Keeley a "Mick bastid."[43] For Keeley, this fight is another beachhead in a yet-to-be-won WWII, and in his dying moments he thinks about international solidarity in the fight against fascism.[44]

Keeley's vigilante killing of Montgomery is also significant, since Brooks uses it to express both the importance of individual responsibility in combatting prejudice and fascism, while voicing a noiresque lack of faith in the ability of official institutions to do so. In *Crossfire*, Keeley's Commanding Officer declares the military's disapproval of Montgomery and his ilk; no such voice of institutional authority is heard in the novel. Captain Finlay, though he condemns the soldiers' killing of Edwards because of his "strange sexual habits," gives no speeches about prejudice as an urgent societal problem—he is merely trying to solve the murder.[45] For example, even after Keeley tells the detective about the existence of Mitchell's alibi (the prostitute Ginny), Finlay, primarily concerned with keeping his job, remains skeptical until he can check it out and declines to arrest Montgomery. Keeley decides then and there to take justice into his own hands.[46] *Crossfire* has Keeley ultimately cooperating with Finlay, who takes the decisive action, shooting Montgomery on the run, an ending that makes more ideological than practical sense, which even Paxton later derided.[47]

More generally, Finlay's expanded role in the film's plot diminishes that of Keeley. The novel's Keeley thinks constantly about the need to combat prejudice—that we are all connected to each other's fate and cannot allow bigotry to go unanswered. In the film it is Finlay who forcefully lectures Leroy after the latter states: "I don't see that this [Monty's two murders] is any of my business anyway." Finlay resorts to the story of his grandfather being murdered one hundred years ago just for being Irish. Leroy, a stand-in for the audience, follows Finlay in enacting a narrative of conversion to the cause.[48]

Along the same lines, the filmmakers reduced the restoration of Mitchell and Mary's marriage to a few lines of dialogue from Keeley about their off-screen rapprochement ("I think they're going to be all right," he tells Finlay). Brooks ends the novel with the reunion of Mitchell and Mary after she and Finlay secure The Man's alibi. None of the characters know that Keeley has

Figure 2.2 Leroy (William Phipps) does not want to be involved in the Samuels murder case, but Captain Finlay (Robert Young), supported by Sgt. Keeley (Robert Mitchum) and a Commanding Officer (Kenneth MacDonald, left), persuade him otherwise. On the wall, F.D.R. looks on in tacit approval.

killed Montgomery; Finlay plans to arrest him later in the day. All Mary can think about is making love to Mitchell to erase any memory of his fling with Ginny.[49] The novel provides a less cohesive sense of restored social order and the role of the police in surveilling crime and achieving it.

While critics took no issue with the ending of Brooks's novel, they pummeled his characterization of Mitchell. In both versions of the story, Mitchell is too absorbed in his own problems to become an ally in the struggle against fascist attitudes and bigotry. Some reviewers pointed out that Mitchell's hypersensitivity to his surroundings and his obsession over his wife's alleged infidelity was more pathetic than sympathetic, as Brooks surely intended. Writing in *The New Yorker*, Hamilton Basso found Mitchell unconvincing, even implausible:

> Although Jeff shows many of the signs of a man headed for a psychoneurotic discharge, Mr. Brooks never once presents him as a psychoneurotic—in fact, there are times when the author seems to imply that Jeff is one of the few healthy-minded men in his outfit—and his peculiar behavior is too absurd for belief. It is no less absurd when Jeff does nothing to find out if the girl involved is the Mary he's married to, declines even to telephone his wife, and clings to his conviction that she has been unfaithful to him—a conviction, unfortunately, upon which all the rest of Mr. Brooks' book depends . . . Jeff, instead of being the sensitive, admirable person that Mr. Brooks tries to make him, is a trivial and rather embarrassingly stupid young man, one who shows all the signs of having been so over-mothered in his childhood that he is as useless to himself as he is to others.[50]

Similarly, then-Sergeant and future Blacklisted screenwriter Walter Bernstein was more blunt on this point, calling the novel "a pretentious book, tough on the outside and soft on the inside": "Sergeant Brooks's hero would be more sympathetic if he were less of a jerk. He represents a class of intellectuals who interpret the world in terms of their own navel. The other characters are equally without depth; there are a great many high-sounding and undoubtedly well-meaning words about anti-Semitism and truth and prejudice of all kinds, but they are spoken by people interested only in themselves."[51]

Whether or not Scott, Paxton, and Dmytryk read these reviews, their decision to begin the film in postwar Washington, D.C. in effect solved this problem. Like the book's harshest critics, Scott felt the overheard rumor in the barracks was too flimsy a basis to initiate the narrative.[52] *Crossfire*'s Mitchell is not filled with jealous, frustrated murderous intent; rather, he is drunk, dazed, and confused, absolutely harmless, which makes him far more sympathetic and reinforces Keeley's claims that he couldn't kill anyone. In the film, Keeley shakes his head in friendly frustration when Mitchell can't account for his time spent with Ginny: "You ought to be kept in a cage." The film's Mitchell is vaguely unhappy: "He's homesick," Keeley tells Finlay. "He's wifesick. Maybe she said something in one of the letters that made him suspicious of her love life, I don't know."

Instead of being driven by Mitchell's "psychoneurosis," *Crossfire* focuses more on the problems of postwar readjustment, then facing millions of the demobilized. Everything seems tenuous, uncertain, and Mitchell is uprooted, ungrounded. "This sort of life doesn't bother some soldiers," Keeley tells Finlay. "It doesn't bother me much. I haven't seen my wife for two years. When I do, maybe we'll pick up again. I don't know, maybe we won't. But I don't worry about it now. Mitchell isn't like that. Mitchell isn't tough. He needs his wife . . ."[53] Samuels can put into words Mitchell's confusion via his "win the war/eat the peanut" analogy: having won the war, soldiers don't know what to do now: "I think it's suddenly not having a list of enemies to hate anymore . . . A whole lot of fight and hate that doesn't know where to go." In the movie theater balcony, Mitchell explains to both Keeley and Mary that Samuels' insights have helped him understand his own anxiety about reintegration into society. The ambiguous, enigmatic Man (Paul Kelly) in Ginny's apartment is Mitchell's older mirror image, due to his own uncertain status in relation to her. He quickly spins out different scenarios regarding his relationship with Ginny (husband, ex-husband, boyfriend, and, in the novel, pimp).

Thus, *Crossfire* sustained and amplified many key elements of Brooks's novels while adding others. Conversely, the film lacks the novel's satire, dark humor, and irony, perhaps because so much of it was directed at eliminated, secondary characters. Brooks is an equal opportunity satirist: a Catholic priest on the base is utterly useless; in a chapter consisting entirely of a monologue, Max Brockey's father, a wealthy assimilationist Jewish bra manufacturer, tries to talk his son out of the boxing match, obliviously claiming "This is America. There is no anti-Semitism here."[54] On the base, Monty harangues the heedless soldiers of the animation unit for not cleaning up after themselves or respecting authority. Portions of his comments were repurposed for his drunken bar scene speech in the film about an "army of stinking civilians," who "don't respect the service," have no manners, and who are constantly stealing.[55] The soldiers regard him in the barracks, as they do in the bar scene in the film, as a tiresome blowhard. In the latter, Mitchell describes Monty to Keeley as "shooting off his mouth."

Brooks also emphasizes the role of movies in shaping the American psyche. As Pettey points out, Brooks via Keeley argues that American soldiers fight well because they combine "realism with sentiment."[56] Films feed that sentimentality. Brooks makes constant references to movie stars, movie scenes, and even film titles. In the brothel, Mitchell tells Ginny that he wants to be an ambassador for lonely men who want to talk to Bette Davis.[57] Keeley understands that Mitchell's desire to see combat is encouraged by combat films, specifically referencing *A Guy Named Joe* (1943):

> It was the Cinderella story all over again. It was winning the war for us, thought Keeley. The infantryman could, without too much trouble, imagine himself as Humphrey Bogart crawling through the music of a jungle, and sooner or later he would kill dozens of the enemy and, before it was all over, end up in a beautiful bar with a girl who wore low-cut dresses and kissed with her mouth open. And an American aviator could place himself in the field jacket of Spencer Tracy, and nonchalantly dive his plane into the funnel of a Jap [sic] aircraft carrier, knowing all the time that he would meet Lionel Barrymore in some leather armchaired heaven and, before the thing ended, have Irene Dunne in his arms.[58]

Keeley's own reflections are flooded by movie scenes, real and imaginary. In the Pacific theater, he notes, "you imagined things in short sequences, like in a movie. You took the girl in your arms and kissed her and made love to her. Then the scene faded from your mind." Other scenes follow. Stateside there is no fade-out, however: "After you made love to her she was still there. And you didn't know what to say or do."[59] Brooks also parodies low-budget Westerns by describing those playing in the theater where Mitchell hides out: "The horse was a beautiful animal and the country through which he was galloping was beautiful and Jeff thought it was a beautiful story and he wished he could be somewhere riding a horse . . . And then he remembered he had no horse and he couldn't ride and he didn't even know where the Tonto Pass was."[60]

By contrast, in *Crossfire* we hear only a newsreel playing when Mitchell arrives and swelling orchestral music when Mary and Mitchell are reunited. As Langdon points out, the movie theater itself is also a noir convention: "This, too, is a quintessentially noir scene, redolent of the lounge spaces described by Vivian Sobchack: the shadowy theater, bright light spilling from the high window of the projectionist's booth and diffusing into murky darkness below . . ."[61] Such overt self-referentiality is not a hallmark of Brooks's subsequent scripts and films; but combined with Brooks's evocative prose, such scenes and passages demonstrate that he was thinking cinematically as well as meditating on how popular cinema figures in the lives and perspectives of his contemporaries, shaping their thoughts about life, love, and war.

*The Brick Foxhole* is undeniably a mixed achievement, but it provides an intriguing look at Brooks's earliest coherent conception of American society and the American male, by diagnosing what Judith E. Smith calls "the pressures on masculinity in wartime" and a variety of responses to them.[62] Brooks uses the hard-boiled detective framework to shape his experiences during

WWII into a multifaceted, tough noir exposé that readers everywhere recognized for its shocking frankness. His experiences, like his first book, cast a long shadow across his subsequent work—most obviously in *Key Largo*, *Brute Force*, *Crisis* (1950), *Lord Jim* (1965), and *In Cold Blood* (1967)—and found resonance in American popular culture.

We should also note the striking relevance of *The Brick Foxhole*'s and *Crossfire*'s diagnosis of the social ills of American society in 1945. Montgomery's cruel killing of crime suspects and innocents like Edwards, and Bowers's killing of a Black soldier (both of them unpunished) makes them forerunners of the recently visible repulsive killers, whether police or civilian, of George Floyd, Treyvon Martin, and a host of other unarmed Black citizens. In *Crossfire*, Finlay concludes his story of his Irish grandfather's murder by saying, "That's history. They don't teach it in schools, but it's history just the same." That history of injustice and racism *has* been taught since the film's release, but now reactionary forces seek to end such lessons by outlawing curriculum and banning books. Brooks foresaw the emergence and rise to power of autocratic, anti-democratic and fascist white nationalist movements and leaders. His work often emphasizes the fragility of true American democracy, as well as the urgent need to fight for it, then and now.

\*

My thanks to R. Barton Palmer and Homer Pettey for their editorial acumen.

## NOTES

1. Douglass K. Daniel, *Tough as Nails: The Life and Films of Richard Brooks* (Madison: University of Wisconsin Press, 2011), p. 35.
2. Jennifer E. Langdon, *Caught In the Crossfire: Adrian Scott and the Politics of Americanism in 1940s Hollywood* (New York: Columbia University Press, https://hdl-handle-net.proxy.library.emory.edu/2027/heb.99024), Chapter 5, "You Can't Do That: From *The Brick Foxhole* to *Crossfire*." Langdon provides the most detailed analysis of Brooks's novel and the adaptation process. The trio's previous film, *Cornered* (1945), portrayed the need to defeat the remnants of European fascism worldwide.
3. Ibid., Chapter 6, "It *Can* Happen Here: Noir Style and the Politics of Antifascism in *Crossfire*."
4. Daniel, *Tough as Nails*, pp. 14–35.
5. Richard Brooks, *The Brick Foxhole* (New York: Harper & Brothers, 1945), pp. viii–ix.
6. Ibid. p. 9.
7. Langdon, *Caught In the Crossfire*, Chapter 5.
8. Orville Prescott, "Books of the Times: Unsuited to a Military Life," *New York Times*, May 28, 1945: p. 17.
9. William Grimes, "Richard Brooks, 79, Screenwriter and Director of Dramas, is Dead," *New York Times*, March 13, 1992: p. 38.

10. Brooks, *The Brick Foxhole*, p. 5. Mitchell's suspicion of Mary's infidelity does not come up explicitly in *Crossfire*, but in the novel, when the couple are finally reunited in the movie theater, she explains that she had met Red. But: "There had been nothing. Northing, really. It was the least those at home could do for the boys who came back. A party. A few drinks. A dance. A good-bye kiss. That was all." Mitchell is wracked with guilt for doubting Mary and his own infidelity with Ginny, pp. 212–13.
11. Brooks, *The Brick Foxhole*, p. 28.
12. Ibid. p. 82.
13. Homer B. Pettey, "*Crossfire* and Homeland Insecurity," in Alain Silver and James Ursini (eds.), *Film Noir: Light and Shadow* (Milwaukee: Applause Theatre and Centerna Books, 2017), pp. 261–2.
14. For thorough analyses of *Crossfire*'s visual style, see Pettey, "*Crossfire* and Homeland Insecurity," pp. 256–71; and James Naremore, *More Than Night: Film Noir in its Contexts, Updated and Expanded* (Berkeley: University of California Press, 2008), pp. 114–23.
15. Langdon, *Caught In the Crossfire*, Chapter 5, stresses that the creative team's anticipation of PCA objections were much more of a factor in this major change than the PCA itself.
16. Naremore, *More Than Night*, p. 116.
17. Patrick McGilligan, "Richard Brooks: The Professional," in Patrick McGilligan (ed.), *Backstory: 2: Interviews with Screenwriters of the 1940s and 1950s* (Berkeley: University of California Press, 1991), p. 41.
18. Richard Brooks, "A Novel Isn't a Movie," *Films in Review* Vol. 3 (1952), p. 58. As Langdon, *Caught In the Crossfire*, Chapter 5, notes, Brooks shows little interest in Mr. Edwards, his life history or subjectivity—and by extension that of gay men in or out of the military.
19. *The Brick Foxhole*, p. 35; Langdon, *Caught In the Crossfire*, Chapter 5.
20. Judith E. Smith, *Visions of Belonging: Family Stories, Popular Culture, and Postwar Democracy, 1940–1960* (New York: Columbia University Press, 2004), p. 145; Langdon, *Caught In the Crossfire*, Chapter 5.
21. Brooks, *The Brick Foxhole*, p. 92.
22. Ibid. pp. 85–6.
23. Ibid. p. 87.
24. Ibid. p. 89.
25. Langdon, *Caught In the Crossfire*, p. 131.
26. Captain Finlay is the most enlightened character in the novel on the subject of homosexuality. He wonders to himself if being gay is a matter of nature or nurture (p. 155). He also denounces Edwards's killing: "You soldiers get some peculiar ideas," he tells Keeley after interviewing Montgomery. "A man has strange sexual habits so you take it upon yourselves to straighten him out by murder . . . No uniform gives a man the right to do that" (p. 166).
27. Naremore, *More Than Night*, p. 118, writes:

> And yet, even though Samuels appears motivated by nothing more than decency and concern for a veteran, and even though we are told that he and Mitchell talk mostly about baseball, the scene has a sexual ambiguity. The effect is heightened because of the Socratic intensity of the conversation, because the actor playing Mitchell is boyishly handsome, and because the bizarre setting creates psychological tension. The city streets, bars, and hotel lobbies are surreally crowded with uniformed men, and Dmytryk's mise-en-scene occasionally resembles an expressionist, militarized locker room. In this place, as one character remarks, "the snakes are loose," and nobody seems purely innocent.

The bathroom scene between Monty and Leroy would be another example. The attempt to remove any suggestion of homoeroticism in Hollywood films was perennial—but it also

was particularly urgent for combat films during the war. See Robert Eberwein, "'As a Mother Cuddles a Child': Sexuality and Masculinity in World War II Combat Films," in Krin Gabbard and William H. Luhr (eds.), *Screening Genders* (New Brunswick, NJ: Rutgers University Press, 2008), pp. 111–22.
28. Brooks, *The Brick Foxhole*, p. 165.
29. Smith, *Visions of Belonging*, p. 147.
30. Brooks, *The Brick Foxhole*, p. 163.
31. Ibid. p. ix.
32. McGilligan, "Richard Brooks: The Professional," p. 41. Citing studies in American gay history, Langdon, *Caught In the Crossfire*, Chapter 5, connects the dots: WWII created unique opportunities for gay encounters among soldiers and between soldiers and civilians.
33. Brooks, *The Brick Foxhole*, pp. 101–2.
34. Ibid. pp. 105–8. These two characters are Brooks's most overt homage to one of his literary idols, Sinclair Lewis, whose *Elmer Gantry* Brooks would later adapt and direct.
35. Prescott, "Books of the Times," p. 17.
36. Richard Wright, "A Non-Combat Soldier Strips Words for Actions," *PM* (Sunday Magazine Section), June 24, 1945: p. 16.
37. Sinclair Lewis, "Obscenity and Obscurity," *Esquire*, June 1945: p. 51.
38. Prescott, "Books of the Times," p. 17.
39. Niven Busch, "A Yell of Pain in War," *The Saturday Review of Literature* 28:22, June 2, 1945: p. 12.
40. Dan Norton, "'The Brick Foxhole,'" *The New York Times*, June 3, 1945: p. BR 9.
41. Langdon, *Caught In the Crossfire*, Chapter 5.
42. In *Crossfire*, a number of Keeley's punchy dialogue exchanges with Finlay are taken verbatim from the novel; so, for that matter, are The Man's speeches about his relationship to Ginny. Among other things, Brooks demonstrated an ear for crisp dialogue.
43. Brooks, *The Brick Foxhole*, pp. 223–5. Keeley's other ally in defending democratic values is Max Brockey, the Jewish solder who boxes "Whitey" on the base and assists Keeley and Mitchell in various ways. Brockey was eliminated from *Crossfire*, though Samuels's distinguished war record recuperates Brockey's physical bravery.
44. Ibid. p. 220.
45. Brooks, *The Brick Foxhole*, p. 166.
46. Ibid. pp. 208–9.
47. Screenwriter John Paxton later characterized this climactic scene as "dramatically crude, in lousy taste" given Finlay's "improbable marksmanship." Quoted in Langdon, *Caught In the Crossfire*, Chapter 6.
48. As Langdon, *Caught In the Crossfire*, Chapter 5, puts it: "*The Brick Foxhole* also works as a narrative of conversion in which the main characters move from tolerance of intolerance and self-absorption in their own petty troubles, to the realization of the essential interconnectedness of all humanity and the necessity of individual responsibility and risk-taking to defeat fascism."
49. Brooks, *The Brick Foxhole*, p. 238.
50. Hamilton Basso, "Notes from Purgatory," *The New Yorker*, June 2, 1945: p. 68.
51. Sergeant Walter Bernstein, "Stateside Army," *The New Republic*, 113:4, July 23, 1945: p. 10. The character of Keeley contradicts much of Bernstein's characterizations—most of the time Keeley *is* concerned, in thought and deed, with the bigger picture of the war. Overall, Bernstein took umbrage at Brooks's focus on a part of the army and the army experience at the expense of the whole—stressing the rarity of fascistic soldiers, the triumphant battle against fascism abroad and the typically better-adjusted soldier. His perspective was clearly influenced by his service abroad.

52. Langdon, *Caught In the Crossfire*, Chapter 6.
53. *The Brick Foxhole* includes a subplot involving Keeley and his wife Helen, who, in contrast to Mitchell and Mary, both understand that their spouse has been unfaithful during the war. Their relationship is tenuous. Moreover, when they are reunited in D.C., we learn that Keeley has to get stupefyingly drunk and allow Helen power over him in order to make love with her. His willingness to submit to this routine inspired *Times* critic Prescott to describe Keeley as "a wise and clever man, a loyal friend and an efficient killer. But he was a hopeless drunk and the spineless victim of the sadism of his own wife. There are no characters in 'The Brick Fox Hole' [sic] who are both strong and decent." Keeley and Helen are about to make love when Keeley learns from Brockey that Mitch is hiding out in an all-night movie theater. He leaves his wife to protect his buddy. See Prescott "Books of the Times," p. 17. *Crossfire* reduces this storyline to Keeley's comment to Finlay about his own marriage.
54. Brooks, *The Brick Foxhole*, p. 39.
55. Ibid. pp. 76–80.
56. Brooks, *The Brick Foxhole*, p. 24; Pettey, "*Crossfire* and Homeland Insecurity," pp. 262–3.
57. Brooks, *The Brick Foxhole*, pp. 135–6.
58. Ibid. p. 24.
59. Ibid. p. 202.
60. Ibid. pp. 186–7.
61. Langdon, Langdon, *Caught In the Crossfire*, Chapter 6.
62. Smith, *Visions of Belonging*, p. 146.

CHAPTER 3

# The Muted Voices of Conscience and Responsibility in *Crisis* (1950)

*Alan Woolfolk*

> A realistic analysis of the problem of human society reveals a constant and seemingly irreconcilable conflict between the needs of society and the imperatives of a sensitive conscience. This conflict, which could be most briefly defined as the conflict between ethics and politics, is made inevitable by the double focus of the moral life. One focus is in the inner life of the individual, and the other is in the necessities of man's social life. From the perspective of society the highest moral ideal is justice. From the perspective of the individual the highest ideal is unselfishness.
> —Reinhold Niebuhr, *Moral Man and Immoral Society*[1]

In Richard Brooks's directorial debut in *Crisis* (1950), based on a short story by George Tabori from which Brooks adapted the screenplay, Brooks depicts the personal crisis of an American couple caught up in the post-WWII political crisis of an authoritarian South American regime, loosely evoking the rule of Juan and Eva Perón in Argentina. On the surface, the film is a conventional melodrama about the intrusion of politics into the private life of prominent American neurosurgeon Eugene Ferguson (Cary Grant) and his wife, Helen Ferguson (Paula Raymond), as Dr. Ferguson is given little choice but to perform surgery on an unpopular dictator, Raoul Farrago (José Ferrer), in order remove a brain tumor to save his life and necessarily the life of his corrupt regime. However, *Crisis*, which was originally titled *Ferguson*, also attempts to raise important moral questions centered on tensions between the imperatives of the individual conscience and the demands of political and social responsibility that are only partially articulated and incompletely addressed. Consequently, the film works as neither an outright

Hollywood melodrama nor a thought-provoking drama about the moral dilemmas of politics. Not surprisingly, *Crisis* received unimpressive reviews when released, lost money at the box office, and has not been re-evaluated by critics and scholars in hindsight as a stronger film than originally judged. Nonetheless, *Crisis* deserves further consideration despite its flaws, or perhaps because of them, as the inaugural film of a master director who was notable for his insistence upon artistic excellence, his passion for addressing matters of social justice, and his sensitivity to the demands of individual identity and conscience.

## SPECTATORS

*Crisis* begins with Eugene and Helen Ferguson on vacation in an unidentified South American country (Brooks traveled to Colombia and toured South America in preparation for directing the film, but he was forced to film in the studio by M-G-M), attending a *jai alai* match with the time described as "now."[2] In the opening scene, an unidentified man plants a bomb in an automobile outside a *fronton* covered with political posters of Farrago where the *jai alai* match is in progress. Although Farrago is not initially identified, it soon becomes increasingly apparent that he is the country's unpopular and tyrannical president, as the *jai alai* match concludes inside the *fronton* with an altercation involving the president's brother and team players, and the crowd erupting into disorder and fighting as soldiers intervene. As this scene unfolds, the Fergusons are portrayed as spectators swept up in a series of events that they do not understand and cannot control, first inside the *jai alai fronton*, where it becomes apparent that they do not know even elementary Spanish, and then outside again, when the car bomb explodes with Eugene pulling Helen away from the blast to protect her. The Fergusons continue, however, to act, back at their hotel, as if they are nothing more than detached spectators, as Eugene completes their room checkout, calls Helen on the house phone to meet him, and dismisses the attempts of a military colonel to speak to him on the hotel phone. As they drive back to their cruise ship, the Fergusons present themselves as a privileged and conventional postwar American couple, with Helen acting deferentially and talking about completing their vacation shopping on Fifth Avenue, and Eugene expressing his love for her, while both remain oblivious to the developing political realities of their immediate situation. Even when they are stopped at a military roadblock, their passports are taken, and they are forced to ride with the now identified Colonel Adragon (Ramon Novarro) to an unknown destination, they seem to underreact, expressing more umbrage than outrage.

Eugene dominates these scenes and the ones that follow with an insouciance and smugness that seems out of place and too reminiscent of Cary Grant in earlier film roles, as a waiting train is commandeered, an entire railway car is emptied of disgruntled peasants from the countryside, the Fergusons are placed onboard under guard, and they travel overnight through snow-capped mountains towards the Presidential Palace. On awakening the next morning, Eugene wanders around the railway car with a native blanket draped over his shoulders engaging in a series of comedic interactions that work at cross purposes to the personal and political drama unfolding. For example, when Eugene finds himself without water in the restroom, he secures from a friendly peasant some liquor with which he ostentatiously brushes his teeth and gargles, and then remarks to Helen when she asks about his new mouthwash that it is "moonshine rinse," as he offers her coffee that he has brusquely taken from the colonel's breakfast table after insulting him. All of this seems oddly incongruous with the serious intent of *Crisis*, but these scenes nonetheless serve to reinforce the impression that the Fergusons continue to imagine themselves as privileged, disengaged tourists, even as they almost blithely speculate on the possibility that they have been kidnapped.

The Fergusons's detachment ends abruptly when bullets are fired at the car in which they are riding with the colonel and the bulletproof glass next to Eugene is shattered as the colonel attempts to protect him, soldiers return fire, and they finally approach the heavily guarded Presidential Palace. But it is not until they meet the imperious but cordial Isabel Farrago (Signe Hasso), the wife of the President, and Eugene demands to know why they have been arrested and "held prisoners like criminals," that he and Helen learn President Farrago is gravely ill with a brain tumor. At this point, as Isabel pleads with Eugene and Helen for him to examine her husband, the viewer learns that Eugene is a renowned neurosurgeon from Johns Hopkins University. When Eugene responds to Isabel's comment that he is "modest" with the retort that he is "never modest," and then responds to Isabel's next remark that "some people want my husband to die" with the reply "*not a doctor*," we know that Eugene has ceased to be a spectator. Some complex combination of conscience and pride has been set in motion.

## CONSCIENCE

In the scenes that follow, Eugene quickly exhibits his expertise as a medical doctor and his astuteness in evaluating his personal situation as he rapidly assesses both the condition of Farrago and the implications of the developing political crisis for himself and Helen. He meets and examines the arrogant and fiery Farrago, who engages in a tirade about his military commander's inability to put down the popular rebellion and the need to show courage.

As Eugene observes Farrago having difficulty lighting his cigarette, he begins to conduct a series of tests on Farrago that are interrupted by a seizure

Figure 3.1 Neurosurgeon Eugene Ferguson (Cary Grant) meets dictator Raoul Farrago (José Ferrer).

and then followed by further tests of his vision. Upon completing his examination, the results are obvious, but Eugene remains evasive about committing to surgery, all the while carrying out a negotiating strategy. He tells Farrago when asked if he can be trusted that "you can't" trust him. When Isabel and even Helen plead with Eugene to help, he relents but demands that their passports be returned and raises the question of his fee. A short while later when Helen and Eugene are in private, Helen learns that Eugene had decided to operate from the moment he saw Farrago's condition. Although Helen is taken aback and informs Eugene seemingly in jest that he has a "vicious streak," he clearly has accurately assessed their predicament, telling her that they are caught in the middle of a national crisis without friends and few rights. "Have you thought what could happen? Suppose he dies . . .?" Even so, Eugene only understands the implications of the political crisis in terms of their immediate personal crisis. Eugene's astuteness should not be mistaken for an exercise in Aristotelean *phronesis.*

Eugene is driven by the Hippocratic moral imperative to attend to the health of his patient. When Helen suggests that he not perform the operation, Eugene's response is understated: "I've got to. I've already committed." Dictator or not, he will attempt to save Farrago's life as a matter of conscience. But Eugene also tells Helen that he has not been given a choice, that he "dislikes force of any kind by anybody." As Eugene reluctantly agrees to convert the elaborate reception area outside Farrago's bedroom into an operating room, Eugene and Farrago engage in another extended discussion in which Eugene returns to the theme of freedom. After showing little patience for Farrago's attempted humorous remarks about being "a good patient" and his egotistical anecdotes about how he rules his country, Eugene rejects Farrago's invitation to dine with him, informing him that he has another invitation and that he "insists on freedom." However, Eugene's invocation of freedom seems to be more personal than political, merely a question of individual agency and rights. Eugene sounds very American insofar as he invokes a notion of freedom that makes no reference to the virtues of republican government, the rule of law, free and fair elections, and the like. Even Eugene's comment to Farrago that he considers his "enemies" on the streets to be his "friends" rings hollow, in that Eugene appears to know very little about the people and history of the country that he is visiting. Indeed, the whole premise of the film begs the question of why Eugene and Helen are even vacationing in a country that is obviously in the midst of a political crisis and on the verge of a violent overthrow of the government.

Eugene is presented as an apolitical but dedicated and conscientious doctor, who is determined to follow through on his commitment to his morally corrupt patient. These two points are driven home in the next scene in which Eugene and Helen dine with the genial American oil executive, Sam Proctor (Leon Ames), at a local restaurant. First, Eugene has no meaningful response to Proctor's description of the questionable business arrangement whereby his company and Farrago share the profits from the country's oil that is extracted. He expresses no outrage that Farrago receives thirty percent which he deposits in a Swiss bank account. Second, when Proctor tells Eugene to "forget the operation," that he can arrange a car to get them out of the country, Eugene responds that he "can't do that," that "the man will die" from "a meningioma of the left temporal lobe." The discrepancy between the two responses is telling: Eugene is driven by the strict moral demands of his medical profession, but he is unable to see the larger political and moral issues at stake. The medical interdict to "do no harm" means saving the life of an egotistical and dangerous dictator with the consequence that he will certainly continue to harm others. Removing Farrago's tumor will enable the tumor of the body politic to grow.

RESPONSIBILITY

Brooks's concern for social justice was a consistent theme throughout his life as a writer and director that is perhaps most evident in his early novel *The Brick Foxhole* (1945), which focused on prejudice against homosexuals in the military (adapted for the film *Crossfire* [Edward Dmytryk, 1947] with the prejudice changed to anti-Semitism), and the successful, critically acclaimed film *Blackboard Jungle* (1955), which Brooks wrote the screenplay for and directed. In *Crisis*, Eugene is confronted with the political and social reality of Farrago's rule when Sam takes Eugene and Helen, at her prompting, to a local restaurant to have "some fun." At the restaurant, importunate patrons quickly introduce themselves to the Fergusons and plead with Eugene not to perform the operation on Farrago. An internationally acclaimed guitarist, Guillermo Cariago (Vicente Gómez), asks Eugene if he will "save the life of this tyrant?" and Eugene learns that Cariago has pledged not to play again until "my people are free." Roland Gonzales (Gilbert Roland), who is clearly a leader of the revolution, bluntly tells Eugene that he should simply make a slip with his surgeon's knife once Farrago's head is open. Rosa Aldana (Teresa Celli), the wife of the proprietor of the restaurant, angrily tells Eugene that perhaps it would be better if the doctor were dead. But Eugene remains guarded and circumspect. Even when Cariago decides to play his guitar again in honor of Eugene, he remains unmoved. However, when Colonel Adragon arrives with a contingent of soldiers, strikes Rosa several times for her brazenness, and informs Eugene that he and his party should leave, Eugene does act.

Much to the amazement of the restaurant guests, Eugene asks Colonel Adragon why he must leave and informs him that he will resist arrest, forcing him to either beat him unconscious or shoot him, thereby creating problems for his boss. Outmaneuvered, the colonel retreats and the crowd breaks into cheers under the leadership of Gonzales. Eugene then follows this unexpected act of resistance with a gesture of compassion towards Rosa, offering her ice for her bruised face and telling her that he wishes "there was something more I could do about it." In both instances, Eugene continues to act on the basis of an ethic of conscience, rather than an ethic of responsibility.[3] He dislikes being forced to do anything against his will. His insistence on freedom apparently extends to others. Similarly, his commitment and compassion as a doctor obviously includes attending to individuals in distress. Eugene acts from a sense of duty, rather than calculating how just political ends may be achieved. He is moved to relieve the suffering of individuals, but not the misery of some larger population of humanity through a consideration of political means and ends. Consequently, to the extent that the crowd in the restaurant imagines that the good doctor is with them, they are mistaken. Eugene will not be moved to expedient but morally questionable action by the widespread injustice of the Farrago regime, nor will he be moved by the passionate imperatives of what is called "the social question," to which he appears, less to his credit, immune.[4] As Eugene proceeds to exit the restaurant, Gonzales announces that "there is something you can do for all of us," but Eugene responds with a simple "good night" as he leaves.

In his seminal essay, "Politics as a Vocation," Max Weber took exception to adherents of an ethic of conscience (or *Gesinnungsethik*, frequently translated as an "ethic of ultimate ends") because he contended that such believers feel "'responsible' only for seeing to it that the flame of pure intentions is not quelched . . . To rekindle the flame ever anew is the purpose of . . . quite irrational deeds, judged in view of their possible success. They are acts that can and shall have only exemplary value." In Weber's critical view, such believers evade difficult problems of political responsibility. "No ethics in the world can dodge the fact that in numerous instances the attainment of 'good' ends is bound to the fact that one must be willing to pay the price of using morally dubious means or at least dangerous ones—and facing the possibility of or even the probability of evil ramifications."[5] However, Weber himself in turn evades difficult questions concerning the corrupting influence of "morally dubious means." The Hippocratic interdict to "do no harm" defines the essence of the medical profession. *Crisis* suggests that an ethic of responsibility (Weber's or any other) allows for exceptions that would destroy the practice of medicine with little chance of preventing greater harm. Removing the tumor from the body politic is a false promise because of the corrupting influence of corrupt means.

*Crisis* presents yet another example of an ethic of conscience subjected to political pressures in the case of the priest, Father del Puento (Pedro de Cordoba), who is twice asked to support the regime, in the second instance to declare a day of prayer for Farrago. In both instances, Father del Puento refuses, explaining in the first instance that he is under "God's law" and in the second that he cannot "use prayer for political reasons." For both Eugene and Father del Puento, the corrupting influence of politics appears to be clear. However, in the case of Eugene, the extent and the depth of the corruption only gradually comes into focus as he is further exposed to the political means of not only Farrago but also the revolutionaries.

## METHODS AND MEANS

The political means of the revolutionaries are put into relief as Eugene methodically proceeds with preparation for surgery with a team of untested local medical personnel, including Farrago's personal physician (Antonio Moreno). The order and precision of these preparations and the subsequent execution of the surgery form a stark contrast with the revolutionary violence and disorder present from the opening scenes of the film that prepare for the final overthrow of the Farrago regime. The contrast between the execution of the surgery and the methods of the revolutionaries is further highlighted by the fact that the revolutionaries, under the leadership of Gonzales, kidnap Helen prior to the surgery to ensure that Farrago does not survive the operation. However, the communiqué informing Eugene that Helen is being held as a hostage never reaches him. Consequently, Eugene operates on Farrago in ignorance of the threat to Helen. Once Eugene successfully completes the operation, there is a lull of a few days during which Farrago appears to recover and the populace, including the revolutionaries, are left in suspense as to the outcome of the surgery, while Eugene remains unaware that Helen has been kidnapped. In their parallel states of mutual unawareness, Eugene and Gonzales are a study in contrasts, with Eugene holding the superior moral position. Whether Gonzales would really harm Helen is unknown, but he has already demonstrated his willingness to employ coercion and violence in the name of the revolution to achieve his ends. Whether Eugene would intentionally kill Farrago, if he knew that Helen's life was at stake, remains an open question that the film does not answer to its discredit for reasons that are discussed below. Even so, to overdraw the parallel between Eugene and Gonzales risks suggesting that they are potentially morally equivalent, when the evidence is clear that they are not.

Definitive evidence of the shortcomings of the revolution is presented in the closing minutes of the film with the downfall of the Farrago regime imminent, when Eugene finally learns in disbelief from Gonzales that Helen has been kidnapped and held hostage. Upon learning this, Eugene refuses to tell Gonzales if Farrago survived the operation and immediately returns to the Presidential Palace to confront Farrago, although it is not clear to what end. Upon first confronting Isabel, Eugene learns that in fact she did intercept the communiqué from Gonzales and is completely indifferent to the fate of Helen. By the time Eugene reaches Farrago, he is on the verge of a massive brain hemorrhage and within a matter of minutes collapses and dies, all the while raving about how indispensable he is to his country. While the callousness of the Farragos is quite predictable, Gonzales's response a few moments later is more revealing in that he suddenly no longer cares how Farrago died (having already set Helen free), but instead explains to Eugene in the midst of the revolutionary celebration and chaos how he will become the new leader in paternalistic language that is strikingly similar to Farrago's earlier comments.

Gonzales's revealing comments to Eugene, just prior to being shot in the midst of the revolutionary disorder, that the people "are excited, like children," that "they will learn, I will teach them," and that they will "always need a leader" are simply a less explicit version of comments made by Farrago prior to his operation. On that occasion, Farrago informs Eugene that freedom "would not work here . . . you have to be educated to freedom," and concludes with the comments that "people are stupid" and "cannot help themselves . . . only I can help them." While the parallel between Farrago and Gonzales is overdrawn, it serves to underscore the cyclical and cynical nature of politics depicted in the film that leaves little hope for a genuine ethic of responsibility.

It is not surprising that *Crisis* was banned in a number of Latin American countries upon release because of its pejorative depiction of the region's politics. Nonetheless, V. S. Naipaul made a similar point some years later prior to the return of Juan Perón to power in Argentina in 1973:

> The nation appears to be playing a game with itself; and Argentine political life is like the life of an ant colony or an African forest tribe: full of events, full of crises and deaths, but life is only cyclical, and the year always ends as it begins.[6]

What is missing from *Crisis*, however, is any serious consideration of the role of populist politics in perpetuating this cycle. Although Farrago makes one comment about how he hates "poverty and disease," the point is not developed: "the social question" of the misery of the masses is not addressed as critical to understanding the dynamics of the populist politics of South America.[7] More significantly, *Crisis* fails to develop the final and definitive crisis that was in the original screenplay but cut from the film because it was censored by the Breen Office that enforced the Production Code for the motion picture industry.[8] *Crisis* contains no genuine crisis of conscience.

## THE ABSENT CRISIS

In Brooks's original screenplay, Eugene goes to Farrago's quarters in the climactic scene with a gun, clearly intending to kill him in order to save Helen's life. However, the Breen Office deemed "an act of murder that is portrayed as acceptable and justifiable" as not allowable under the Code. Consequently, Brooks decided to rewrite the scene, with Eugene confronting Farrago unarmed and without clear intentions.[9] But since Farrago suffers a brain hemorrhage and dies shortly after the confrontation begins, the question of Eugene's intentions becomes a moot point. The possibility of the good doctor confronting a profound moral crisis because he is forced to do precisely what he must not and cannot do to preserve his very integrity as a physician, yet does, was eliminated from the narrative of the film in favor of an ending that is both evasive and hypocritical.

The revised ending of *Crisis* is evasive because it perpetuates a false myth created by the film that adherents of an ethic of conscience face neither difficult choices nor the prospect of a guilty conscience. Eugene, after all, is never seriously tempted to deviate from his commitment to saving Farrago. The original ending subverted this myth. As it stands, *Crisis* closes with the dying Gonzales crying out to Eugene, "Save me, doctor," and Eugene answering with the plaintive soliloquy, "Same old cry, down through the ages. Save me doctor,

Figure 3.2 The death of Gonzales (Gilbert Roland).

save me anybody." As a consequence, an inner struggle is avoided. Eugene does not have to confront what he is capable of under extreme circumstances. Rather, he indulges in a moralizing cry about the eternal shortcomings of the world that hypocritically confirms his own moral superiority.

The moral tension in *Crisis* could have been raised in two ways. First, the film might have intensified what Niebuhr called the "constant and seemingly irreconcilable conflict between the needs of society and the imperatives of a sensitive conscience" by presenting a stronger and more compelling vision of "the conflict between ethics and politics."[10] This could have been accomplished through a much more effective representation of the ideal of justice underlying the politics of the revolutionaries, rather than a depiction that merely accents the corruption of the leadership. Eugene is never really tempted to kill Farrago because his moral certainty and smugness is not seriously challenged. He is confronted with nothing that would realistically result in a conversion to the revolutionary cause because he seems largely indifferent to corruption, which extends to the revolutionaries anyhow, and remains physically and psychologically removed from any significant exposure to the misery of the population that might persuade him to act otherwise. Consequently, *Crisis* fails to create the minimal tension between an ethic of conscience and an ethic of responsibility necessary for a genuine moral drama about the conflict between ethics and politics.

Second, *Crisis* does not create the necessary tension between an uncompromising set of moral demands and the trials of personal life, even though the film repeatedly promises to do so. Eugene affirms time and again his commitment to saving the life of Farrago as his concern for the safety of Helen grows, culminating with her boarding a train to leave the country after the riot at the Fernandez memorial. Yet, *Crisis* never gets to the point of seriously challenging Eugene's high principles, with the result that Eugene remains untested. He does not traverse Keats's famous "vale of Soul-making," nor is he even presented with that option at the close of the film. The originally scripted ending would have explicitly opened this door. While Eugene possesses the necessary "intelligence," he does not seem to have acquired what Keats calls an "identity" because of his moral self-righteousness and smugness. Faced with the necessity of killing Farrago in order to save Helen's life, Eugene would have been confronted with, in the words of Keats, "a world of Pains and troubles" necessary "to school an Intelligence and make it a soul."[11] Instead, he is let off the spiritual hook and will suffer no guilty conscience.

This may seem an unfair charge. Yet, Brooks went on to explore crises of conscience in later films. The topic clearly fascinated him. In *Blackboard Jungle*, which Brooks wrote and directed, as mentioned earlier, WWII veteran Richard Dadier (Glenn Ford) must endure his own particular vale of Soul-making as a teacher at an inner-city vocational high school, who in the end must decide either to abandon the school and move on to a more comfortable teaching position or to stay. Brooks returned to the subject of a *crise de conscience* again, most notably in *Lord Jim* (1965), which was, of course, an adaptation of Joseph Conrad's well-known novel. Brooks wrote the screenplay, produced, and directed the film, having purchased the movie rights in 1957 in anticipation of one day having the opportunity to direct a film adaptation.[12] But when compared to his earlier acclaimed films such as *Cat on a Hot Tin Roof* (1958) and *Elmer Gantry* (1960), which Brooks directed, *Lord Jim* was not a successful film, thanks in no small measure to the befuddled performance of star Peter O'Toole. Nonetheless, the subject matter could not have been more important and illuminates *Crisis*, as well as other films, directed by Brooks.

*Lord Jim* as both a novel and a film is a study of an individual who identifies with a militant idealized image of himself as a sailor in the merchant marine, but who suffers from a catastrophic failure to live up to those ideals. While Brooks perceived Jim as an individual in need of a "second chance," he may not have understood the extent to which the references to Jim's "superb" and "exalted egoism" in the novel by the narrator Marlow gloss over the significance of Jim's internalization of militant ideals and the dynamics of his public conception of himself.[13] Such militant ideals and public self-understandings had already grown weak in the late modern world by the time Brooks began directing films in the

1950s and have only grown weaker since. But Brooks intuitively understood that deeply internalized militant conceptions of the self continued to persist in certain professions, even as our culture as a whole had grown more tolerant of remissions from these ideals. Hence, Brooks explored the militant ideals of the merchant marine (at the turn of the twentieth century) in *Lord Jim*, the trials of the teaching profession in *Blackboard Jungle*, the hypocrisies of the ministry in *Elmer Gantry*, and of course the code and commitments of the medical profession in *Crisis* because he was fascinated by the moral dynamics of the self. Eugene's moral certainty and smugness are in the end evidence of his own deeply internalized ideal conception of himself in *Crisis*. Unfortunately, the film that Brooks directed and created does not present the protagonist with an identity-defining crisis that would have immeasurably elevated the drama of the good doctor's confrontation with himself and others.

## NOTES

1. Reinhold Niebuhr, *Moral Man and Immoral Society: A Study in Ethics and Politics* (New York: Charles Scribner's Sons, 1960), p. 257.
2. Douglass K. Daniel, *Tough as Nails: The Life and Films of Richard Brooks* (Madison: The University of Wisconsin Press, 2011), pp. 8–9.
3. The distinction between an ethic of conscience and an ethic of responsibility is probably best known through the work of Max Weber. See Weber's classic statement "Politics as a Vocation," in *From Max Weber: Essays in Sociology*, translated, edited, and with an Introduction by H. H. Gerth and C. Wright Mills (New York: Oxford University Press, 1958), pp. 77–128. Reinhold Niebuhr presented perhaps the best-known defense of an ethic of conscience in the twentieth century (see note 1 above).
4. On "the social question," see note 7 below.
5. Weber, "Politics as a Vocation," p. 121.
6. V. S. Naipaul, *The Return of Eva Perón with the Killings in Trinidad* (New York: Alfred A. Knopf, 1980), p. 101.
7. T. G. Masaryk memorably characterized "the social question" as "the great fact of all the economic, social, moral, and material misery that confronts us constantly, whether we look at the luxury of the rich or the poverty of the proletariat, whether we observe life in the cities or in the country, in the streets or in the home. The social question? Today that means unrest and discontent, aspirations and fear, and the hope and despair of thousands and millions . . ." (*Masaryk on Marx*, edited and translated by Erazim V. Kohák [Lewisburg, PA: Bucknell University Press, 1972], p. 25). For an analysis of the social question with reference to the American and French revolutions, see Hannah Arendt, "The Social Question," *On Revolution* (New York: The Viking Press, 1962), pp. 53–110.
8. Daniel, *Tough as Nails*, pp. 8–9.
9. Ibid.
10. Niebuhr, *Moral Man and Immoral Society*, p. 257.
11. John Keats, *Complete Poems and Selected Letters of John Keats*, Introduction by Edward Hirsch, Notes by Jim Pollock (New York: The Modern Library, 2001), p. 505.
12. Daniel, *Tough as Nails*, p. 152.

13. Daniel, *Tough as Nails*, pp. 154–5. Joseph Conrad, *Lord Jim*, with a general Introduction by Albert J. Guerard (New York: Dell Publishing Company, c. 1961), pp. 381, 384. Note the following passage in the penultimate paragraph of the novel: "But we can see him, an obscure conqueror of fame, tearing himself out of the arms of a jealous love at the sign, at the call of his exalted egoism. He goes away from a living woman to celebrate his pitiless wedding with a shadowy ideal of conduct" (p. 384).

## FILMOGRAPHY

*Blackboard Jungle* (M-G-M, 1955). Directed and screenplay by Richard Brooks.
*Cat on a Hot Tin Roof* (M-G-M, 1958). Directed by Richard Brooks. Screenplay by Richard Brooks and James Poe.
*Crisis* (M-G-M, 1950). Directed and screenplay by Richard Brooks.
*Crossfire* (RKO, 1947). Directed by Edward Dmytryk. Screenplay by John Paxton. Based on the novel *The Brick Foxhole* by Richard Brooks.
*Elmer Gantry* (Elmer Gantry Productions through United Artists, 1960). Directed and screenplay by Richard Brooks.
*Lord Jim* (Columbia and Keep Films through Columbia, 1965). Directed, produced, and screenplay by Richard Brooks.

CHAPTER 4

# *Deadline—U.S.A.* (1952): A Fox Film of Fact

R. Barton Palmer

Richard Brooks achieved quick success as both a screenwriter and a novelist, but when he turned to directing he found the going much tougher initially. His first two projects as director, the sub-Hitchcockian thrillers *Crisis* (1950) and *The Light Touch* (1951), were sourced in women's magazine fiction, the rights to which had previously been purchased by M-G-M, then ruled by the legendary Louis B. Mayer, with whom Brooks had signed the long-term contract that would decisively shape his early career. Because he was an experienced screenwriter, M-G-M was willing to grant him this limited control over story, thinking that he would get the most out of what he had been given. Shot and then completed with no notable difficulties, *Crisis* and *Touch* demonstrated that Brooks could see to more or less scheduled conclusions projects that turned out to be somewhat suspenseful and entertaining, with characters who are far from unengaging. He ably directed the star performers (Cary Grant and Stewart Granger) in the lead roles; in *Touch* he oversaw effectively the substantial contributions of the established headliner George Sanders and sensational newcomer Pier Angeli.

For whatever reason, however, Brooks proved unable in both cases to remedy (or at least mask) effectively the weaknesses of what he adapted for the screen. Commenting on the myriad narrative problems in the "pulp magazine story" screened in *Crisis*, Bosley Crowther offered the director a backhanded compliment: "it is remarkable that Mr. Brooks has been able to get any substance of even passing consequence on the screen."[1] This judgment is perhaps a bit harsh since it slights the film's effective staging of the *crise morale*, à la Graham Greene, endured by Cary Grant's surgeon, Dr. Eugene Ferguson. On vacation with his wife in Latin America, he has been kidnapped to perform a life-saving operation on a brutal dictator, Raoul Farrago (José Ferrer). Helen Ferguson

(Paula Raymond) has in turn been abducted by Farrago's political opposition, who tell him that her life is forfeit if Ferguson does not let his patient die. True to his oath, Ferguson does his best, but Farrago dies anyway, and later Helen is released. Director and star found themselves as part of a story that, if compelling, at numerous points could have made better sense. Miscasting might have been part of the problem. Grant seems to have landed somehow in the wrong film genre, and he was saddled with a "B" list female lead with whom he could find little personal connection. For his part, Brooks failed to coach Raymond into anything more than a barely adequate performance (for all its faults the film does show promise: see further Woolfolk in this volume).

Neither release generated much in the way of audience interest, and both ended up in the red, with the substantial loss suffered in *Touch* particularly galling for the studio. With the exception of the Raymond casting decision and the sub-literary sources, Mayer had provided Brooks with material for *Crisis* from which he, arguably, could have developed better results. *Touch* had the advantage of a good-sized budget that allowed for extensive location work in Sicily, with its focus on international intrigue and romance interestingly anticipating the greater success of other sunny European-sited films later in the next decade or so, including *Roman Holiday* (1953), *Three Coins in the Fountain* (1954), *To Catch a Thief* (1955), *A Certain Smile* (1958), *Bonjour, Tristesse* (1958), and *Light in the Piazza* (1962) all based on story materials that are also hardly free from melodramatic cliché and plot absurdities. With *Dollars$* (1971), which pleased most critics and did decent business, Brooks would later demonstrate that he could turn out a first-rate romantic/adventure film, but this genre never resonated with his métier, which, like that of Joseph L. Mankiewicz, tended toward the literary in terms of both sources and treatment.

One can see a kind of logic in the two first assignments Brooks was given. After all, he had done excellent work on the screenplay he helped fashion for *Key Largo* (1948), a drama that centered on a moral and psychological issue not all that different from the one explored in *Crisis* (see Pettey's discussion of his work on that film in the Introduction). Similarly, the complex juggling of several lines of action he helped work out in his script for *The Killers* (1946), with its exploration of betrayal, temptation, and conflicted loyalties, suggests the kind of treatment that was needed to remedy similar problems with the heist plot and its unpredictable aftermath in *Touch*. Given the director's professional history, Mayer and company likely thought the bright young man could make something reasonably successful from these genre materials, which were inexpensive but then not pre-sold in the least.

In the opinion of his biographer, these were projects in which Brooks could find "no special interest," and that lack of investment can be sensed from what he puts on the screen. Working on them had not excited the "passion" he needed to engage his storytelling talent and demonstrate—as he would many times in his subsequent career—that he could turn out a serious film that was also first-class movie entertainment.[2] After these box office failures, Brooks needed no fortune teller to foresee that his career as a director would soon be over if he did not do better the next time. It suits perfectly the auteurist paradigm that, with the system not providing him with the opportunity to make films that succeeded both critically and in terms of box office, he would make a sharp turn to a project that was as personal as his contract would permit.

Brooks's response to failure was not to politic with his erstwhile employers at M-G-M to provide him with a more promising property. Instead, in a move that would establish him as something of a maverick, Brooks took the situation into his own hands by composing an original screenplay for his next project, which would eventually be titled *Deadline—U.S.A.* This project could hardly have been more different from those he had been working on. Even more surprising, the script he had in mind fell into the postwar production series of message pictures and would never suit studio head Mayer, though Dore Schary, the head of production who replaced him as studio head during early 1951, would have found the subject matter and treatment more congenial; by the time Schary was in charge, however, *Deadline* was being developed with a cross-town rival, Twentieth Century-Fox, whose studio chief, Darryl F. Zanuck, was pleased to have it as part of the series of realistic socially conscious dramas Fox had been specializing in since the war. Schary was more enthusiastic about this kind of film and of Brooks's interests more generally. He would, for example, be very much in favor of *Blackboard Jungle* (1955), also a message picture of sorts, that Brooks made a few years later when back at M-G-M.

Brooks's script for this new project told the story of the efforts of a crusading editor, Ed Hutcheson (Humphrey Bogart), who tries to prevent the sale of his paper, *The Day*, to its chief competitor, *The Standard*, even as he dedicates himself and his reporters to proving that a nationally prominent crime boss, Tomas Rienzi (Martin Gabel), had ordered the murder of his erstwhile mistress in order to conceal his bribery of candidates in a recent election. *The Day* and its indefatigable editor would thus achieve what none of the official institutions of law enforcement despite years of investigation had managed to do. This story embodied material and themes that, if in some ways generic and resonant with the message picture series, also reflected the screenwriter's experience as a journalist, as well as his liberal political views.

This new story was a fictional creation, fabricated from conventional elements of the contemporary crime melodrama, but with a villain at its center who was drawn from recent headlines. Rienzi seems a fictional version of New York City crime boss Frank Costello (1891–1973). Costello, the so-called prime minister of the Mafia, had been a notorious figure since Prohibition, but he had recently come again to national notice during the 1951 New York City hearings of the Senate Special Committee on Interstate Organized Crime, chaired by Estes Kefauver. The proceedings were a considerable public sensation. They completed a national circuit of major cities that transformed Kefauver into one of America's best-known political figures. As a result of his appearance before the committee, Costello's photo, to his considerable chagrin, appeared on many a newspaper front page around the country over a period of weeks, lending him a celebrity that rivaled that of his senatorial inquisitor.[3]

Further unwanted publicity for this figure from the New York underworld was provided by *Deadline*'s opening sequence: an authentically detailed account of a gangster, who was a dead ringer for Costello thanks to Gabel's casting, undergoing a version of the grilling that the mobster had, famously and not long ago, faced from Kefauver and his staff, likely while Brooks was working on the screenplay. Extraordinarily, this hearing had been televised by local New York City station WPIX 11, and it became one of the most important early "live" events for the new medium.[4] The film evokes this event with a crowded mise en scène that includes camera, lights, microphones, and technicians, all of which Brooks's camera carefully captures. His script for this brief sequence is based closely on the line of questioning to which Costello was subjected and which the mobster deflected adroitly with mischievous humor, as recorded both in the committee's report and also in newspaper accounts of the event. With this reconstruction of recent history, *Deadline* became in some sense a true event film.

Like the Kefauver investigation, *Deadline* is a response to a nationwide phenomenon, what historian William Howard Moore refers to as the "Postwar Crime Scare," a concern in many cities around the country about what was perceived as an increasing prevalence of organized gambling and associated vices such as prostitution and loansharking.[5] Crime commissions were established in Kansas City (Missouri), Gary (Indiana), and elsewhere, but the crusade would soon go national. On May 2, 1950, after a bitter fight, the United States Senate passed Senate Resolution 202 establishing a five-member special Committee on Organized Crime with a substantial budget of $150,000 and a charge to conduct over a period of fifteen months investigations of criminal conspiracies, usually involving political corruption, to be held in fourteen American cities. This would be, Kefauver bragged, a "national crusade, a great debating forum, an arouser of public opinion on the state of the nation's morals."[6]

Though a purely administrative, not a legislative, action, the establishment of this committee turned out to be era-defining, as Americans through the committee's hearings (held publicly in all the different cities) and various timely publications were informed about the existence of a shadowy alternative economy that often operated with the collusion of local authorities. The federal government's involvement in discovering the extent of such activity, often linked to otherwise legitimate businesses, was in response to numerous local and regional requests for action. In particular, the year before, the American Municipal Association (now the National League of Cities) had asked the federal government to investigate what many of its members believed was a serious threat: the flourishing of organized crime networks, some with interstate connections, that, profiting from gambling, loansharking and prostitution, managed to buy influence over local governments, even turning some municipalities into virtual criminal enterprises.[7]

With its hooks to current events, its intricate but easy to follow plotting, and its characters drawn in some depth, *Deadline* appealed immediately to Zanuck, who was interested in factual fiction properties, but only those that could be charged with entertainment value and express serious themes. As was his practice, the producer took a hand in shaping the property for the market in ways that had proven successful with similar projects. He believed that such films of fact needed to be provided with entertainment value in order to be successful at the box office. These films should possess what he called "factual technique" and "factual dramatization," and they should be centered on a "vital personal story" that involved "characters whom we understand and appreciate."[8] He had been producing such films at Fox for some years, the most successful of which had been Elia Kazan's *Gentleman's Agreement* (1947), whose main character, Phil Green (Gregory Peck), is yet another crusading journalist, one who this time sheds a harsh light on the social problem of anti-Semitism, especially as it plays out in the tony suburban precincts of Fairfield County, while he also romances a young widow from that set, Kathy (Dorothy McGuire).

This series of films, which includes *Deadline*, had a long life, enduring because of Zanuck's interests to the last years of the decade, although the fashion for these factual films had been waning for some time. Zanuck's production of *Island in the Sun* (1957), directed by Robert Rossen, followed the pattern set a decade earlier by *Agreement*; it too was an adaptation of a controversial novel (by Alec Waugh) that dealt with a current issue (race relations in the British West Indies) in a realist, almost documentary style (much of the film was shot in Barbados), but its several vexed romances and political intrigue possessed an entertainment value that justified a substantial budget. When *Island* generated controversy during its U.S. release because of its focus on a black/white romance, Zanuck was pleased to enjoy the free publicity thereby provided, even though exhibition in the American south was harmed by the frank racial themes.[9] While engaged with *Deadline*, he was also working with director Joseph L. Mankiewicz to impose the same pattern on his espionage adventure project, based on *Operation Cicero*, an account written by one of the German agents involved. Retitled as *Five Fingers*, the film would also appear in 1952 and achieve the respectable box office success enjoyed by *Deadline*. Zanuck's eight-page memo to Brooks outlined suggested improvements, minor and major, similar to those he had made in the case of *Fingers*, most of which Brooks adopted since they suited his vision of what the film should be.[10]

In *Deadline*, the committee questioning fails to reveal evidence that would put Rienzi out of business, as we are soon informed. It is only the subsequent criminal investigation organized by *The Day* that brings him down. Here real life and fiction diverge. Costello did land in jail not long after the Kefauver show left town, serving a sentence for contempt. Further, disabling legal troubles soon followed (details in de Stefano). In *Deadline*, Rienzi's fall from prominence, however, is engineered by intrepid journalists (Hutcheson is pure fiction, not a composite character). Costello was stymied by government lawyers working with New York authorities and the Senate investigators, rather than by an intrepid editor devoted to a Pulitzer-like code of public service.

If it does so through a fabulized turn of events, *Deadline* speaks a larger truth in suggesting that Rienzi (Costello) is "finished." Brooks accurately sums up what the next few years had in store for the crime boss: some time spent in prison, then "retirement," and finally irrelevance as his generation of Mafiosi (including one-time collaborator Lucky Luciano) passed from the scene. For obvious legal reasons, Brooks (as Welles did with Hearst in *Citizen Kane*) had to take care not to make Rienzi and his real-life model too similar, but the detailed recreation of the gangster's famous encounter with the Senate investigators left no doubt among the cognoscenti as to the director/writer's intentions. As a result of both casting and presentation, Gabel's Rienzi certainly looked the part.

By the early 1950s, Costello, thanks to widespread publicity, had become the very image of organized crime, and of the Mafia in particular. And so Brooks must have been surprised that *Deadline* was not appreciated by the critics for this *à clef* frame, which lends its fictionalized version of a recent event (the decline of Costello as a major crime figure) the urgent timeliness expressed by its title.

An "A" production, *Deadline* purveys, if with more intellectual depth and acting talent, the cinematic journalism of many successful "B" noirs of the period that focused on urban corruption and organized crime. Most important of these was Robert Wise's *Captive City* (1952), released in March 1952, just two weeks after *Deadline* premiered, which also features the takedown of a crime boss and uses the Kefauver investigations as a hook (the senator, never camera shy, appears in the film's epilogue). *The Phenix City Story* (1955), written by Crane Wilbur and directed by Phil Karlson, would be the apotheosis of the period's anti-crime, factual fiction series. The film is celebrated for its riveting presentation of events that took place in that Alabama city, a famously corrupt watering hole for soldiers from nearby Fort Benning. Like *Captive City*, it also uses footage of actual participants in the story. As in *Deadline*, the successful criminal investigation is based on the fact with some alteration for dramatic effect. All three films communicate the same message: that the country's institutions have recognized the widespread and destructive power of organized crime, long mistakenly tolerated as a harmless social evil, and are

Figures 4.1a, 4.1b  Frank Costello and, below, Martin Gabel as Tomas Rienzi.

now determined to get this illegal activity under control. Interestingly, in both *Captive* and *Phenix*, as in *Deadline*, journalists are among those most active in uncovering and destroying organizations making a profit from vice and the resultant government corruption.

Zanuck was interested in production standards that would justify a substantial budget, hence the casting of leading performers. He had been producing such films at Fox for some years, the most successful of which had been *Agreement*. It is certainly possible, even likely, that Brooks, in the wake of that film's considerable success with critics and middlebrow viewers, conceived his project from the beginning as a Fox film. If so, that would explain why what was provisionally titled "Newspaper Story" fit so perfectly, after the adjustments that Brooks eagerly adopted, into the series of similarly prestigious and profitable films of fact that had become a Fox specialty since *The House on 92nd Street* (1945).[11] Like Kazan's call for tolerance and empathy, *Deadline* would argue for a substantial change in the national culture, for the reform of a social evil (the gambling that was then the lifeblood of organized crime). Anti-crime/vice fervor had been a feature of mainstream (that is, essentially mainline Protestant) American progressivism since the publication of Walter Rauschenbusch's *A Theology for the Social Gospel* (1917). In making *Deadline*, Brooks was aligning himself, at least for the moment, with a non-sectarian and non-partisan movement toward sweeping social change that had been gathering strength especially among urban elites during the last decade and is a distinct feature of Kefauver's reformism.[12]

Zanuck approved a production plan that would require first-rate performances from a full roster of well-known secondary players, all of whom would get acting moments that lent the story a rich texture, making canny use of the studio's contract performers (Ethel Barrymore, Jim Backus, Richard Kiley, Warren Stevens, Paul Stewart, Joyce McKenzie, and Audrey Christie). Using name actors in substantial secondary roles had worked effectively in *Agreement*, with John Garfield's effective characterization as Gregory Peck's Jewish friend adding authenticity both to the Gentile cast (Garfield was a prominent Jewish member of the Hollywood community) and also to the story, most of whose characters are Gentiles. Even though Zanuck, interested in saving money, would have preferred casting Fox contract players Peck or Richard Widmark, Brooks would make sure that Bogart, the iconic star of the era's crime melodramas with whom the director had become friendly while both were working on *Key Largo*, would be cast as the lead. Significantly, Zanuck did not refuse the young director's request; he obviously had substantial hopes for the project. Indeed, studio marketing made the best of the production's roster of sterling players. The film's trailer emphasizes that *Deadline* offers the pairing of two Hollywood performers whose abilities have recently been recognized by Academy awards: Bogart for *The African Queen* and Hunter for *A Streetcar Named Desire*.[13] Reflecting Zanuck's understanding of the market, Fox attempted to promote *Deadline* as much for its production qualities as for the suspenseful and engaging aspects of the story it had to tell. It was quite a change from the director's experience thus far at M-G-M.

To add entertainment value, Zanuck convinced Brooks to emphasize a more mundane secondary theme: Hutcheson's failed attempts to woo back his ex-wife Nora (Kim Hunter), who is planning to remarry. This was not to add "romance;"

instead, as their dramatic exchanges make clear, the relationship between the two was intended to add a homeyness to Hutcheson's character that made him "rounder," more appealing, sharpening the sense of the personal price he had paid and still pays to devote himself to his profession and to the greater social good. *Deadline* was thus shaped to fit the pattern that had proven successful in *Gentleman* where the romantic connection between Phil and Kathy, who almost separate because of her reflexive prejudice, is worked deftly into the main plot. With the troubled relationship between Hutcheson and Nora given more focus, Brooks's project would pursue a kind of cinematic journalism that put some emphasis on the banal everyday; the scenes between Bogart and Hunter are not glamorized in the least, but are sustained by engaging acting and dialogue that oscillates intriguingly between humor and poignancy. This *tranche de vie* suggests a kinship with the realist approach of frequent Fox collaborator Louis de Rochemont, and the RD-DR filmmaking company he formed early during the postwar era in collaboration with *Reader's Digest*.

The characters and action in *Deadline* are fictional, but they reference actual events and personalities in the news, just as did RD-DR docudramas such as *Lost Boundaries* (1949), which deals with "passing," and *The Whistle at Eaton Falls* (1951), which, utilizing character types, dramatizes postwar labor difficulties.[14] *Deadline* finds its themes in addressing the threat to serious investigative journalism occasioned by the consolidation of newspapers under one corporative control, and by the emergence of media conglomerates, an especially troublesome development because of the key, sustained role that newspapers might play in fighting crime, an American myth strengthened by postwar developments that was amazingly persistent though only partially true. The film does not challenge this view of the social and political importance of print journalism.

Faithful to the formula worked out by Zanuck, the film also finds room for that most conventional form of entertainment value: the pleasures of genre. Brooks uses his reconstruction of the Kefauver interrogation of Costello as a frame for a thoroughly fictional, and in many ways quite predictable, crime story: Rienzi's murder of a troublesome mistress and the sleuthing that reveals his complicity. This framing is similar to the reshaping of the source material that Zanuck had approved for *Five Fingers*, the last half of which is taken up with the British investigation of the agent, Diello (James Mason), who outwits them after a suspenseful chase, only, ironically, to be caught once seemingly safe in South American exile. In its focus on reporting, *Deadline* drew not only on Brooks's years of working in journalism, but the crime story reflects his association at an early stage in his film career with Mark Hellinger, another journalist turned director, who, before a premature death, had achieved notable success with the urban crime dramas *The Killers* (1946), to which Brooks contributed a story treatment, and *Brute Force* (1947), for which Brooks wrote the screenplay. Hellinger's final and perhaps most famous film, *The Naked City* (1948), was very much in the same tradition. *Killers* and *City* were both structured as investigative narratives in which violence plays a central role. Even more importantly, both had a semi-documentary or realist feel, even though neither was based on actual events or engaged with a serious political or social issue (similarly, the chase sequence in *Five Fingers* was shot largely on locations in Turkey). With the exception of its true event ambitions and civic reform tendentiousness, *Deadline* would follow closely down the path that Brooks and Hellinger had marked out, which is to say that it would also fit into what critics would later call the *film noir*, a genre in which *Five Fingers*, with its anti-hero main character also resonates.

As in his other noirs such as *Dead Reckoning* (1947), Bogart's character doggedly oversees to its successful conclusion a criminal investigation motivated by a desire for revenge. Similarly, Hutcheson is outraged by both the crime and Rienzi's violent attempt to intimidate the *Day* reporter he assigns to cover him. This righteous anger, at once personal and professional, marks as deeply noir his quest to discover the crucial evidence. With this "scoop," the paper would thereby have an exclusive, and presumably long-running, story that would boost circulation and perhaps persuade the owners not to sell. Yet this journalistic triumph cannot change anything in Hutcheson's personal and professional circumstances. Before the discovery of the vital evidence against Rienzi, the sale is ratified in civil court, and the paper is thus still doomed, though not before rolling out a last edition that contains all the details needed to insure the crime boss's arrest and conviction.

With its noirish mixture of professional triumph and failure, this finale leaves Hutcheson on the moral high ground, but with no clear way ahead, recalling the equally bleak but uplifting ending of *Knock on any Door* (1949), in which Bogart's articulate defense attorney, Andrew Morton, fails to prevent his juvenile delinquent client from going to the electric chair for murder. Even so, Morton effectively claims a kind of ideological victory when he delivers an impassioned speech to the jury, arguing that such crime is to be blamed more on social ills, including economic inequality, than on a young man's culpable lack of self-control. One wonders if that speech, a spectacular performance moment that pushes the cause of judicial reform, had any influence on the similar sequence that Brooks created with Bogart in mind for *Deadline*. Hutcheson is granted a platform for the kind of virtue-signaling in which the film of fact often trades when at the civil trial that decides the fate of *The Day* he pleads in vain, but with great eloquence, for the paper's continued independence and, more generally, for the power of a truth-seeking press.

Ironically, Hutcheson's attempts to woo back Nora, who is about to marry a well-off businessman as the film opens, appear also at film's end to have met with no success. Their marriage collapsed years before and is beyond resurrecting. His monomaniacal efforts to find the evidence against Rienzi, including putting himself in danger of assassination, have shown Nora that the man she loves is dedicated above all else to his profession. She is present (if not at his side) in the film's last scene, but only to witness Hutcheson giving the order for the presses to roll as they print the paper's final issue. Rienzi is on the phone, listening, as Hutcheson taunts him: "That's the press, baby. That's the press," relishing with unrestrained schadenfreude the moment of his triumph and what it portends for the mob boss and for organized crime in general.

These images, and the sound that issues from them, are "real," with *The New York Daily News*'s printing machines actualizing, because of the presence of these realia in the fiction, the power of mass journalism to inform the public and move official institutions to action. This is also something of a self-reflective moment. That power is now harnessed by serious filmmaking, which has the ability to include what is now *in* the diegesis but not *for* it; in this medium as well opinion can be formed and important issues brought to light. With this harnessing of the contemporary real, a larger truth is communicated to viewers along with this message to Rienzi: the authenticity and indeed in some ways facticity of what the film has shown, with the point of obvious reference being Frank Costello and his place atop the efficient machine of organized crime. This is a story, of course, already made known to the public through the related media of newspapers, radio, and television in a commonality of purpose that the film portrays. In the spirit of the larger project pursued by Zanuck, Brooks worked diligently with the Fox production team to create the most important effect of the period's "film of fact": the sense that the border in this film between fact and fiction, between the world of the story and the world of the viewer, has been rendered permeable for a purpose that goes beyond mere entertainment. Location shooting involved extra expense and a substantial logistical burden for a story that unfolded mostly in indoor dialogue scenes, so these aspects of the film's production offer important evidence that both filmmaker and executive producer were committed to making sure that *Deadline* was seen not only as authentic but, importantly, as less fictional, and thus as more prestigious, than the usual studio product.

Indications are that he largely succeeded. *Deadline*, so reviewer Glenn Erickson enthuses, is "one of the best newspaper sagas ever ... smartly directed, designed and photographed ... one of Richard Brooks's best pictures." This studied professionalism and technical excellence, he concludes, provides the film with a deep sense of authenticity as it dramatizes the hectic routine at the fictional *The Day*: *Deadline* "drops us into a marvelous newspaper environment" where the drama unfolds "with dialogue so natural that it can't be accused of overdone stylization or hardboiled *cliché*," an effect achieved by Brooks's no-nonsense script and the naturalistic performances of

Figure 4.2 Brooks emphasizes the editor's (Humphrey Bogart) passionate control of the production of the newspaper.

the many experienced professionals in the cast.[15] Bosley Crowther, acknowledging Brooks as a fellow journalist, similarly praises the director for making "a quite authentic picture of a down-to-earth newspaper shop," adding that "really good newspaper pictures are few and far between."[16]

Brooks's push for verisimilitude was considerably aided by the painstakingly detailed art direction of Lyle Wheeler (the so-called "dean of Hollywood art designers") and George Patrick, as well as the set design work of both Thomas Little and Walter M. Scott. The film's sound stage interiors are remarkable for their provision of a series of adroitly interconnected office and conference spaces that make it possible for the staging in depth of the various activities of the staff, both individually and collectively, in getting out the news. Veteran cinematographer Milton Krasner had already established himself as one of the premier cameramen working in what would later be called the noir style. The photography in *Deadline*, its expressionism palpable but not showy, contributes substantially to the natural feel of the drama it records. According to Zanuck, "If you start out with a feeling of authenticity you immediately have the audience on your side and they tell themselves that while this seems an incredible story, it must be true."[17] As the producer suggests, such veridicality would in most cases be only truth-seemingness used to foster viewer investment in the narrative; in *Deadline* it also serves the larger rhetorical aim of connecting the film to the current scene.

*Deadline* is also a personal film in that it reflects the interest both the director and producer had during their careers in making films that offered positive images of American culture and institutions by addressing (and in this case providing a provisional answer to) current social problems and events. Uniquely among studio heads, Zanuck felt a strong commitment to films that were earnestly journalistic in their presentation of facts and opinions; he was distressed when met with failure in an attempt to screen former presidential nominee Wendell Wilkie's *One World*, a bestselling and passionate plea for a global unity intended to mitigate the disaster caused by WWII.[18] He was also disappointed by the box office performance of *Wilson*, a 1944 biopic that he was personally very committed to, in part, I believe, because of President Woodrow Wilson's passionate fight to establish the League of Nations with the U.S. as a charter member.[19] Given Brooks's personal investment in the story he had to tell and Zanuck's enthusiastic endorsement, it is thus no surprise that *Deadline* responds with righteous passion to one of the most pressing issues in postwar America, concerns over a growing national crime wave, with widespread illegality infecting the operations of state and local government.

Bogart plays Hutcheson as a crusader who is deeply committed to the public service that newspapers are uniquely qualified to provide. In this advocacy he speaks eloquently and obviously for Brooks, who spent much of his early adult life pursuing forms of journalism before writing a novel, *The Brick Foxhole*, that offered, in addition to a crime story à la Raymond Chandler, an engaged commentary on those forms of destructive prejudice (anti-Semitism and homophobia) that he saw as a blight on the national body politic (see the chapter by Bernstein in this volume). As he points out, Brooks was not as focused on homophobia as he was on white racism against Blacks and Jews). In railing against social evils, Brooks showed himself a deep admirer of the journalistic tradition of Joseph Pulitzer and the eminent position enjoyed by his *New York World* until its controversial demise in 1931, an event that, fictionalized and updated, provides an important part of the narrative framework in *Deadline*. Talking to a reporter at the time he was writing the script, Brooks revealed that he "wanted reality and promised to deliver it."[20] The film shows that he was true to his word.

In line with Brooks's enthusiasm for Pulitzer-style journalism, *Deadline* celebrates the unique power of the press, which flows from its independence and that legal protection afforded to free speech, to influence society for the collective good.

This theme had already been developed in a previous Fox release, *Call Northside 777* (1947), which was made in conjunction with producer Louis de Rochemont and *Reader's Digest* editor in chief DeWitt Wallace. Based on a true story with which some liberties are taken, Hathaway's film traces the successful struggle of a reporter, P. J. McNeal (James Stewart), to uncover the evidence needed to prove the innocence of a man wrongly convicted years

Figure 4.3 In order to forestall the newspaper's sale, Hutcheson (Bogart) passionately defends the freedom of the press in court.

before. Another semi-documentary film of the period, Fox's *Boomerang!* (1947), directed by Kazan and with the participation of de Rochemont, also deals with an investigation that proves the innocence of a man convicted for murder, albeit with no reporter involved. In *Northside*, McNeal's work on the case starts out as an attempt to "make news" by creating a sympathetic story whose sensationalism will boost circulation and hence his own career, but he quickly becomes committed to a search for the truth, which the police intend to keep hidden in order to protect their reputation. The film thus illustrates a central element of Pulitzer's concept of the modern newspaper; in the words of George Juergens, the famous publisher "used sensationalism to achieve something more than a cheap reputation. The splash on page one attracted readers, but the editorials on page four educated them, uplifted them, crusaded for them."[21]

While Brooks was developing the script for *Deadline*, Billy Wilder's *Ace in the Hole* (1951) explored the darker side of sensationalism. The film portrays newspaper journalism as a medium that can be hijacked to arouse an unsavory interest in tragic events, manufacturing the news rather than reporting it. As Bosley Crowther somewhat harshly suggests, *Ace* offers "not only a distortion of journalistic practice but something of a dramatic grotesque."[22] All three of these newspaper stories (along with a dozen or so others) were developed as part of the industry-wide production series now labeled *film noir*.[23] The newspaper noirs directed by Hathaway, Wilder, and Brooks are notable for their exploration of the complex legacy of modern American journalism, as shaped by the rivalry between Joseph Pulitzer and William Randolph Hearst during the closing decades of the nineteenth century and the first two of the twentieth. Wilder sees only that mass-market journalism has an inherent interest in exploiting and, if need be, creating the sensational, regardless of any damage thereby caused. Brooks, in contrast, defends the position that a free press, properly impartial and respectful of its duty to discover and report the darker truths about society and its institutions, is necessary for the proper functioning of a modern democracy, which depends on a well-informed electorate. The temptation to cater to prurient interests by focusing on muckraking for its own sake or "yellow journalism" must be resisted, not exploited for professional gain.

In addition to its representational and dramatic authenticity, the action that unfolds in Brooks's artful simulacrum of a newsroom is also much of its moment, journalistically speaking. A central element of the complicated narrative engages a then-current widespread phenomenon in the business: the monopolizing consolidation of the papers operating in single markets, as well as the formation of national and regional chains. This is a development that continues today and is just as decried now as it was then by journalistic purists. As a result, in the early postwar era a number of large and medium-sized cities were left with only one serious daily to cover and interpret the news. This is the fate it seems the film's New York City will suffer if *The Day*, its financial health quite shaky, disappears. As *Deadline* opens, the heirs of *The Day*'s now-dead founding owner, Mr. Garrison, who had committed the paper to honest and responsible reporting, are preparing to sell out to a more profitable tabloid, ironically termed *The Standard*. If sold, *The Day* will then be no more, its staff, facilities, and subscribers either absorbed by this erstwhile competitor or simply disposed of along with Garrison's high-minded ideals.

*The Standard* caters to what we might euphemistically call readers' less respectable interests, and it has a larger circulation as a result. That paper's editor without any qualms puts a risqué photo of a half-naked murdered woman on the front page, an opportunity to promote salaciousness that editor Hutcheson rather piously rejects; he decides to run the story in the issue's back pages along with a tastefully cropped version of the crime scene photo. Interestingly, *The Day*'s reporters soon tie the young girl's murder to Rienzi, who had hitherto carefully avoided arrest and foiled official investigations despite a long career as a so-called "mob boss." Hutcheson and *The Day* reporters gather the evidence and testimony that reveals he ordered the murder, which is itself connected to Rienzi's involvement in a political bribery scheme. At film's end, in a strong move against organized crime, his eventual prosecution is assured for both crimes.

The development of this "story," which promises to be vital to the then-ongoing national struggle against organized crime, becomes the main focus in *Deadline*, with the full meaning of the title becoming clear only in its final sequences. The crime had seemed at first an instance of "ordinary" urban violence, of only local interest, with the pictorial record of its aftermath providing an opportunity for exploitative sensationalism, but it turns out to be key to an investigation that leads to revelations of national significance. The trajectory of the narrative thus follows closely the Pulitzer model that had transformed his *New York World* into the nation's most important paper through establishing investigative reporting as the goal of journalistic seriousness. Joseph Pulitzer believed, as Juergens reports, "that the press had a responsibility to serve the public," which he met in part "by running sensational articles exposing criminals and culprits to punishment for their misdeeds."[4] Hutcheson fulfills his aim to "blow the syndicate wide open," but he is disappointed in his hope that "with a story like this they'd never shut us down."

The circumstances of the paper's death, especially the self-serving greediness of the founder's heirs, recalls, as Brooks meant it should, the sale of the *New York World*, following the success of his heirs in breaking Pulitzer's written will (he had died in 1911) that the paper not be sold. As Pulitzer had feared, Roy Howard, owner of the Scripps-Howard newspaper chain, bought his rival in order to put it out of business. The three thousand staff were summarily fired. The story that became *Deadline*, Brooks admitted, was intended to memorialize the *World*'s demise, shedding some glory on Pulitzer's radical transformation of American journalism. At an earlier stage in its development, it was titled "The End of the World." Brooks had worked for a time at the *World-Telegram*, the *World*'s successor, and this film was in some sense a love letter to his former employer.

On one level, then, *Deadline* calls attention to what many, like Hutcheson, saw as an accelerating decline in one of the most vital areas of the national culture. The newspaper business was at one and the same time extraordinarily profitable and hugely influential because it provided information and thus had the power to sway public opinion; these latter functions are, of course, a by-product of the by-the-unit sales of papers and the provision of space for advertisers. For Hutcheson, who admits to caring little about circulation and even less for the opinions of advertisers, *The Day*'s absorption by its competitor would be a betrayal of the passionately principled journalism that is devoted to uncovering important facts that the powerful and criminally minded would prefer remain hidden. At a key moment, he chastises the heirs for thinking of selling and reminds them that their father had always thought that a civic-minded advocacy was at the heart of the paper's founding mission, enshrined in a statement of principles from which he quotes: "This paper will fight for progress and reform. We will never be satisfied with simply printing the news." Here Brooks obviously references the similar homage in *Citizen Kane* (1941) to investigative journalism, and the role of William Randolph Hearst in promoting it in the *New York Journal* through the principled contract with the paper's readers that Welles's film obliquely references.[25]

Such a view of journalism is based on the assumption that there are powerful forces, inside government and civil society, whose operations are opposed to the common good. "Reform" is thus needed if society, presumed incapable of effective self-regulation, is to "progress," an effort in which high-minded journalism finds its true purpose, and for which its independence is a necessary qualification. By the early 1950s, a so-called "free" press had become deeply ensconced in the national culture as an investigative force necessary to the identification and amelioration of social/political wrongs; for many it was a kind of complement to the official justice system. A corollary, supplied by wartime and postwar experience, was that the suppression of independent journalism under both fascism and communism had permitted public opinion to be molded in ways contrary to the common good. Official anti-communism at the time made much of the absence of independent journalism behind the Iron Curtain, and the threat to the U.S. from purported communist influence in the media. The treason trial of Hungarian Cardinal József Mindszenty, a key Cold War event, was the subject of Felix E. Feist's *Guilty of Treason* (1950), a fiction film sponsored by and using information gained from the American Overseas Press Club. The film's narrative frame is supplied by yet another heroic newsman, just returned from Hungary, who can bear witness to communist opposition to free speech and a free press.

Needing a constant and disinterested surveillance of their operations, the institutions of democracy, dependent on supposedly free-thinking individuals informed of the truth, could not in a struggle between competing ideologies otherwise survive—this is, at least, the story that Americans had become quite accustomed to telling themselves as the Cold War lurched from crisis to crisis. *Deadline* demonstrates that the press could succeed in the discovery and remediation of egregious public wrongs, a necessary task that, as the story reveals, the institutions of government can fail for one reason or another to carry out. In supporting the enduring value of the Pulitzer/Hearst tradition, *Deadline—U.S.A.* promotes a central element of the American system and of its supposed inherent disposition toward moral righteousness and respect for the law, in line with views held passionately by both Richard Brooks and Darryl F. Zanuck.

\*

Many thanks to Matthew Bernstein for his helpful comments and suggestions for improvement.

## NOTES

1. Bosley Crowther, review of *Crisis*, *New York Times*, July 4, 1950. https://www.nytimes.com/1950/07/04/archives/the-screen-in-review-crisis-with-cary-grant-and-jose-ferrer-is-new.html?rref=collection%2Fcollection%2Fmovie-guide
2. Douglass K. Daniel, *Tough as Nails: The Life and Films of Richard Brooks* (Madison: University of Wisconsin Press, 2011), p. 66.
3. For details, see Anthony M. De Stefano, *Top Hoodlum: Frank Costello, Prime Minister of the MAFIA* (New York: Citadel Press, 2018) and Thomas Doherty, "Frank Costello's Hands: Film, Television, and the Kefauver Crime Hearings," *Film History* 10 (1998): pp. 359–74.
4. For details, see Doherty, "Frank Costello's Hands": pp. 359–74, and Thomas Doherty, *Cold War, Cool Medium: Television, McCarthyism, and American Culture* (New York: Columbia University Press, 2003).
5. William Howard Moore, *The Kefauver Commission and the Politics of Crime, 1950–52* (Columbia: University of Missouri Press, 1974).
6. For details, see Estes Kefauver, *Crime in America* (New York: Doubleday, 1951).
7. Kefauver Committee Report. https://www.senate.gov/about/powers-procedures/investigations/kefauver.htm
8. R. Barton Palmer, *Shot on Location: Postwar American Cinema and the Exploration of Real Place* (New Brunswick, NJ: Rutgers University Press, 2017), p. 162.
9. As in "Prior to Release of Film Joan Fontaine Gets Filthy Mail on 'Island' Role," *Variety* June 18, 1957. https://archive.org/details/variety207-1957-06/mode/1up?view=theater
10. Daniel, *Tough as Nails*, p. 67.
11. This series is discussed in Chris Cagle, *Sociology on Film: Postwar Hollywood's Prestige Commodity* (New Brunswick, NJ: Rutgers University Press, 2016) and R. Barton Palmer, "The Small Adult Film: A Prestige Form of Cold War Filmmaking," in Homer Pettey (ed.), *Cold War Film Genres* (Edinburgh: Edinburgh University Press, 2019), pp. 62–78.
12. See Moore, *The Kefauver Commission*.
13. See *Deadline* trailer. https://www.youtube.com/watch?v=CniKtNOzzuE
14. See Palmer, *Shot on Location* for detailed discussion.
15. Glenn Erickson, "*Deadline U.S.A.*," September 2, 2016. https://trailersfromhell.com/deadline-u-s-a/
16. Bosley Crowther, review of *Deadline—U.S.A.*, *New York Times*, March 15, 1952. https://www.nytimes.com/1952/03/15/archives/deadline-u-s-a-humphrey-bogart-as-crusading-editor-opens-at-roxy.html
17. Qtd. in Rudy Behlmer, *Memo from Darryl F. Zanuck: The Golden Years at Twentieth Century Fox* (New York: Grover Press, 1993), p. 195.
18. Details in John B. Wiseman, "Darryl F. Zanuck and the Failure of *One World*: 1943–45," *Historical Journal of Film, Radio, and Television* 7 No. 3 (1987): pp. 279–87. https://www.tandfonline.com/doi/abs/10.1080/01439688700260351?journalCode=chjf20
19. For detailed discussion, see Thomas J. Knock, "'History with Lightning': The Forgotten Film *Wilson*," *American Quarterly* 28 No. 5 (Winter 1976): pp. 523–43.
20. Qtd. in Daniel, *Tough as Nails*, p. 68.
21. George Juergens, *Pulitzer and the New York World* (Princeton, NJ: Princeton University Press, 1966), p. 50.
22. Review of *Ace in the Hole*, *New York Times*, June 30, 1951. https://www.nytimes.com/1951/06/30/archives/the-screen-in-review-ace-in-the-hole-billy-wilder-special-with-kirk.html

23. Other newspaper noirs include: *Stranger on the Third Floor* (1940); *The Glass Alibi* (1946); *Big Town After Dark* (1947); *Blonde Ice* (1948); *Abandoned* (1949); *Chicago Deadline* (1949); *Woman On The Run* (1950); *Shakedown* (1950); *Scandal Sheet* (1952); *The Blue Gardenia* (1953); *The Phenix City Story* (1955); *The Big Tip Off* (1955); *Beyond a Reasonable Doubt* (1956); *Hot Summer Night* (1957); *Sweet Smell Of Success* (1957).
24. Juergens, *Pulitzer*, p. 74.
25. See Juergens on Pulitzer, and on Hearst, Kenneth Whyte, *The Uncrowned King: The Sensational Rise of William Randolph Hearst* (Berkeley, CA: Counterpoint, 2009).

CHAPTER 5

# "Man Against the Times": Conformity, Anti-Statism, and the "Unknown" Korean War in *Battle Circus* (1953)

*Ian Scott*

In 1970, Robert Altman's film *M\*A\*S\*H* about a mobile army surgical hospital (the acronym of the title) in the Korean War was a major critical and commercial success. Using the earlier conflict as a stand-in for the horrors of Vietnam at the time, *M\*A\*S\*H* brought in over $80 million in box office receipts and resulted in a Best Screenplay Oscar for the previously blacklisted writer, Ring Lardner Jr. Further awards followed at the BAFTAs, Golden Globes, and the Cannes Film Festival for the movie, actors, and Altman as director. *M\*A\*S\*H* struck a resonant chord in post-counterculture America, its scathing attack on war and dark comedic roots caustically situating it at the heart of the mayhem that Vietnam had become, the medics in the film making light of every conceivable injury that enters their surgical tent. It was a film that fitted neatly into the "New Hollywood" moment and seemed at odds with more conventional war films of the time such as *Patton*, *M\*A\*S\*H*'s studio sibling that was also made at Twentieth Century-Fox. And yet *M\*A\*S\*H* appeared to be defying more than the dying embers of American patriotic sentiment during the chaotic Nixon years. It was taking a swipe at Hollywood principles too. It tapped into anti-war sentiment and yet its comedy ridiculed all manner of subjects and positions, both from the political left and right.

Altman's quirky direction was equally off-kilter, the film a series of raucous situations that add up to a dismembered narrative memorable for its quotable scenes, but somehow detached from a cohesive storyline that might offer answers, even redemption, for the bloody quagmire the United States found itself in as a new decade dawned. As Robert Neimi explains, *M\*A\*S\*H\** the film was, like the novel, anti-authoritarian and episodic, "really just a disjointed series of comic vignettes."[1] For Robert Sklar, it was a picture that nevertheless positioned Altman at the forefront of cinema's "creative dissidence" by the end of the sixties.² And it was a dissidence that the director maintained throughout the following decade, despite Hollywood's rediscovery of its commercial instincts during the 1970s with movies like *Jaws* and *Star Wars*.

A similar creative dissidence infused the career of writer-director Richard Brooks some twenty years earlier. The anti-authoritarianism that Neimi identified in Altman's oeuvre, that sense of kicking against the established order, was a similar facet identified in Brooks's own filmmaking. And in Korea, the focus on a surgical rather than combat unit, and the need to break with the conformity of an industry and society that was too staid and conservative for them both, the filmmakers's themes and subject matter overlapped. *M\*A\*S\*H* then was really an updated version of Brooks's 1953 film *Battle Circus*, the latter being the focus of this chapter and its central conceits about anti-statism and a director working against contemporary norms and expectations.

It is little surprise to learn that conflict, in all its guises, should be another overlapping trait in both directors. Like Altman, Brooks saw military service during WWII. Unlike Altman, who flew sorties for the U.S. Air Force over Borneo and the Dutch East Indies with the 307th Bomb Group, Brooks served out his war based principally at the army's film unit at Quantico in Virginia. He had already commenced his Hollywood career at this point, having secured a contract at Universal in the early 1940s which he then walked out on to sign up with the army, and later remarked on how much the posting taught him about filmmaking that he presumably never learned at the studio. While serving, Brooks took to writing about the experiences he witnessed, a move that resulted in his first well-received novel, *The Brick Foxhole* (1945), which Edward Dmytryk turned into the popular and critically acclaimed *Crossfire* (1947), the adapted screenplay of which was nominated for an Academy Award.

*The Brick Foxhole* was anything but a novel expounding the "good war theory" about WWII. Set in the final weeks of the conflict, the story settles upon the problems and prejudices of military personnel scarred by battle or else hampered by pent-up rage in an atmosphere charged with tension as the war concludes and civilian life intercedes. It was as uncompromising and honest as Brooks dare make it. From there on in, his subject matter, scripts, and directing rarely shifted from these immutable principles; never shirk a challenge, write what you know, seeking the truth is the only way to a good story. A filmmaker who quickly earned a reputation for focusing on injustice and inhumanity that could be inflamed by racism and homophobia, Brooks had designs on being a writer-director from the beginning of his career. It was a reputation that won him fair praise for his ambition, but also quickly earned the sobriquet of an opinionated, sometimes bullying character unable and unwilling to compromise on his vision of the movies he wanted to make. By the time Brooks was ready to receive the accolades of his contemporaries at the end of his career, for example, a *Variety* review of the Director's Guild of America ceremony honoring him in 1990 used the none-too-flattering description, "God's angry man."[3] Like the characters in *The Brick Foxhole*, Brooks lived a personal and professional life that seemed to have an untapped rage about him and the state of the world around him that wouldn't be quietened.

Brooks channeled the prejudice and unfairness in the best of his films into an indignation that benefitted from a reluctance to bend to whim or favor. Starting out in the industry during an era of anti-communist inquiry and inquisition, he wore his heart on his sleeve and championed stories that fought for causes and principles. As biographer Douglass Daniel exclaims, there may have been a part of Brooks that was reluctant to get too heavily involved in the debate over communist infiltration in American life, if not Hollywood in particular, a reason possibly for backing out of some projects that he tore to pieces for, in some collaborators' eyes, no reason at all.[4]

But the early 1950s conceived of a poisonous political atmosphere that threatened reputations and wrecked careers in an instant, so it wasn't a surprise to find artists on edge. The execution of Julius and Ethel Rosenberg in June 1953 for their part in a notorious spy ring that was caught passing on classified information, bitterly divided the nation. In sentencing the pair to death, the judge in the trial, Irving Kaufman, not only affirmed the Rosenbergs's involvement in espionage but also accused them of costing the lives of countless numbers of American soldiers in Korea, a conflict whose time span almost identically matched the length of the case. From the Rosenbergs's arrests in the summer of 1950 to their deaths three years later, one month before an armistice was signed that in effect ended the war in July 1953, the plight of the pair defined American Cold War attitudes at home and abroad.

Amid the domestic upheaval and trauma that reached a zenith with the Rosenbergs's case, however, Korea quickly became what Bruce Cumings describes as the "unknown war."[5] Extensively reported in its initial stages, the conflict soon became restricted in size and scope and developed into a faraway backdrop for further, controversial House Committee on Un-American Activities (H.U.A.C.) purges at home, only occasionally puncturing some of the headlines caused by the weight of H.U.A.C.'s revelations together with the rise—and ultimately fall—of Wisconsin senator Joe McCarthy.

It was into this atmosphere that Brooks emerged as a crusading Hollywood writer with a point to prove and a reputation on the rise. Among those more daring projects that he rejected was *Bad Day at Black Rock* (1955), probably one of his costliest mistakes. Having bad-mouthed the project to writer Millard Kaufman and star Spencer Tracy, it became a critically applauded movie for John Sturges, spotlighting the plight of Japanese Americans and the rancor surrounding the immediate postwar period.[6] As the example demonstrates, Brooks wasn't always at his best championing others' tales, whether he was adapting or directing them, even though his co-writing of *Key Largo* (1948) with director

John Huston was a significant fillip for Brooks's career when Huston became something of a mentor to him, on and off set.

Therefore, by the time Brooks came to film his two key Korean War movies, *Battle Circus* and *Take the High Ground!* (both 1953), his reputation for being "difficult" was already becoming legendary, not least because he was clearly intent on constructing scripts that were really most suitable for his own style of direction rather than anybody else's. Brooks had already penned and received some attention for *Crisis* (1950), his first directorial effort, about a doctor (Cary Grant) and his wife on holiday who are forced to treat an ailing Latin American dictator (José Ferrer). With moral principles colliding against orders and authority, Brooks coaxed strong performances from his leads while hinting at the geopolitical complexities of American influence abroad after the war.

*Crisis*, and *Deadline—U.S.A.* (1952), a home-grown noir about a struggling editor out to save a newspaper while exposing racketeering and murder, were not perfect movies but they had a crusading sensibility that caught the attention. Brooks was at M-G-M by 1953, but these films hadn't yet built enough of a reputation at the studio for him to be able to refuse certain assignments. *Take the High Ground!*, also written by Millard Kaufman, was one such example. Produced by Dore Schary and with Kaufman being nominated for an Original Screenplay Oscar, the film was assigned to Brooks, who made it into a sizeable enough hit without the themes being quite to his personal taste. But *Take the High Ground!* acquired its repute for exposing the toughness of combat training thanks to Richard Widmark's stellar performance as a troubled and sadistic staff sergeant, Thorne Ryan, determined to put his raw recruits through hell. Ryan's aggressive persona would later be imitated by Lee Ermey's drill sergeant in Stanley Kubrick's *Full Metal Jacket* (1987).

*Take the High Ground!* concentrated on the punishing treatment of fledgling G.I.s in training, a typically humanistic story for Brooks as much as a military one, about the demands of the establishment and its controlling force in conformist, Cold War America. That Brooks should take on one Korean War assignment in 1953 was remarkable enough; to direct another from his own script was somewhat astonishing for someone reputedly ill at ease with military stories. Yet Brooks made and released the in-country-based movie *Battle Circus* seven months prior to *Take the High Ground!* in March 1953. Dore Schary had acquired a story called "MASH 66" from husband-and-wife writers Allen Rivkin and Laura Kerr, the acronym for a surgical hospital being lost on audiences at the time unfamiliar with military vernacular and titles. So, the "first" M.A.S.H. had its name changed as Brooks set to writing a screen treatment of Rivkin and Kerr's story. It was an alteration designed to accommodate a sense of relentless movement that the storyline was meant to emulate, of erecting and dismantling a small community as it moved from place to place wherever the battlefield happened to be.

*Battle Circus* would prove to be less commercially successful than *Take the High Ground!*, and yet it remains a curious but strangely affective distillation of battleground realism, corny romance, and prophetic crises of the American soul to come, notably its own allusions to Vietnam, a kind of complementary conflictual philosophy to Altman's *M\*A\*S\*H* seventeen years later. Like that movie as well as *Take the High Ground!*, Brooks brought what Jim Cullen calls a "sardonic feel" of anti-statism to proceedings that considered the ethical facets of war in an era of political obstinacy.[7] Moreover, Brooks's filmmaking in this instance, often conditioned by obligations to studio routine, was, this chapter argues, far more oracular than has been previously acknowledged. *Battle Circus*, like its companion picture a few months later, points toward the corrosive effects of war captured in even fiercer close-up by Altman's and Kubrick's later movies. But it is also much more about displacement; a displacing of values, propriety, and perspective as Cold War America demanded more from its citizenry—loyalty, vigilance, and conformity—that Brooks took to be deflections from the profound injustices at the heart of postwar poverty, racism, and violence.

In the story, Ruth McCara (June Allyson) arrives with a bunch of other female medical recruits at her new assignment as part of the 8666th M.A.S.H. unit during the early stages of the Korean War. A naïve rookie initially, Ruth is straightaway thrown into the reality of medical duties under fire when an attack

Figure 5.1 Major Webbe (Humphrey Bogart) carries Ruth McCara (June Allyson) to safety during an air attack.

on the unit sees her protected by medical officer, Major Jed Webbe (Humphrey Bogart). Webbe shepherds Ruth out of harm's way as enemy fighters strafe the M.A.S.H., only to put himself in the firing line a few scenes later when rescuing injured personnel and helicoptering them off the battlefield while under heavy fire.

Hard-drinking and womanizing, Webbe's no-nonsense unreconstructed attitude to the thankless task of saving and repairing G.I.s thrown into battle—something of a mirror to Brooks's own personality—alienates Ruth at first, until she learns he is much admired by those under his command, even though she's overwhelmed by the burden of Webbe's obvious attentions from the moment she arrives.

Romance between McCara and Webbe eventually ensues and is meant to undercut the harsh realities of death and destruction that surround them. As the M.A.S.H. ships out once more to a new location, their convoy comes under further fire, and Webbe shelters Ruth again, a cue to ask her why she ended up in Korea. "To get in the war, like everyone else," she replies. "Everyone!", exclaims Webbe, wondering what anyone back home knows about this conflict, a clear signal in Brooks's script of its increasingly forgotten nature by 1953. The two of them fall into a flirtatious pattern, but Brooks can't quite settle on an emotional register for the pair. They eventually wine and dine, only for Webbe to declare he wants a no-strings relationship without saying why, while Ruth sometimes accepts the romantic challenge from Webbe but occasionally thinks better of it and reveals a much tougher feminine sensibility, all of it floating between physical attraction and casual indifference. Just when Ruth perceives a possible future for them, she is repeatedly revulsed at Webbe's lack of tact as well as his hostile attitude toward authority—even as a major in a position of power he declares to his commanding officer, Lieutenant Colonel Whalters (Robert Keith), that he doesn't want to lead anything—and it is the last of these elements that leaves the most impression in *Battle Circus*.

Webbe's indiscretions can be seen to be a part of a wider cynicism at the world unfolding around him that, his character hints at, he had once idealistically pitched for. His skeptical outlook indeed sustains the film's occasional punches at the war, the politics of the time, and the establishment conformity that fifties America was seen to be indulging in. At one breakfast meeting in the mess tent, Webbe entreats Ruth to sit with him and chat, asking whether she would be interested in dinner later. She reminds Webbe that she's only here to win the war, to which he replies wryly that while they're winning the war maybe they can enjoy themselves a little too.

Brooks's approach to war in general and Korea in particular is encapsulated in these offhand critiques, a much subtler method than the pseudo-WWII machismo that other productions gravitated toward. With anti-communism prevalent, motion pictures found increasingly little room to divert from ethical and political clarity in war movies especially. Yet Brooks reacted to the restrictive atmosphere of the early fifties by bucking the trend for studio convention while advocating a style of pulpy, semi-realist storytelling that was arresting for both critics and audiences.

Hollywood faced all sorts of challenges within this constrictive environment, bedeviled as it now was by H.U.A.C. investigations like so many other institutions at the turn of the 1950s. The Cold War's first "hot" conflict on the Korean peninsula had demanded and got a response from the studios. However, the popular and accepted view of historians has been to associate Hollywood with a retreat away from the war. As Tony Williams asserts, in comparison to WWII movies in particular, Korea generally became toxic at the box office, especially so after the conflict descended into stagnation.[8] Ernest Giglio even suggests that "the Korean War was not so much forgotten as ignored by Hollywood."[9]

Williams counters Giglio's point if not his own, however, in acknowledging that there were exceptions to Hollywood's reticence, particularly among low-budget productions, where going against the grain of conventional war narratives proved fruitful and conceptually challenging. Samuel Fuller's gritty *The Steel Helmet* (1951) stood out in this respect for its somewhat uncensored account of American losses early in the war, a trick he repeated the same year, with a somewhat bigger budget at Twentieth Century-Fox, in *Fixed Bayonets!*, this a story by Lamar Trotti about a platoon protecting a defensive position against the odds for which Fuller himself wrote the screenplay. The director knew what he wrote about. Fuller had been a G.I. in the 1st Infantry Division during WWII, taking part in landings in Sicily and Normandy as well as experiencing brutal combat across Europe that served him well not only for *The Steel Helmet* and *Fixed Bayonets!* but a series of WWII films throughout his career.

J. Hoberman's account of the making of *The Steel Helmet*, however, is instructive in noting just how much American Cold War aims and ideology were still in the formative stages of development in 1950–1. Following a unit of lone survivors and inexperienced G.I.s, focused on the battle-hardened Sergeant Zack (Gene Evans), the film documents the group's fight for survival, eventually ending up in a firefight with North Korean forces in and around a Buddhist temple in which only a few Americans, including Zack, survive. Accused of propaganda, of being too violent, and yet at the same time of inciting racism toward both the one principal Black character in the film – a medic accused of desertion by some in the unit – and the Koreans and Chinese, Fuller's film managed to survive scrutiny by the Defense Department and the Breen Production Code Committee, both of whom couldn't quite decide whether he was lamenting the war or fixating on how America could win it. *The Steel Helmet*, exposing cinema audiences to the conflict for the first time, and surviving all manner of backlashes from critics and some patrons alike, was a hit on the back of a miniscule budget and extraordinarily short shooting schedule, attempting to replicate the conflict on screen only six months after it had commenced.[10] Taking on board his own experiences, Fuller's film was therefore perceived as being both a retread of the "good war" philosophy as well as an explicit wake-up call to the potential terrors that WWIII would bring.[11]

On the back of Fuller's two films, Korea proved to be anything but forgotten in Hollywood, then, though the combination of increasing public uncertainty about the war and less financial investment in such pictures after Fox's comparative failure with *Fixed Bayonets!* prevented the conflict from having anything like the impact WWII continued to enjoy at the box office. Indeed, several later 1950s productions, taking their cue from Fuller, rather resembled WWII in all but name. Both Mark Robson's *The Bridges at Toko-Ri* (1955) and Lewis Milestone's *Pork Chop Hill* (1959) would bring aerial combat to the fore—in the former—and the courageous battle realism of Fuller's film—in the latter—combined with the delicate state of negotiations to end the war in 1953, of which the militarily insignificant but symbolic hill of Milestone's title became one of the bargaining chips. Suggesting a replication of heroism and derring-do straight out of the previous global conflict, the more specific aspects these films pointed out about the war in Korea were its drudgery, and the brutality of combat in cold, windswept landscapes. matched in other movies such as *Prisoner of War* (1954).

If the war had a presence in Hollywood, mild propaganda in the form of the Howard Hughes-produced *One Minute to Zero* (1952), only a year after *The Steel Helmet*, demonstrated what happened when movies had to bend to the whims of the political zeitgeist and got watered down as war became unpopular with the masses. *The Bamboo Prison* (1954) and the later and more celebrated *The Manchurian Candidate* (1962) by contrast established a tone within some pictures for investigating the various alleged abuses, including accusations of prisoners of war being brainwashed by the North Koreans, a situation that *The Steel Helmet* had alluded to back at the start of the war.

So, while the conflict raged on and Americans became ever more distracted by events at home, Korean War films made only moderate impressions with audiences, but were hardly absent without leave through the 1950s. Rejecting some of the obvious themes that defined these and other war movies of the time, Brooks relocates *Battle Circus*'s humanity to another place, a different picture of Korea from other productions. He directs it toward assistance for refugees displaced by the fighting, treatment of enemy soldiers, and a savior trope within the M.A.S.H. team that sees them fixated upon the recovery of a young Korean boy injured by shrapnel who is in effect adopted by Sergeant Strait (Keenan Wynn) for the benefit of reflecting the American's compassion toward his foe. Ruth urges Webbe to circumvent the rules in order to save the boy with a risky operation, a procedure Colonel Whalters steps into and questions why resources are being used in this way. Webbe saves the young boy on the table who allegedly "never had a chance" with a massaging of his heart those watching can barely believe works, and which placates Whalters, for a time.

A similar reach-out to the Korean population features in Altman's *M\*A\*S\*H*, although with an implied cynicism that is ultimately wrapped up in Niemi quoting Robert Kolker's analysis of the later movie. At best, Kolker claims, *M\*A\*S\*H* is of its time, but with a "smugness" inherent in characters that are at once part of the military and yet who act as privileged commissioned officers, allowing their countercultural nonconformity to be given free rein while challenging little, least of all why they are in Korea and what the war really means.[12]

Webbe, by contrast, grows more seriously disillusioned with the conflict in each passing scene. The anti-statist sentiment in Cullen's analysis may be harder to locate in *Battle Circus* than other movies the director made, but it's there periodically. It arises in Bogart's approximation of an army doctor whose personal failings are presented as a symbol of the war's pointlessness as much as they are a suggestion of professional or moral failings that have transpired in a previous stateside occupation. After one especially risky landing for the medical supply helicopter at night, where Webbe is nearly shot, he retreats to his tent with a record player and a bottle of scotch. Threatened with a court martial the next morning by Whalters for excessive drinking on the job, Webbe protests that the "war is catching up with me, its futility, stupidity." Shaking his head, he pointedly remarks that they are on to a *third* world war in his lifetime, wondering if whiskey is in fact as common as conflict in this century. For 1953, even allowing for a greater public disaffection at large with the war, these are no idle remarks for a Hollywood movie.

Webbe's comments match much of the film's melodramatic though sometimes stilted action. Most events involve "shipping out," of people, of facilities, and ultimately of the army itself from the war. Released only a month before that brutal battle at Pork Chop Hill, *Battle Circus* is accurate only in so far as a series of unrelated confrontations—indeterminate bombing raids, the nighttime ambush while the helicopter is landing fresh blood supplies, and the climax's exodus by the M.A.S.H. unit toward safer ground while under fire— all circumscribe a war fought on various fronts, against resolute but faceless enemies, on terrain that is as indiscriminate as the attacks themselves. As the climax nears, an injured enemy soldier fearing for his life, who is brought into the unit for treatment, pulls out a grenade in the surgical tent, threatening to blow himself up while taking everyone else with him. Ruth calms the soldier down and takes the grenade off him, to the astonishment of her admiring male colleagues, while Webbe continues to operate on a patient.

Webbe later loses the soldier on his table, and he and Ruth, exhausted and traumatized by the incident in the tent with the North Korean, both accept a shot of whiskey from Whalters as a peace offering and recognition of their efforts. But the unit has one more dangerous move to negotiate, retreating behind their own forward lines and getting the injured to a hospital train, casualties that now include Whalters hit in the leg in yet another air assault. In a hurry to leave their current location, M.A.S.H. 66 burn some of their tents and paperwork as the enemy closes in. In clearing out his own tent, Webbe finds a half-drunk bottle of whiskey. In a symbolic gesture, he pours it over the papers, setting fire to the tent. Ruth is injured in the bombing but only concussed and the convoy plot their retreat.

## CONCLUSIONS

"The one major theme in any movie I've made is that of men against the times."[13] Brooks spoke these words in retrospect, staring at his career from the standpoint of the 1970s. But in looking back, notably at *Battle Circus* as a staging post in Brooks's progression from a studio director finding a voice for himself to a filmmaker who would go on to make such striking cinematic pictures as *Blackboard Jungle*, *Cat on a Hot Tin Roof* and *In Cold Blood*, a sense of social disconnection matched the anti-statism that Brooks remained true to for much of his career. In truth, he was always attracted to characters who were, as his quote suggests, born out of their times. They are angry too, at the world, but also with themselves, with what they perceive to be a bind not of their own making. Korea is a bind not of Jed Webbe's making in *Battle Circus*, but a bind nonetheless born of a Cold War frustration on his part with singularity and inevitability.

As John Bodnar explains in *The Good War in American Memory*, the pro-military stance of the 1950s that produced the need for defence against communism in South-East Asia cut across political divides and hardened public opinion, even while people lost faith in the Korean War. The senatorial campaigns of John F. Kennedy and Richard Nixon at the start of the decade may have pitted themselves domestically in opposing camps—one for increased welfare provision, the other against government intervention—but when it came to America's global obligations, a universal mantra they both expressed by the time of their 1960 presidential battle was the need for a strong military. Not a Pax Americana, as Kennedy liked to describe it, although in Webbe's eyes nearly a decade earlier, that's exactly what it was turning out to be.

Bodnar also alludes to the power and presence of organisations like the American Legion reinforcing the message, with the Legion's head, Erle Cocke, stating in 1950 that America's "unrelenting battle" left no room for "weaklings."[14] The relentlessness Cocke was referring to, and which his organization of over a million WWII veterans had no qualms about calling for a stronger stance and ever greater vigilance against, were the forces of communism congregating in this corner of South-East Asia. Bodnar acknowledges that the American Legion was not wholly against the breakout of liberal internationalism that took hold in other arenas of American society after the war, but Cocke did make the somewhat sensational claim that the Korean conflict should be left to the military and taken out of the hands of civilian politicians entirely.[15]

The ensuing battle for the philosophical heart of America's postwar military mission played out in public in 1951 in the battle between American general Douglas MacArthur's gung-ho, victory-at-any-cost fearlessness ranged against President Harry Truman's political calculations for war on the Korean peninsula, a sacrifice to stalemate worth making, thought Truman, to avoid WWIII and unacceptable American losses in a conflict the president conceived of as "limited."[16] Truman won the political battle in Washington but lost the publicity war in America at large. MacArthur was treated as a homecoming hero in 1951 when ordered stateside by an irate Truman and, whatever the eventual limitations of the war in Korea, the militaristic ambitions of U.S. global intervention whenever and wherever necessary was reinforced by a reverence for MacArthur's cult of personality. It was only Dwight Eisenhower's campaign for a peaceful settlement in the 1952 presidential election that changed the nature of public perception, a stance that won popular support and confirmed the peculiarity of Korea in America's Cold War cultural and political imaginary.

It is this curious juxtaposition of events and beliefs in a period of deep political conflict that is at the heart of Richard Brooks's *Battle Circus*. "Broken dreams and dashed hopes were a regular theme in Brooks's work," Douglass Daniel explains. Authority, ambition, and arrogance were all watchwords that either could be encouraged, thwarted, or rejected within his characters and stories, many of them dating back to his radio writing, constructing short fifteen-minute sketchbook stories for N.B.C. at the turn of the 1940s.[17]

In the final scenes of the film, the tortuous path over jagged slopes to safety sees the unit lose vehicles on the hillside terrain, forcing them to retreat further on foot, a gaggle of personnel seeking shelter in open sight of the enemy if it had a mind to locate them. Whalters, losing blood from his leg and hope for his unit, calls for assistance and, finally, the army marches over from the opposite hill into the exposed valley to rescue the unit from where it is holed up. Ruth, spotting the reinforcements, runs to greet them and to reunite with Webbe who, in heading off to seek support and protection for the M.A.S.H., has promised that he would find his way back to her.

It's a highly conventional ending to a somewhat conventional film, and yet one that reasserts thwarted ambition and the arrogant pursuit of resolution when no resolution is in sight. In an interview over twenty years later, Brooks lamented the end of heroism the film marks as the only true belief at play in the story, a sense of personal sacrifice for no greater good or duty that Webbe understands all too well. Heroism "went out when we became ashamed of ourselves. We became a spectator nation," insisted Brooks.[18]

That shame arguably has its roots in Brooks's vision of what the Korean War had become in 1953. Not just the shame of combat as a means of forcing legitimacy upon actions and the training of young men and women for wars without end, but conflicts as "common as whiskey," like Webbe says. Shame too, in losing any sense that heroism goes hand in hand with a vision of a better and brighter future, that clearer path which had been promised at the end of WWII but what Korea, in its relentless drudgery and sacrifice, was now killing as an ideal.

"Back home I thought I knew what the war was about," says Ruth at one point to Webbe. "Now I'm not so sure, everything seems such a waste." *Battle Circus* is not necessarily Richard Brooks's finest hour, but it's a film that within its conventional studio straitjacket allied to Bogart's hard-bitten cynicism ties Hollywood to a more critical conception of war, one that Stanley Kubrick would follow up on in *Paths of Glory* (1957) only a few years later and in more graphic detail with *Full Metal Jacket* in the 1980s. Its anti-statism is a theme also taken up by Robert Altman in the midst of another endless engagement in South-East Asia over the following decades in *M\*A\*S\*H*. Brooks in *Battle Circus* was therefore doing nothing if not signaling the work of a filmmaker who was, like the characters he put up on screen, a man against the times.

## NOTES

1. Robert Niemi, *The Cinema of Robert Altman: Hollywood Maverick* (New York: Columbia University Press, 2016), p. 24.
2. Robert Sklar, *Movie-Made America: A Cultural History of American Movies* (New York: Vintage, 1994), p. 325.
3. David Robb, "'Angry' Richard Brooks is honored by guilds," *Variety* Vol. 341, Issue 3 (October 29, 1990): pp. 8, 75.
4. Douglass K. Daniel, *Tough as Nails: The Life and Films of Richard Brooks* (Madison: University of Wisconsin Press, 2011), p. 83.
5. Bruce Cumings, *The Korean War: A History* (New York: Modern Library, 2011), p. 79.
6. Daniel, *Tough as Nails*, pp. 83–5.
7. Jim Cullen, *Sensing the Past: Hollywood Stars and Historical Visions* (Oxford: Oxford University Press, 2013), p. 30.
8. Tony Williams, "Beyond Fuller and M.A.S.H.: Korean War Representations in Film, Genre, and Comic Strip," *Asian Cinema* Spring/Summer 2009: p. 3.
9. Ernest Giglio, *Here's Looking at You: Hollywood, Film, and Politics* (New York: Peter Lang, 2003), p. 166.
10. Beverly Merrill Kelley, "Isolationism in *The Steel Helmet*," *Reelpolitik II* (Oxford: Rowman & Littlefield, 2004), pp. 177–203.
11. J. Hoberman, *An Army of Phantoms: American Movies and the Making of the Cold War* (New York: The New Press, 2011), pp. 147–51.
12. Niemi, *The Cinema of Robert Altman*, p. 29.
13. "Director Richard Brooks Demands Authenticity," *Boxoffice* Vol. 105, Issue 9 (June 10, 1974): W8.
14. John Bodnar, *The Good War in American Memory* (Baltimore, MD: Johns Hopkins University Press, 2010), p. 63.
15. Ibid. pp. 67–8.
16. Ibid. p. 74.
17. Daniel, *Tough as Nails*, pp. 22–3.
18. "Director Richard Brooks Demands Authenticity," *Boxoffice*.

CHAPTER 6

# Captured Interiors: Female Performances in *The Last Time I Saw Paris* (1954) and *The Happy Ending* (1969)

*Daniel Varndell*

> A dream world glimmers in the background of the soul.
> —Søren Kierkegaard, "Repetition"[1]

In *Looking for Mr. Goodbar* (1977), Richard Brooks demonstrated a keen eye for directing a female star (Diane Keaton) in a complex psychological role exploring sexual and relationship mores at a time when such values were being radically redefined. Brooks is much less well known, however, for earlier films exploring similar discontents arising from women's liberation, such as *The Happy Ending* (1969). In that film, he directed Jean Simmons in a role that explored marriage and motherhood at a time when the U.S. was still coming to terms with the impact of Betty Friedan's *The Feminine Mystique* (1963). Over a decade before that, in *The Last Time I Saw Paris* (1954), Elizabeth Taylor played a woman caught in the vicissitudes of a relationship unsettled by shifting assumptions about a woman's role in postwar society. In *Paris*, Brooks's use of costume and color accentuated a counterthrust to the story's Fitzgeraldian literary roots about a husband "cracking up," placing emphasis on the frustrations of Taylor's spirited wife. In *Happy Ending*, Brooks used narrative focalization through memory and escapist fantasy to centralize Simmons's (Oscar-nominated) performance, providing an emotional heft to a story about a woman demanding more from life and marriage. While both films anticipated Brooks's more famous *Goodbar*, they each warrant attention as signal works exploring the psychological and emotional depth of women reflecting—even anticipating—shifts in gender politics to come.

## BABYLON REVISITED

By the time it was republished in the short-story collection *Taps at Reveille* (1935), F. Scott Fitzgerald's "Babylon Revisited" (1931) was already being considered among his finest pieces of short fiction. The story introduces an alcoholic American businessman, Charlie Wales, on his return to Paris shortly after the 1929 crash in which he lost all his money. Now sober and successful in a new business, Charlie has returned to Paris to be reunited with his daughter, Honoria, who has been living under the guardianship of his sister-in-law, Marion, following his mental collapse and the death of his estranged wife, Helen. As he prepares to win Marion over and convince her of his trustworthiness, Charlie reflects on the two years he wasted in Paris drinking and partying. He is unsurprised to find Marion bitter and reluctant to part with the child, and still blaming him for her sister's death. But what does surprise him is his experience of Paris. As he checks in on his old haunts, Charlie is disturbed by the emptiness of the old bars and dismayed by the strong whiff of desperation. All his old friends have gone and even the streets lack the bustle and energy they once possessed. Unfamiliarity soon turns to estrangement, and regret hardens into shame as Charlie rues his life choices. A barman asks if he lost a lot of money in the crash. Charlie confirms he did, but that he "lost everything I wanted in the boom."[2] If only he can win back his daughter and escape to a new life in Prague, he thinks. But the old life haunts Charlie. After a hard-fought battle to gain Marion's approval is snatched from him following an unpropitious encounter (not untypical of Fitzgerald), Charlie's image as a reformed man lies in tatters. His appeal for custody denied, Fitzgerald ends the story with Charlie sitting crestfallen and embittered in a bar, nursing a whiskey. Despite wanting it, however, he refuses the offer of a second drink and wonders whether Helen would have wished him to be alone.

It is a poignant story of deep regret and one that might have appealed to Brooks for any one of several reasons. Brooks and Fitzgerald shared certain life experiences. They both lived itinerantly for a time. Fitzgerald, because his parents were déclassé, and his father moved the family around for work. Brooks, because his parents were poor, prompting him to leave his native Philadelphia to strike out on his own in the world.[3] Both were seen as outsiders who could be "aloof and overbearing" (as Fitzgerald has been described)[4] and "cantankerous and irascible" (as George Stevens Jr. said of Brooks).[5] Both men were intelligent but underperformed at school, yet excelled at writing short fiction. While struggling with his studies at Princeton, Fitzgerald published many stories, reviews, and poems in the *Nassau Literary Magazine*. And just as Brooks was ready to give up on Hollywood, he convinced a network executive at NBC to pick up a radio show called *Sidestreet Vignettes*, which required him to write five fifteen-minute stories a week. Both signed up for military service as wars raged in Europe (neither was deployed). But perhaps more than any other reason, Brooks might have been attracted to "Babylon Revisited" for the way Fitzgerald bared his soul in this semi-autobiographical piece. Like Charlie, Fitzgerald lived a high and fast life in Roaring Twenties' France; he struggled in his marriage, struggled with alcoholism, and struggled to retain custody of his daughter.[6]

Such brutally honest introspection would have appealed to Brooks. As he raced to keep up with the busy writing schedule at NBC, he spent his days literally scouring the streets for new material. He was not above plagiarism, he admitted, nor recycling his stories.[7] But sometimes he drew on his own life experience. In "The Iconoclast," a short story published in 1941, Brooks wrote about a man who drove his wife away with his brutish manner, which is not dissimilar, notes his biographer, Douglass K. Daniel, to how the author had treated his first wife, Jeanne Kelly. In "The Iconoclast," Brooks's protagonist finally admits to himself that his loneliness is a fitting punishment for a man so bent on destroying his relationships.[8] At their best, Daniel notes, Brooks's *Sidestreet Vignettes* focused on "the back streets and little men" linked thematically by "broken dreams and dashed hopes"—characters and themes Brooks took into his screenwriting. He "was at his most strident when decrying the cruelties of human nature and urging compassion and love."[9] But love and cruelty are not always so distinct in these works.

As Charlie is a reformed man in "Babylon Revisited," any cruelties in his past are recollected only briefly, and quickly suppressed by the third-person limited point of view. While he feels ashamed of his past actions, the shameful acts go undescribed—with one exception. During his meeting with Marion to convince her to sign custody of Honoria over to him, she queries his sobriety. When he mentions socializing with Helen, Marion flinches, begging him not to talk about her sister. She points out she is only being dutiful to Helen before telling Charlie, "Frankly, from the night you did that terrible thing you haven't really existed for me." Charlie is silenced. Marion continues, "I'll never in my life be able to forget the morning when Helen knocked at my door, soaked to the skin and shivering, and said you'd locked her out," at which Charlie grips the sides of his chair, unable to account for his actions.[10] He protests that Helen died of heart trouble not pneumonia, but Marion remains unmoved ("'Yes, heart trouble.' Marion spoke as if the phrase had another meaning for her."[11]) He finally manages to win Marion's consent, but his initial elation leads to a fitful sleep haunted by memories of "that night." He dreams of Helen speaking reassuringly to him from beyond the grave, wearing a white dress and rocking on a swing. He is initially reassured by this vision, until Helen goes on swinging, "faster and faster all the time, so that at the end he could not hear clearly all that she said."[12]

It is a powerful image, of the kind Freud described as typical of unconscious wish-fulfillment. Having suppressed the disturbing feeling of guilt, the dreamer (Charlie) fantasizes Helen as forgiving. But as with all wishing in dreams, fulfillment and coherence at the "manifest" level succumb to the depths of "latent" uncertainties and incomprehension. I'm less interested in pursuing the Freudian reading, more in the idea of emotions and thoughts bubbling up into concrete literary images (the "white dress"). Before analyzing Brooks's adaptation of "Babylon Revisited," let me quote these words from a conversation Brooks had with George Stevens Jr. on the difference between writing words and directing pictures:

> Movies are different from the written word. When you read something or you go to the theater and the dialogue comes from the proscenium, you have to translate those words. You may do it quickly as you read or as you hear, but it is an intellectual reaction. Now if all the words are put together and structured properly, your secondary reaction may be emotional—or it ought to be. But film, like music—they are very closely related—is almost exactly the opposite. Your primary reaction is emotional. If the scenes are structured properly, you may have a secondary impulse which is intellectual. But the first reaction is emotional.[13]

In Fitzgerald's story, the emotion of Charlie's unresolved guilt over his treatment of Helen appears to him in this image of the white dress. An image provoked by a thought. Brooks's adaptation of "Babylon Revisited," I want to suggest, presents images as emotion. What feelings are triggered, the film seems to ask, when sighting this color in that dress, worn by this woman moving in that way? What kind of thinking follows in the wake of such images— thinking which might "speak" more than the narrative will "tell"? That which is "manifest" in the color and form will yield a "latent" content, unlocking the passions and cruelties of the past.

## SEEING PARIS

In truth, Brooks didn't choose Fitzgerald's story. When M-G-M acquired the rights to Julius J. Epstein and Philip G. Epstein's adaptation of "Babylon Revisited," Brooks was tasked with rewriting the story to shift the action from the end of the "Jazz Age" to the contemporary postwar era. In retrospect, Brooks noted this as one of two reasons the film "comes apart" (the other being its sentimentality).[14] In this critical reassessment of the film in 1977, Brooks (who was notoriously sensitive to criticism) echoed the contemporary critical reaction to the film by reviewers like Bosley Crowther, who felt that what Fitzgerald managed to evoke of the "reckless era of golden dissipation" in a "few words" and "subtle phrases," Brooks expanded to a "nigh two-hour assembly of bistro balderdash and lush, romantic scenes . . . a great florid rush of warm romance." He found the story trite and the motivations thin; the writing glossy and pedestrian, and the acting forced.[15] The charge of sentimentalism is perhaps fair. It is also floridly romantic (neither of which I particularly mind). But I struggle to agree with Crowther's view that Brooks's film bloats Fitzgerald's taut construction. Aside from the need to expand the story (there is simply not enough material in the source text for a feature film), Brooks uses Fitzgerald's text as a frame narrative to plunge into the protagonist's troubled Parisian past.

The film begins with titles over a backdrop of a Paris skyline immediately identifiable by the prominence of the Eiffel Tower. As the credits finish rolling, American journalist Charles Wills (Van Johnson) disembarks the metro and strides onto the sidewalk to hail a taxi. The jaunty score by Conrad Salinger suggests a confidence typical of American males arriving in postwar European cities blighted by fighting (I'm thinking of Joseph Cotton's entrance into blitzed Vienna in *The Third Man* [1949]). But the impression is immediately undercut by a flicker of uncertainty in Charles's face. This flicker deepens into a slight frown when Brooks cuts (*Paris* was edited by John D. Dunning) to Charles standing on a bridge gazing into the river Seine. The score now plays the main theme—a soft, wistful rendition of the Kern-Hammerstein hit, "The Last Time I saw Paris" (1940).[16] A ponderous expression creeps onto Charles's face as he notices a tugboat and smiles to himself, lost in a thought. He moves less purposefully now, taking in his surroundings. The music changes again as Charles arrives at a fairground. As he watches the frolicking children, he stares into space, troubled by that thought again. Finally, he wanders into the Café Dhingo. Now the "Paris" theme in Salinger's score is picked up by a slow, diegetic rendition of it on piano, the lyrics sung (in French) by a chanteuse (the singer is Odette Myrtil). At first, Charles smiles in recognition of this place, his hand reconnecting with the familiarity of the grain of a wooden rail around the bar. His attention is seized, however, by a huge mural on the wall depicting a stunning woman standing in a fountain, bursting from a vivid yellow dress. Charles looks up into her eyes and Brooks cuts to the woman's face.

Cutting back to Charles, a brief wistful smile animates his face before it sinks back into the troubled countenance from before. He is snapped out of this uncomfortable reverie by the appearance of a barman (Kurt Kaszner) he recognizes. They delight in their reunion and share a drink. When Charles refuses a second the barman raises his eyebrows, reminding him how crazy things were after the war. Too crazy, Charles grimly supposes, before raising his eyes to a framed picture titled "U.S. Troops in Paris." Via a stunning jump cut, Brooks zooms into and then cross-fades to the moment Paris was liberated from Nazi occupation several years earlier.

Figure 6.1 Wistfully, Charles Wills (Van Johnson) stares at a mural of a woman standing in a fountain.

The song, from which this film got its title, had been popular for years. Regarding its popularity, Hammerstein explained that "everyone feels that way about Paris, even the people who've never been there."[17] For many Americans, Paris existed purely as a "city of the imagination." In *The Other Paris*, Luc Sante describes this "imagined Paris" as the "City of Light, the city of fine dining, seductive couture and intellectual hauteur . . .," the city, that is, of nostalgia.[18] Interest in Paris during WWII was piqued in the imaginations of Americans partly because of the Nazi occupation, and partly for its romanticization in films like *Casablanca* (1942).[19] The French film director Cédric Klapisch has written that "the problem with the postcard view of Paris, the one that just shows the Eiffel Tower and the accordion player, is that it tries to whitewash the landscape and show a false reality."[20] Sante suggests a more nuanced view. It is not that this Paris is false, but that it hides the "other Paris," as he calls it, the shadow city of "the poor, the outcast, the criminal, the eccentric, the wilfully nonconforming."[21] It is specifically a representation of Paris as a place to which one only travels in the imagination. One can contrast, for example, the Paris of Humphrey Bogart's nostalgic reminiscing in *Casablanca*—the memory of which he and Ingrid Bergman will "always have"—with that of Jean Gabin and Mireille Balin in *Pépé le Moko* (1937). While Bogart's Rick invokes Paris romantically to frame his heartbreak, the Parisians Pépé and Gaby invoke the different "Parises" of their childhoods (hers from the upmarket western districts, his from the rougher, working-class areas). Brooks's Paris is decidedly closer to Gaby's than Pépé's, but it is more substantial than the "false reality" of the "postcard view" we see in the title sequence. But while the bars in Fitzgerald's Paris are already darkened by shades, Brooks introduces Paris as the "City of Light" first, before gradually lengthening the shadows.

At the start of Charles's flashback, we find him pushing through jubilant crowds at a V. E. Day parade, dancing and celebrating in front of the Arc de Triomphe. Dressed in military uniform (having served as a war correspondent for the *Stars and Stripes*), Charles spins from one embrace to another and then into the arms of a dark-haired beauty who plants a smacker on his lips before peeling away with a smile and a wave. Charles cranes his neck to look for her, but she has already disappeared into the thronging crowds. He enters the Café Dhingo and introduces himself. Another similar-looking dark-haired girl introduces herself as Marion Ellswirth (Donna Reed). Clearly interested in Charles, she invites him to a party. He accepts, and is warmly greeted by Marion's father, James Ellswirth (Walter Pidgeon), an affable rogue living beyond his means and ever on the cadge. Marion has dressed to impress, wearing a bright red buttoned-up dress. But Charles's eye is caught by a figure all in black. It is the woman from the parade, who introduces herself as Helen Ellswirth (Elizabeth Taylor), Marion's sister. In this scene, Brooks uses color in an unusual and quite remarkable way. While Marion is the one wearing the eye-catching color in a room filled with dull dresses and dark suits, it is to Helen that Brooks's camera, emulating Charles's eye, is drawn. Her black outfit both blends in and stands out from the crowd, just as Marion's red dress both pops out and, strangely, appears to recede into the margins of the frame.

This counterintuitive logic is played with, and sometimes inverted, throughout Brooks's film. The color and intensity of Helen's dresses, coupled with the attention and focus of Charles's interest in her, is crucial to Brooks's visual communication of the emotional complexity of their tempestuous relationship.[22] For Charles does choose Helen, leaving an embittered Marion to marry the dependable Claude (George Dolenz). After a blissful (but too brief) honeymoon period, life after the war becomes difficult for Charles and Helen, who struggle to make ends meet. While working as a hack for a local rag, Charles is deflated by a succession of rejection letters from editors refusing to publish his novels. The couple's financial woes are exacerbated by the arrival of a baby girl, Mr. Ellswirth's playboy lifestyle (funded by Charles), and Helen's carefree attitude to life. While he begins to despair, she gambols about the town, socializing and drinking, and in a moment of abandon leaps into the fountain in a striking yellow dress. Later that night, at the Café Dhingo, Helen is immortalized by a local artist who paints a mural of her misbehavior. But as she gushes in the warm glow of the enraptured patrons—all of whom gaze upon her with a sense of wondrous desire—disquiet creeps into her face at the reaction of Charles, who silently fumes at her immaturity. From the perspective of the narrative focalization, this scene is the inverse of the party on V. E. Day: while Helen is just as celebrated as she was then, here it is she who is dressed in the vibrant gown. But Charles barely sees her. He quickly leaves the room to find their daughter, Vicki (played by 1950s child actress Sandy Descher), and Brooks takes his camera with him, leaving Helen and her bright yellow dress behind.

Their fortunes change, however, when worthless Texan oilfields gifted to them as a wedding present from Helen's father suddenly strike rich. Charles quits his job and joins the partying lifestyle, quickly developing a taste for the high life. But as their money woes subside, the cracks in their relationship widen. Now it is Helen who is sober. She begins to long for home (America), and references Thomas Wolfe's *You Can't Go Home Again* (1940) while referring to her life in Paris as a kind of exile. She often asks Charles to take her home from the parties they attend, but he is usually too drunk to notice or care. He begins openly flirting with other women to provoke her. "Let's go home," Helen asks Charles one day (at the fairground from the opening scene). "Home, *America*," she clarifies, adding that she is desperately unhappy in Paris. He dismisses her, insisting things will change. She says, "Let's go back, before we crack up." But things don't change. Charles ignores Helen's warning and takes a beautiful, rich divorcée, Lorraine (Eva Gabor), out racing in Monte Carlo. The event is a damp squib, however, and Charles storms into the Café Dhingo in search of Helen. He finds her enjoying the company of a young, handsome tennis player, Paul (Roger Moore), wearing a dazzling red dress. Blinded by jealousy, Charles behaves boorishly to instigate a fight with Paul. He loses and returns home in a drunken rage. Before passing out on the stairwell, he latches the door. Unable to get into their home or rouse Charles from his stupor, Helen walks through freezing rain to her father's house, and arrives soaked through, collapsing into his arms. She is hospitalized with pneumonia. Helen wakes briefly to find Charles devastated and begging her forgiveness. She recalls that once, not long after they'd first met, he'd lost her umbrella and let her walk home alone. Back then she caught the flu, and he'd remarked on how susceptible she was to illness from exposure. "You took my umbrella," she softly chides him, adding that she will always love him and asking him to take care of Vicki. She dies. "I wanna go home," Charles gasps. "*All* the way home."

Brooks's film is sentimental. But while Fitzgerald's story is (brilliantly) focalized through the regretful self-recriminations of a present Charlie rueing a past we never really see (his Babylon is only ever *re*visited), Brooks's adaptation invites us to see the ideal past against which the present appears so vapid, so colorless. At least two-thirds of Brooks's film takes place in Charles's flashback, culminating in Helen's demise and his grief-stricken breakdown. The film then returns to Charles in the present as he seeks out Marion and Claude to beg for the return of his daughter. He is greeted with cold disdain by a vengeful Marion, who rejects his request as per Fitzgerald's source. But here Brooks adds a twist, changing the ending of the original story. A late intervention by Claude forces Marion to confront the fact that she is withholding Vicki not in the child's best interest, but to punish Charles whom she never forgave for choosing her sister over her. Recognizing this truth, Marion releases her resentment and reunites Charles with his daughter. Brooks ends his adaptation with them walking off into the same future Charlie in Fitzgerald's story has lost (hence Crowther's charge of sentimentalism).

But what Crowther misses, for me, is the power of those vividly present dresses, especially the disjunct between the insistence of that yellow screaming to be looked at, and the ease with which Charles (and Brooks) turn away. It is different from the disinterest Jeff (James Stewart) shows in Lisa (Grace Kelly) in Hitchcock's *Rear Window* (1954), since Hitchcock's camera is quite clearly adoring of Kelly's dresses (right out of a *Vogue* magazine), despite Jeff's distractibility. In *Paris*, we experience those colors in ways Charles appears not to. Take the yellow dress, for example. Since the fourteenth century, writes Michel Pastoureau, yellow had (like red) been associated with prostitution, and was only beginning to be rehabilitated as a color in late twentieth-century painting.[23] "Yellow is indeed a color that is seen," writes Pastoureau, "a color that stands out. That is why it is frequently reserved for clothing or objects that must attract the eye, surprise the viewer, enliven the view."[24] However, note the difference between Van Gogh's gushing proclamation of yellows in a letter to his brother, which he describes thus: "sulfur yellow, lemon yellow, golden yellow. How lovely yellow is!," and the scathing opinion of Wassily Kandinsky, who complained that,

> bright yellow wounds the eyes, the eye cannot bear it: one thinks of the ear-splitting sound of a trumpet. It irritates, stings, excites . . . Yellow torments man, it imposes itself on him like a constraint, intruding with a kind of unbearable brutality.[25]

Clearly, Kandinsky was speaking only for himself, notes Pastoureau. But in *Paris* we are invited to see Helen's yellow dress as both "lovely" and "unbearable." The yellow signifies both her vitality and Charles's vitiation, first by framing her as a mesmerizing screen presence, then by pulling us away from her as we follow him into the slough of despond. The color also reaches back, of course, to the moment in the frame narrative when Charles stood before the mural in the present day, that smile morphing into a grimace as both emotions—lovely and unbearable—prompted the entire flashback.

The red is perhaps more complex still. In the first party scene, Helen's lack of color (she wears black) draws our attention more than Marion's bright red dress which, despite her best efforts, will not make her stand out for Charles. And when Helen wears red on "that night," associations are conjured that Marion's wearing of the color do not. Of red, Pastoureau notes the complexity of its meaning. Having fallen out of fashion (along with yellow) around the time of the Reformation (because it was too garish for an increasingly modest sixteenth-century Europe), red came to express emotions like dread, fear, shame, anger, or confusion. It was also the color of punishment, hence a disturbing or dangerous color.[26] But red is also the color of seduction and sensual pleasure. "Dressed in any color other than red," notes Pastoureau, "Marilyn [Monroe] would not be entirely Marilyn."[27] So it proves for Taylor in this film. While yellow is the color which transports Charles back to the old Paris, red is the color of the painful memory which stains it.

Maurice Merleau-Ponty wrote that a "red dress a fortiori holds with all its fibers onto the fabric of the visible, and thereby onto a fabric of invisible being. A punctuation in the field of red things . . . it is also a punctuation in the field of red garments."[28] In saying this, he didn't mean to pass a general comment about red dresses per se, but to indicate that there is no singular "red dress." Rather, an experience of *this* red dress in *this* visual spectacle "makes diverse regions of the colored or visible world resound at the distances," such that it becomes "less a color [red] or a thing [dress] . . . than a difference between things and colors, a momentary crystallization of colored being or of visibility."[29] It becomes an example of what phenomenologists like him call *qualia*, which refers to one's personal experience of a color or feeling. It is a red that inflicts pain because it is a memory of a color, the exposure of an unthinking cruelty with mortal consequences, and a future world blighted by remorse. Thus, in between the Fitzgeraldian frame narrative of loss and regret, Brooks's film goes on a Proustian "search of lost time," one that springs from the vibrancy of colors. Helen no longer appears as a mere dream girl dressed in white on a swing; she is vividly re-membered in seducing black, indelible yellow, and painful red.

## CRACKING HAPPINESS

When Helen begs Charles to take her back to America, she tells him it is to avoid a "crack up." If *Paris* shows a marriage that doesn't so much "crack up" as "fall apart," then marital cracking was more decidedly the subject of Brooks's *The Happy Ending* (1969). Like *Paris*, here was another film that many critics disliked, and audiences avoided. It also had some supporters. Charles Champlin declaimed it as "deeply felt and as personal as any from the celebrated European auteurs," and noted a performance by Simmons of "shattering intensity and importance." Rex Reed also raved about Simmons and described the ideas in the film as "difficult to get across, because they depend so much on richness of detail and an abundance of dialogue that is small but intelligent."[30]

The film was intensely personal to Brooks, and partly biographical. He was still married to Simmons, but it was an uneasy union. The marriage was under strain from Brooks's workaholism and Simmons's alcoholism, so he wrote the film to help his wife confront her problem.[31] The story is about a woman approaching her sixteenth wedding anniversary and questioning the foundation of her marriage. On the surface, she appears to have it all: successful husband, loving daughter, large house, beautiful home. But her days are filled with pill popping and vodka sipping, getting her hair done and her nails manicured, and shopping, shopping, shopping. She meets up with similarly embittered wives who snidely gossip behind one another's backs. All are fearful their fading looks will drive their increasingly distant husbands into the arms of younger women.

It is also a film that returns to Brooks's notion of exploring thinking through the primacy of emotion experienced through powerful images. In this case, the portals aren't colors but Hollywood cinema itself, as an introduction to the opening sequences will show.

The film begins with a whirlwind romance as two young lovers, Mary (Jean Simmons) and Fred Wilson (John Forsythe), marry in haste. She abandons college to do so, and, as they say their vows, imagines a series of images from classical Hollywood marriages (Norma Shearer wedding Leslie Howard in *Smilin' Through* [1932]; Spencer Tracy giving Elizabeth Taylor away in *Father of the Bride* [1950], and so on). As Fred lifts Mary's veil to seal their nuptials with their first kiss as husband and wife, a title appears on screen announcing, "The End," at which Brooks slowly dissolves to a blue sky panning down. A cut (the film was edited by George Grenville) reveals Mary gathering the newspaper from the lawn. It is sixteen years later. Her movements are languid, even lumbering. With some effort she hauls herself back inside to be greeted by Fred as he dresses for work. He smiles and declares his love (she weakly smiles). Then he asks her to fix his eggs ("Be a good girl," his eyes say, if not his lips). Mary listlessly plods through the motions while the radio announces Nixon's first day in office along with a string of commercials aimed at housewives. If the ennui with which Mary mechanically goes about fixing her husband's eggs doesn't suggest "trouble in paradise," then her apathy at their vivacious teenage daughter, Marge (Kathy Fields), and impassivity towards the irritating radio broadcasts (Brooks loathed Nixon[32]) frame her as a woman numb to these stimuli. Any semblance of domestic bliss is punctured when Brooks cuts back up to Fred. No longer smiling, he urgently rifles through their bedroom, apparently searching for something. He finds what he is looking for wrapped in a brown paper bag and tucked inside one of Mary's boots—it is a half-consumed bottle of vodka. On his way to work, Fred instructs their housekeeper, Agnes (Nanette Fabray), to keep an eye on his wife.

As Mary prepares for a big party to mark their sixteenth wedding anniversary, she finds herself "thrown" into uncomfortable memories marking their marital strife. The first is a memory of their fifteenth wedding anniversary party, at which she recalls (and embellishes) witnessing Fred flirting and sharing a kiss with a beautiful blonde. The scene plays in flashback. Disgusted, Mary takes refuge in her room with a bottle of vodka and a rerun of her favorite film romance, *Casablanca*. When the party finishes, Fred impatiently asks if she is coming to bed, to which she storms "back to Humphrey Bogart, Peter Lorre, and Claude Rains!" He fires back that they are "Dead, dead, dead!," at which she screams, "Dead and buried, they're more alive than we are!" In another memory, one from much earlier, the movies once again pull up short when it comes to expressing the bliss of eternal marriage. When as a child Marge (Erin Moran) asks why all the stories in Hollywood end after "married," Mary soothes that they don't, because they live "happily ever after," and "when people love each other very, very much, there is no end." But now, in the present, such words don't mean what they once did. She can repeat her favorite movies, but they always end at the beginning of marriage (or "beautiful friendship"). To say "I do" is to pledge oneself to the future, to eternity. But those words don't prepare one for living in it, or through it. The married couple, Kierkegaard wrote, must solve this "great riddle of living in eternity and yet hearing the hall clock strike."

"A clean break is something you cannot come back from," wrote F. Scott Fitzgerald in a 1936 essay, "because it makes the past cease to exist."[33] But feeling trapped in her marriage, Mary decides to do just that. Haunted by the ghosts of anniversaries past, she cannot face anniversary sixteen. Instead, she books a one-way ticket to the Bahamas. As Fred despairs at his ruined party, Mary bumps into an old college pal, Flo (Shirley Jones), on the plane. Flo consoles Mary, before admitting she is anti-marriage. Instead, Flo enjoys being the "other woman" in a relationship with a married man, Sam (Lloyd Bridges). When Mary raises an eyebrow at this, Flo reasons that "you can't break up a home that isn't already cracked." That 1936 essay by Fitzgerald was, of course, his famous essay, "The Crack-Up," in which he reflected on the experience of cracking "like an old plate."[34] For Fitzgerald, cracking up was not the same as breaking down, nor was it the result of some sudden, dramatic blow from the outside. Rather, "there is another sort of blow that comes from within—that you don't feel until it's too late to do anything about it."[35] He concludes that there is little he could do but run away to a remote town where no one knew him, for "absolute quiet to think out why I had developed a sad attitude toward sadness, a melancholy attitude toward melancholy and a tragic attitude toward tragedy—*why I had become identified with the objects of my horror or compassion.*"[36] Brooks might never have read Fitzgerald's essay, but I'd be astonished if this were the case (on the plane, Mary asks Flo, "Why can't I love the man I love?").

Mary is invited to stay with Flo and Sam until she can paste herself back together. In a beautiful moment, she relaxes on a quiet beach just listening to the waves with her face turned up to the sun's rays. A young couple in love ask her to take their picture. She briefly sees herself and Fred in the viewfinder, young and carefree. Later, Mary allows herself to be seduced by a slick young Italian, Franco (Bobby Darin). But as they prepare to make love, she works out he is an American gigolo preying on rich women. However, rather than respond angrily, Mary pities Franco (seeing in him something of the desperate "kept women" who pretend and go on pretending until pretending is all they are and have). More painful memories surface. As she splashes in the midnight surf, Brooks disorientatingly cuts to a wailing siren as Mary is rushed to hospital to have her stomach pumped, having swallowed a large quantity of pills. She had attempted suicide after getting a facelift to stay young and fresh for Fred, only to discover he was "away on business" (that is, being unfaithful). But perhaps the most powerful of these recollections in the film comes when Mary is humiliated by Fred in a department store after racking up huge debts on expensive clothes, her drinking now out of control. As he cuts off her allowance and demands she return the clothes, Mary laughs and teases but soon enough comes to a screeching halt. She retires to her favorite bar and drinks one vodka after another while listening to Michael Dees singing, "What Are You Doing the Rest of Your Life?" on the jukebox.[37] As Mary sits and sits and sits (and drinks and drinks and drinks), we suddenly get it. Even here, in this dark, secret place, she feels paradoxically both exposed and invisible. Soon enough, Fred enters and insists she return home, but Mary flees, only to crash into a police car.

Back in the present, Mary is coming to terms with her situation. Her time in retreat ends when Flo announces that Sam is leaving his wife to marry her. Nervous, Flo asks Mary how to make a marriage work. "I've no idea!" Mary gasps, bidding them both luck before running off. Sam calls to ask where she is going. "Home!" she replies (echoing *Paris*).

Mary is like the pseudonymous hero of Kierkegaard's essay, "Repetition." Having gone in search of the ideal of contentment (a "happy ending"), he finds himself close to perfect happiness until . . . "suddenly something began to irritate one of my eyes, whether it was an eyelash, a speck of something, a bit of dust, I do not know, but this I do know—that in the same instant I was plunged down almost into the abyss of despair."[38] Arising from these depths, Kierkegaard's hero struggles to find meaning in the now-jaded world. "I am nauseated by life," he moans, "it is insipid—without salt and meaning . . . One sticks a finger into the ground to smell what country one is in; I stick my finger into the world—it has no smell."[39] Perhaps Fitzgerald was familiar with Kierkegaard's essay on "Repetition," for he writes in "The Crack-Up" that "a man does not recover from such jolts—he becomes a different person and, eventually, the new person finds new things to care about."[40]

But Brooks's film is about a woman. How can she become a new person when the odds are stacked against her? Everything suggests she will return to Fred. But she does not. When Mary returns from the Bahamas she leaves her husband, reconciles with Marge, and takes up classes at night school. In the final scene, Fred finds her outside her college and asks what went wrong. "I love you, same as ever," he declares. But she points out that while she still loves him too, "we're not the same anymore." He tries once more to convince her to come home, to which she poses a question: "If right now we were not married—you were free—would you marry me again?"[41] He falters, and she smiles a sad smile back. And there the film ends.

*

I can't agree with Brooks's view of marriage in *Happy Ending*, but like *Paris* this film captures what Adam Phillips says: that we either suffer from what "sabotages our intimacies," or we suffer from the "notions of intimacy that we have inherited."[42] It has been said of Brooks's *Sidestreet Vignettes* that they depicted a "man's world . . . seen mostly through a male perspective of dilemmas involving work, honor, and duty," and that "women invariably appeared to be either deceitful and conniving or impossibly virtuous."[43] But *Paris* and *Happy Ending* are proof that the man who made *Looking for Mr. Goodbar* didn't suddenly wake up to the fact that women were insisting they had interior lives, too. He had already been making films about those lives. Unlike the successful *Goodbar*, these two might be lumped in with Brooks's "failures." But I prefer to think of them as illuminating images from a past that was already bursting with yearning and desire, aiming at a future on the cusp of being written.

## NOTES

1. In *The Essential Kierkegaard*, ed. Howard V. Hong and Edna H. Hong (Princeton, NJ: Princeton University Press, 2000), p. 105.
2. F. Scott Fitzgerald, "Babylon Revisited," in *Babylon Revisited and Other Stories* (Richmond: Alma Classics, 2014), p. 25.
3. Douglass K. Daniel, *Tough as Nails: The Life and Films of Richard Brooks* (Madison: University of Wisconsin Press, 2011), pp. 16–17.
4. Richard Parker, "F. Scott Fitzgerald," in *Babylon Revisited and Other Stories* (Richmond: Alma Classics, 2014), p. 264.
5. George Stevens Jr., "Richard Brooks," in *Conversations with the Great Moviemakers of Hollywood's Golden Age* (New York: Vintage Books, 2007), p. 534.
6. Parker, "F. Scott Fitzgerald," p. 268.
7. Daniel, "Tough as Nails," p. 22.
8. Ibid. p. 20.
9. Ibid. pp. 22–3.
10. Fitzgerald, "Babylon Revisited," p. 15.
11. Ibid. p. 17.
12. Ibid. p. 19.
13. Quoted in Stevens Jr., "Richard Brooks," p. 537. Brooks said this not long after shooting *Looking for Mr. Goodbar* (1977), after nearly thirty years as a filmmaker.
14. Quoted in Daniel, "Tough as Nails," p. 79.
15. Bosley Crowther, "Capitol's Film Inspired by Fitzgerald Story," *New York Times*, November 19, 1954; digitized version accessed January 10, 2022, https://www.nytimes.com/1954/11/19/archives/capitols-film-inspired-by-fitzgerald-story.html

16. The song was composed by Jerome Kern (who provided the music) and Oscar Hammerstein II (lyrics), and was popularized in the film *Lady Be Good* (1941), for which it won the 1941 Academy Award for Best Original Song.
17. "The Last Time I Saw Paris," *Time Magazine*, December 23, 1940; digitized version accessed January 10, 2022, https://web.archive.org/web/20090201051156/http://www.time.com/time/magazine/article/0,9171,765092,00.html
18. Luc Sante, *The Other Paris* (London: Faber and Faber, 2017), inside sleeve; p. 3.
19. Also written (with Howard Koch) by the Epstein brothers.
20. Quoted in Cynthia Lucia, "The Last Time He Saw Paris: An Interview with Cédric Klapisch," in *Cineaste* January 1, 1997, Vol. 23 [1]: p. 10.
21. Sante, "The Other Paris," inside sleeve.
22. The gowns for this film were designed by Helen Rose. See the "The Last Time I Saw Paris, 1954," *Academy Film Archive*, accessed September 17, 2021, http://collections.new.oscars.org/Details/Archive/70077669
23. Michel Pastoureau, *Yellow: The History of a Color*, trans. Jody Gladding (Princeton, NJ and Oxford: Princeton University Press, 2019), p. 191.
24. Ibid. p. 193.
25. Ibid. p. 194.
26. Michel Pastoureau, *Red: The History of a Color*, trans. Jody Gladding (Princeton, NJ and Oxford: Princeton University Press, 2017), p. 182.
27. Ibid. pp. 186–7.
28. Maurice Merleau-Ponty, "The Visible and the Invisible," in *Basic Writings*, ed. Thomas Baldwin (London and New York: Routledge, 2004), p. 250.
29. Ibid.
30. Quoted in Daniel, "Tough as Nails," pp. 189–90.
31. Ibid. pp. 187–8.
32. Ibid. p. 186.
33. F. Scott Fitzgerald, "The Crack-Up," in *The Crack-Up*, ed. Edmund Wilson (New York: New Directions, 1993), p. 81.
34. Ibid. p. 72.
35. Ibid. p. 69.
36. Ibid. p. 80–1.
37. This beautiful original song, with music by Michel Legrand and lyrics by Alan and Marilyn Bergman, was nominated for an Academy Award.
38. Søren Kierkegaard, "Repetition," in *The Essential Kierkegaard*, eds. Howard V. Hong and Edna H. Hong (Princeton, NJ: Princeton University Press, 2000), pp. 109–10.
39. Ibid. p. 112.
40. Fitzgerald, "The Crack-Up," p. 75.
41. Daniel notes that Brooks did not tell John Forsythe about the closing line, "a trick to film Forsythe's uncertainty as to how to respond to the question." Daniel, "Tough as Nails," p. 189.
42. Adam Phillips, *Promises, Promises: Essays on Psychoanalysis and Literature* (New York: Basic Books, 2001), p. 200.
43. Daniel, "Tough as Nails," p. 23.

# FILMOGRAPHY

*The Happy Ending* (United Artists, 1969). Directed by Richard Brooks.
*The Last Time I Saw Paris* (M-G-M, 1954). Directed by Richard Brooks.

CHAPTER 7

# *Blackboard Jungle* (1955): A Cinematic Education

*Steven Rybin*

Although the film authorship of Richard Brooks has received little attention in cinema studies, his 1955 film *Blackboard Jungle* has certainly not been ignored. While Brooks himself is not at the center of very much of this discourse, scholars have nevertheless dissected the film from a range of perspectives. This work includes examinations of the film's depiction of an interracial, urban vocational school in the mid-twentieth century, and its representation of American high-school pedagogy during this period more generally.[1] The film's subversive incorporation of rock 'n' roll music has also attracted scholarly interest (see Reinsch).[2]

Few writers, however, offer substantive consideration of the film as an adaptation of Evan Hunter's 1954 novel *The Blackboard Jungle*. Douglass K. Daniel, in his study of Brooks, does offer a helpful itemization of some salient differences between novel and film:

> First, [Brooks] took an anecdote told by one teacher about another—the teacher had once turned his back on his class and a student threw a baseball, taking a chunk out of the blackboard—and put Dadier in place of the teacher under fire. In the book, Dadier's wife, Anne, suffers the stillbirth of their son. However, [the script of the film] allows the baby to be born alive if prematurely, perhaps trying to keep the overall tone upbeat. [Brooks] also makes student Artie West more menacing in the film, showing West leading the afterschool assault on Dadier and the other teacher.[3]

This chapter will go beyond charting differences between the two works, looking closely at a handful of selected passages from the book and moments from the film to underscore some of Brooks's significant choices as a director. Brooks was of course informed by Hunter's novel, but he also had his own set of filmmaking problems to solve, relatively independently of the antecedent text. Brooks's choices as a director have effects of their own, ones that do not simply illustrate a pre-existing text but engage in a complex dialogue with it.

What follows rests on the idea that Brooks's creative act of translating *The Blackboard Jungle* to the screen intersects in various ways with the subject matter of his film. Rather than use cinema simply as an instrument for the dutiful replication of a pre-existing text or the reproduction of established ways of thinking—like an instructor or school official boringly plodding through a predetermined PowerPoint lecture or mission statement might today—*Blackboard Jungle* questions those who might instrumentalize cinema toward ideologically reproductive ends. The film, which memorably opens with the rebellious rhythms of a Bill Haley and the Comets rendition of "Rock Around the Clock," sharply critiques the pedagogical over-reliance—then and now—on mimetic thought, even when such thought is framed by those in positions of administrative or faculty power as ostensibly "progressive." In doing so, the film underscores the many important, and expansive, pedagogical encounters that can occur in complex and unpredictable spaces—some institutional, others more personal—in which behavior, far from being imitated, "learned," or dully replicated, is unpredictable and subject to complex, interpersonal forces that the administration of classroom space cannot predetermine. Brooks's adaptation ultimately amounts to a cinematic education, an object lesson in how a range of mainly psychological ideas from a literary source are not imitated but rather reimagined as external, socially situated action on film.

ADAPTING AUTHORITY

Teaching is a notably vexed and stressful profession in both literary and cinematic versions of *Blackboard Jungle*. In the novel, an afternoon conversation in a local bar between Rick Dadier and his colleague and fellow teacher Josh (played by Richard Kiley in the film) highlights the difficulty of translating the benefits of the teacher's education to a group of students largely unwilling to receive knowledge:

"The things we learned in school. The Ed courses. What a bunch of horse manure."
"Right," Rick said, nodding his head.
"Damn right," Josh agreed. He paused for a moment, studying the open rim of his glasses. He scratched his head and then asked, "What was I saying?"

"Ed courses," Rick said, silently, congratulating himself upon having remembered.

"Oh yes, Ed courses," Rick waited for more, but Josh had apparently said all he cared to say about the subject.

"A bunch of horse manure," Rick supplied. "Tell you to give difficult kids board erasers to clean. Well, I got a question for the bigshot Ed Psych experts."

"What's that?" Josh asked lazily.

"What do you do when you got thirty-five difficult kids? There ain't that many board erasers in the city of New York."[4]

Appearing a third of the way through the novel, this conversation between two teachers, after a long first week on the job at North Manual Trades High School in the Bronx, encapsulates much of Hunter's treatment of pedagogical labor. Josh, alienated from his years of English Education training after just one week on the job, joins Rick in drowning his sorrow in drink after a day of work. The dialogue points to a hierarchy within the socioeconomic world of the labor market for teachers, with the Education Psychology "experts," noted by Josh, who pontificate about education from administrative perches, contrasted with the blood, sweat, and tears of the more creative and improvisatory type of work Josh wants to do in the classroom. (Hunter's choice of writing Josh as a character interested in great jazz music is an astute one, and the film wisely retains this trait.) The passage also highlights, in its setting in a bar, the therapeutic nature of alcohol in assuaging the psychological stress the teacher carries after long hours of largely ineffectual, disappointing work. Both novel and film, which treat this scene similarly, also invest the conversation between Rick and Josh with slightly ironic humor, Hunter's word choices and prose stylization conveying not only the increasingly inebriated states of both characters, but also making a punchline—"There ain't that many board erasers in the city of New York"—out of a very real problem: a surplus of underprepared, difficult kids, and a lack of the adequate resources with which to teach them.

What drink alleviates here is not simply the distinctive failure of one individual teacher to "reach" students. Both film and novel carefully paint this failure as a larger, institutional one. More trenchantly, the film questions the very limits of the kinds of mimetic, reproductive thought many institutions, then as now, encourage. The book begins with Rick Dadier heading to the trade school for a job interview, which will be his first teaching gig out of college. During the interview, the chairman of the school notes that Dadier speaks softly. When asked to do so, Dadier subsequently demonstrates his proficiency for projection through, notably, a work of adaptation, reciting a passage from *Henry V* in the small space of the chairman's office:

Rick felt his voice at the pit of his diaphragm. "*Once more unto the breach, dear friends, once more,*" he quoted loudly, strongly, "*or close the wall up with our English dead. In peace there's nothing so becomes a man as modest stillness and humility: but when the blast of war blows in our ears, then imitate the action of the tiger.*"[5]

This passage from *Henry V* and its intimations of war prefigure what will turn out to be the warlike encounters between teachers and students in the school. If the reader intimates the novelist's irony, however, it is notable that Dadier, still rather green before winning the job at this point in the book, does not, or not yet. He is earnestly replicating a canonical text in a bid to win a job which will bid him to encourage students to repeat, rehearse, and memorize pre-existing works in a similarly rote way. Hunter keeps the scene focused on Dadier and the school official, refraining from any mention of the effect of Dadier's sonorous reading of the Shakespeare on those around the office who might hear it.

The book's crafting of this scene contains very little description of the space of the chairman's office and Dadier's place within it. The film, which retains Dadier's reading of *Henry V*, must present the spatial relationship between Dadier and his potential employer and, further, must convey their confrontation within this space in ways that make cinematic sense. The scene begins with the school's principal, Warneke (John Hoyt), welcoming Dadier into this office. Initially, the two men are balanced in the composition of the shot, with Warneke on the left and Dadier on the right. The development of the scene shortly makes clear Warneke's position of power in the school and in relation to Dadier, with Ford taking a seat, per the principal's instruction, as Hoyt remains standing. Hoyt's stern voice and rigid posture, along with his positioning in the frame above Ford, clearly position his character as in possession of a social and professional power Dadier does not possess. Warneke, looming above Dadier, is thrown slightly by the fact that Dadier has attended Sarah Lawrence—"but that was an all-girls' school," Warneke objects, as Dadier goes on to explain the shortage of spots available in higher education for men returning home from the war. Warneke, given his profession, would already be in possession of such knowledge about the recent historical and social currents affecting the labor market for teachers. Given this, his prompting of Dadier to explain the nature of his educational training, as well as his experience in the navy, takes on the quality of a stern, older man testing a nervous, younger one for his ability to meet the demands of the classroom.

Ford positions himself throughout this early stretch of the scene in a slightly passive way, his arms slouched across his briefcase and his words descending into mumbles. This aspect of Dadier's character at this moment is presented here less as some inherent facet of his psychology and more as an effect upon that psychology of his placement in this principal's office, with Warneke's assumption of a stern and rigid presence generating jitter in Dadier. To test whether or not Dadier has the ability to project authority in the classroom, Warneke, upon hearing Dadier's mumbled responses, queries whether or not Dadier can project his voice in a room of squirrely students. Here, Ford ably provides Dadier with just such projection, speaking the words from *Henry V* in a bold, theatrical, and confident way. As in the novel, his theatrical authority wins him the job. Interestingly, however, Brooks makes a choice here that is not present in the antecedent text. Rather than remain inside the space of the principal's office as Dadier recites Shakespeare, as Hunter does in the book, Brooks cross-cuts to shots underscoring the contingent effects these words have on the men and women sitting immediately outside in the waiting room to Warneke's office. In particular, Brooks underscores a shot of Dadier's future colleague, Joshua, moved by Dadier's rendition of *Henry V* and mouthing the words to the play as he hears them spoken. Joshua is, like Dadier, a sensitive, intelligent man, whose love for music—he will unsuccessfully attempt to share his love of jazz with students later in the film—parallels Dadier's apparent affection for the stage. The cross-cutting, which at the cue of Dadier's words freely floats from the office to the space of the waiting room, also suggests the possibility that whatever knowledge and performative skill Dadier possesses can transcend the barriers of the institution in which he works. Perhaps he will be able to provide something other than rote instruction to which difficult students do not respond. But no students are present in this scene and these powers of pedagogy will be put to the test as the film goes on.

## THE CLASSROOM AS SOCIAL SPACE

If the scene in the principal's office offers us an example of Dadier's skilled ability in adapting his knowledge and skills to the unique demands of a particular position, the classroom scenes put this talent to the test in an altogether different and uniquely challenging space. In the novel, Hunter's initial descriptions of Dadier's encounters with his students rest on the growing realization that Dadier's assumptions about what teaching is all about are tested by, unsurprisingly, actual students in an actual classroom—conveyed to the reader in the novel in the form of an interiorized monologue in which Dadier's naïve ideas and abstract, theoretical training are set into counterpoint against unpredictable classroom behavior. This is a space occupied by unruly young men who invert the assumptions about power evident in the scene in the principal's office: just because Dadier stands above them in an ostensible position of authority does not mean they lack the guile to chip away at whatever measure of confidence he brings to this predetermined position.

Hunter expresses this idea vividly. On his first day of teaching, Dadier encounters a belligerent classroom. After a blunt threat disguised as a query, in which the student asks him whether or not he has ever fought thirty-five guys at once, Hunter describes Dadier's psychological reaction to this insolence:

> Rick heard the question, and it set off a trigger response in his mind which told him, *This is it, Dadier. This is it, my friend.* He narrowed his eyes and walked slowly and purposefully around his desk. The boy was seated in the middle of the room, and Rick walked up the aisle nearest his desk, realizing as he did so that he was placing himself in a surrounded-by-boys position. He walked directly to the boy, pushed his face close to his, and said, "Sit down, son, and take off that hat before I knock it off!"
>
> He said it tightly, said it the way he'd spoken the lines for Duke Mantee when he'd played *The Petrified Forest* at Hunter. He did not know what the reaction would be, and he was vaguely aware of a persistent fear that crawled up his spine and into his cranium. He knew he could be jumped by all of them in this single instant, and the knowledge made him taut and tense . . .[6]

Using literary resources of interiority and physical description, Hunter describes not only the psychological impact of the boys' insurrectionist words but also how these words shake Dadier to his core—a fear, now persistent, crawling "up his spine and into his cranium." Stress is placed on the very mind and body of the teaching figure—who is also a performer, as Hunter's reference to *The Petrified Forest* reminds us.

As a director working within Hollywood filmmaking conventions, Brooks needs to find another, externally expressive solution to these descriptions of psychological torment, frayed authority, and spinal anxiety. Literary fear must become cinematically expressive; a classical film narrative is driven by action and by the placement of the camera, not by reproducing or simply imitating the metaphorical descriptions or psychological interiority expressed in a book. Brooks finds his solution, in this scene, through the composition of the shot and the comportment of his actors. And where the book chooses the literary equivalent of a shot-and-reaction shot structure—with Hunter descriptively darting back and forth between Dadier's attempts to control a pedagogical space full of antsy students on the one hand, and the disruptions of those students on the other—Brooks insists on keeping as many of the encounters between Dadier and his students in single shots and with multiple planes of the image sharply in focus, underscoring the idea that the classroom is a collective space with tensely frayed edges. In order to achieve this sense of space and its emotional valence, Brooks and his cinematographer Russell Harlan "turned to a relatively new film stock, Eastman Tri-X Panchromatic Negative

Film, which dramatically increased depth of field without requiring a tremendous amount of light".[7] This choice results in scenes that underscore Dadier's reactions to his class not through interior dialogue or explicit performative references but through staging and shot composition.

These choices also reveal that Brooks is just as interested in the social and institutional origins of classroom behavior. What the film is expressing is not so much a series of individual, psychological reactions to institutional failure (which might be said to be the focus of the book), but rather the concrete, physically manifested ways that institution fails its faculty and its students on a daily basis. In the film's first extended sequence in the classroom, Dadier prepares his materials in the front of his class while students slowly amble to their desks. Two particularly unruly kids, Artie (Vic Morrow) and Belazi (Dan Terranova), initially refuse Dadier's command to take their seats, and linger in the back of the classroom in resistant chatter. When Dadier implores them to sit, Artie asks, in a tone of belligerence that is Morrow's steady resource throughout his performance, "Why?" The presumed authority of the teacher in the classroom is explicitly rejected as justification for Artie to listen to anything Dadier commands. Brooks, tellingly, keeps this moment in a single shot, framing Ford from behind (the camera is apparently positioned at some point to the left and behind his teacher's desk) and keeping both teacher and class in focus in the way Eastman Tri-X enables him to do. Tellingly, however, we cannot see Glenn Ford's facial expressions in this moment: as he approaches Artie and Belazi, we see their sullen disaffection, and the riled attention of their seated, fellow students to this melodramatic situation, but

Figure 7.1 Dadier (Glenn Ford) framed from behind as he tries to control the class.

we only see the back of Dadier, his ostensible presence as an authority figure signaled by the presence of Glenn Ford's back in the frame but set into counterpoint with a camera that, for the moment, refuses to locate that authority in a discrete personality.

This describes the spatial development of many of the classroom scenes in the film, in which Dadier is often placed in a larger context that only occasionally shows how Glenn Ford expresses his character's psychological and expressive reactions to the rebellious students. Just as often, the film is concerned with the reactions of the students themselves—as both individuals, and as a fragile collective—suggesting that Dadier's presumed role of authority, and his superior knowledge, guarantee no pride of place in a social space fraught with unease and uncertainty.

When Brooks does choose to cut to closer shots and reaction shots in the classroom scenes, it is not only to enable an actor to express a reaction or an emotion, but more meaningfully to suspend the flow of physical action in a moment of suspension and ambiguity. One such moment occurs after the aforementioned confrontation between Dadier and the two unruly students during the first extended classroom sequence. Hitherto keeping most of this sequence in a long shot that situates Dadier and his students in the same image, Brooks eventually cuts to a medium shot of Glenn Ford writing his last name for the students in chalk on the blackboard. The students are kept momentarily out of frame, but they—or, at least, one of them—violently announce their presence from the contingent realm of offscreen space, chucking a baseball and damaging the part of the board on which Dadier is writing his last name. For a moment, the room goes silent, and Ford is given by Brooks a stretch of screen duration upon which to etch a response. The most charged moment in the scene is the one between the chucking of the baseball and before Ford's turn-of-head, which keeps the various possible ways Dadier might respond in suspension for a quietly thrilling moment. After the baseball interrupts Dadier, he tosses his chalk in the air and catches it, an indication of both Dadier's awareness of the pointlessness of proceeding with conventional classroom procedure at this point and of his ability to improvise, demonstrating his skill in turning a functional piece of chalk into a potential expressive response to an unexpected baseball. Just what this response will be, we do not yet know; as in the book, the uncertainty of the teacher's comportment in the physical classroom—and this despite all of his predetermined pedagogical "training"—is one of the film's central concerns. In the Hunter book, however, as Daniel notes, this moment of baseball interruptus does not involve Dadier, but is rather an anecdote told to him by another teacher.[8] By transposing this slice of narrative to Dadier's own classroom experience, Brooks gives Ford not only the opportunity to play with the expressive object of the chalk—indicative itself of the film's need to transform the book's psychological interiority into physical action—but also an opening to play with tensions between onscreen and offscreen space. After the moment with the baseball, Dadier lands on a quip, remarking that whoever threw the ball has no future on the Yankees' roster. The class laughs and recognizes Dadier as a hipster, a cool one: but he is also cloaking that coolness in authority, and so the kids quickly find ways to turn this to their advantage, converting the quasi-aristocratic, French last name "Dadier" into the hip "Daddy-oh!," a moniker that Dadier will resist throughout the film even as it evokes the rock 'n' roll music marking the film he is in.

For Brooks, though, cinema may be as hip, if not more so, than rock 'n' roll, and even though "Rock Around the Clock" left them dancing in the aisles on the film's premiere, it is the director's commitment to film as a potential source for creative pedagogy that is ultimately more lasting and substantive. Intriguingly, Brooks adds a touch of cinematic reflexivity to his adaptation, with a reference to the apparatus of cinema itself, signaling his interest in the medium of cinema as a source for expansive, non-mimetic learning. In the novel, Hunter includes a scene in which Dadier, finding that he needs to change his tactics in light of an inattentive and unruly group of kids, brings a narrative from a popular storybook into the classroom. He reads it and finds that this new approach is working, to a point. But then he is, again, interrupted:

> He'd brought an adventure magazine to school, figuring he'd start a new regime by showing some friendship toward the boys, by reading them a story from a popular publication rather than a textbook. The story was a good one, if not a classic masterpiece, and he read it well, injecting life into the descriptive passages, giving the dialogue real meaning. He had reached the climax when the machine shop erupted.
>
> It started as a dull whine, and he barely glanced up from the printed page. The whine increased in volume until it sounded like a runaway buzzsaw. Rick looked up with honest bewilderment on his face, and he saw the boys in the classroom begin to smile. He lifted his eyebrows, shrugged, and started to read again.
>
> The buzzsaw began to click, and then it began to clank, as if someone had thrown a monkey wrench into the gears and the gears were pounding hell out of it. The entire room seemed to vibrate from the sound. The windows rattled, and the pencils lying on his desk began doing an impromptu jig.[9]

Hunter subsequently underscores Dadier's, and the students', reactions to the interruption of the machine shop class into English pedagogy, a rare moment in which the students are actually on the side of their instructor. Both teacher and students break into astonished laughter at the sound of the machinery's obnoxious interruption of the adventure story: "He knew they were not laughing *at* him," Hunter goes on:

> He knew they were, just for the moment, sympathetic with his problems, looking at themselves from where he stood in front of the room, realizing they were not exactly angels, and laughing because this added sound barrier was making a tough job tougher. They laughed with him because, just for the moment, they saw things as he saw them, and perhaps as they actually were.[10]

Hunter's prose here achieves the difficult feat of describing intersubjectivity in a suspended moment and within a very particular social space. At various points through this passage, the annoyance of Dadier by the interruption of the machinery is sharply conveyed, as is his rather charming earnestness, as a teacher, in reading this popular adventure yarn to his students—an effort to reach them through something other than, or in addition to, canonical literature. Here, we get the sense of this classroom as an alive space, one in which not only Dadier lives and works but also one that might be animated by unanticipated interruptions—here, the machinery causing pencils on a desk to jump almost as if the scene were in an animated film; and as a space filled with the subsequent recognition by the students, touched perhaps by their instructor's willingness to bring a familiar popular text into the classroom, that their teacher is indeed a human being, and that they are perhaps not angels, a kind of recognition which is indeed rare in Hunter's description of the students' psychological comportment.

Brooks will include these sounds of adjacent classrooms as a source of interruption in his film, but not in the context of Dadier reading a popular narrative. Instead, and intriguingly, the scene in which Dadier brings a popular story into the classroom, in his search for an alternative pedagogical tactic, involves not a reading of a popular adventure story but rather his projection in 16mm of a short animated film adaptation of "Jack and the Beanstalk" to his class. In this sequence, Brooks alternates between shots of Dadier monitoring the projector with the class arranged diagonally across the frame, the projected images of the animated film flickering on the screen in front of the classroom, to shots of the students reacting, mainly with amusement, to these images (or, in some shots, keeping all three in frame; see Figure 7.2). Brooks also cuts to shots of students, and one teacher, looking in at this unusual pedagogical use of film from outside the classroom, implying the atypical, innovative, non-mimetic aspects of Dadier's new approach.

While these images of Dadier screening the film suggest a momentary ability to wield some productive control over the attention of his students, shots of the class underscore the relatively unamused reactions of Artie and Belazi, suggesting lingering problems with particular students who will continue to

Figure 7.2 Dadier projecting an animated "Jack and the Beanstalk" to his class.

challenge Dadier even after he has calibrated his teaching strategies. Nevertheless, Dadier, after the cartoon is over, is able to orchestrate a relatively productive discussion about ethics in relation to the behavior of the animated Jack and the giant, the energy of which Brooks conveys, in part, through cuts from Dadier to various groups and individual students who express their immediate reactions to the film they have just seen. The rhythm of the cutting across the various responses of the students complements the energy in the classroom that Dadier has created, an energy that appears generative and contingent rather than imitative and reproductive. Most intriguingly, Brooks, rather than literally illustrating the antecedent text, has here synthesized elements of the scene from the novel in which Dadier reads an adventure story to his class. Rather than being interrupted in his description of an adventure story by mechanisms from the machine shop class adjacent to his classroom, the film's Dadier has used a machine—a 16mm projector—to his advantage, effectively combining both machinery and adventure story in the form of a pedagogical filmstrip. Through this combination and synthesis of some of the Hunter novel's ideas, Brooks's film inscribes the cinema itself as part of a new mechanism of creative, aesthetic pedagogy, effectively positioning the discourse of *Blackboard Jungle* not simply as entertainment with a "message" but as part of a complex debate about how classroom space might become animated.

## MILLER'S LESSONS

For many viewers both upon the release of *Blackboard Jungle* in 1955, and today, the complex relationship between Glenn Ford's Rick Dadier and Sidney Poitier's

Glenn Miller remains of central interest. In his analysis of Poitier's career as an actor and a star, Aram Goudsouzian notes that Poitier's character in *Blackboard Jungle* had less to do with the actor's previous roles, which tended toward virtuous or humble figures, and more to do with "the emergent hero of 1950s American youth culture: silky, sullen, sexually charged," in the then emerging, Method-inflected tradition of James Dean and Marlon Brando.[11] Goudsouzian, further, perceptively notes that "Poitier's character was the black version of this culture hero, lending him an extra element of subversion—a hint of a new racial order within the teenage rebellion."[12] However, Sharon Willis, in her book-length study of Poitier's star text and its impact on audiences, is more ambivalent about the productively rebellious nature of this persona, underscoring instead the ways in which Poitier's star image itself embodied a kind of pedagogical authority within American culture of the 1950s and 1960s:

> In the move away from the therapeutic iconography that characterized his early social problem films, the pedagogical scenarios that multiply through Poitier's films suggest that whites cannot seem to transmit what they learn: each white person needs private tutoring in race relations. With startling consistency, his black mentor arrives by accident to enlighten white people, often by reminding them of what they already know. Having accomplished his task, by means that remain obscure or mysterious, the mentor disappears.[13]

Although her study closely examines the pedagogical functions of Poitier's persona, Willis mentions *Blackboard Jungle* only in passing. Placing her view of Poitier's work in juxtaposition with Goudsouzian's underscoring of Poitier's "hint of a new racial order" through a more "silky, sullen, sexually charged" figure is productive, however, because it enables us to see how Brooks's *Blackboard Jungle*, in a sense, has it both ways. The film is consistent with the pedagogical function of Poitier's star persona in cinema that Willis critiques: it is apparent that he does teach Dadier something the teacher couldn't get through his conventional, bourgeois education and professionalization, even though, in some sense, the film implies that the sympathetic, if frustrated, Dadier "already knows" it. But the fact that Miller must in some way teach the teacher, and that Dadier must learn on his own to become receptive to this interaction, points not to some intrinsic or essential failure of any particular group of people but rather to the larger failure of institutions of learning to offer something other than mimetic thought. The teachers and the students, in other words, largely have to find it on their own. In this sense, the fact that both Dadier and Miller grow as people through their personal relationship—one that occurs just as much outside the space of the classroom as within it—might not be a limit of the film's politics but a key part of its rebellious critique of the kinds of normative, mimetic teaching practices the film so vividly shows to be failures.

In the book, Miller functions as a figure who is mainly there to teach the teacher how to connect to an African American student—and, by extension, all of the students in the school, whose personal backgrounds are in various ways different from Dadier's own—when Dadier's own methods of pedagogy fail to do the trick. We do not go very far inside the interiority of Miller in the novel (nor do we get very far inside any of the students); he is presented from the outside—in terms of the description of his appearance, and manner of speech—and primarily through how Dadier himself sees him. When Hunter does offer some description of Miller from a relatively objective point of view, we are still left with something of a caricature, a character—in dialect and attitude—meant to stand, in large part, as a larger symbol of his race rather than as an individual figure, and further, a symbol of his race's encounter with the white schoolteacher rather than an autonomous person. This is partially a function of the book's intention to show how this trade school operates as a machine, in which the students are seen mainly—and from the outside—as problems that are both the product of and a blockage to the functioning of an educational institution. It is also a function of Hunter's choice to focalize most of the novel through Dadier's perspective. In these respects, the novel *Blackboard Jungle* is to some extent a symptom of the very institutional limitations it is working to critique.

Although Brooks makes a similar choice in the film to focalize his story through Glenn Ford's Dadier, the film's style, as I've already noted, works to situate Dadier in a larger context of both culture—the rock n' roll that scores the film's opening credits, for example—and cinema, shifting the novel's primary focus on psychological content and conflict to a focus on external action. Although *Blackboard Jungle* is consistent with that aspect of Sidney Poitier's star persona that is frequently instrumentalized, as Willis has sharply shown, as a means to educate naïve or ignorant members of the audience about racism, Brooks, to his credit, cinematically explores and reflects upon the larger causes generating that very instrumentalization. In doing so, the film furthers its critique of the instrumentalization of pedagogy—even, and perhaps especially, in situations in which the student is "educating" the teacher, highlighting the reactionary failure of modern educational systems that perpetuate mimetic, uncreative thought (even when in the guise of ostensible "progressivism"). Brooks goes further than the novel in showing how the unfortunate necessity of, to borrow Willis's phrase, this "private tutoring in race relations" between Miller and Dadier in the face of the larger institutional failure of the school in which they teach and learn is in fact not something the film is endorsing, but something it is critiquing.

In the book, Dadier gives a lesson on social prejudice by attempting to persuade students of the evils of racial and ethnic slurs. The substance of his lesson is not much more than "treat your neighbor as you would like your neighbor to treat yourself," but to Dadier's credit, he situates this conventional lesson in a relatively complex racial and ethnic context, connecting the universal idea of respect to the social problem of racism. But in order to critique these slurs, he must represent them by speaking them. The charge of the slurs on the soundtrack, spoken by a man who does not appear to be consciously racist—and as spoken by Glenn Ford, whose characterization of Dadier as a thoughtful, sensitive, if frustrated, man, does not necessarily prepare us for this language—carries its own charge. Subsequently, Dadier learns that a student has—perhaps willfully—misunderstood his lesson, complaining to the principal about his perception of Dadier's citation of prejudiced language in the classroom. Dadier, in both book and film, but without any concrete evidence, suspects it is Miller who has reported him. As in much of the book, this suspicion is conveyed in the form of Dadier's internal monologue, which traces his line of thinking after his meeting with the principal:

> The real bastard is whoever dumped the idea into his [Small's] empty head. Miller, of course. Miller. Goddamn Miller to Hell! Goddamn Miller and his tricky goddamn handsome smile! The little bastard is like a snake; every time he bites, he spreads a little more venom. I wish I were Max Schaefer. I'd clobber the little bastard until he couldn't do a pushup if he had four arms.[14]

In the passages preceding this internal monologue, Hunter clearly illustrates the ineffectuality of the administration of Manual Trades to deal effectively with the problem of racism. The reader is treated to a dialogue between Dadier and Principal Small, an aptly named man who dutifully berates Dadier for citing racial slurs while failing to understand the larger point the teacher was trying to make. Hunter's emphasis on Small's reactions suggests that the novelist is himself refraining from judging the rightness or wrongness of Dadier's pedagogical approach, and instead focuses on the failure of the larger institutional forces at play in the school. The depiction of Small is of an administrator who is more concerned with public displays of his own virtue and less with the concrete, material, and economic institutional forces conspiring to put Dadier in such awkward pedagogical positions in the first place. And, yet, ultimately, Hunter's focus is on the psychological effects this encounter between teacher and administrator has on Dadier.

In the film, Brooks takes Hunter's approach further, giving us a keen sense of Dadier's frustration—Glenn Ford's performance again deserves much credit here, as does the work of the young Sidney Poitier—and framing that frustration in a cinematically complex sequence. Hunter, admittedly, does occasionally suggest Dadier's own complicity with the racial problems his institution fails to address. At one point in the book, in another of the novel's many internal monologues, Dadier's frustration with Miller is nearly articulated in the form of a racial epithet:

> *The little bastard*, he thought. *The little black* . . .
> He stopped abruptly.
> Hey now. Hey now, what the hell was that? Now just what the hell was that?
> *Nothing, it just* . . .
> . . .
> *It's not because he's black*, Rick thought. *That has nothing to do with it.*[15]

But in the film Brooks adapts this internal monologue to the form of external action, and spoken dialogue between characters. After the film's depiction of his fraught meeting with the principal described above, Dadier encounters Miller in the hallway. Suspicious that Miller is the one who suggested to the administration that Dadier was endorsing, rather than critiquing, racist terms in the classroom, he corners Miller on the staircase. As Dadier presses Miller with his suspicions, Brooks's framing of Ford and Poitier on the staircase, positioned from a slightly low angle and placing Dadier in an ostensible position of power in this social context (see Figure 7.3), underscores the relatively ironic aspect of that power in this school—Dadier, as one who must answer to men like the principal, is ultimately not so powerful a figure in this institution, even though he may appear as one to some students.

The conversation escalates—as Brooks eschews cutting, preserving the tense aspect of the encounter in the form of its duration—and Dadier threatens

Figure 7.3 Dadier confronts Miller (Sidney Poitier) on the staircase.

to take a swing at Miller, and a moment after this comes close to uttering aloud to Miller the same prejudiced phrase the novel's Dadier edges up against in the previously cited passage. With his gestures, movements, and vocal inflections here, Poitier memorably embodies many of the qualities of "silky" rebelliousness Goudsouzian notes as crucial to his persona, while also eschewing some of the pedagogical qualities Willis sees as central. That is because Brooks is not interested here in showing us Miller (and Poitier) "teaching" Dadier (or the viewer) anything. Brooks is painting for us, through cinema, one effect of the collective failure of an institution to meaningfully address a problem that creates a rift between teachers and the students they are supposed to be educating. This shot is less a "personal tutorial" in racism and more a symptom of the institutional, administrative failure of Manual Trades, and by implication many institutions of higher learning, to reform a mimetic, reproductive structure which is not working.

By underscoring the larger social context of the school in the film *Blackboard Jungle* as well as the interpersonal action at play within it, Richard Brooks effectively translates the primarily psychological content of the novel into a concrete, physical, and cinematic experience. The result is a film that, although of course partially a product of its cultural moment like all creative works are, still has much to teach us about the failure of institutions and their members—particularly those that signal themselves as ostensibly "progressive"—to meaningfully address the material, economic, and social causes of prejudice. Both Ford and Poitier give remarkable performances in conveying the pressures this institutional failure places on individuals, but it is above all Brooks, as their director, who teaches us a thing or two about what it means to creatively grapple with these matters in cinema.

## NOTES

1. See Adam Golub, "They Turned a School into a Jungle! How *The Blackboard Jungle* Redefined the Education Crisis in Postwar America," *Film & History* 39:1 (2009): pp. 21–30; Beth McCoy, "Manager, Buddy, Delinquent: *Blackboard Jungle*'s Desegregating Triangle," *Cinema Journal* 38:1 (1998): pp. 25–39; Daniel Perlstein, "Imagined Authority: *Blackboard Jungle* and the Project of Educational Liberalism," *International Journal on the History of Education* 36:1 (2000): pp. 407–24; and Jennifer Stoever-Ackerman, "Reproducing U.S. Citizenship in *Blackboard Jungle*: Race, Cold War Liberalism, and the Tape Recorder," *American Quarterly* 63:23 (2011): pp. 781–806.
2. See Paul N. Reinsch, "Music over Words and Sound over Image: 'Rock Around the Clock' and the Centrality of Music in Post-Classical Film Narration," *Music and the Moving Image* 6:3 (Fall 2013): pp. 3–22.
3. Douglas K. Daniel, *Tough as Nails: The Life and Films of Richard Brooks* (Madison: University of Wisconsin Press, 2014), p. 87.
4. Evan Hunter, *The Blackboard Jungle* (New York: Open Road, 1999), pp. 118–19. Originally published in 1954.

5. Ibid. p. 16.
6. Ibid. p. 77.
7. Daniel, *Tough as Nails*, p. 91.
8. Ibid. p 70.
9. Hunter, *The Blackboard Jungle*, p. 139.
10. Ibid. p. 140.
11. Aram Goudsouzian, *Sidney Poitier: Man, Actor, Icon* (Chapel Hill: The University of North Carolina Press, 2015), p. 103.
12. Ibid. p. 104.
13. Sharon Willis, *The Poitier Effect: Racial Melodrama and Fantasies of Reconciliation* (Minneapolis: University of Minnesota Press, 2016), p. 4.
14. Hunter, *The Blackboard Jungle*, p. 240.
15. Ibid. p. 211.

CHAPTER 8

# Hunting and the Economics of Adaptation: *The Last Hunt* (1956) and *The Professionals* (1966)

*Homer B. Pettey*

As director and screenwriter, Richard Brooks adapted two popular, postwar Western novels about destructive financial conditions at the closing of the American frontier: Milton Lott's *The Last Hunt* (1954) and Frank O'Rourke's *A Mule for the Marquesa* (1964). Both novels confront human greed and excessive violence as inherently American traits, as well as part of its Manifest Destiny to achieve territorial and economic conquest. Both novels reveal the necessity of men to adapt to menacing natural and commercial environments in the West. Both novels focus upon the technical skills of hunting, whether bringing down bison or bringing down men. Both the novels and Brooks's adapted films—*The Last Hunt* (1956) and *The Professionals* (1966)—involve the sexual kidnapping of a woman as the central metaphor for ruthless capitalistic conquest of the American West. At work in the novels and films can be found an economy of adaptation that plays out in unchecked overconsumption and systems of brutal exchange. Economics of adaptation for America includes not just man in the wilderness, but also the wild within mankind. Risk, whether bringing buffalo hides to market or returning for pay a wife to her capitalist husband, does not function by the simple gain–loss mechanics of equilibrium, but rather by irrational, unpredictable greed and fear. Ironically for Brooks, the film productions took on extreme risk–reward consequences of their own, whereby he discovered that blood-guilt of American Western history did pay off at the box office, and that a heist-like caper would proffer significant financial and artistic gains. In some respects, then, Brooks's relationship to the industry oddly mirrored the economic fixations in the novels.

Brooks wrote the adapted screenplays for both *The Last Hunt* and *The Professionals*. As with his other adaptations from the fifties and sixties, such as *The Blackboard Jungle* (1955), *The Brothers Karamazov* (1958), *Elmer Gantry*

(1960), and *Lord Jim* (1965), Brooks did not shy away from controversial and iconoclastic subject matter. *The Last Hunt* and *The Professionals* represent Brooks's attempts to redirect the image of the West, to reinterpret the underlying values of the Western, to create new archetypes of Western masculinity, and to critique assumptions about economic progress in American Western history. Challenging cinematic formulas would characterize much of Brooks's career, and *The Last Hunt* and *The Professionals*, while relying upon standard elements of codified morality and societal justice in typical Westerns, undercut and replace them with new visions of the destructive and violent history of the West. In many respects, both films are forerunners of revisionist and anti-Westerns of the late sixties and early seventies, such as Sam Peckinpah's *The Wild Bunch* (1969).

Peter Lev points out that the "late 1940s and early 1950s were an important time of transition for the Western," due to thematic shifts that André Bazin noted in "superwesterns" by embedding social, political, and psychosexual subplots into the standard formulaic Western.[1] In this sense, then, the new Westerns adapted the previous black-and-white morality of the genre in order to convey new postwar social and existential concerns. In many respects, *The Last Hunt* and *The Professionals* take the "superwestern" a step further, with the inclusion of economics and a critique of American western expansion as pervasive themes. In *The Professionals*, the socially and economically supported professional hunters, as Jeffrey Wallmann points out, "succeed not because of morals but of superior skills."[2] For *The Last Hunt*, superior hunting skills lead to devastation and self-destruction.

In his study of the Western as American social history and commentary, John H. Lenihan situates Westerns, such as *The Last Hunt* and *Broken Arrow*, that include Native American characters in the mid-1950s as reflections of the civil rights transition after *Brown v. Board of Education*: "Taken in their totality, however, both films cast a dark shadow over the nation's frontier epoch, which emerges less as a precedent for progress than as a presage of contemporary bigotry and violence."[3] Along with *The Searchers* (1956) and *Fort Massacre* (1958), *The Last Hunt* was among a handful of Westerns "addressing white bigotry against Native Americans."[4]

Addressing professionalism in Westerns, Noël Carroll broadly suggests that *The Professionals*, primarily through the character Jake Sharp (Woody Strode), an expert with a bow and arrow, ignores racial distinctions in favor of technical skills, so much so that in the end, "professionalism appears justified in the service of society," not separate from the ends of society.[5] Carroll's sweeping claim of social values misses the economic subtext of the film and its critique not of good and evil so much as of the predatory capitalist class. Indeed, the morality of the professionals in the film, as in the novel, centers not on a social ethos, but upon a risk–reward strategy, whereby consequences become reduced to payment for task completed. Lee Clark Mitchell casts *The Professionals* among several Westerns whose main characters, primarily "misfits, loners, bullies, mavericks, and sociopaths," may well be technical experts of their destructive crafts, but they are on the fringes of society, where morality has been eroded by the economics of zero-sum games, hunting only to acquire money, not social acceptance.[6] Certainly, misfits, losers, and one psychotic characterize the four-man team of *The Last Hunt*.

Structurally, both films share similar plots and themes, particularly the skills and knowledge of a hunting party confronting dangerous prey: buffalo in *The Last Hunt* and Mexican revolutionaries in *The Professionals*. Both films break from traditional Western formulas, whereby the knightly code of honor and the masculine code of the West have been replaced by monetary pursuit. In both films, professional hunters kill with moral and social impunity, exchanging carnage for financial gain. Both films focus upon four male professional hunters who represent fringes of American society. In *The Last Hunt*, beleaguered bison hunter Sandy McKenzie (Stewart Granger) teams up with bloodthirsty, sociopathic novice Charles Gilson (Robert Taylor), and they hire two skinners, veteran buffalo skinner Woodfoot (Lloyd Nolan) and jejune, bi-racial Native American Jimmy O'Brien (Russ Tamblyn). McKenzie represents the dying of the frontier as much as Gilson represents the root cause of the West's death, while Woodfoot embodies the history of the destruction of the buffalo and the West from the Prairies to the north and Jimmy represents the effects upon the marginalized peoples of the West.

In *The Professionals*, a four-man team of field-specific experts work for ten thousand dollars each to return the kidnapped Mexican wife (Claudia Cardinale) of a wealthy rancher and mine-owner, Mr. Grant (Ralph Bellamy), by infiltrating the revolutionary stronghold of a former Villa comrade, Raza (Jack Palance), and rescuing Mrs. Grant. Team leader, Rico Fardan (Lee Marvin), earns his living through his superior knowledge of guns, the primary means of death in the West, as does explosives specialist Bill Dolworth (Burt Lancaster), whose fetish for dynamite symbolizes the newest technology of death. The opening credit sequence of *The Professionals* has Lee Marvin demonstrating the loading and firing of a 1916 Browning-style machine gun, a weapon of mass killing. Both Fardan and Dolworth served as mercenaries along with Raza in numerous Mexican revolutionary skirmishes, reinforced in the opening title shot with an adobe wall with the inscription Viva Villa. In the novel, *A Mule for the Marquesa*, the professional team consists of five members, but Brooks in his screen adaptation combined the bomb-maker Fred Bisley with the womanizer, "*jolies mesdames*" mansion-owner Bill Dolworth.[7] To join Fardan and Dolworth, Grant enlists two other specialists, sentimental horse-lover and wrangler Hans Ehrengard (Robert Ryan) and bow-and-arrow shootist, tracker, and bounty-hunter Jake Sharp (Woody Strode). In the novel, Woody Strode's character is a half Mexican and half Irish-Mormon, Danny Rios, who worked on the Grant ranch. Along with his career as a supporting action star in John Ford's Westerns *Sergeant Rutledge* (1960) and *The Man Who Shot Liberty Valance* (1962), as well as his acclaimed gladiator role in Stanley Kubrick's *Spartacus* (1960), Strode fulfills the significant historical role of the African Americans in the West as Native American hunters, but also as U.S. Army soldiers, remnants of the Buffalo Soldiers of the lengthy Indian Wars, now fighting against Villa along the border.[8] The opening credit sequence reinforces these roles for African Americans, with Strode riding and leading a chained Native American to a U.S. Marshall office. By their specialties, Ehrengard and Sharpe represent not the new West, but the old West, those modes of traditional transport and antique weaponry that Fardan and Dolworth are making more and more obsolete. Moreover, as the novel makes clear, because of the Mexican Revolution, the West has transformed profoundly, both politically and economically:

> Grant asked this of a man named Henry Fardan, in the sixth year of the Mexican Revolution, three months after the United States had embargoed munition shipments to Villa, three days after Villa had stopped the mine train near Santa Ysabel, Chihuahua, and shot sixteen American engineers. Carranza was in the President's chair and Obregón, commanding the government armies, was slowly destroying the remnants of Villa's power in the north; and bandits innocent of all political pretensions were raiding villages and ranches on the American side of the river, and Americans were shooting Mexicans on sight.[9]

The plot of *The Professionals* underscores precisely this history, with the now politically cynical Fardan and Dolworth, the new Westerners, reducing revolutionaries to mere obstacles to their economic gain, and Mr. Grant, the new Western law, also viewing Mexicans as expendable.

Both films include a woman who intrudes upon the professional quartet: Maria (Claudia Cardinale), the supposedly kidnapped Mexican wife of the wealthy Grant (Ralph Bellamy) in *The Professionals*, and the innocent, sexually exploited Sioux girl (Debra Paget) in *The Last Hunt*. In both films, the fate of the rescued woman grants some semblance of morality to otherwise violent tales of rapacious capitalism besieging the frontier. In many respects, Richard Brooks adapted two novels that challenge cinematic assumptions about traditional Westerns. In both films, Maria and the Sioux girl are viewed in economic terms. In *The Professionals*, before the team departs the treacherous canyons with Maria Grant, Dolworth, who volunteers to stay behind to decoy and thwart Raza and his men, reminds Fardan, "You take care of the goods," their payday object, Maria. Even though Raza and Maria are lovers and Fardan and Dolworth realize "We've been had," the professionals still continue with their mission, delivering Maria to Grant at the end, to fulfill the contract. In the novel, as they flee Raza's men, Fardan wonders about their situation, understanding Maria's economic and emotional motivations, but not her husband's:

> She had gambled for the biggest stakes in her world, and victory demanded the strongest demonstration. And Grant? What should they do about Grant? Did Grant know what he wanted in return for love? Or was it possession that he felt, the greedy pride in owning a beautiful object?[10]

In the novel, Danny Rios shoots Raza dead. In the novel, when Maria questions Fardan about why he did not inform Grant about what she has done, he simply responds: "He paid the price."[11] For the film, Brooks creates a romantic ending, with the professionals delivering Maria to Grant, but then letting her take the wounded Raza back to Mexico. In the end, the professionals fulfill their contract, as Marvin informs Bellamy: "We made a contract to save a lady from a nasty, old kidnapper, who turns out to be you."

In *The Last Hunt*, aside from the short scenes of bargirls in the town saloon, the Siouan girl's sexuality fulfills Charlie's lust and greed as much as bison hides do. In the novel, Charlie reduces the Sioux to "a kind of varmint," to slaves with bone-picking just "Nigger work," and Sioux women to merely an economic object, symbolized by Charlie's tobacco pouch of "a squaw's breast as a souvenir."[12] Lott devotes much of the novel to the mechanics of shooting, to the proliferation of bison killing, and to the specifics of skinning hides, in

Figure 8.1 The professionals ride off at the end; from left to right, Robert Ryan, Lee Marvin, Burt Lancaster, and Woody Strode.

order to reveal Charlie's mounting psychosis, as well as to achieve the work's most disturbing scene:

> It was hard getting a start, but once he got a little edge between his thumb and finger, the rest was easy. He was surprised to find the skin so thick and tough. Somehow he had expected it to tear easily and stick hard to the flesh.
>
> It was tedious work, though, compared to a buffalo. Sweat came out on his face as he worked and dripped off the end of his nose onto the dark-muscled flesh. There was a warm smell of meat mixed with the Indian smell that he could hardly stand. He found himself holding his breath for long intervals, then sucking in air through his mouth so as not to smell it.[13]

Charlie treats the Siouan girl very much the way he debases Native Americans to animals and hides. In the novel and film, Charlie sleeps with the Siouan girl, as a form of power lust. McKenzie, although disapproving of Charlie's objectification and cruel treatment of the girl, remains silent for most of the film. In the end, however, McKenzie frees the girl and they become the target of Charlie's last hunt. Again, Brooks transforms the novel's ending into a romantic tale, with McKenzie and the girl surviving a blizzard night in a cave, while Charlie, having killed a buffalo and wrapped its carcass around him, freezes to death, a fitting end to a blood-crazed hunter. In the novel, Charlie does not hunt McKenzie and the girl, who escape midway through the book, but instead is lost in a blizzard tracking down the last buffalo. Charlie kills the last buffalo, quickly skins the hide, rolls himself within it, only to discover a short time later that he is trapped,

Figure 8.2 The last image of Charlie (Robert Taylor) frozen to death within the newly killed buffalo's hide.

immobilized by the frozen hide. For both films, Brooks obviously wrote Hollywood endings, comedies of marriage—McKenzie with the Siouan girl; Maria with Raza—as a way to make the shaky morality and violent narratives more palatable for audiences.

*The Last Hunt* deals with the historic time period of the Spring of 1882 to the Winter of 1883–4 that signaled the horrendous decline in bison by Sioux populations and hide-hunters in the American West, from what had been estimated a population of thirty to seventy-five million animals at its peak.[14] John Hanner explains that by the early 1880s, after the defeat of the Sioux in 1877, white hunters in the Dakotas achieved the greatest kills in 1882 with "the extermination of the northern herd complete—at least for commercial purposes—by the fall of 1883."[15] In his historical work on buffalo and the New West, *Last Stand*, Michael Punke, author of *The Revenant*, recounts the dismal, progressive destruction of the bison:

> In 1882, the Northern Pacific Railroad alone shipped 200,000 hides to eastern processing facilities, an amount that filled an estimated 700 boxcars. In 1883, the railroad shipped 40,000 hides. In 1884, the total harvest fits in a single boxcar, and according to a Northern Pacific official, "it was the last shipment ever made."[16]

Brooks begins the film with an opening disclaimer about the subject matter and time period of the script:

> In 1853 the American plains thundered with the sound of 60,000,000 buffaloes. Thirty years later, at the time of this story, the hunters and Indians had recklessly slaughtered these herds to a bare 30,000 survivors.

The inclusion of the Sioux among the slaughterers reveals Brooks's well-grounded knowledge of the history of this devastation. In the film, Charlie fights and kills Siouan hunters, whom he sees as unworthy competitors. George Colpitts cites statistics on Siouan meat-hunters for large companies: "fresh meat equivalents of bison purchased exclusively by the Hudson's Bay Company for transport grew from 482,000 pounds in the 1840s, to 579,870 in the 1850s, 615,625 in the 1860s, and 864,053 pounds in the 1870s, on the eve of the bison herds' collapse."[17] The Sioux of the Great Plains transformed from collective to more individual or small group associations, all due to the need for providing buffalo skins and meat in exchange for commodities. As the demand for buffalo increased, the Sioux changed from winter hunters after denser winter coats to summer hunting parties in order to meet demand and to remain viable in the marketplace.

Market forces for buffalo robes expanded bison hunting beyond the Sioux, as did the need for a source of ready protein for railroad workers:

> After buffalo robes became popular, Euro-Americans slaughtered buffalo for profit. Railroads provided the impetus for wholesale slaughter. Professionals hunted to provide meat for the railroad crews. William "Buffalo Bill" Cody allegedly killed 4,200 bison to supply food for workers. Trains often slowed down and opened windows so people could shoot buffalo. Market hunters approached hunting from an economical perspective. They despised sportsmen who had nothing to lose if they failed. For economic reasons, professionals shot only what the market could sell. Killing more would only raise their costs. Once they had their kill they needed to sell their meat.[18]

Even beyond the global market for buffalo robes, the American marketplace demanded buffalo products to replace industrial, commercial, and personal uses for leather processing, thereby accelerating the number of white hunters and "market-oriented Indians" into the fields:

> At a time when many day laborers struggled to make a dollar a day, a single bison hide robe could bring anywhere from $3–5, although by the 1870s, the robe trade had disappeared as the harvest became centered around greater efficiency in leather processing and prices dropped.[19]

Price decline did not thwart skin-hunters, but ensured they redoubled their efforts to bring in even more hides for eastern tanneries and those in Europe, as M. Scott Taylor cites for the British market:

> In addition to sole leather, the tough buffalo hides found use as industrial belting for machinery in England and elsewhere on the European continent. Many secondary sources make this connection, but primary source evidence is also available from English business directories. For example, Slater's Royal National Commercial Directories at the time list numerous tanners, hide merchants, and leather belt manufacturers in their directory of trades. These businesses list as products buffalo hides, buffalo skips, buffalo hide shavings, buffalo pickers, and strapping for cotton gins.[20]

With such a great demand for buffalo products, even in a somewhat dwindling market in the Dakotas, the reward of continued hunting greatly outweighed the immediate, but not the long-term, risk. By 1895, when it became protected in the United States, estimates reflect that bison lost "99 percent of its habitat and numbered only 800 animals in the wild and another 1,000 in parks or ranches."[21]

In the novel *The Last Hunt*, with the exception of novice hunter Charley, Sandy, Woodfoot, and Jimmy had already been buffalo hunters before retreating to more civilized but failed lives of rancher, drifter, and jobber in town respectively. Sandy convinces Jimmy to join the newly formed hunting party as a skinner for profits, even from the thinner-haired summer pelts: "'Summer hide?' 'Sure, it pays as good as prime now. They use it for leather. You on?' Jimmy nodded."[22] Their party will observe the steady decline in the animal population, with much of the film showing lengthy shots of buffalo after buffalo being brought down, mostly concentrating the camera on the bloodthirsty Charley. To the opening sequence, Brooks added a disclaimer so that audiences will understand not only that numerous killings of buffalo in the film were real, but also the necessity for the animals' deaths:

> We were permitted to photograph the required annual thinning of the largest buffalo herd in America. The shooting of the buffalo is the assignment of expert Government riflemen.

While Lott's novel achieved considerable popularity, even in contention for a Pulitzer Prize, the grim subject matter was certainly a risk for Brooks.

Brooks's adaptation choices for his scripts, particularly the endings in comedies of marriage, were themselves necessitated by market forces affecting studios with dwindling audiences. Studios needed to make strategic choices in subjects and directors to remain solvent. 1956 resulted in a blockbuster year for Warner Bros. studio, with audiences flocking to experience the spectacular cinematography of *Giant*, adult-content features of *Baby Doll* and *The Bad Seed*, and the television spin-offs of *Our Miss Brooks* and *The Lone Ranger*. John Ford's Technicolor VistaVision Western epic *The Searchers* for Warner Bros. received mostly high praise from reviewers. M-G-M, where Brooks directed two films in 1956, *The Last Hunt* and *A Catered Affair*, had released fewer successful extravaganzas than Warner Bros.; its *Lust for Life*, about Vincent van Gogh, lost nearly seven hundred thousand dollars in audience profits. The mid-1950s saw major reductions in film releases by the major studios, including M-G-M, which produced only twenty-four films in 1956 as compared to forty-four in 1953.[23] M-G-M set its sights on big-scale production costs for musicals, which accounted for around a quarter of its output, such as Gene Kelly's obsessive experimental *Invitation to the Dance*, which had no dialogue, just expressive dance and miming, and which failed at the box office. Two old-style musicals, however, returned audiences to theatres—*Meet Me in Las Vegas* with Cyd Charisse's legs and *High Society*, its biggest profit margin maker, a remake of *The Philadelphia Story*—combined the two films grossing approximately $7.5 million profit at the box office.[24] Discounting the epics from other studios, the other film grosses for M-G-M in 1956 ranged from meagre to industry averages: *I'll Cry Tomorrow* ($6.5 million), *Friendly*

*Persuasion* ($4.1 million), *Forever Darling* ($2.6 million), *Fastest Gun Alive* ($2.2 million), *Bhowani Junction* ($2.1 million), *Somebody Up There Likes Me* ($2 million), *Tea and Sympathy* ($2 million), and *Forbidden Planet* ($1.6 million).

With *The Last Hunt* grossing just over $1.7 million and ranking 57th out of the top 109 films for 1956 in terms of domestic rentals, Brooks fell into the lower profit margin category.[25] Although not a top earner, Brooks did make a profit with *The Last Hunt*. Fittingly, *The Last Hunt* had its world premiere in Sioux Falls, South Dakota, with director Brooks and stars Stewart Granger and Russ Tamblyn in attendance.[26] In *Variety*, under "Picture Grosses" for February 1956, *The Last Hunt* recorded $14,000 during its newcomer week.[27] A month later, as part of twenty-two pre-release openings in the Midwest,[28] in Cincinnati, *The Last Hunt* held its own with audiences, edging out *Our Miss Brooks*, but not *I'll Cry Tomorrow*.[29]

With *The Last Hunt* and *The Professionals*, Brooks gambled on two very different but exceptional works of literature, because he understood the economic, if slim, value of presenting fascinating adult-content genre pieces in film. Significantly, Brooks continued to work on adaptations of literary works over the next decades, even though this mid-decade year revealed weak box offices. For the next two years, a relentless Brooks stuck to literary adaptations, with *Something of Value*, *The Brothers Karamazov*, and the very profitable *Cat on a Hot Tin Roof*. Certainly, it was not studio budgets for production that lessened his films' profits, since *Cat on a Hot Tin Roof* had a budget nearly similar to *The Last Hunt*, but pulled in around eight times the profit over production costs. 1956, then, was a seminal year for Brooks, who had to make risk–reward and zero-sum profit margin decisions when negotiating with the studio suits at M-G-M.

*The Last Hunt* had two astounding and dread-inducing CinemaScope effects, with the screen dominated not only by the thundering of a massive herd of buffalo, but also their wholesale massacre. *Variety* recognized that *The Last Hunt* was "somewhat off the beaten path for wild west shows" and that Brooks's screenplay adaptation showed "marked talent for construction and organization of material that will likely stir revulsion among the sensitive and score with the 'he men' of the audience."[30] In his *New York Times* review of *The Last Hunt*, Bosley Crowther characterized the shock effect on the audience of the initial scenes of the Federal Government's "thinning" of a protected herd of buffalo at Custer State Park in South Dakota as "startling and slightly nauseating," although he did understand Brooks's aim "to display the low and demoralizing influence of a lust for slaughter upon the nature of man" and recognized the Western allegory that equated "Indian-hating with a lust for slaughter."[31] *Picturegoer* was far less appreciative of the film's comparison of buffalo eradication with Sioux starvation, because that theme becomes so embedded in "a tedious tale of white man against white man, with a cute Indian maiden as the prize, that you're apt to lose sight of it."[32] That the film made money should be surprising with these kinds of reviews that reduce the film's message to sickening scenes of wholesale slaughter and a trite love triangle ending. In retrospect, *The Last Hunt* survives as one of Brooks's extraordinary adaptations, on which he gambled, then hunted, and found appreciative audiences.

A decade later, Brooks would not only find an audience, but also secure significant profits with *The Professionals*. It fared well for Columbia Pictures in 1966, with North American rental figures of $8.8 million.[33] After some financial woes in the late 1950s, Columbia expanded its production and distribution to British epics, such as *Lawrence of Arabia* (1962) and *A Man for All Seasons* (1966), both box office successes.[34] Brooks had a number of very successful screen adaptations under his belt by 1966, but found himself in competition with major adult popular literature also adapted to film. Ian Fleming's sex-and-violence Bond novels, *Dr. No* (1962), *From Russia with Love* (1963), *Goldfinger* (1964), and *Thunderball* (1965), would be adapted before the release of *The Professionals*. There were also star-studded war epics adapted from popular novels, including *The Guns of Navarone* (1961) and *The Great Escape* (1963). And there were also a few very well-received Westerns, such as *A Fistful of Dollars* (1964) and the comic *Cat Ballou* (1965). Making a Western again meant Brooks needed to find the right material that could support an all-star cast, have epic visual quality, and contain an adult theme. In 1966, Columbia Pictures released twenty-nine films, so *The Professionals* amounted to another risky project for Brooks.[35] At the end of the year, *The Professionals*, however, topped Columbia's list, particularly with its opening first week in November with "a terrific $86,000" and setting records at Broadway theatres.[36]

A full-page advertisement for the world premiere of *The Professionals* in *Variety* had the word "EXCITEMENT," the X highlighted to match the crossed X of a rifle-ammunition bandolero in the middle of the page, with Burt Lancaster, dynamite bundle in hand, at the top of the V of the X, a well-armed Lee Marvin on the left V of the X, Woody Strode with bow and arrow and a rifle-pointing Robert Ryan on the right V of the X, and at the open V at the bottom of the X a busty, suggestively open-legged Claudia Cardinale. Clearly, Columbia Pictures wished to exploit the violent and sexual content of the film in order to secure as large an audience as possible.[37] What *The Professionals* shared with many of the blockbusters listed above remained the violent adult content of the plot and scenes, which The National Catholic Office for Motion Pictures criticized:

> In this adventure fantasy certain elements of treatment (rationalized brutality, erotic situations and coarse language) which would be morally intolerable to any but an adult viewer should, in the opinion of this office and its consulters, qualify the film for an advisory adult classification from the Production Code Administration of the National Picture Ass'n of America.[38]

Of course, in the mid-1960s, such an attempt at audience restrictions could only boost attendance and profits for Columbia Pictures. With stiff competition from the adult-oriented Bond films of the early 1960s, Brooks and Columbia certainly chose the right vehicle to hunt down the largest possible audience. As part of its monthly retrospective average of twenty-four key sites for sampling audience and current rentals in the United States and Canada, Mike Wear for *Variety* reported that *The Professionals*, even during "the pre-Christmas doldrums" and bad winter weather, found huge audiences, almost matching *Hawaii* for general viewers and surpassing *Dr. Zhivago* and *Alfie* among adults.[39]

Brooks himself helped promote *The Professionals* by allowing screenings through Columbia for distributors and in Denver for "a contingent of top New York-based executives" for general sales, advertising, and "national exploitation."[40] Much of the pre-release build-up for *The Professionals*, such as in Minneapolis, was "aided by hard-hitting newspaper ads and much advance word-of-mouth excitement," obviously from local reviewers.[41] Six months ahead of its Thanksgiving-Christmas season release, Columbia pictures began strategies for promoting and distributing *The Professionals*: "Mo Rothman, Columbia Pictures vice-president in charge of global distribution; Rube Jackter, vice-president, Robert S. Ferguson, vice-president in charge of advertising and publicity, Norman Jackter, Richard Kahn and Milt Goodman went to Hollywood to view an early rough cut of Richard Brooks' 'The Professionals'."[42] Along with the excitement for the star-studded cast, *The Professionals* received glowing reviews for the technical filmmaking of this action adventure, in particular:

> Pictorial values are excellent, since Conrad Hall's Technicolor-Panavision camera has caught the dusty mood of the Southwest. Maurice Jarre's score is brisk and effective. Willis Cook handled the explosive effects which add substantially to the excitement. Sound editing and recording are noteworthy in view of the exterior lensing in many desert and canyon areas.[43]

Additionally, industry and theatre exhibitors honored Brooks for the box office success of *The Professionals*, such as his "being kudoed because of the business his current Columbia release" made at the Midwest at Show-A-Rama in Kansas City.[44] Distribution strategies and ad campaigns took on global significance, as evident from the 488,904 admissions at Toho Kakudai cinema chain in Tokyo, making *The Professionals* "second only to 'Lawrence of Arabia' as Columbia's all-time earner in Japan."[45] As an odd bit of self-reflective irony, the last reel of *The Professionals* was stolen from the United Artists Theatre in Louisville, Kentucky, reported as "a stunt for profitmaking," but "costly unwanted publicity."[46]

Westerns about hunting parties remain rare for the genre. Still, valid analogies can be drawn among the concept and practice of hunting, contractual relationships, economic competition within the industry, and filmmaking for targeted audiences. Lesley Brill's *Crowds, Power, and Transformation in Cinema*, although not discussing Westerns or the film industry directly, offers pertinent insights into these analogous areas associated with Brooks's *The Last Hunt* and *The Professionals*. The point remains not to draw overly extended or false analogies, but rather to provide another way to interpret the complexities of adaptation and filmmaking. Brill reads films through an admittedly limited, yet provocative lens that relies upon the master work by the Nobel Laureate of Literature, Elias Canetti's *Crowds and Power*. Brill reserves his enlisting of and analysis of Canetti's views on hunters and packs for Hitchcock's *North by Northwest* (1959).[47] Moreover, Brill places Roger Thornhill as an isolated victim beset upon by hunting packs: "From the point of view of *Crowds and Power*, however, Thornhill is not struggling with crowds but with packs: the originary units of crowds, but distinguishable from them in their size and the constraints upon their growth."[48] Hunting packs, whose aim Canetti clearly defines in economic terms, aptly applies to the hunting parties of *The Last Hunt* and *The Professionals*:

> The truest and most natural pack is that from which our word derives, the hunting pack; and this forms wherever the object of the pack is an animal too strong and too dangerous to be captured by one man alone. It also forms whenever there is a prospect of a mass of game, so that as little as possible of it shall be lost. If the slaughtered animal is very large, a whale or an elephant for example, its size means that it can only be brought in and divided up by numbers of men working together, even if it was originally struck down by one or two individuals. Thus the hunting pack enters the stage of *distribution*. Distribution need not always be preceded by hunting, but the two stages, or states, are closely connected and should be examined together. The object of both is the *prey*; and the prey alone, its behaviour and nature, whether alive or dead, determines the behaviour of the pack which forms with it as object.[49]

As an example of such packs, Canetti includes the ceremonial interrelationship within the Mandan buffalo dance, in which the participants become both "buffaloes and hunters simultaneously," as the buffalo dancers themselves succumb to the enticement of this ritual:

> The buffalo, whose aspect and motion are so well known, resemble me in that they like dancing and allow themselves to be lured to a festivity

by their disguised costumes. The dance lasts for a long time, for it has to take effect over large distances. From far off, the buffaloes sense a pack and succumb to its attraction so long as the dance continues . . . As in the increased pack, in a state of continuing excitement they are stronger than a loosely-grouped herd and draw the buffaloes irresistibly into their orbit.[50]

Such an aesthetic dance corresponds to the manner by which the hunters merge with their prey, feel their prey, and understand their prey. Ritualizing that experience of hunter and prey certainly applies to the audience experience of observing and identifying with hunting packs and their aims in film. Clearly, the plots of both Brooks's films conform to Canetti's definition of the hunting pack; whether the small group of hunters go after bison or after Mexican revolutionaries, the plurality of prey only expands the means of killing, not the size of the hunting pack. Moreover, distribution describes not only the hierarchy of the shooters and skinners in *The Last Hunt*, but also Mr. Grant and his distributive wealth to the contracted hunting professionals. Taking a step further, hunting and distribution can apply to the process of finding a work to adapt, creating that aesthetic, cinematic movement that coalesces theme and content, and then distributing gains to those who were chief in the hunt (read director and studio). Again, such analogies are not meant to impose strict readings upon Brooks, adaptation in general, or his films. Instead, they hint at new insights into the relationships among text and adaptation, director and film, and film and audience experience. To avoid correlatives between script adaptation and literary text, or between cinematic craft and thematic content, or between directorial exercise and audience shaping, is to negate essential, if precarious, power relationships that are the essence of filmmaking. Like the hunter, Brooks understood his role as master over and subject to the prey, an always reversible situation whereby Brooks the director, as evidenced by his Hollywood endings for *The Last Hunt* and *The Professionals*, not only relied upon audiences, but necessarily had to succumb to them. Ultimately, among the many admirable qualities of *The Last Hunt* and *The Professionals* remains the way their cinematic archetypes force audiences to re-envision their own role in the hunter–prey paradigm that has always been at the heart of the economy and history of the American West.

## NOTES

1. Peter Lev, "Westerns" in "Genres and Production Trends, 1950–1954," *The Fifties—Transforming The Screen, 1950–1959* (Berkeley and Los Angeles: University of California Press, 2003), p. 54.
2. Jeffrey Wallmann, *The Western—Parables of the American Dream* (Lubbock: Texas Tech University Press, 1999), p. 166.

3. John H. Lenihan, *Showdown—Confronting Modern America in the Western Era* (Urbana and Chicago: University of Illinois Press, 1980), p. 73.
4. Johnny D. Boggs, *The American West on Film* (Santa Barbara, CA: ABC-CLIO, 2020), pp. 96–7.
5. Noël Carroll, "The Professional Western: South of the Border," in *Back in the Saddle Again—New Essays on the Western*, eds. Edward Buscombe and Roberta E. Pearson (London: The British Film Institute, 1998), p. 57.
6. Lee Clark Mitchell, *Westerns—Making the Man in Fiction and Film* (Chicago, IL: University of Chicago Press, 1996), p. 225. Mitchell cites Will Wright's overview of professional fighters in Westerns as "men willing to defend society only as a job they accept for pay or for love of fighting, not from commitment to ideas of law and justice" [Will Wright, *Sixguns and Society: A Structural Study of the Western* (Berkeley, CA: University of California Press, 1975), p. 85].
7. Frank O'Rourke, *The Professionals* (New York: Avon Books, 1966), p. 31.
8. For a detailed account of the black soldiers and the border, see Gerald Horne, *Black and Brown—African Americans and the Mexican Revolution, 1910–1920* (New York: New York University Press, 2005), p. 145.
9. O'Rourke, *The Professionals*, p. 11.
10. Ibid. p. 171.
11. Ibid. p. 176.
12. Milton Lott, *The Last Hunt* (Boston, MA: Houghton Mifflin Company, 1954), pp. 205, 101, 207.
13. Ibid. p. 214.
14. Andrew C. Isenberg, "Environment and the Nineteenth-Century West: Or, Process Encounters Place," in *A Companion to the American West*, ed. William Deverell (Oxford: Blackwell Publishing, 2004), p. 82. Isenberg claims that with the introduction of steamboats on the Missouri River in the 1830s, by the 1850s "Indian hunters in the plains annually supplied Euro-American traders with an estimated 100,000 bison robes" (p. 83).
15. John Hanner, "Government Response to the Buffalo Hide Trade, 1871–1883," *Journal of Law and Economics* XXIV (October 1981): p. 246.
16. Michael Punke, *Last Stand—George Bird Grinnell, The Battle to Save the Buffalo, and the Birth of the New West* (2007; New York: HarperCollins, 2020), p. 135.
17. George Colpitts, "A Métis View of the Summer Market Hunt on the Northern Plains," in *Bison and People on the North American Great Plains—a deep environmental history*, eds. Geoff Cunfer and Bill Waiser (College Station: Texas A. & M. University Press, 2016), p. 216.
18. Randal Fulkerson, "Leisure in the West," in *The World of the American West*, ed. Gordon Morris Bakken (New York: Routledge, 2010), p. 355.
19. Sara Dent, *Losing Eden—An Environmental History of the American West* (Chichester: Wiley Blackwell, 2017), p. 85. See also Margaret Walsh, *The American West. Visions and Revisions* (Cambridge: Cambridge University Press, 2005): "Not only did buffalo tongues become a more widespread delicacy and buffalo hide, complete with hair, become popular, but a new technique for converting hide into commercial leather also made the buffalo a valuable commodity. Moreover, the bones could be ground into fertilizer" (p. 98).
20. M. Scott Taylor, "Buffalo Hunt: International Trade and the Virtual Extinction of the North American Bison," *The American Economic Review* 101.7 (December 2011): pp. 3169–70.
21. Kurt Russo, "The Flora and Fauna," in Bakken, *The World of the American West*, p. 28.
22. Lott, *The Last Hunt*, p. 17.
23. Lev, "Appendix 1. Number of Feature Films Released by the Eight Major Distribution Companies, 1950–1960," *The Fifties*, p. 303.

24. Lev, "The American Film Industry in the Early 1950s," *The Fifties*, p. 15. M-G-M curtailed musical production after the profit losses for *The Band Wagon* (over one million dollars), with *Brigadoon* and *Silk Stockings* losing over one million, three hundred thousand dollars (p. 15).
25. "Top Film Grossers for 1956," *Variety*, January 2, 1957: p. 4.
26. "Granger, Brooks, Tamblyn To 'Last Hunt' Opening," *The Hollywood Reporter*, February 15, 1956: p. 2.
27. "'Hunt' Smash 24G, Mpls; 'Darling' 8G," *Variety*, February 22, 1956: p. 8.
28. "'Last Hunt' Premieres," *The Hollywood Reporter*, February 9, 1956: p. 3.
29. "'Hunt' Paces New Cincy Pix, $11,000; 'Brooks' 81/2G, 'Cry' Hot 12G, 2d," *Variety*, March 28, 1956: p. 8.
30. "The Last Hunt (C'Scope—Color)," *Variety*, February 15, 1956: p. 6.
31. Bosley Crowther, "Screen: Out Where the Buffalo Roam; 'The Last Hunt' Has Premiere at State," *New York Times*, March 1, 1956: p. 37.
32. "The Last Hunt," *Picturegoer*, May 19, 1956: p. 18.
33. Joel W. Finler, "Box Office Hits 1914–2002," *The Hollywood Story* (London and New York: Wallflower Press, 2003), p. 359.
34. Finler, "Columbia," in "The Major Hollywood Studios," *The Hollywood Story*, p. 83.
35. Paul Monaco, "Appendix 1—Number of Feature Films Released by the Seven Major Distribution Companies, 1960–1968, 1970," *The Sixties—1960–1969* (New York: Charles Scribner's Sons, 2001), p. 269.
36. "B'way Helped by Voting Day Holiday; 'Professionals' Giant 86G, 'My Wife' Big $43,000, 'Liquidator' Lusty 31G," *Variety*, November 9, 1966: p. 9.
37. Advertisement, *Variety*, November 2, 1996, p. 18.
38. "Lack of PCA 'Adult' Rating for 'Professionals' Flayed," *Boxoffice*, November 28, 1966: p. 10.
39. Mike Wear, "'Hawaii,' 'Professionals' as December Pace Setters; 'Alfie' & 'The Bible' Zingy; 'Paris Burning' Ranks 7," *Variety*, January 11, 1967: p. 20.
40. "'Professionals' Shown For Mountain Showmen," *Boxoffice*, September 26, 1966: W-8.
41. "'The Professionals' 250 in Minneapolis," *Boxoffice*, December 5, 1966: NC-1.
42. "Col. Officials to Hollywood To View 'Professionals,'" *Boxoffice*, June 13, 1966: p. 10.
43. "The Professionals (Color-Panavision)," *Variety*, November 2, 1966: p. 6.
44. "'Professionals' Biz Wins Brooks A Nod," *Variety*, January 18, 1967: p. 13.
45. "'Professionals' Smash $527,000 in Tokyo Run," *Variety International*, March 22, 1967: p. 27.
46. "'Professionals' Theft," *Boxoffice*, December 19, 1956: ME-1.
47. For Lesley Brill's sensible approach to employing Canetti's work, see his Introduction for *Crowds, Power, and Transformation in Cinema* (Detroit, MI: Wayne State University Press, 2006), p. 5: "In the following essay on individual movies, *Crowds and Power* is less frequently 'applied' than enlisted to direct our attention to aspects that might otherwise go unnoticed or that have proved difficult to describe or categorize. That is, *Crowds and Power* serves at least as much to offer clues about where to look as to provide suggestions about the meaning of what we find. Put another way, Canetti allows us to ask questions more precisely than we have done and to ask some others that we have not asked at all."
48. Ibid. p. 133.
49. Elias Canetti, *Crowds and Power*, trans. Carol Stewart (New York: Farrar Strauss Giroux, 1984), pp. 94–5.
50. Ibid. p. 112.

CHAPTER 9

# The Curse of Money: Negotiating Marriage in *The Catered Affair* (1956)

*Elisabeth Bronfen*

An oval silver serving plate, placed on a patterned tablecloth, serves as the backdrop for the credit sequence of *The Catered Affair*. The names of those involved in the film are superimposed, one after the other, over this festive object. Yet for each brief moment of transition between these names we see only the plate. Over and again, our gaze is thus drawn to the spot at the center of the ornate decorations engraved over most of its surface. The lighting is such that while the edges of the plate are brightly lit, this unadorned centre appears like a vortex. Its blurred oval shape, in which dark and light are indiscernibly enmeshed, serves as a visual counterpoint to the clear lines of the engraved pattern that surrounds it. If the credits momentarily screen out this uncanny blob at the center of the silver plate, it, in turn, persistently returns to our field of vision as well. Before the drama has even set it, we are led to expect that something will trouble the spirit of festivity which is being announced with this serving dish.[1]

## MARRIAGE AND ITS DISCONTENT

Something is, indeed, haunting the film's heroine Aggie Hurley (Bette Davis), who wishes to give her daughter a lavish wedding reception. Jane (DebbieReynolds) and her bridegroom Ralph (Rod Taylor) had planned for a quiet early morning ceremony in church with only the immediate family present. They are keen to get an early start on their drive to California, where they intend to spend their honeymoon. Aggie, however, persists in wanting for her "this one fine thing with all the trimmings." On the evening of the day on which she has found out about her daughter's plans, she comes to Jane's room to apologize for a quarrel they had earlier on in the kitchen. Because Jane, annoyed at the fuss her mother is making, is lying on her bed with her back turned toward her, Aggie sits down beside her. To plead her case, she makes a confession that draws into focus the murky kernel at the heart of her own marriage. She recalls how she herself never had a proper wedding, only a rushed affair on a Saturday morning, in a worn-out cotton dress, "not fit to be seen on the street with, let alone be married in." The excessive trimmings she wants for her daughter are meant to undo the shame she has been living with ever since.

Yet imagining something better for her daughter is more than just an antidote to her own bad memories. Aggie is also driven by a more diffuse sense of discontent. As she explains, she wants Jane to have "something to remember when, well when the bad days come, you're all wore out, you're grown old, like me." The catered affair she insists on is, thus, not only conceived in terms of a solace, but also in anticipation of the sorrow that is her current situation. Though she thinks of it in terms of finally being able to splurge on her daughter after not having had the economic means to do so previously, her gift comes with a threat. Aggie envisions that the romantic hope her daughter is currently entertaining will be replaced by the sober experience she has had of married life. There is a touch of maternal cruelty involved in her prophecy. She is asking Jane to imagine that she, too, will grow old, that for her daughter things will become as sad as they did for her.

If, up to this point in their conversation, Jane repeatedly looks at her mother, only to turn her face away from her again, this is the moment she sits up on her bed. She is finally willing to give in to her mother's request. In the reverse shot we see Aggie, eagerly leaning toward the daughter who has now become her accomplice. Her face, which had previously worn an expression of forlornness, is reanimated. The cheerful banter that follows between them regarding all the arrangements that will have to be made once more covers up the dismal picture, which Aggie had painted for her throughout that day. It is unclear whether Jane's response is out of pity for her mother, or whether, having been infected by her warning, she, too, now wants to repress the possibility of unhappiness lying in store for her. Either way, she is now willing to partake in Aggie's fantasy of a catered affair, which both know to be a protective fiction.[2]

This joint fantasy is, however, pitted against a different dream, namely the one that is the subject of the very first scene of the film. After driving his cab all night, Aggie's husband Tom (Ernest Borgnine) returns to his station in the Bronx and finds his friend Sam eagerly waiting for him. For twelve years they have been saving and waiting to go into business together. Now, Sam has found someone who is willing to sell his taxi and the medallion that goes with it. A down payment of $500 must be paid within a week. As he shakes hands on the deal with his friend, Tom breaks into a broad smile. His return home, in turn, is staged in stark contrast to the camaraderie between these two men. From the moment Tom enters the apartment, we are shown that he and Aggie are living separate emotional lives that seem to have no common ground. Jane's wedding plans launch a string of heated discussions between them, all of which circle around the question of how much money they will give their daughter, even though Jane repeatedly claims that she wants nothing. While Tom keeps bringing up the issue of how little he can afford such an extravagant expense, Aggie, to whom it has become a question of duty, keeps raising the amount she intends to spend.

Not only are their dreams incompatible. Paying for a catered affair in the style Aggie wants, threatens to wipe out the very savings Tom has intended to use to buy the taxi medallion. At the same time, both are also reticent about their wishes. The incessant bickering is their modus vivendi for not confiding, but also not listening to each other. Tom can't tell his wife about the prospect of going into business with Sam, which had made him so happy in the previous scene. Aggie, in turn, can't convey to him how trapped she feels in the routine of her everyday. She has resigned herself to a life in which everything is always going to be the same "day after day, year after year." While she can tell this to her daughter, Jane, in turn, seeks to ward off the monotonous picture her mother is painting for her. By assuring Aggie that her union with Ralph will be different, she not only avoids hearing the advice the older woman has to pass on to her. More importantly, she isn't listening to what her mother is saying about herself.

Nor does her husband want to listen to the comparison Aggie has been drawing between herself and her daughter ever since she found out about the wedding plans. Once Jane has left for work, Aggie goes to their bedroom. Tom has closed the blinds to shut out the daylight and is lying in bed. While she is sitting on a chair with her back to him, only looking over her shoulder now and then, she not only speaks about her dream of giving her daughter a real wedding. She also confides in him that she has been telling Jane about what marriage is really like once it becomes an ordinary everyday affair. She soon realizes, however, that what she is saying is of no concern to her husband. Tom has fallen asleep and begun to snore. For a few moments she sits in the darkened room, staring wearily into space. Her posture suggests how, as his wife, she feels unheard and unseen. As is so often the case when he comes home tired from work, he has paid no attention to her words, as though he had no interest in knowing her. Aggie gets up and goes to the door to turn off the light. While hovering on the threshold, she repeats a phrase from her previous monologue, only now it is filled as much with accusation as it is with remorse: "what it was like being married." Given that her husband is already asleep, she is clearly speaking only to herself. She then closes the door, leaving Tom by himself in the dark. The shot is a visual epitome of the sadness haunting her marriage.

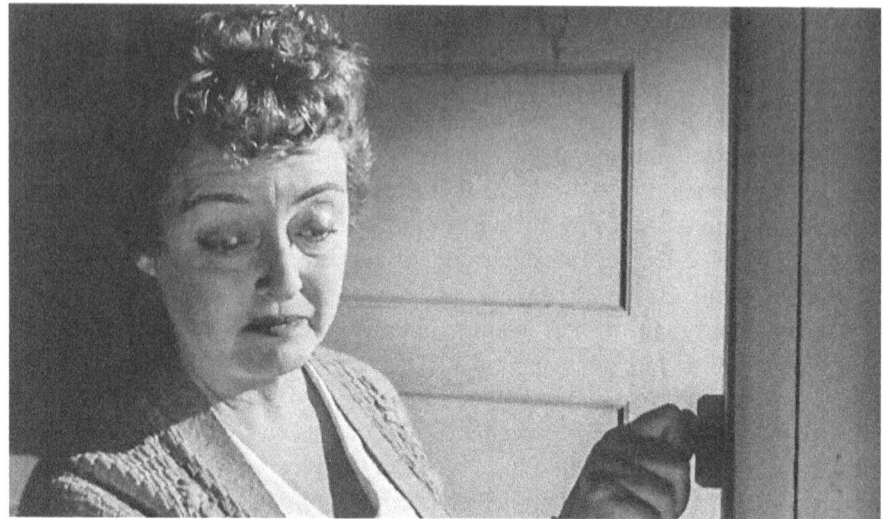

Figure 9.1 Aggie's (Bette Davis) quiet desperation.

Aggie is shown to be completely alone with her quiet desperation, as locked out from her husband's dreams as he is from her self-reflections.

Yet later that evening, after a dinner with Ralph's parents, the film also draws Tom's solitude into focus. Not only has Mr. Halloran, a prospering real estate agent, offered the newlyweds a full year's rent on an apartment. His boasting about the reception he gave his daughter has fuelled Aggie's sense of competition. While she accompanies her guests to the door, Tom remains at the dinner table, alone with the empty coffee cups and the filled ashtray. The anguish on his face signals that he has come to resign himself to the fact that his hope of making the down payment on the taxi medallion is about to be shattered. He, too, is alone with his anguish, unable to speak to his wife about how painful it is for him to relinquish his dream. Instead, even as Aggie gets more and more carried away with the idea of doing something opulent for her daughter, his squabbling about how the cost will wipe out his entire savings increases.

What both are unable to address is how Aggie's vain wishes for Jane's reception have taken the place of her marital discontent, at the heart of which lies her own shotgun marriage. The catered affair for her daughter is a proxy for the opportunities Aggie believes she has missed out on. As such, her self-absorbed planning of the event has inherited the interest which was formerly directed at her regret. This interest, however, is ambivalent. In the creation of this substitute, the way she has come to read her own improper wedding ceremony as having been the harbinger of her discontent as a wife has set up a memorial to itself. The catered affair with all the trimmings that she is trying so desperately to pull off recalls the very sense of something profoundly missing in her marriage, which it is meant to screen out.³ Implicitly, it acknowledges the very thing the catered affair is meant to disavow.

In his exploration of the meaning of marriage, Richard Brooks thus offers up a telling genre hybrid, thereby underscoring the difference between the two generations of women in the Hurley family. The daughter is conceived as the heroine in a romantic comedy. She has been earning her own living because her father didn't have the money for her to go to college. Marriage to a man who has successfully embarked on his academic career promises her the upward mobility so typical for the cultural optimism of the 1950s. It also signals a shift in gender conceptions prevalent in this postwar period. There was a great push to get women, who had been successful as profession workers during the war years, to give their jobs back to the veterans and return into the domestic sphere. The comedy genre helps sweeten the heroine's transition from working woman to wife, predicated as it is on presenting the two young lovers as perfectly in tune in their expectations of the future. The mother, in turn, is conceived as the heroine of a melodrama equally typical for this period. She feels her home to be a cage and not a very golden one at that. Marriage for an immigrant family during the Depression was an economic not a romantic affair, and she has since come to accept the curtailment of any notion of happiness she may have harbored when she was her daughter's age. Given the constant worry about money that continues to overshadow her life, there is no optimistic change she can hope for. Instead, she is living in what the transcendentalist Ralph Waldo Emerson famously called silent melancholy.

## REMARRIAGE COMEDY AS A RESPONSE TO MELODRAMA

In his writings on Hollywood, the philosopher Stanley Cavell repeatedly turned to the two genres, comedy and melodrama, when exploring the meaning of marriage in the American cultural imaginary. Yet he suggests a further generic distinction, calling films that find a way of resolving the conflicts on which melodrama is predicated comedies of *remarriage*. These particular comedies transcend the difficulties melodrama explores, he argues, precisely by rediscovering the possibility of marital happiness *after* it seems to have been lost. In both melodrama and the comedy of remarriage (and as such in contrast to the standard romantic comedy), the heroine is a married woman, faced with the possibility that her orderly life may be shattered into fragments, because a running quarrel is forcing the couple apart. The dramatic development in both genres does not revolve around the question of whether the lovers are made for each other. Instead, the distinction between the two is whether, on the one hand, the couple will get together *again*, or whether, on the other hand, the two married people will irrevocably dissolve their union.

Both resolutions, furthermore, hinge on a moment of self-recognition on the part of the heroine and the transformation concomitant with this.

In the remarriage comedy this anagnorisis brings with it a mutual acknowledgment between the husband and wife. As Cavell puts it, "the reconciliation of genuine forgiveness; a reconciliation so profound as to require the metamorphosis of death and revival, the achievement of a new perspective on existence."[4] In melodrama, the heroine's transformation, in turn, is predicated on the realization of her isolation, on the recognition of her "unknownness" to her husband, who can conceive of her only as an extension of himself, not as a woman separate from him.[5] The heroine's demand for acknowledgment in this case results in her recognition that her husband will never understand why she is discontented with their marriage. Because a reaffirmation of their initial marriage vow, and with it a reconciliation, is no longer possible, the only option she has is to divorce. According to Cavell, the two genres are companion pieces because if Ibsen's *A Doll's House*, as the prototypical melodrama, establishes a problematic regarding the unsustainability of marriage, then the remarriage comedy can be seen as constituting a response to this danger. As he notes, it does so precisely because it explores "how the miracle of change may be brought about and hence life together between a pair seeking divorce become a marriage."[6]

Classic Hollywood's appropriation of the melodrama formula doesn't always end in the dissolution of a marital union. Not all of Nora's cinematic sisters pull the door shut behind a home they can no longer live in. Yet every heroine in a Hollywood melodrama plot must accept how curtailed her claim on personal happiness is. She must resign herself to the fact that she will not be able to realize the dream of marriage she once had for herself. The comedy of remarriage, in turn, explores what it would take to remain in the home; albeit in a home that has been transformed by virtue of the heroine's rediscovery of her desire for the man who has been at her side all these years. Owing to her anagnorisis, she is able to transform herself into his wife *again*, the same yet also different. As a result, the couple finds a way to walk in the direction of their dreams together once they have come to understand that it is a dream they share.

An essential aspect of Cavell's definition of the remarriage comedy is that the running quarrel between the couple, which threatens to shatter their union, be seen as a conversation of love, because "a willingness for marriage entails a certain willingness for bickering."[7] He bases this claim on an idiosyncratic reconceptualization of the passage from John Milton's *Doctrine and Discipline of Divorce*, in which the Puritan poet claims that "a meet and happy conversation is the chiefest and noblest end of marriage." For Cavell, however, the word "conversation" conveys an entire mode of association, a form of life, such that in the films that belong to this genre, "the central pair are learning to speak the same language."[8] While in remarriage comedy this conversation can be revived, because its spark was always sustained by the couple's verbal battling, in melodrama the heroine realizes that she is not speaking the same language anymore as her husband. There are no longer any grounds for resuming a conversation long defunct.

To conceive of marriage as a meet and happy conversation, which must be reaffirmed in the face of the possibility of it being dissolved, furthermore, implies an open-ended willingness to self-perfectibility. Both husband and wife must do the work of achieving their promise to realize themselves as a couple, even if this goal is never fully achieved. In melodrama, such a pursuit of self-realization means putting an end to the marriage in the face of a defeat of any meet and happy conversation. Falling silent proves preferable to any inadequate dialogue that can no longer be salvaged. According to Cavell, the choice of solitude remains compatible with a desire for self- perfectibility. Walking away from a marriage which, because it is unsatisfactory, is experienced as a form of living death, of being but a shadow of one's full self, means overcoming a sustained state of melancholia. At issue in this case is "the transfiguration of mourning as grief into morning as dawning and ecstasy."[9] The act of transformation may leave the heroine to accept the curtailment of her dreams, yet she anticipates the dawning of a new day of her own choosing. In the remarriage comedy, in turn, the dawning of a new day for the couple that has come to reaffirm their marriage, means rediscovering a way to talk not just on that morning, but to sustain this conversation throughout all the days that will follow.

Before looking in more detail at how *The Catered Affair* pits the daughter's discovery of what marriage might be against her mother's sober assessment of what it has been for her, a final aspect of Cavell's discussion of the remarriage comedy's response to melodrama needs to be raised. Both genres, he argues, interrogate the sustainability of a marital union not only regarding a personal claim to happiness but also as a barometer of the inner agenda of the American nation at the cultural moment to which a particular Hollywood film speaks. Like the reaffirmation of a successful conversation between two married people, the American project is also an ongoing process and the silver screen one of the most prominent sites where the nation constantly reflects on its own promise; to be more precise, on whether the perfectibility it had, from its inception, made a claim to is still achievable. Cavell's revisitation of Milton's tract on divorce, after all, also draws on the claim that "no effect of tyranny can sit more heavy on the commonwealth than this household unhappiness on the family."[10] In aligning political tyranny with marital unhappiness, the covenant of marriage emerges as a miniature of the covenant of the commonwealth. As Cavell argues, much as in a satisfactory marriage, "one may be said to owe the commonwealth participation that takes the form of a meet and cheerful conversation."[11] For Hollywood genre cinema, the possibility of reavowing a marital bond or dissolving it completely can, thus, be seen as speaking to the covenant a particular film imagines not only between two married people, but also between this couple and the American project. The couple's reaffirmation of vows serves as a miniature for a pledge of national allegiance that has been reconfirmed. The silver screen renders it of collective interest as a cultural reflection on the state of the union.

## THREE STARS AND THEIR SCENES

With *The Catered Affair*, Richard Brooks explores the questions Cavell raises in his discussion of these two genres in terms of generational difference. He not only asks how marriage can be rediscovered by the mother, but also what this means for the way the daughter, as a representative of a changed worldview, comes to think about what it means for her to marry for the first time. As such, he is as preoccupied with the inner agenda of postwar American culture as were the Depression and WWII films Cavell discusses. For this, the choice of the stars is telling. When Debbie Reynolds was cast as Jane, she had already become the cheerful face of young postwar Americans, confident that they would enjoy a prosperity not necessarily available to their parents. Four years earlier she had starred in *Singin' in the Rain* (1952), where she played a young entertainer who is initially hired by a Hollywood studio to give her smooth voice to a silent movie star. The voice of the older actress betrays her lower-class background and thus doesn't fit the glamour roles she is supposed to continue to play. During the premiere of the film with which she hopes to transition into sound film, however, this dubbing scheme is revealed, and Debbie Reynolds comes to replace her predecessor, both onscreen and as the bride of the hero. Chosen for the role of Jane, this new Hollywood embodied the upwardly mobile woman of her generation, poised to leave behind all the hardships of the past decades.

When Bette Davies accepted the role of Aggie, which several other actresses had turned down, she was already one of the greatest stars of Hollywood melodrama. Her intense, forlorn yet also resilient gaze was as iconic as her inimitable way of delivering lines. The audience would have remembered how, at the end of *Now, Voyager*, she tells the man whom she can never marry, yet whose troubled daughter she has decided to adopt, "Oh, Jerry, don't let's ask for the moon. We have the stars." That she is paired with Reynolds, furthermore, anticipates a very particular exchange between the two generations. A few years earlier, she had received an Oscar nomination for her role of an older actress in *All About Eve* (1950), who is being stalked by a younger one, eager to step into her shoes. In contrast to *Singin' in the Rain*, however, while her rival succeeds in becoming a Hollywood star, Bette Davis remains a fixture on Broadway.[12]

Finally, Ernest Borgnine had previously garnered critical praise for his performance of an Italian-American butcher in *Marty* (1955), also set in the Bronx. In the screenplay by Paddy Chayefski, on whose television play *The Catered Affair* was based, he has little self-esteem and calls himself a fat, little, ugly man. Yet when he meets a shy, plain-looking librarian at the Stardust Ballroom one Saturday night, he discovers in her someone he can finally have a conversation with. Although his friends and even his mother will try to talk him out of this affair the next day, he will not be discouraged from courting her. Despite his social awkwardness he stands his ground because she has made him discover something in himself.

The meaning which the controversial wedding reception assumes in the interactions between the three members of the Hurley family, thus works with the star image each of these performers brings to their role in *The Catered Affair*. To begin with Aggie, Bette Davis plays the aging mother as a woman who has resigned herself to not reaching for the moon but who, in this one instance, wants surrogate happiness through a daughter from whom she has always felt a certain distance. A quintessential scene is the one in which Jane is being fitted by a seamstress for her lace wedding dress. Aggie is fully enthralled with her younger self, letting her gaze greedily wander all over Jane's thin body. After her daughter has put on the bridal veil that reaches all the way to the floor, the camera moves into a close-up to accentuate the delight on Bette Davis's face, while she lovingly strokes the delicate tulle.

The bond Aggie suddenly feels toward her daughter among all these wedding clothes compels her to make a confession while Jane is changing in the dressing room. Aggie not only recalls how it was "the curse of money over us all our lives" which was responsible for her lack of maternal care, but also discloses the original scene for her shame. Her father, who met Tom one day at the Union Hall, had offered him $300 if he were to marry his daughter. Aggie is standing in front of a mirror while she is speaking, so we see Bette Davis both from the front and the back as she confronts her daughter with this ugly incident. One could read the doubling in the mirror—disclosing the two sides of this maternal figure of authority—as a visual marker for how Aggie's confession troubles the very romance which she nominally seeks to sustain with her insistence that Jane get a "wedding to remember all her life." Her daughter is now burdened with a story about her own origin she had never heard before. At the same time, we are led to understand that Aggie's insistence on getting her husband to squander his savings is also a way of paying him back in kind.

Backhanded revenge also comes to the fore in the scene at the Hotel Concourse Plaza, where Aggie has asked to meet her husband so they can jointly decide on the details of the catered affair with the manager. When Tom, for whom this is one of the quintessential episodes, arrives, he is clearly impatient with his wife's romantic sentimentality. Unwilling to be taken in by the grandeur of the ballroom, he wants to get the issue of the cost, which so greatly irks him, over as soon as possible. When Aggie keeps asking for more elaborate trimmings, they once again bicker about the one thing that has always been their common ground—the curse of money. While Tom initially resists throwing away his life savings, and with these his dream of a business of his own, he ultimately gives in to his wife's whim.

Yet both his anger and his subsequent sense of defeat bring a degree of irony into the scene. Because we are observing this exchange from his perspective, we are called upon to regard Aggie's excitement at the most lavish of the wedding cake ornaments as a desperate attempt to make her husband literally pay for having forced her to scrimp all her life. Her refusal to take his position into account underscores the folly of an enterprise which not only makes her blind to anything that disturbs her wish but also only barely covers up the despair so close beneath the surface of her rapture. The camera captures the horrified disbelief on Ernest Borgnine's face in a close-up, before he walks out of the manager's office without saying a word, leaving his wife to order everything on her own. As he walks through the ballroom, muttering the names of some of the costly trimmings he feels he can't afford, an attendant is shown sweeping away all the confetti still lying on the floor from a previous wedding celebration. This debris is the visual counterpoint to the voice of the manager, listing the prices of everything Aggie has ordered, which we hear on the soundtrack. If these long strips of paper announce the ephemerality of the ceremony that will also ruin him financially, Ernest Borgnine is shown as a man who, as in *Marty*, will stolidly bear a burden until he figures out a way to cast it off.

In the case of Debbie Reynolds, it is the star image of the cheerful young newcomer, which Richard Brooks develops to a singular purpose of his own. Throughout *The Catered Affair*, Jane's ability to talk to Ralph openly about what troubles her serves as a counterpoint to her parents' reticence. A lap dissolve serves as the transition from Tom's silent retreat from the Hotel Concourse Plaza and a discussion between Jane and Ralph in his studio apartment. For a moment the two, standing in his kitchen, with Jane drying the dishes and him smoking a cigarette, are juxtaposed over the confetti hanging in strips from the ceiling of the ballroom; as though these decorations were a spectral harbinger of the end of their own wedding reception. Because Ralph is trying to convince his bride to cancel all the arrangements, Jane sits down on his bed. Once she begins talking about all that has troubled her ever since she announced her wedding plans to her parents, he sits down on the other side of the bed and patiently listens to her. As she leans toward him, the camera captures her in a close-up. Her mother's story of complaint has infected her, and, seeking to ward off the idea that her married life might become a repetition of the life her parents lead, she wants him to confirm that theirs will be different.

Tellingly, for her it is a question of words shared. She confesses to Ralph that she is sure her mother and father never said they loved each other. Moving close to her across the bed, Ralph seductively murmurs, "It's not necessarily something you say, it's something you do, it's the whole way you live, that's love." Jane, however, haunted by all the things that have been left unsaid by her parents, finds no complete reassurance in his comment. As they move closer together, the camera captures a close-up of both their faces. They have fallen into a deep shadow. Only when Jane shifts her position, now lying next to Ralph with her face to the ceiling, does she fall back into the light. The way Debbie Reynolds plays her suggests that Jane's previous undaunted optimism is now troubled by an uncertainty she can't quite grasp. She begs her future husband never to stop telling her what he feels about her. Yet Jane's insistence that he keep up their language of love acknowledges the very possibility of falling silent in the face of marital misunderstandings which it is meant to disavow. The fact that both their faces remain partially shaded, even after they have kissed, further suggests that the doubt Aggie has raised in her daughter's mind will remain even after she has moved out of her home.

## WAKING UP TO A NEW MORNING

The dramatic resolution Brooks finds for his interrogation of the legitimacy of marriage involves self-recognition on the part of both heroines. Together, their insights culminate in the Hurley family awakening from the romantic dreams and financial nightmares that began the morning Jane told her parents about her wedding plans. She is, in fact, the one to call the catered affair off. In the kitchen, where the most vehement arguments have taken place throughout the film, she finally screams at her parents. She wants them to stop their mutual accusations and, instead, to see what a rift all the wedding arrangements have already caused in the past two days. In her passionate outpouring, she not only accuses them of being at the point "of breaking up," but also gives voice to her fear that her own marriage is endangered: "Ralph is so sore he may walk out on the whole thing."

The response, on the part of Aggie, is that she withdraws once more into the personal sadness which her reception plans had momentarily displaced. While Tom gets up and calls the Hallorans to tell them about the change in plans, she remains alone at the kitchen table, her back turned to him. She is looking down at the floor, with her head casting a large shadow on the wall. She is shutting everyone out, making the deliberations she is now forced to entertain unknown to everyone but herself. By refusing to speak even to her daughter, she is, however, also fostering the guilt that had initially compelled Jane to give in to the catered affair in the first place. Later that evening, Jane will confess to Ralph that she will never forget the look on her mother's face. Her distress mounts as she imagines what her parents' home will be like without her, "the two of them alone, living there the rest of their lives, never talking, never loving." The battle in the kitchen has, once again, raised the specter of her marriage turning into a repetition of her mother's. Although, as Ralph kisses her forehead, he assures her that they will never be like that, the close-up that captures this gesture shows her face fully illuminated, while his is turned away from the camera. What we are shown, as in the previous scene, is a vignette of her anticipation of a quiet despair of her own. The blind confidence she exhibited at the beginning of the film is irrevocably gone.

It is with a touch of dramatic irony that Richard Brooks makes use of Jane's dismal image of her parents' future to bring about Aggie's anagnorisis. That same evening, her brother Jack, who has been living with them for the past twelve years, is moving out because, he, too, is finally getting married. As Aggie watches him pack his suitcase it dawns on her that she will be living all alone with her husband for the first time in her life. The camera follows her as she goes to her bedroom where, witnessed only by us, sitting on the chair next to her marital bed, her face buried in the sheet, she finally breaks into tears. This pathos gesture of desperate loneliness is the turning point leading to the self-recognition on which the transformation of her marriage is predicated. Once Tom comes to her, she soon composes herself. Throughout the harsh argument that ensues, she is in the process of preparing herself for the night. As she unpins her bun and lets her hair fall down her back, she speaks to him directly about her shame. He accuses her of being no fancy bargain and she retorts: "You got your $300 worth." His first impulse is to forbid her to ever mention those $300 to him ever again. Yet the fury she has inspired brings him not only to confess how often he had wanted to leave her, but also to speak openly about his own shame about not having been able to afford their daughter's college education.

Although throughout his diatribe Aggie combs her hair while remaining silent, we sense that she is listening to Tom. They are both sitting on the bed, their backs turned to each other. While she is in the background, the camera focuses on Tom as he now articulates what she, too, has come to realize: "It's just me you've got left in your old age. It's me you've got to worry about." Aggie is not yet able to show her sympathy. Instead, she continues to wistfully braid her hair, even after Tom has left the room in anger. Yet the morning after, she has gained a recognition of her circumstances such that something can change. She is now able to tell Jane what her daughter has been surmising all along, even while it is something she seems to only now have come to fully realize herself. She confides in Jane that she and Tom were never alone together from the first day they were married. Furthermore, because her relatives and then the children were always there to distract them, they also "never talked together once [. . .] in all that time together."

Being able to finally put into words what has been troubling her for so long brings with it a sense of relief. Aggie's face lights up in expectation as she insists that nobody will ever move in with her again. In fact, she embraces the idea of being "all alone. Something new, your Pa and me together." The reverse shot offers a close-up of Jane's face, who remains puzzled at her mother's unexpected response. Asked why she isn't angry anymore, Aggie explains, "How can I be mad at what has been my whole life and will be to the end?" To draw into focus the transformation that has taken place for both the mother and the daughter, the mise en scène places Aggie throughout their dialogue in the brightly illuminated part of the room, while Jane remains enveloped in a dark shadow. Her bemused gaze signals that something is dawning on her as well, namely that marriage may well mean sustaining affective contradictions. The bickering between her parents was never anything other than their version of the satisfactory conversation between two people which, according to Cavell, assures the renewed affordance of marriage.

Aggie has, indeed, awoken from her sustained sadness into a morning filled with hope. Once Jane has left for church, we see her sitting on the chair in her bedroom, patiently watching Tom, who is still asleep. Only when he wakes does she rise and pull up the blind, letting the sun in. Tom, also, has had a change of heart and declares, "About last night, you were right." She immediately corrects him, saying that she was wrong. What matters, she adds, is that the two of them will be at the ceremony together. Her stress on their being there with each other prompts Tom to see in the marriage about to be forged a gage of his own. "It's a long time *we've* been married," he murmurs to her and, picking up his challenge, she responds by asking, "Too long a time?" What follows is Tom's version of the unshaken trust in their marital bond, which she had spoken about to Jane in the earlier scene. With moving conviction, he assures her, "To know somebody, it's like a day Aggie." The smile they share is almost shy, as though they were themselves astonished at what has just passed between them. If Jane is beginning a new life, they are reaffirming their long time together, but doing so in a new key. The strangeness to each other, which has remained with them all this time, proves to be the sentiment that also assures the endurability of their marriage. They have so much still to discover.

In his concluding remarks on *Woman of the Year* (1942), Cavell notes that this comedy doesn't present marriage as a distraction from a somber world, "but as the scene in which the chance for happiness is shown as the mutual acknowledgment of separateness, in which the prospect is not for the passing of years (until death parts us) but for the willing repetition of days, willingness for the everyday."[13] In *The Catered Affair*, Aggie's acceptance of such a repetitive everyday, which will no longer be the source for lonely desperation, takes the form of a pact, involving not only her husband but also his friend Sam. While Tom was still sleeping, she had made a deal with him. The cab, in which he arrives to drive them to the church where the others are already waiting, is the one they now own together. When Tom shows his surprise at being told this news, Sam calls out through the open window to Alice to confirm their new joint ownership.

A close-up of her face, registering her silent response to her husband's astonishment, is immediately followed by one of Tom, who has broken into the same huge grin we saw in the first scene of the film. He eagerly opens the backseat door and is about to get in before realizing that Alice has been hovering just behind him. The editing moves to a close-up of Bette Davis, tilting her head backwards while breaking into her iconic laughter. What exactly she is laughing at we don't know. At the husband, who, in his overwhelming happiness, almost forgot her? At the joke she has played on him, a joke which, to boot, demonstrates not only her largesse but also her control? Is she laughing at herself and the folly of the last few days? Or is she simply enjoying his happiness?

What follows, once they are both seated in the back, recalls the final shots of many sophisticated comedies that came before. First, having made themselves comfortable, they smile at each other. Then Tom lovingly places his left arm around Aggie's shoulder, who is looking at the interior of the cab with pride. We get no image of the ceremony in the church. Instead, the final shot shows them driving into the morning, toward the horizon. Having discovered something about each other which, perhaps, they had already known all along, they are now looking forward together, toward a series of shared tomorrows. If the dramatic resolution which the remarriage comedy offers has displaced the threat of this couple's dissolution, it has also reaffirmed the resilience of the

Figure 9.2 Aggie's laughter of reconciliation.

American project that was always also under scrutiny. The business on which the Hurleys are about to embark with this newly acquired cab promises to be a financial success as well.

## NOTES

1. In his article "The Uncanny" (1919), *The Standard Edition*, Vol. 17 (London: The Hogarth Press, 1955), Sigmund Freud writes about the uncanny as an event or an experience which, disturbing the ordinary, produces a sense of strangeness. Key to his definition is that, far from being something unfamiliar, it gives voice to an experience that, initially familiar, has come to be repressed only to return in a new guise. Applied to the notion of marriage which the film deliberates, the union between Aggie and Tom Hurley is predicated on the repression of something they knew from the moment they took their vows, but which had to be repressed for them to sustain their married life; yet something which hovers on the fringes of their shared life.
2. In his early writings on hysteria, Freud coined the term "protective fiction" (*Schutzdichtungen*) to describe the way repressed memory traces can be converted into a narrative one can live by when they become distorted by compromise. These protective fantasies, however, not only cover up the disturbing knowledge which produces the very displeasure that is meant to be covered over. The German word *Dichtung* also refers to a sealing gasket. Regarding the psychic work of displacement, one could say it keeps the unpleasurable knowledge from spilling over into consciousness. A protective fiction thus seals the junction between these two realms, even while it is marked as precisely such a mitigating tool. See "Extracts from the Fliess Papers" (1892–9), in *The Standard Edition*, Vol. 1. (London: Hogarth Press, 1950/1966).
3. See Freud's article "Fetishism," in *The Standard Edition*, Vol. 21 (London: Hogarth Press, 1961), although his discussion explicitly focuses on sexual discontent.
4. Stanley Cavell, *Pursuits of Happiness. The Hollywood Comedy of Remarriage* (Cambridge, MA: Harvard University Press, 1981), p. 19.
5. See Stanley Cavell, *Contesting Tears. The Hollywood Melodrama of the Unknown Woman* (Chicago: University of Chicago Press, 1996), p. 197.
6. Cavell, *Pursuits*, p. 23.
7. Ibid. p. 86.
8. Ibid. p. 87.
9. Cavell, *Contesting Tears*, p. 212.
10. Cavell, *Pursuits*, p. 150.
11. Ibid. p. 151.
12. As Douglass K. Daniel writes in *Tough as Nails: The Life and Films of Richard Brooks* (Madison: University of Wisconsin Press, 2011), p. 101, Bette Davis called her performance in this film a personal favorite and counted Richard Brooks among her best directors.
13. See Stanley Cavell, "The Uncanniness of the Ordinary," in *In Quest of the Ordinary. Lines of Skepticism and Romanticism* (1988; Chicago: University of Chicago Press, 1994), p. 178.

CHAPTER 10

# Adapting Modernism: Richard Brooks and *The Brothers Karamazov* (1958)

*Douglas McFarland*

*The Brothers Karamazov* poses particular problems for screen adaptation. That the novel is simply long and filled with a multiplicity of primary and secondary characters is less an obstacle than its formal structure and individual characterization. *The Brothers Karamazov* is a generically hybrid work, made up of Socratic dialogue, philosophical and theological digressions, soliloquies, and intellectual set pieces, all of which occur within the framework of a character-driven nineteenth-century novel. Moreover, the moral and psychological identities of the novel's primary characters are woven in both overt and subtle ways into the abstract ideologies that permeate the narrative. When Richard Brooks made the decision to adapt Dostoevsky's novel, he took on the daunting challenges of the text itself, as well as the demands of the studio system. M-G-M agreed to finance the project with the expectation that it would appeal to a wide audience and hence, would make money. In attempting to balance the need to attract an art-house audience receptive to sophisticated cinema and concurrently to satisfy corporate demands, Brooks pleased no one.

Yet however compromised the film might be, it does reveal much about Brooks as a writer and director, and looks ahead to some of his most successful work. His adaptation of *The Brothers Karamazov* (1958) marks a critical stage in Brooks's career. Prior to this film, he had adapted little of what we might call high literature. *The Blackboard Jungle*, Evan Hunter's novel about young urban delinquents, and Robert Ruark's bestselling *Something of Value*, both previously adapted by Brooks, come nearest to what one might call consequential works. But after *The Brothers Karamazov*, Brooks would move onto the material of Tennessee Williams, Sinclair Lewis, Joseph Conrad, and Truman Capote. Near the end of his career he would take on the boldly transgressive *Looking for Mr. Goodbar* (1977). While his adaptation of *The Brothers*

*Karamazov* is significantly flawed, it nevertheless positioned Brooks to engage more sophisticated and challenging material in the future.

Brooks's adaptation in the same year of Tennessee Williams's *Cat on a Hot Tin Roof* (1958) benefitted more than any other from his struggles with Dostoevsky. The film proved to be arguably his most successful. Brooks received Academy Award nominations and, if one values such things, the film did very well at the box office. In his lectures on Dostoevsky for his Russian Literature course at Cornell, Vladimir Nabokov, although generally dismissive of the novelist, does offer one insight particularly important for Brooks. Nabokov asserts, "I want to stress again the fact that Dostoevsky was more of a playwright than a novelist. What his novels represent is a succession of scenes, of dialogues, of scenes where all the people are brought together—and with all the tricks of the theatre." He adds, "Considered as novels, his works fall to pieces."[1] It is precisely the often overlooked theatricality of *The Brothers Karamazov* that emerges in Brooks's adaptation as the most significant aspect of the film. But because Brooks will not fully relinquish the religious and philosophical deliberations embedded in Dostoevsky's novel, the film lacks a thematic and aesthetic coherency. Yet the film fascinates precisely because of its flaws. We are afforded the opportunity to witness a director in the process of discovering his own strengths as a filmmaker. When Brooks went on to adapt Tennessee Williams's stage play, he brought with him his recently gained experience with theatrical filmmaking and was provided a context in which that experience might be fully exploited.

THE NOVEL

Before proceeding to the film itself, I think it necessary to have a greater understanding of Dostoevsky's novel. Helpful to this endeavor are two overlapping critical approaches to Dostoevsky in general and to *The Brothers Karamazov* in particular. Joseph Frank, the author of the definitive three-volume critical biography of Dostoevsky, argues that the novel is one of the great humanist works of western culture: "*The Brothers Karamazov* achieves a classic expression of the great theme that had preoccupied Dostoevsky since *Notes from Underground*: the conflict between reason and Christian faith . . . and evokes comparison with the greatest creations of Western literature."[2] Frank compares the novel to works by Dante, Shakespeare, Milton, and Goethe. This could not be more evident than in the chapter entitled "The Grand Inquisitor," a poem written by Ivan, the enlightenment rationalist, and recited to Alexi, the youngest brother and a novice in the church. Christ has returned to earth during the Spanish Inquisition and is interrogated by a "Cardinal Grand Inquisitor." The Inquisitor rationalizes that the Christian freedom Christ brought into the world has been mercifully eradicated by the Catholic Church in order to "make people happy."[3] The ensuing exchange between Christ and the Inquisitor is interwoven with a rich patterning of biblical and historical allusions. Moreover, in a more general sense throughout the novel, philosophical and religious positions are not detached from character. Frank argues, "No other novelist can rival Dostoevsky's ability to develop his themes, and reveal the moral-psychological sensibility of his characters, through the discussion of seemingly abstract ideas."[4] The relationship between character as a symbolic representation and character as psychological agency poses the most difficult challenge Brooks will face. Admirable as it might be, his insistence on remaining faithful to the complex construction of personal identity in *The Brothers Karamazov* will undermine critical points in his adaptation.

René Girard offers a much different and no less valid approach to Dostoevsky, and one that speaks to the most successful aspects of Brooks's film. Girard is more interested in the dramatic and psychological elements in *The Brothers Karamazov*, rather than its intellectual insights. In *Deceit, Desire and the Novel*, Girard argues that triangular desire forms the modernist basis for individual identity and interpersonal relationships. Triangular desire is quite simply mediated desire. In other words, in desiring an object the individual imitates the desire of another. The object of desire is merely a mask to conceal the individual's dependence on another individual. Human agency is not made up of spontaneous acts but rather by what it lacks. Identity is nothing other than a profound and unrelenting feeling of absence. Human relationships thereby form a complex web of interpersonal desires and conflicts. This results, Girard argues, in a world in which "there is no longer any love without jealousy, any friendship without envy, and any attraction without repulsion. The characters [especially in Dostoevsky's works] insult one another, spit in each other's faces, and minutes later they fall at the enemy's feet, they abjectly beg mercy."[5] Indeed, there are multiple examples of triangular entanglements of desire in *The Brothers Karamazov*: Fyodor/Dimitri/Grushenka; Dimitri/Ivan/Katerina; Dimitri/Grushenka/Polish Officer; Grushenka/Katerina/Dimitri; Fyodor/Dimitri/Mother; Fyodor/Smerdyakov/all three Brothers; Alexi/Fyodor/Father Zosima. For Girard these vectors of desire, more than ideas, inform *The Brothers Karamazov*. I am not arguing that Brooks has somehow consciously adopted Girard's reading of Dostoevsky, but that in the most penetrating scenes of the film Brooks responds to those elements of the novel that Girard identifies: the dense interplay of competing desires, the failure of spontaneity, and the frustrated need for authenticity.

## THE OPENING CREDITS

So what of the film itself? Let me begin with the opening credits since they immediately reveal the inconsistent cross purposes and conflicting expectations embedded in the film. The first image the audience sees is the corporate logo of Metro Goldwyn Mayer: the pretentious Latin; the mangy and aged lion; the growling that is a feeble expression of corporate power; and literally the words "Trade Mark." An ominous tolling of a single bell rings out over the image, creating an odd tension between the visual and the aural, the corporate and the atmospheric. The ensuing cut to the film credits is startling; for the audience now encounters the image and soundtrack of a modernist film. Against a black background the Karamazov family, the father and his four sons, is depicted in primary colors with thick black lines forming edges at the borders of the figures, dappled over with white impressionistic specks. The images resemble the work of the modernist painter Georges Rouault, especially in *The Three Judges* in which academic aesthetics of the late nineteenth century are replaced with an absence of perspective, little shading, primary colors and the breaking up of space into panels. The artwork on the screen also suggests the aesthetics of stained glass and Russian peasant woodblocks.

The figure of Dimitri, the eldest of the brothers, is depicted on one side of the screen; Alexi, the youngest, on the other. Dimitri stands against a background of intense red. His black boots, red shirt and aggressive posture express masculine power. Alexi is depicted in a Christ-like pose with hands folded in prayer. Their typologies are provided nuance by the aesthetics of the visual effects I have pointed out. Between these figures are the images of the father and his two other sons: Ivan, the rationalist, and Smerdyakov, the illegitimate epileptic brother. At the center of the screen is what appears to be the face of Fyodor, the Karamazov patriarch. That face dominates the entire tableau. The head is tilted slightly upward to emphasize a gaping mouth that is either fiercely

Figure 10.1 Opening credits image of Rouault-like stained glass of the Karamazovs.

in pain or rabid in desire. But one also senses that this might be Smerdyakov possessed by a frenzied epileptic fit. Regardless, that figure provides an aura of violent passion exerting its will over the images surrounding it.

The opening score works alongside the artwork to fashion an unsettling and particularly modernist tableau. The music is divided into two parts. The first is suggestive of the symphonic intensity of a movement in a score by Mahler. A discordant and unexpected piano phrase dramatically intrudes, just before the music changes to a peasant dance full of primitive energy and simplistic harmonies. And then near the end of the credits the symphonic music returns. This mixture of the sophisticated and the primitive in both the visual and musical opening of the film reflects one of the important characteristics of the modernist art form. It would be unfair to compare "Lara's Theme" in the opening of David Lean's romanticized Russian film *Doctor Zhivago* (1965), but the contrast couldn't be more telling. There is every expectation that what follows in Brooks's film will be a demanding and perhaps unsettling experience for the audience.

## OPENING SCENES

Brooks introduces the major characters in four set pieces in the first thirty minutes of the film. Since they are critical in understanding the strengths and weaknesses of the adaptation, I will spend some time with them. The film opens with a distant shot of the youngest Karamazov, Alexi (William Shatner), walking through a town toward his father's house. Alexi is a novice in the church and is appropriately dressed in a dark cassock. Above the town perched on a hilltop is the (painted) image of a church spire. Alexi's robe skirts the dirt of the unpaved street, as if it were in jeopardy of becoming soiled. An exaggerated number of animals fill the street: pigs, chickens, geese, dogs. The innocent, youthful figure of William Shatner, in his first film role, is met by a Tsar's officer atop a powerful horse entering the main street. Secular authority and the material conditions of the world are juxtaposed to Alexi's spiritual vocation. The symbolism of the scene, however, is sophomoric and most importantly lacks cinematic imagination. There is no attempt to express the dichotomy of material and immaterial through lighting, camera angles, art direction, or other techniques. This scene provides immediate evidence of a failure to incorporate abstract ideas into the film in any cinematically meaningful way.

The next scene hyperbolically contrasts Alexi's Christian vocation with his father's degeneracy. Brooks plunges the audience into a frenetic bacchanalia. Fyodor (Lee J. Cobb) pours wine down the throat of an ecstatic blonde-haired woman (Gloria Pall) whose arms have been tied on a bedpost behind her head. Fyodor's mouth moves along her leg until it reaches her naked foot. Fast-paced and frenetic music adds energy to the sensual abandon. There is, needless to say, little subtlety, no sense that Fyodor is anything other than a degenerate. On the other hand, Dostoevsky's Fyodor is a multifaceted character. He is a profligate, a buffoon, a wicked ironist, and a clever manipulator of others.

However, the introduction of the eldest of the four sons, Dimitri (Yul Brynner), reveals the real strength of the film. It is divided into two parts. The first takes place in a tavern where Dimitri plays cards, runs up credit, and demonstrates an aggressive and potentially violent masculinity. But in the aftermath of this scene, Brooks takes us into Dimitri's bedroom, his private space and one less dependent on symbols and hyperbolic displays than on the scrutiny of character and interpersonal relationships. The camera looks up at Dimitri from a medium close-up. He still seems proud and aggressive, but his face is now half covered with a dark shadow. The room itself is darkly lit and filled with patterned shadows. We find ourselves in an intimate environment where a greater sense of psychological depth seems possible. It is also an enclosed theatrical space. Here Brooks is responsive not to the intellectual concerns of Dostoevsky's novel but to its series of staged dramatic encounters. The theatrical spaces that Nabokov identifies become for Brooks the most successful settings in the film.

Dimitri's room contains other figures, both literal and evocative. Alexi has brought the money from Fyodor that Dimitri has demanded. Brooks seems disinterested in the symbolic status of Alexi. He is a mere intermediary. When Alexi leaves, the camera follows him down a darkly lit Escher-like staircase and then turns to follow Katerina (Claire Bloom) upward toward Dimitri's room. Her presence brings emotional and psychological weight to the scene. She has come to receive money from Dimitri with which she can prevent her father from going to prison. Dimitri has told Katerina that he would give her the money if she would sleep with him. Money, sexual desire, sexual blackmail, familial conflict, duplicity, and criminality quickly fill this interior space. Dimitri hands Katerina the money, and she dutifully sits on the bed and begins to undress. In a POV shot from Dimitri's perspective, the camera looks down on Katerina as she unbuttons her blouse. She is surrounded by the darkness of the room, against which the small exposed area of her white flesh above her breasts stands out. In an uncanny way, one feels as if her pose has been captured by a still camera. We hover over that moment just before she undoes another button, a button with no symbolic significance, but a button that literally signifies a sensual undressing. Through her gestures and expressions Bloom generates a transgressive eroticism much more powerful than the flamboyantly unbridled romp in Fyodor's house. I say transgressive not only because of Katerina's victimization but also because there is a hint that she desires this moment. She moves to the bed without hesitation, and Bloom conveys in Katerina's face not simply resignation but expectation as well. The bed on which she sits is shrouded in darkness, the literal site where complex, unsettling desires are about to be acted upon. Needless to say, Brooks has created a powerful scene with a wealth of psychological depth.

But there is more. The camera now reverses itself and looks up at Dimitri. We expect masculine desire to be etched in his face, but he has a calm, almost benign, expression. He tells her to dress. He does not intend to follow through with their bargain. But he does reveal that he asked her to marry him sometime in the past and that she refused. This suggests that Dimitri has been disingenuous and merely desires revenge for her refusal. He would punish Katerina not by having her body, but by psychologically degrading her. And of course there is the money, a medium to exert power in the world. The money he gives Katerina has come from Fyodor, who has acquired it through Dimitri's deceased mother. And the money is to be used to free Katerina's father from punishment for embezzlement. The room is evocatively crowded with family members and the tensions that perhaps only families can generate.

The ensuing set piece transpires at a railroad depot. Ivan (Richard Basehart), the rationalist brother, and Smerdyakov (Albert Salmi), the epileptic bastard child, await the arrival of Katerina. Pressured by his half-brother and in keeping with his typological role, Ivan states that without God there is no morality and since God does not exist, neither do any ethical obligations. This comes across as a wooden statement, a syllogism if you like, rather than the flawed logic of a character struggling to rationalize the human condition. When Katerina does arrive, Ivan falls spontaneously and irrationally in love with her. Rational self-control apparently has no defense against desire. The tension between spontaneity and mediated desire, to use Girard's term, will emerge as an important theme in the film. But here, in the clear, bright sunlight, the bland performance by Richard Basehart and the absence of any cinematic depth render this non-theatrical scene ineffective at best.

Brilliantly effective, however, is the accompanying scene inside a carriage occupied by Fyodor and Grushenka (Maria Schell). She will shortly emerge as one of the most important figures in the film. The coach is a small self-enclosed theatrical space where Fyodor and Grushenka dramatically interact with one another. The first shot of Grushenka is a medium close-up of her profile. A white translucent veil covers her head, giving off an aura of virginal innocence. Her face is tilted slightly downward at an angle, suggesting a Madonna-like modesty. But Brooks utilizes the most significant cinematic technique yet in the film. He shoots her profile through a tinted green filter that disqualifies her innocence. It is not the green of spring but an eerie and disquieting shade of green. The image is unsettling and calls into question the reliability of our own spontaneous response to Grushenka. But most obviously it conveys her duplicitous nature. The pose is one she has taken to manipulate her carriage companion. This is not mere symbolism but a representation of character achieved through subtle cinematic skill.

Fyodor cynically tells Grushenka that Dimitri's future bride, Katerina, has money. He chuckles and surmises that Dimitri is a Karamazov since his son understands the way of the world and the purposes of women. Grushenka, without any trace of innocence, but with a coy smile, asks, "Is she pretty?" We sense she feels competitive and that she understands women are valued for their appearance. Then finding a way to torment Fyodor, she adds that she would like to meet Dimitri. He turns toward her with an expression of jealous suspicion. Multiple configurations of triangular desire have quickly opened up in this enclosed space: father/son/Grushenka; father/son/Katerina; Grushenka/Katerina/Dimitri. And, of course, in this world there is always the assumed power of money. Fyodor asks Grushenka to come to his room that night. An envelope with money will await her. "Maybe," she responds. "I thought you liked money," Fyodor says. "Mostly," she coyly responds. Fyodor turns to face her with his head now beneath hers. Grushenka's power, not her innocence, is manifest. He asks her again to come that night, and she responds with another "maybe," and this is followed by several more "maybes." She takes on the role of what Girard terms the "coquette." Girard writes, "The coquette does not wish to surrender her precious self to the desire she arouses, but were she not to provoke it, she would not feel so precious."[6] The world contained within the coach is a microcosm of the world at large, an existential environment, if you will, in which a false sense of autonomy depends on the manipulation of the desire of others and the control of one's own. In his representation of Grushenka, some might accuse Brooks of anti-feminism. I would argue, however, that there is not necessarily anything gender-specific about this coy manipulator of desire. Grushenka is important because she exposes a world. Of less importance, if any at all, is that she exposes herself as a predator of men. The need to be an autonomous individual is manifest across the spectrum of characters. But autonomy, and this is very much what Girard means, is in conflict with authenticity. That is, the means employed by these characters to achieve autonomy is mediated means. For Dimitri, it is primarily money; for Alexi, the imitation of Christ; for Ivan, Voltaire; for Fyodor, de Sade; for Grushenka, the indifference and irony of the coquette. We need not exclusively accept Girard's theories in order to see that Brooks's landscape is populated by characters caught up in interwoven patterns of desire and need. Brooks has seized upon that element in the novel, the existential relationship between self and other that Girard identifies, and explores it in a series of contained theatrical scenes of character interaction.

## DIMITRI AND GRUSHENKA

The vicissitudes of the relationship between Grushenka and Dimitri, hinted at in the coach scene, follow through the remainder of the film. Two familiar factors emerge as significant in their first meeting: money and spontaneous desire. Dimitri learns that Grushenka has acquired the IOUs he had given to his father. He is indignant and confronts Grushenka, who is ice skating with others at a frozen pond. The dramatic interaction between the lovers is diluted by Brooks's refusal to relinquish formulaic ideologies; in this case, a Freudian ideology. The money that Dimitri demands from his father had belonged to his mother, and thus he hates his father for standing between them. One might say that the issue of money merely disguises (this is basic to Freud) a resentment by the son for the father's interference in his relationship with the mother. That Freudian theme is overt in what follows. Grushenka stands out in stark red tights, a red scarf, red gloves, and a red muff. Because she holds Dimitri's credit slips and because the source of monetary power initially fell to Dimitri's mother, Grushenka has taken over the role not simply of the father, but the mother as well. When Dimitri confronts her, this mother substitute coyly flirts with him: "Oh, you have come to pay me . . . or to beat me. I might like that." She tells Dimitri that Fyodor has asked her to marry him and that this would make her his mother. She mockingly asks, "You wouldn't beat your mother?" As Frank pointed out, Dostoevsky was able to skillfully meld character and idea. For Dostoevsky, Alexi's embrace of Christianity seems real, seems in keeping with who he is, how he acts, how he attempts to discover meaning. But Brooks invariably fails in his attempts to emulate Dostoevsky in this way. Ideas, in fact, impede our encounter with the film's major characters. The Freudian scheme is mechanically imposed and brings us no closer to understanding the relationship between Dimitri and Grushenka. At the conclusion of the episode the couple ride off in a display of simplistic erotic desire. Dimitri vigorously whips the horses to achieve greater and greater speed. Grushenka takes the whip from him, stands, and whips the horses with equal if not greater energy. All that is lacking is a climax, ensuing exhaustion, and perhaps a cigarette.

There is, however, one instance in the set piece that provides significant thematic meaning. After the initial exchange between Dimitri and Grushenka, their interaction suddenly moves from flirtation to a moment in which they spontaneously fall in love. The camera moves in for a medium close-up of their faces as Dimitri kisses her. The close-up conveys a sense of genuine intimacy between the lovers. They have carved out their own self-contained space. Desire is unencumbered, but not in the sense that passion is free from restraints. The spontaneity of their love is free from money, jealousy, hatreds, familial pathologies, and, in Girard's understanding, free from mediated desire. Perhaps it is here in this still moment of spontaneity that Brooks has hit upon the one possibility for redemption in the film. The only chance for authenticity comes in the form of a love that strips away the masks of mediated desire.

## BAD FAITH ABOUNDS

As I have argued, the portions of film in which Brooks most effectively engages the thematic significance of Dostoevsky's novel transpire in theatrical stage-like settings. A scene in Katerina's drawing room, coming later in the film, provides a setting in which the interaction among the characters and the revelation of internal motivation play out in richly complex ways. Once again in his role as messenger, Alexi has come to tell Katerina that Dimitri will never see her again; he has committed himself to Grushenka. When Alexi is announced, Katerina quickly pulls a curtain shut that conceals a small nook. The audience does not know Katerina's purpose but she clearly feels the need to keep someone or something hidden. An aura of concealment and duplicity immediately hovers over the players. Katerina greats Alexi with a disingenuous deflection: "You see with the eyes of god." Alexi is the least compelling and least effective figure in the film. His innocence might have afforded him a space to provide detached moral commentary. But in this case his innocence is merely mocked. Brooks quite simply has no interest in passing moral judgment; he prefers instead to create environments in which his very human characters struggle with each other and with themselves.

Katerina's irony directed at Alexi is soon accompanied by self-deception. She asserts that what Dimitri feels is not love for Grushenka but merely carnal desire. Her misreading of her rival's relationship with Dimitri is at best a rationalization. But as if to prove that she speaks the truth, Katerina turns and dramatically pulls open the drape to reveal Grushenka, who has all along been listening from her concealed nook. There is something almost Jacobean about the stagecraft. It resembles the scene in *Hamlet* in which the King and Polonius conceal themselves behind the arras to secretly overhear an exchange between Hamlet and Ophelia. An aura of surveillance permeates Elsinore castle. It is a fragmented and duplicitous world, politically, socially, and psychologically. Brooks's adaptation obviously does not rival *Hamlet*, but there is something Shakespearean about this scene. When Katerina dramatically pulls the curtain back to reveal what she believes will vindicate her, the audience sees Grushenka sitting, listening, and staging herself in a pose, acknowledging and taking advantage of her sudden position as the dramatic focal point. She has a remarkable look on her face, a hyper-sweetness that invokes coy cunning. We sense she is about to step out and take command of the stage.

And so she does. Katerina puts her arm around her perceived formal rival, addressing her as "my darling Grushenka." And in an almost absurd instance of misreading, Katerina claims that her rival has come as an "angel of peace." The irony she had used in naming Alexi as a representative of God now backfires on her in referring to Grushenka as an angel. Katerina boasts that she and

Grushenka will cure Dimitri of his mere "obsession." Grushenka's face glows with a mask of angelic innocence, suggesting that yes, in fact, she has come on an altruistic mission to release Dimitri from her hold so that Katerina may have him. But she soon morphs into a different figure. No longer angelic, her face takes on a playful and menacing aspect. Just as Katerina intended a dramatic display when she pulled the curtain aside, now Grushenka dramatically drops her mask to mock Katerina: "I did not give my word . . . you kept talking, talking, talking." And then, "I said nothing . . . promises are so binding . . . now yes, now no . . . I am so changeable." Her motives are elusive. She may feel resentment toward her wealthy rival. She may feel a prideful need to punish Katerina's simplistic and arrogant misreading of her. Or perhaps she does this merely for sport, merely for the rush that ironic mockery can provide. Brooks has taken us into a room figuratively with no exit. The importance of the scene lies less, perhaps, in the specific set of psychological perspectives and relationships than with the depiction of an all-encompassing environment, existential in nature, in which the objectification of the other is a guiding principle, a space stripped of any possibility of authenticity.

And now Grushenka engages in an act of sardonic observation. "Jealousy is driving you mad," she tells Katerina. She claims Katerina is incapable of real physical passion, simply the passion of resentment and jealousy. Then Grushenka coyly bends her head down to kiss the hand of Katerina. But she pauses and pulls her lips back and smiles like one of Girard's "coquettes." Katerina loses her temper, slaps Grushenka and calls her a "slut." And now Grushenka drops any hint of irony and simply attacks. She reminds Katerina that she was ready to sell her body to Dimitri for 5,000 rubles: "You sell yourself very high . . . it's only the price that is different." Then returning to irony, she smiles and curtsies. Into the swirling mix of this compelling and destructive exchange, Ivan arrives. Katerina welcomes him, either unaware of his love for her or turning her own irony against him, perceiving him to be a weaker opponent. Ivan reacts bitterly to her disingenuous welcome: "You want me so you can punish me with impunity." He becomes even angrier and accusatory: "The more he [Dimitri] insults you, the more you love him. You love him because he insults you." Ivan's adoption of reason as a defense against the absurdities, amoralities, and contradictions of the human condition here falls to the wayside. Perhaps in this instance Brooks has managed to fuse ideology and character. Ivan's embrace of enlightenment values now appears as a weakness, generated by need rather than by free choice.

I have taken considerable time with this scene because perhaps more than any other it suggests the film Brooks might have made. Here is a scene in which Brooks thrives in staging the dramatic intensity of human interaction. But scenes such as this appear sporadically and inconsistently in the film. Apparently Brooks wanted to include the "Grand Inquisitor" as a set piece in his adaptation.[7] As I pointed out earlier, questions of faith, revelation, and especially the freedom of a Christian are addressed in that chapter of Dostoevsky's philosophical novel. The studio apparently blocked its inclusion, and that may have been a blessing. But it does tell us something about Brooks. I cannot look into his face and and tell you what I see. But I suspect that Brooks was seduced by the intellectual sophistication of Dostoevsky. His attempt to include that sophistication only dilutes the visceral energy of the theatrical interactions of the characters. As I stated earlier, Brooks will immediately move on to source material without these abstract intellectual snares. Brooks's struggles with Dostoevsky, however disappointing the outcome, helped prepare him in his next film to successfully take on the imaginative world of Tennessee Williams.

REVENGE

In the final act of the film, revenge takes center stage. Katerina, Smerdyakov, the illegitimate epileptic brother, and perhaps most significantly, Brooks himself, seek retribution on various levels. The bare outline of the plot has been building toward the trial of Dimitri, who has been falsely accused of murdering his father. The courtroom climax, however, lacks the dramatic resonance one might expect. By providing the court with damning evidence against Dimitri, Katerina takes revenge for Dimitri's perceived betrayal. That she easily and unemotionally then reverses herself suggests that Dimitri no longer occupies her psychic sphere. The revenge of Smerdyakov is much more significant. It arises from the festering resentment over his status as Fyodor's bastard child, as well as the irrational and violent unpredictability of the "falling down sickness." He has contrived to frame Dimitri for the murder of Fyodor that he himself has committed. The scene in which he reveals his machinations to Ivan is shot with green and red filters, tilted camera angles, and the histrionic and capricious gestures of Smerdyakov. Brooks uses his cinematic imagination to convey the aberrant energy of the epileptic. When Ivan brings court officials to hear Smerdyakov's confession, his brother has already hanged himself. His body dangles at the end of a rope in the interior of a closet. This enclosed space is an escalation of Grushenka's hidden nook in Katerina's drawing room. Here the theatrical gesture seems more baroque than modernist, more akin to the stagecraft of Webster and Ford than to Shakespeare. The efficacy of the law and Ivan's rationality are overwhelmed by the force of Smerdyakov's deceit, jealousy, and self-violence. For this moment, Brooks has brought us full circle to the opening image in the credits, specifically the stained-glass icon of a howling face. The overriding tone is conveyed by lighting, striking music, and the constraint of the enclosure itself. Smerdyakov, the misshapen outsider, has taken his final revenge on Dimitri, his well-proportioned and manly half-brother.

But it is Brooks's own personal revenge that brings the film to its deeply ironic and subversive conclusion. In the final chapters of his novel, Dostoevsky foregrounds Christian values. Brooks undermines those values. In Brooks's version, although Dimitri nobly refuses to confess to a crime he did not commit, in his final courtroom speech he exhibits an apparently redemptive self-awareness. He acknowledges his destructive masculine aggression, his profligate behavior, and his careless treatment of others. In prison, Dimitri seems at peace, almost beatific. He wears a crucifix around his neck. The cell is fully lit, and sitting against the wall is an old prisoner reciting passages from the Bible, including the Lord's Prayer and words of Christ prior to his crucifixion. The site of Christian contrition and conversion is a stale and unconvincing one, fashioned without imagination and filled with shallow symbols. It is as if the world of desire and need conveyed so richly in earlier scenes through a cinematic imagination, has been wiped clean.

Spiritual release is soon supplanted by literal escape. Ivan has bribed the guards and arranged for the lovers, Dimitri and Grushenka, to flee. Contrition is apparently less redemptive than money. However, before the two lovers can complete their journey to the secular happiness awaiting them, Dimitri insists that they stop at the pathetic abode of Snegiryov (David Opatoshu), whose son (Miko Oscard) is dying of influenza. The boy's sickly body is wrapped in blankets. An icon of the Madonna hangs on the wall. Earlier, Dimitri had become enraged that Snegiryov held his IOUs. He publicly confronted him, slapped his face, and demanded they meet in the morning for a gentlemen's duel. Snegiryov's already frail son witnessed his father's demeaning humiliation and is mocked and pelted with stones by the other boys. Dimitri has now come seeking the boy's forgiveness. He stands over the deathbed and offers not a humble and self-effacing apology, but rather gifts; not frankincense and myrrh, but a toy cannon and his own military medals. The boy refuses, as if he recognizes the shallowness of this misguided attempt by Dimitri to find forgiveness through symbols of war and masculine aggression. But before leaving in defeat, Dimitri turns back to the boy and tells him what he thinks the dying child wants to hear. He falsely claims that he was frightened of the boy's father, afraid that he would be killed since his father had been known as an excellent marksman. The boy hypocritically accepts the fabrication. He embraces his father and blessedly asserts, "I am so proud of you." In this final theatrical space, Christian humility and forgiveness is displaced by the seductive temptation of pride. In Dante's scheme of Purgatory, pride forms the very foundation of the six other deadly sins. Pride is the sin that must be expunged before the journey to the heavenly garden can even begin. With an absence of self-awareness, believing that he is now truly free, Dimitri rides off with Grushenka to his earthly paradise. Pride does not impede release but becomes its very means. This ending to the film deconstructs the conclusion to Dostoevsky's novel, in which the child is truly a figure of Christ, surrounded as he is by his twelve friends, his twelve disciples.

Under the apparent requirement of a happy ending, Brooks has sardonically sabotaged the validity of the lovers' escape. He mocks the corporate studio and the film's intended middlebrow audience; he may even be mocking happiness itself, or at least a shallow form of it. But the value of the film does not lie in this final subversive gesture, and certainly not as a coherent work of art. Yet its flaws should not detract from those moments in the film in which Brooks develops his skill, perhaps even gaining the confidence, for staging the enclosed psychological spaces of a family at odds with itself. For his next project there will be no need for revenge. Tennessee Williams's *Cat on a Hot Tim Roof* will provide Brooks with the material in which he might freely express his cinematic talents.

## NOTES

1. Vladimir Nabokov, *Lectures on Russian Literature* (New York: Harcourt Inc., 1981), p. 130.
2. Joseph Frank, *Dostoevsky: A Writer in His Time* (Princeton, NJ: Princeton University Press, 2010), p. 848.
3. Fyodor Dostoevsky, *The Brothers Karamazov*, trans. Richard Pevear and Larissa Volokhonsky (New York: Farrar, Straus, and Giroux, 2002), p. 251.
4. Frank, *Dostoevsky*, p. 857.
5. René Girard, *Deceit, Desire and the Novel*, trans. Yvonne Freccero (Baltimore, MD: Johns Hopkins University Press, 1965), p. 41.
6. Ibid. p. 105.
7. Douglass K. Daniel, *Tough as Nails: The Life and Films of Richard Brooks* (Madison: University of Wisconsin Press, 2011), p. 120.

CHAPTER II

# Haunted: *Cat on a Hot Tin Roof* (1958)

## David Sterritt

Tennessee Williams regarded the making of a play as both a profoundly personal and inescapably collaborative enterprise, conceived by the playwright but shaped by contributions from directors, producers, and other participants in the creative process. Screen adaptations carry this reality a step further, and an intellectually inclined auteur of the order of Richard Brooks was bound to exert a powerful influence on the contours of *Cat on a Hot Tin Roof*, even as he respected many vital properties of the hugely successful stage version. As the playwright Edward Albee has observed, this drama is almost as famous for its revisions as for its final text, and in fact there is no definitively final text, since Williams kept tinkering with it as decades passed. He was less than fond of Brooks's rendering, which premiered in August 1958, but he was surely pleased with its enthusiastic reception, and for Brooks the project merged seamlessly into the remarkable decade of literature-related creativity that started with *The Brothers Karamazov*, released just six months earlier, and concluded with *In Cold Blood* in 1967.

Like its source, the film centers largely on the physically stalled marriage of morose, alcoholic Brick (Paul Newman) and sensual, frustrated Maggie (Elizabeth Taylor), leading many observers to regard it as a study of a troubled young man's veiled homosexuality. Yet while that interpretation is useful, Williams had a deeper agenda, using a domestic situation rife with misunderstanding and mendacity as grist for a poetic essay on the meanings and mechanisms of memory, which are thrown into relief as Brick and Maggie struggle with fraught recollections of a dead friend, whose neediness and vulnerability they feel they once betrayed, and with the larger-than-life presence of Big Daddy (Burl Ives), a dying patriarch whose history reflects the decadent sway of capitalism, clannishness, and masculine entitlement. Its compromises notwithstanding, Brooks's film brings these themes to the screen with intelligence and force.

## PHASES

*Cat on a Hot Tin Roof* passed through many phases on its way from Williams's imagination to Brooks's cameras and thence to movie theaters in the United States and beyond. It originated as a short story titled "Three against Grenada," which Williams wrote during a time of heavy drinking, loneliness, self-hatred, and bewilderment—a miserable "term in Purgatory," he called it—and later revised as "Three Players of a Summer Game," published in *The New Yorker* in 1952. The male protagonist, a tall, hard-drinking Mississippi planter named Brick Pollitt, still retains "the slim grace of his youth" and has "not yet fallen beneath the savage axe blows of his liquor." But at the outset of the narrative he is in the process of "throwing his life away, as if it were something disgusting that he had suddenly found in his hands," leaving his wealthy and practical-minded wife, Margaret, to manage the business matters pertaining to his 10,000-acre plantation, a task she handles "as though she had her lips fastened to some invisible wound in his body through which drained out of him and flowed into her the assurance and vitality that had been his before his marriage."[1] This story was a very personal one for Williams, according to biographer John Lahr, who sees Brick's alcoholic immobility as a parallel for "the creative and emotional still water" in which Williams was languishing at that time, as in many periods over the decades of his career. Brick loves liquor "as if he had married it or given birth to it," Williams wrote in the first version of the story, "it is his child now and his lover. Everything else disappears behind the comforting veil of his liquor or is seen through it with indifference and dimness," and his retreat to the bottom of a bottle evidently mirrored Williams's own strategic withdrawal to a "crustacean world" where he could find some social quiet if not some spiritual peace.[2] The illustrious playwright, short-story writer, novelist, and essayist was in an unhappy place, and so was Brick Pollitt, last seen in the backseat of his fancy car, "pitching this way and that way ... like a loosely wrapped package being delivered somewhere" as Margaret boldly pilots them through town "exactly the way that some ancient conqueror ... might have led in chains through a capital city the prince of a state newly conquered."[3] This is a much weaker and more pitiable man than the Brick who emerged in the story's fabled offspring, the three-act drama *Cat on a Hot Tin Roof*. He is also a very far cry from the Brick in Brooks's film, played by Newman in a performance that earned Academy Award and BAFTA nominations for best actor of 1958.[4]

Brick was the first of the drama's characters to take literary form, but two other characters inject similar amounts of psychological complexity and emotional energy into Williams's drama and the movie that Brooks and his collaborators derived from it. One is the character who gives the narrative its name: Margaret Pollitt, nicknamed Maggie the Cat in recognition of her complicated personality, marked by traditionally feline qualities of craftiness and skittishness along with a streak of independence that helps her make an ultimately successful journey through the stormy seas of her strange and difficult marriage. She is vibrant and authentic, and Taylor's performance in the film earned the same Academy Award and BAFTA nominations that Newman garnered. The other key figure is Big Daddy Pollitt, a magniloquent patriarch who fully lives up to his sobriquet; in Williams's play as originally written he was not present in the third act, but he was given a central part in the resolution of the drama when Williams rewrote the last act at the urging of Elia Kazan, who directed the first Broadway production. Big Daddy is mortally ill with cancer, but even as a dying man he is an awesome presence; as critic Gene D. Phillips has observed, he "holds the family together by being the hub around which the rest of the Pollitts revolve, and he . . . holds the play together for the same reason."[5] He was played by Burl Ives on Broadway and on the screen in a superb performance that manages to be simultaneously thunderous and subtle. Each of these three characters—Brick, Maggie, and Big Daddy—is both archetypal and idiosyncratic, constituting an ensemble as quintessentially human as any that Williams or Brooks ever created.

The drama takes place primarily in the Pollitt mansion, where members of the family have convened to celebrate Big Daddy's birthday. Brick limps about on crutches, nursing an ankle he broke the night before in a failed attempt to relive his former athletic glory, and drinks the steady stream of liquor that sustains his alcoholic lifestyle. He also quarrels with Maggie, who has good reason to fear that the obvious deficiencies of her household—her rocky relationship with Brick, his dependence on booze, their failure to have a child—will induce Big Daddy to bequeath his land and fortune to Brick's older brother, Gooper (Jack Carson), a lawyer with a disagreeable wife named Mae (Madeleine Sherwood) and a passel of rowdy children, or "no-neck monsters," as Maggie disdainfully calls them. Fresh from a high-stakes medical examination, Big Daddy is jubilant that tests have found him free of a suspected cancer, but before long the family physician reveals to Brick and Gooper that Big Daddy has indeed been stricken and will probably die within a year.

That evening, Big Daddy confronts Brick over his irresponsible behavior and Maggie joins the colloquy, tracing Brick's distress to the suicide of his best friend Skipper, who killed himself by jumping from a building. Maggie played a role in this tragedy. She had hatched a plan to seduce Skipper for two essentially selfish reasons: to show that Skipper's affection was not dictated by homosexual longing for Brick, and to shatter Brick's faith in Skipper's friendship, of which Maggie was jealous. Her machinations failed when Skipper proved unable to have sex with her, and Brick has never forgiven her for the suicide that followed. Yet he places most of the blame for Skipper's death on himself, believing that it resulted from his refusal to heed despairing phone calls from his suffering and needy friend.

Brick unburdens himself about these matters to Big Daddy, who now knows that he is fatally ill, and the father and son come to terms during a long conversation in the basement, a roomy bin of accumulated items (strongly recalling the superfluity-stuffed mansion in Orson Welles's 1941 *Citizen Kane*, which this scene inevitably recalls) that film scholars R. Barton Palmer and William Robert Bray call "a dollar-book Freudian symbol for what the two men have been repressing as well as a treasure trove of symbolic objects, the things that each man has hitherto mistakenly lived for."[6] Some of the items stored there encapsulate Big Daddy's history as an avid and acquisitive capitalist, which is precisely what he hopes his favorite son will become by following in his oversized footsteps; others evince Brick's faded celebrity as a football star, captured with ironic luster in dust-gathering trophies and a large photograph of the once-gifted athlete poised for action on the gridiron.

In the meanwhile, Gooper and Big Mama (Judith Anderson) hash out disagreements and demands regarding the settlement of the Pollitt estate—the towering power of money in the Pollitt dynasty is not extensively explored but is a thinly veiled undercurrent in the drama—and Maggie gives Big Daddy an unexpected birthday gift, announcing that she is pregnant with Brick's child. Whether a fact, an aspiration, or perhaps a self-fulfilling prophecy, this news instills hope in Big Daddy, increases the chance that Brick and Maggie will inherit his all-important estate, and points to a possible end of Brick's immersion in self-obsessed gloom.

Figure 11.1 Brick (Paul Newman) confronting Big Daddy (Burl Ives) among the capitalistic and athletic trophies of their pasts.

## CHANGES

Williams had a distinguished record in the commercial theater when *Cat on a Hot Tin Roof* reached the stage in 1955. *The Glass Menagerie* had established him as a major new talent in 1944, although Irving Rapper's 1950 movie version, scripted by Williams and Peter Berneis, received a far cooler response, and *A Streetcar Named Desire* had a revolutionary impact when Elia Kazan's production arrived on Broadway in late 1947, followed by Kazan's similarly acclaimed 1951 film version. *Summer and Smoke* proved less popular when it premiered in 1948, but it fared well in an Off-Broadway revival four years later, and while *The Rose Tattoo* proved disappointing at the box office, it earned Tony Awards for actors Eli Wallach and Maureen Stapleton, scenic designer Boris Aronson, and the play itself as the best of 1951. The failure of the proto-postmodern *Camino Real* in 1953 may have reminded Williams that he was most at home in the relatively intimate psychological terrain that he had probed so astutely in his major hits, and *Cat on a Hot Tin Roof* was rooted firmly in that territory, using a day in the life of a Mississippi Delta family as a microscope through which such profoundly human themes as alcoholism and denialism, mendacity and manipulation, homosexual desire and heterosexual frustration, and fear of impending death are scrupulously dissected and examined.

The initial Broadway run of the play incorporated alterations that Williams made at Kazan's urging: Big Daddy no longer leaves the action after the second act but reappears in the third; Brick's last encounter with him induces a modicum of change in his previously stagnant personality, producing a more sympathetic and responsive attitude toward Maggie than before; and Maggie shows less hostility toward Mae and more closeness to Big Daddy and Big Mama, adjustments that presumably make her a more appealing figure for the audience. Williams was not happy with these modifications. His reasons for acceding to them can be traced to "his concern to get his work out to as wide an audience as possible" and also to a lapse of confidence in what theater scholar Brian Parker describes as his "extraordinary method of composition," which called for dashing off "draft after draft at high speed without prior planning in order to try to tap subconscious levels of experience."[7] The published play contained two versions of the third act, the original one and the one produced on Broadway, and Williams continued to alter the play in subsequent decades, as he did with various other plays and stories after they had ostensibly been completed. For him as for many cultural creators, a work of art was less often definitively completed than reluctantly abandoned.

M-G-M bought the rights to Williams's play as a starring vehicle for Grace Kelly, then gave the plum role of Maggie to Taylor when Kelly took early retirement from her screen career. (Montgomery Clift was considered for the role of Brick before Newman landed it.) Joshua Logan and then Joseph L.

Mankiewicz were initially slated to direct; also in the running for a while was George Cukor, whom the M-G-M producer Pandro S. Berman vetoed on the grounds that the great director of women's films saw the drama "in terms of a homosexual piece," contradicting Berman's vision of a safer, more sanitized rendition, as Brooks biographer Douglass K. Daniel recounts.[8] A number of screenwriters, including such luminaries as Arthur Laurents and Ernest Lehman, declined the project before Brooks signed on to write and direct, with Lawrence Weingarten as the producer of record. During this preliminary stage the studio enlisted screenwriter James Poe to outline the structure and action of the film; his credentials included a screenwriting credit for Robert Aldrich's 1955 melodrama *The Big Knife*, adapted from Clifford Odets's play, and a co-screenwriting credit (with John Farrow and S. J. Perelman) for Michael Anderson's 1956 epic *Around the World in 80 Days*, adapted from Jules Verne's novel and produced by Mike Todd, who was Taylor's husband from 1957 until his death in a plane crash ten days after *Cat on a Hot Tin Roof* went before the camera.[9] Poe's subsequent projects include Peter Glenville's excellent 1961 movie version of Williams's own *Summer and Smoke*.

Poe approached *Cat on a Hot Tin Roof* with an eye to expanding the scene of action as much as possible, visualizing incidents not seen on the stage; the most important of these relate directly to Skipper's suicidal leap, which is foreshadowed when he drunkenly confides to Brick that he has "never been much of a man with girls" and occurs while Brick tries frantically to talk him down on the phone. As critic Gene D. Phillips observes, this treatment "makes Skipper's death something totally beyond Brick's control," whereas in the play he feels an overwhelming sense of culpability for his friend's tragic demise.[10] Poe's tendency to err in the direction of "sweetness and light" culminates in the final scene, showing Big Daddy and Big Mama together in contented harmony while Brick and Maggie await the birth of their expected child; the screenwriter's overly optimistic vision may have been partly motivated by the desire to please everyday moviegoers, thus avoiding the brouhaha raised by *Baby Doll*, directed by Kazan from Williams's original screenplay, in 1956.[11] In any event, Brooks threw out nearly all of Poe's efforts and embarked on a treatment that did not rely on flashbacks to get crucial points across.[12] This comported with Williams's pride in the structure of the play, which was his favorite among his works, not only because its characters are "amusing and credible and touching" and because the second act gives Big Daddy a "kind of crude eloquence of expression," but also because the drama "adheres to the valuable edict of Aristotle that a tragedy must have unity of time and place and magnitude of theme."[13] The action has a single setting; the three acts run contiguously from start to finish; and Brooks constructed the movie along the same lines.

Still and all, Brooks's adaptation introduces major modifications to Williams's play, some of which evidently reflect second or third thoughts on the filmmaker's part. In a *New York Times* interview early in 1958, he stated his intention to "put [the play] on the screen just as it was on the stage," saying that he did not want "to open it up, to give it action for the screen," since action "doesn't require running around . . . You can have action on the screen with only two people talking to each other."[14] This is what one would expect from the director who discarded Poe's strongly opened-up treatment of the text. Yet the very first moments of Brooks's film unquestionably "open [the play] up" by means of a character "running around," or rather running in a straight line, as the inebriated Brick seeks to recapture his long-gone athletic prowess by clearing hurdles on a high-school track field, an incident described in the play but enacted on the screen, complete with the blunder that breaks Brick's ankle and puts him on crutches for the remainder of the drama. This provides the movie with a vivid and attention-getting introduction, especially since Newman jumped the hurdles without resorting to a stunt double, but it hardly aligns with Brooks's statement that it would be "criminal" to render the play "ordinary" by means of eye-catching changes. Nor did the film emerge as the "black-and-white picture on a regular-size screen" that Brooks described a couple of months before the camera rolled.[15] According to Daniel's biography of Brooks, it was actually Berman who wanted black-and-white photography as a cost-saving measure, infuriating Brooks, who called this a "crazy" approach for a film starring "one of the world's most beautiful women" and recruited that woman's husband, the high-powered Hollywood wheeler-dealer Todd, to demand a color showcase for his wife.[16] This view prevailed, and the movie was shot in Metrocolor with an ample 1.85:1 aspect ratio. One more element of the film susceptible to being called "ordinary" is the artfully constructed realism of its ambience; describing the settings and furnishings of the Pollitt house in some detail, Williams adds that the stage set "should be far less realistic" than his particularized description implies, with "walls below the ceiling [that] dissolve mysteriously into air" and are "roofed by the sky" and "stars and moon suggested by traces of milky pallor, as if they were observed through a telescope lens out of focus."[17] Perhaps inevitably for a commercial production, the onscreen Pollitt residence is as grounded and naturalistic as M-G-M's ace designers—art directors William A. Horning and Urie McCleary chief among them—could make it.

Additional issues and challenges were inherent in the nature of the project, which was controversial from its earliest stages. The play had opened four days after the premiere of Brooks's high-school drama *Blackboard Jungle* in March 1955, immediately garnering loud applause from theatergoers, high praise from critics, and keen interest from Hollywood figures, including producers at M-G-M, the illustrious studio where Williams had once labored as an unhappy scriptwriter for a fleeting six months in 1943. Hollywood was very much under the ponderous thumb of the Production Code Administration, the studio-sponsored censorship office where long-time chief Joseph I. Breen had recently been replaced by Geoffrey Shurlock, his somewhat more lenient successor. Brooks had skirmished with censors before—several American cities banned *Blackboard Jungle*, which the guardians of decency in Atlanta, Georgia, called "immoral, obscene, licentious" and a threat to "the peace, health, morals and good order" of the citizenry—and it was clear that *Cat on a Hot Tin Roof* would push the morality envelope even further.[18] Potential problems included vulgar language spoken by Big Daddy and others, as well as the thinly veiled suggestion of homosexuality in Brick's rapport with his late friend Skipper, which led Shurlock to warn the independent producer Hal Wallis that "it would be necessary to remove every inference or implication of sex perversion," thereby killing Wallis's interest in purchasing movie rights to the play.[19] A more heterosexual problem was Maggie's determination to get Brick into bed and conceive his child, which Shurlock deemed "a very definite Code problem by reason of over-emphasis on this extremely delicate relationship."[20]

Treatment of homosexuality would certainly be the hardest difficulty to overcome, given the aversion to that topic among power brokers in Hollywood and in American culture at large. A substantial part of Brooks's solution was to deny that homosexuality was all that important to the drama in the first place. "There was no indication by Williams in the play that Brick was a homosexual," he told *The New York Times* while preparing the production. The idea that Brick was gay, he added, was just "an impression that grew out of the close relationship with his old college athlete chum . . . who was never seen on the stage."[21] This fit with Berman's view that homosexuality was "not important to the story that he believed should be told," centering on "a father and son who could no longer communicate."[22] According to this interpretation, the misery weighing on Brick stems "not necessarily [from] homosexual repression nor even homophobia" but rather from guilt over "the lack of compassion that made him hang up on Skipper's drunken confession."[23]

It is far from clear, however, that Williams regarded Brick as "heterosexual, not a closeted gay man"; certainly he did not see Brick as unequivocally straight when he called for the character's sexuality to have an "aura of ambiguity . . . created by his passivity and stubborn silences."[24] And the strength of that ambiguity was one of the important elements at stake in Williams's ambivalent responses to some of the revisions that Kazan prevailed on him to make, believing that the mystery of Brick's inner self was "the poem of the play, not its story but the poem of the story."[25] By the time the play was headed toward its first rehearsals, moreover, Williams refurbished his earlier, "somewhat tentative" ideas about this, writing to Kazan that "in the deeper sense, not the literal sense, Brick *is* homosexual with a heterosexual adjustment," belonging to a tribe whose "innocence [and] blindness [make] them very, very touching, very beautiful and sad." And very vulnerable, because "if a mask is ripped off, suddenly, roughly, that's quite enough to blast the whole Mechanism, the whole adjustment, knock the world out from under their feet, and leave them no alternative but—owning up to the truth or retreat into something like liquor."[26] This sounds like Brick, although Brooks's conception of him appears to deny that he has a mask to rip off, only a mopey, depressive nature that needs lifting out of its perhaps transitory gloom.

When the screen adaptation opened, more than one critic readily saw Brick as something like the "homosexual with a heterosexual adjustment" that Williams had decided he was. "The film reviewers concluded that Brick was a homosexual," film scholar Maurice Yacowar writes with a wry touch, "largely because he would wipe away a kiss from Elizabeth Taylor, one suspects!"[27] Brooks expressed a similar suspicion without the wry touch: "On the screen it would be difficult to accept Brick's rejection of Maggie, played by the beautiful, sensual Elizabeth Taylor," he conceded when the film was in release. "What audience would believe that Brick would refuse to go to bed with Maggie, would refuse her advances? Not many men in the movie audience would reject Elizabeth Taylor. Not many women in the audience would understand why Brick turns her down."

But if Brick isn't overtly or covertly gay—as Brooks put it, "writing the homosexuality out of Brick's character" was the biggest change he made to the play—why indeed is there such a barrier between him and his conspicuously desirable spouse? To resolve this conundrum, or at least render it less obvious, Brooks made it appear that the actual root of Brick's rejection of Maggie and attachment to Skipper is a bedrock immaturity and inability to shoulder adult

Figure 11.2 Elizabeth Taylor, seductive and voluptuous as Maggie.

responsibilities, unfortunate traits that temporarily obscure but do not permanently erase his profound connection with the wife he has loved deeply all along. To get this across without wordy explanations, Brooks adds a telling gesture just after Brick and Maggie finish an extended conversation in the bedroom: Maggie impulsively embraces Brick and he pushes her away and flees to the bathroom, where he finds her nightgown hanging on the door and spontaneously buries his face in it, thus revealing his need for her and assuring the audience that "he must be rejecting Maggie for reasons other than loss of manhood."[28]

For many moviegoers, this way of handling the issue was fine. The anonymous critic for *Harrison's Reports* wrote that although "[s]ome slight and necessary changes have been made in the story to clean it up for this screen version ... the considerable talk about sex still is as frank and forthright as anything ever heard in a motion picture."[29] Even the hitherto skeptical Cukor, who had believed that homosexuality was indispensable to the drama, was pleased with how the finished film turned out: "The story is so persuasive," he remarked, "that the lack of this strong motivational element of the plot wasn't even missed on the screen."[30] For others, the "strong motivational element" was not lacking at all; one critic declared, "Brick is the best dramatized study of homosexuality I have seen."[31] In the end, however, immaturity and irresponsibility seem like incomplete explanations of Brick's actions and motivations. As an element interweaving with and complicating guilt-ridden homosexual tendencies, the immaturity factor is a dramatically plausible slant on Brick's psychology; but as a substitution for those guilt-ridden tendencies it seems thin, not to mention contrary to what Williams ultimately decided was at the heart of Brick's unhappiness. Even the mostly sympathetic Daniel concludes that the adaptation of *Cat on a Hot Tin Roof* demonstrates that Brooks was "not always the rebellious, iconoclastic champion of truth he wanted to be."[32] Williams himself was forthrightly incensed. The play was "one of the most bitter social criticisms" he had written, he said in 1973, but the adapters "sweetened that film up so it was hardly recognizable," taking out "everything that was direct, everything that was strong social criticism."[33] In a frequently quoted (perhaps apocryphal) remark, he called to people lined up outside a theater showing the film, "This movie will set the industry back fifty years. Go home!"[34]

The playwright's wrath notwithstanding, Brooks's film became M-G-M's highest earner of 1958, topping the box office for several weeks and parlaying its $2.3 million budget into more than $17.5 million in returns over the years.[35] Not every critic greeted it warmly but many found much to commend, and the film's reputation has been generally high in subsequent years. *Chicago Sun-Times* critic Roger Ebert hailed it as a "searing portrait of the human condition" and *New Yorker* critic Pauline Kael wrote that despite "hocus-pocus about the reasons" for Brick's lack of desire for his wife, "Taylor looks very desirable, and the cast is full of actors whooping it up with Southern accents."[36]

## HAUNTINGS

The earliest draft of *Cat on a Hot Tin Roof* was headed with an epigraph comprising the final quatrain of William Butler Yeats's poem "To a Friend Whose Work Has Come to Nothing," first published in 1914.[37] The quoted words proffer advice on remaining positive in the face of seeming defeat:

> Amid a place of stone,
> Be secret and exult,
> Because of all things known
> That is most difficult.[38]

*Cat on a Hot Tin Roof* abounds in stony secrets and elusive truths: about the foundations of Brick's alcoholism and depression, about Big Daddy's diseased body, about Gooper and May's covetous hunger for the family estate, about Maggie's genuine love for her husband, concern for her father-in-law, and desire to carry their heritage and hers into a new generation. As the drama reaches its conclusion, Maggie's pregnancy announcement gives her cause for the sense of pleasure alluded to in Yeats's poem, and Brick and Big Daddy also have reasons to rise above the moroseness that has hitherto weighed them down. But these delayed and partial victories are not enough to arouse the exultation evoked by Yeats, which may be why Williams replaced his lines with part of Dylan Thomas's more famous poem "Do Not Go Gentle Into That Good Night." The lines that Williams quotes from this villanelle, written in 1947 and published in 1951, are again the final quatrain:

> And you, my father, there on the sad height,
> Curse, bless, me now with your fierce tears, I pray.
> Do not go gentle into that good night.
> Rage, rage against the dying of the light.[39]

These words shift the focus from Maggie's endurance and "capacity for survival" to the theme of dying father and conflicted son, as Brian Parker notes in his analysis of the play's textual genealogy.[40] This change makes good sense, but the epigram from Yeats seems equally appropriate, and at one point "A Place in Stone" was the provisional subtitle of the play. One wonders if Williams's rejection of Yeats's lines is revealing in itself, suggesting possible discomfort with their hint of pleasure in coping with what Brooks called the "deep secrets of the past" often found in Williams's plays, "the kind of secret that boils up at a crucial moment when it must be confronted by the characters."[41]

Mendacity and denial haunt those characters. Some of their secrets and lies, surrounding Big Daddy and his illness, are resolved in a relatively straightforward way; others, surrounding Skipper and his suicide, constitute an enormously fraught shadow that may never be entirely exorcised, notwithstanding the relief offered by the reconciliation of Brick and Maggie in the final scene. The psychospiritual tension brought to bear on their marriage by Skipper's ghostly presence points to *hauntology* as a means of exploring Williams's play and Brooks's film. Two senses of that term, as summarized by the theorist Colin Davis, are pertinent here. One, formulated by the philosopher Jacques Derrida, the chief proponent of hauntology as a complement to the relatively concrete precincts of ontology, posits the *specter* as an ultimately unfathomable intruder that is "neither present nor absent, neither dead nor alive."[42] The other, set forth by the psychoanalytic theorists Nicolas Abraham and Maria Torok, posits the *phantom* as a metaphorical "dead ancestor in the living Ego, still intent on preventing its traumatic and usually shameful secrets from coming to light," using deception and misdirection to that end.[43]

Specters and spirits are different hauntological entities, Davis notes: "Phantoms lie about the past whilst spectres gesture towards a still unformulated future."[44] But the imprints of both are detectable in the Pollitt household, where obfuscations of the past and uncertainties about the future are chronic conditions of everyday life, and baneful influences from bygone days brood over a perilously unstable present. No movie in Brooks's filmography better instantiates the cryptic workings of hauntology than *Cat on a Hot Tin Roof*, although some—*The Brothers Karamazov*, *Elmer Gantry* (1960), *Lord Jim* (1965)—also have elements that Derrida's bold concept can usefully illuminate. It is gratifying that a haunted play by a haunted playwright would result in an honored film by an honored filmmaker.

## NOTES

1. Tennessee Williams, "Three Players of a Summer Game," *The New Yorker* Vol. 28 No. 37 (November 1, 1952): pp. 27–8.
2. John Lahr, *Tennessee Williams: Mad Pilgrimage of the Flesh* (New York: W. W. Norton, 2014), p. 236.
3. Williams, "Three Players of a Summer Game," p. 36.
4. Brooks's film earned five Oscar nominations: Best Picture, Best Actor for Newman, Best Actress for Taylor, Best Director for Brooks, Best Adapted Screenplay for Brooks and James Poe, and Best Color Cinematography for William H. Daniels. It also received three British Academy of Film and Television Arts (BAFTA) nominations and assorted nods from the Directors Guild of America, the New York Film Critics Circle, the Writers Guild of America, the Golden Globes, and the National Board of Review.
5. Gene D. Phillips, *The Films of Tennessee Williams* (Philadelphia: Art Alliance Press, 1980), p. 139.
6. R. Barton Palmer and William Robert Bray, *Hollywood's Tennessee: The Williams Films and Postwar America* (Austin: University of Texas Press, 2009), p. 170.
7. Brian Parker, "Swinging a Cat," in Tennessee Williams, *Cat on a Hot Tin Roof* (New York: New Directions, 2004) p. 183.

8. Douglass K. Daniel, *Tough as Nails: The Life and Films of Richard Brooks* (Madison: University of Wisconsin Press, 2011), p. 126.
9. Michael Todd's untimely death in a plane crash on March 22, 1958, ten days after *Cat on a Hot Tin Roof* started shooting, came while Taylor was bedridden with a virus. The production was suspended for Todd's funeral, then restarted without Taylor as she recuperated from the tragedy. She returned on April 14, in shaky health but game to continue.
10. Phillips, *Films of Tennessee Williams*, p. 142.
11. *Baby Doll* earned a C rating (Condemned) from the Legion of Decency, a Roman Catholic watchdog organization, and was denounced from the pulpit by Cardinal Francis Spellman of New York, who had never made such a move before. "Cardinal Scores *Baby Doll* Film," *New York Times*, December 17, 1956: p. 28.
12. Phillips, *Films of Tennessee Williams*, pp. 142–3.
13. Tennessee Williams, *Memoirs* (New York: New Directions, 2006), p. 168.
14. Thomas M. Pryor, "Hollywood *Cat*," *The New York Times*, January 5, 1958: section X: p. 7.
15. Ibid.
16. Daniel, *Tough as Nails*, p. 129.
17. Tennessee Williams, *Cat on a Hot Tin Roof* (New York: New Directions, 2004), p. 16.
18. "Metro Fights Atlanta Lady Censor Who Banned *Blackboard Jungle* Outright," *Variety* Vol. 199 No. 1 (June 8, 1955): p. 5.
19. "*Cat on a Hot Tin Roof*." *AFI Catalog of Feature Films* (n.d.). Retrieved November 12, 2021. https://catalog.afi.com/Catalog/moviedetails/52496
20. Daniel, *Tough as Nails*, p. 125.
21. Pryor, "Hollywood *Cat*," p. 7.
22. Daniel, *Tough as Nails*, pp. 125–6.
23. Parker, "Swinging a Cat," pp. 180–1.
24. Ibid. p. 180.
25. Tennessee Williams, *The Selected Letters of Tennessee Williams, Volume II: 1945–1957*, ed. Albert J. Devlin (New York: New Directions, 2004). Quoted in Lahr, *Tennessee Williams*, p. 302.
26. Letter, Williams to Kazan. Quoted in Lahr, *Tennessee Williams*, p. 304.
27. Maurice Yacowar, *Tennessee Williams and Film* (New York: Frederick Ungar, 1977), p. 43.
28. Daniel, *Tough as Nails*, p. 127.
29. "*Cat on a Hot Tin Roof* with Elizabeth Taylor, Paul Newman and Burl Ives," *Harrison's Reports* Vol. 40 No. 33 (August 16, 1958): p. 130.
30. Phillips, *Films of Tennessee Williams*, p. 147.
31. Baker, "Cat on a Hot Tin Roof." Quoted in Yacowar, *Tennessee Williams and Film*, p. 43.
32. Daniel, *Tough as Nails*, p. 128.
33. John Calendo, "New Again: Tennessee Williams," *Interview* (April 1973). Reprinted in interviewmagazine.com (June 4, 2014). Retrieved August 9, 2021. https://www.interviewmagazine.com/culture/new-again-tennessee-williams
34. Michael Billington, "*Cat on a Hot Tin Roof*: Tennessee Williams's southern discomfort," *The Guardian*, September 30, 2012. Accessed July 4, 2021. https://www.theguardian.com/stage/2012/sep/30/cat-on-a-hot-tin-roof
35. "National Boxoffice Survey," *Variety* Vol. 212 No. 6 (October 8, 1958): p. 4.
36. Roger Ebert, "A Searing Portrait of the human condition," *Chicago Sun-Times*, October 12, 2007: p. B6; Pauline Kael, *5001 Nights at the Movies: A Guide from A to Z* (New York: Holt, Rinehart, and Winston, 1982), p. 98.
37. William Butler Yeats, "To a Friend Whose Work Has Come to Nothing," in *Responsibilities and Other Poems* (New York: The Macmillan Company, 1916), p. 34.

38. Brian Parker, "A Preliminary Stemma for Drafts and Revisions of Tennessee Williams's *Cat on a Hot Tin Roof*," *The Papers of the Bibliographical Society of America* Vol. 90 No. 4 (December 1996): p. 482.
39. Williams, *Cat on a Hot Tin Roof*, p. 14. Thomas's poem was published in the Italian journal *Botteghe Obscure* and in *In Country Sleep, and Other Poems*.
40. Parker, "Preliminary Stemma," pp. 481, 485.
41. Phillips, *Films of Tennessee Williams*, p. 144.
42. Colin Davis, "Hauntology, Specters and Phantoms," *French Studies* Vol. 59 No. 3 (2005): p. 373; Frederic Jameson, "Marx's Purloined Letter," in *Ghostly Demarcations: A Symposium on Jacques Derrida's "Spectres de Marx"*, ed. Michael Sprinker (Paris: Galilée, 1993), p. 39.
43. Davis, "Hauntology," p. 374.
44. Ibid. p. 379.

# FILMOGRAPHY

*Around the World in 80 Days* (U.S.A., 1956). Directed by Michael Anderson. Screenplay by James Poe, John Farrow, and S. J. Perelman, from the novel by Jules Verne.
*Baby Doll* (U.S.A., 1956). Directed by Elia Kazan. Screenplay by Tennessee Williams.
*Citizen Kane* (U.S.A., 1941). Directed by Orson Welles. Screenplay by Herman J. Mankiewicz and Orson Welles.
*The Big Knife* (U.S.A., 1955). Directed by Robert Aldrich,. Screenplay by James Poe, from the play by Clifford Odets.
*Blackboard Jungle* (U.S.A., 1955). Directed by Richard Brooks. Screenplay by Richard Brooks, from novel *The Blackboard Jungle* by Evan Hunter.
*The Brothers Karamazov* (U.S.A., 1958). Directed by Richard Brooks. Screenplay by Julius J. Epstein, adapted by Philip G. Epstein, from the novel by Fyodor Dostoevsky.
*Cat on a Hot Tin Roof* (U.S.A., 1958). Directed by Richard Brooks. Screenplay by Richard Brooks and James Poe, from the play by Tennessee Williams.
*Elmer Gantry* (U.S.A., 1960). Directed by Richard Brooks. Screenplay by Richard Brooks, from the novel by Sinclair Lewis.
*The Glass Menagerie* (U.S.A., 1950). Directed by Irving Rapper. Screenplay by Peter Berneis, from the play by Tennessee Williams.
*In Cold Blood* (U.S.A., 1967). Directed by Richard Brooks. Screenplay by Richard Brooks, from the book by Truman Capote.
*Lord Jim* (U.K./U.S.A., 1965). Directed by Richard Brooks. Screenplay by Richard Brooks, from the novel by Joseph Conrad.
*A Streetcar Named Desire* (U.S.A., 1951). Directed by Elia Kazan. Screenplay by Tennessee Williams, adapted by Oscar Saul.
*Summer and Smoke* (U.S.A., 1961). Directed by Peter Glenville. Screenplay by James Poe and Meade Roberts, from the play by Tennessee Williams.

CHAPTER 12

# A Bite of Salvation

*Murray Pomerance*

> All gold rushes are essentially negative.
> —F. Scott Fitzgerald to Gerald Murphy, September 14, 1940

## PREAMBLE

More than once as a youngster in the 1950s I watched Oral Roberts laboring in prayer on the little television screen, inside his giant tent that could seat thousands. I had seen such a tent only once before, when in Cecil B. DeMille's *The Greatest Show on Earth* (1952) the Ringling Bros. circus filled the big top. The word that Roberts used most emphatically—his language was peppered with "Lord"s and "Jesus"s and "prayer"s and "Come up, my daughter"—was: *heal*. He summoned divine agency to bring remedy to one destitute soul after another, quivering, quaking, palsied, lame, blind, mute, the whole gamut. And one at a time, like guests in some odd talk show (or the sufferers marching to the springs in Fellini's *8 ½* [1963]), they would head to the platform and allow him to lay hands upon them. He would open his fingers upon a trembling head, look up to the heavens (that is, the top of the tent), clamp his eyes shut, and scream, "Heal!!! Heal this ailing man!!! Heal this woman!!!! Heal!!!!!!" While I watched him, stunned but entirely uninformed, I did not know that, along with Jay Silverheels, who was Tonto in my weekly episodes of *The Lone Ranger*, I was seeing in Roberts one of the very earliest Native Americans of my experience, and certainly an indigenous pioneer to the mass media. He was Choctaw American. Perhaps he had the power of a shaman. In screen truth, however, in snowy black and white, while he screamed and while his hands shook with the force that causes hands to shake when one is devout in prayer, he looked white to me. White, white, and blistering white. White thunder. White lightning. In

Figure 12.1 Elmer Gantry (Burt Lancaster) amuses Sister Sharon Falconer (Jean Simmons) at their first meeting on a train.

Richard Brooks's *Elmer Gantry* (1960), Sister Sharon Falconer (Jean Simmons) copies this routine again and again, once with a deaf penitent (Max Showalter) calling the fire of Heaven to descend through her fingers.

Roberts founded his Pentecostal Ministry in 1947, by which time Sinclair Lewis's satirical novel had been in print for twenty years, and revivalists like Billy Sunday, Aimee Semple McPherson, and Billy Graham were heating up the environment with fervor. These folk, but Graham especially, were models for the film, writes Burt Lancaster's biographer Kate Buford, although this was "carefully denied by the director and star":

> Several months after Lancaster's anti-HUAC [House Un-American Activities Committee] speech at the Commodore Hotel in January 1949, thirty-year-old William Franklin Graham converted six thousand Californians under a huge canvas tent, exhorting them with fiery rhetoric to find the answers to their postwar fears in Jesus (a *Gantry* press release claimed the movie was shot in Los Angeles because the area had "spawned so many religious cults and sects that it seemed only fair").[1] In what became his great evangelist "crusade" of the 1950s, during which sales of bibles reached an all-time high, Graham had a style markedly similar to [Billy] Sunday and McPherson, only more mainstream and global. Brooks kept a file labeled "Billy Graham" stuffed with newspaper and magazine articles on which he pencil-marked the

salient characteristics. Graham's delivery was a "machine-gun speed" with "restless pacing on the platform" often covering a mile and a half in one session, leaving him soaking with sweat . . .[2]

All of that comes through in Lancaster's sales-pitch performance.

Lewis's subject, an underpinning platform upon which the brave characters struggle with one another in agony (and where the choir dutifully harps), is evangelism in America's heartland of the late 1920s and early 1930s, pre-Dust Bowl America. "For more than a century after the founding of the Republic," Max Lerner writes, "there was a complacent assumption that Nature's plenty need not be guarded and would resist forever the withering hand of time and man,"[3] but the farmer knows better. At the time of the novel, roughly one in four citizens of America lived on and in some way worked farms. Changes were in the wind, mechanizations, urbanizations, shifts of population. And the Dust Bowl of the 1930s put paid to the idea of God's garden in the West. The "healing grace and . . . elixir of sturdiness and integrity in contact with the soil," which since the nineteenth century had been so elemental in mid-America, a veritable characterization of the rural personality—characterize and thus be taken for granted—now took on emphasis and became, for many, the subject of or motivation for desperate prayer. That the land should remain fertile against infestations. That the climate should continue to bless in its cyclicity. That the increasingly urbanized and capitalized American population should remain eager to buy the farmer's produce for the table. Farm life was a rich life, and also an uncertain one. "The march of mechanization on the farm is clear."[4] Lerner quotes the modernist prophet Louis Bromfield: "Farming as a way of life is infinitely more pleasurable and satisfactory when it is planned, scientific, specialized, mechanized, and stripped of the long hours and the drudgery of the old-fashioned, obsolete pattern of the frontier or general farm."[5] But by the late 1920s the "scientific" revolution had not yet come in its fullness; the word "science" and all it stood for was, here and in many other parts of America, suspect in the extreme. It was Divinity to Whom address should be made for the deeply hidden spiritual help the farmer needed to carry on. Engineering couldn't do the trick. And the long hours and drudgery Bromfield mentions brought an adversity to life in its daily form. Pains, weaknesses, injuries, degradations of the body, exhaustions, infections, irritations from contact with animals, and on and on.

Further, notes Lerner, distinctly among farmers of the world the American "is not a village dweller."[6] The lonely if fecund farm under the vast cupola of sky, the long and often dangerous trek over pitted land to reach a neighbor: once farmers could aggregate around a town, they could feel the communal spirit as a fountain of revivification, could flock to its precincts for sustenance in trouble. At the same time, increasing mobility between town and state centers brought on increased contact with strangers, business people, connivers—increased moral danger.

Lerner offers a succinct description of bucolic religion and its frenzied appeal:

> One of the striking facts about American history has been the linkage of the "religion of the fathers" with what [H. L.] Mencken delighted to call the "Bible Belt" mentality—a narrow view of life and morals, a belief in the literal inspiration of the Bible, and a reactionary code of political belief.[7] The passion of the "Hot Gospel" and the archaism of the hell-fire-and-damnation religion have been put to work as a counterforce to the inherent humanism of the Christian teachings. It has enabled a number of demagogues, especially in the rural Midwest and South, to clothe their racist and reactionary appeals in Biblical references. In the big cities the tradition of Charles G. Finney and Dwight L. Moody was continued with modern publicity techniques by Billy Sunday, Aimee MacPherson [sic], and Billy Graham. They were evidence of how broad is the gulf in American religion between the loudly committed and the deeply committed.[8]

Sunday, McPherson, Graham, and Oral Roberts by the time of Brooks's film. And a commitment "loud" in every possible way. The louder the more entertaining, and the more entertaining the more a treasure. If God could be found through harmony and melody, through gay color and pleasing form, the pain of the sufferer might be relieved some, if only in the quest.

Sharon Falconer's revival-meeting tent is described in Sinclair Lewis's novel, a virtual film set:

> The tent was enormous; it would seat three thousand people, and another thousand could be packed in standing-room. It was nearly filled when Elmer arrived and elbowed his majestic way forward. At the front of the tent was an extraordinary structure, altogether different from the platform-pulpit-American flag arrangement of the stock evangelist. It was a pyramidical structure, of white wood with gilded legs, affording three platforms; one for the choir, one higher up for a row of seated local clergy; and at the top a small platform with a pulpit shaped like a shell and painted like a rainbow. Swarming over it all were lilies, roses and vines.[9]

One could easily bring to mind the Divine throne described in Isaiah 6. And one could imagine camera positions, too.

As to the willing if not also utterly humbled attendees flocking to the revival tent to hear one celebrated preacher or another—*Gantry*'s Falconer

(Jean Simmons) is meant to rise above these other types, yet also to be one of them; not an easy task for the character or the actor. Simmons knew how women were thought to exist for soothing and nourishing, not preaching! They mingled with a legion of afflicted and desperate souls, weary of themselves and their iniquities, parched for the waters of true forgiveness and belonging. "They generally, before the end of the meetings, worked up gratifying feeling":

> Often young women knelt panting, their eyes blank, their lips wide with ecstasy. Sometimes, when Sharon was particularly fired, they actually had the phenomena of the great revivals of 1800. People twitched and jumped with the holy jerks, old people under Pentecostal inspiration spoke in unknown tongues—completely unknown; women stretched out senseless, their tongues dripping; and once occurred what connoisseurs regard as the highest example of religious inspiration. Four men and two women crawled about a pillar, barking like dogs "barking the devil out of the tree."[10]

Brooks's doggy barkers seem infused with some spiritual plasm shuttling them beyond all civilization.

Lewis particularly noted how the throng *worked up* feelings, in short, undertook the necessary labor to produce a particular effect. In the film, of course, the actors playing the praying multitude are working up feeling in precisely the same way, and on cue. Entertainment film continually analogizes itself to the revival meeting it depicts (in a sanctified outer space beyond filmic construction).

## AN ADAPTIVE SPIRIT

But part of the thrust of Lewis's prose, snatched easily in Lancaster's too gregarious smile, is American capitalism's *investment* in religious fervor, a passion ready to be harvested and yet, as it were, inconceivable and inexplicable in itself. For both the author and the filmmaker there was not a great deal new in this riddle, which inspired Dostoyevsky in 1880:

> The elder came out to the crowd of pilgrims from the common people who were waiting for his appearance at the gates of the hermitage and who had flocked from all over Russia purposely to see the elder and obtain his blessing. They prostrated themselves before him, wept, kissed his feet, kissed the ground on which he stood, cried out to him in loud voices, the women holding up their children to him and leading sick "shriekers."[11]

Lewis is unguarded about describing the revival shock that, as emotional sign, constitutes the gist of the revival business. Early on, Elmer attends a meeting during Annual Prayer Week (simulated onscreen with a black Baptist congregation who adopt him when he raises his singing voice):

> Young men sobbed and knelt; a woman shrieked; people were elbowing the standers in the aisles and pushing forward to kneel in agonized happiness, and suddenly they were setting relentlessly on a bewildered Elmer Gantry, who had been betrayed into forgetting himself . . .
> Others about him were beating their foreheads, others were shrieking, "Lord, be merciful," and one woman—he remembered her as a strange, repressed, mad-eyed special student who was not known to have any friends—was stretched out, oblivious of the crowd, jerking, her limbs twitching, her hands clenched, panting rhythmically.[12]

A shapely and tumultuous dance of delirium.

Adaptation rests in the heart of *Elmer Gantry* (1960), Richard Brooks's film, but also in the heart of the source novel. Elmer is attracted to preaching (preaching, which bears roughly the same relation to the ministry that healing bears to institutionalized medicine), yet the attraction is not natural to him in that he possesses the vivacious and the enthused, but not the Jesuitical spirit. What he is by nature is a salesman, a *spieler* (from the German: gambler). Regardless of the structure of a piece of merchandise, and regardless of the quality any connoisseur might wish to find in it (even if only to aggrandize the self), there is no commercial "value" that does not originate in a pitch, some skillful orator's ability to describe, praise, extol, even worship something the potential buyer as yet doesn't know how to recognize as valuable. He has the fire. In the context of Sinclair Lewis's story, the salesman's fire is adapted to work under the tent, since here, if anywhere in the vast Midwest, and for the ineffable pleasures of wonder and submission, gather the lost multitudes who do not really know what God wants of them or, for that matter, what they want of God, save their everlasting hope that He will send down a cleansing fire to scour their everlasting sin. They are ripe for the picking.

This very ripeness, in fact, was the disturbance that put many studios off doing the film with Brooks. "I couldn't get anybody to make the movie," Brooks told Pat McGilligan. "Nobody would make it":

> As a matter of fact, we rented space from Columbia to do the movie, but Mr. DeMille and the guy who used to run Paramount [Y. Frank Freeman, vice president of Paramount since the mid-1930s] tried to stop the movie from being made. They thought it was antireligion. They thought it was un-American, not in the sense of Communism, but because it was the wrong image of America.[13]

He added a little tale of his encounter with Lewis at the Astor Bar on Times Square. "If you ever do make this into a movie," the author told young Brooks, "make a movie, don't make a book."[14]

Brooks deftly shows Elmer having the conviction and the spirit but needing the code words, the summoning "Open Sesame" to open the gloomy cave of doubt and despair to the Shaft of Gilding Light. One night, in front of Sharon Falconer's astounded eyes and ears, he makes an arrival in grand style, delivering to his flock not only the keys to their Kingdom but, as he sees it, the key to hers as well. This is the tale of "a very sad incident which I recently witnessed." Lancaster delivers this long speech as a wholesale tour de force, a Shakespearean soliloquy gone mercurial, almost verbatim from Lewis. I give it only in part, as the speech, mounting and mounting to an acrobatic height (ideal for Lancaster, of course), and in its steady ascension calling up images of Christ's Sermon on the Mount, is long, prolix, a tripper off the tongue. It's about Jim Leffingwell—Elmer pseudonymizes Jim Lefferts, a character prominent earlier in the book—who was "the best of good fellows, but he had fatal defects. He drank liquor, he smoked tobacco, he gambled, and I'm sorry to say that he did not always keep his tongue clean" (Elmer is describing, of course, himself). Jim's poor little daughter is stricken, "Oh, what a sad time that was to that household!," but only after the girl's passing does he come to Elmer in sobs, "Oh God, that I should have spent my life in wicked vices, and that the little one should have passed away knowing her dad was a sinner!":

> Thinking to comfort him, I said, "Old man, it was God's will that she be taken. You have done all that mortal man could do. The best of medical attention. The best of care."
>
> I shall never forget how scornfully he turned upon me. "And you call yourself a Christian!" he cried. "Yes, she had medical attention, but one thing was lacking—the one thing that would have saved her—I could not pray!"
>
> And that strong man knelt in anguish and for all my training in—in trying to explain the ways of God to my fellow business men, there was nothing to say. *It was too late!*
>
> Oh, my brothers, my fellow business men, are you going to put off repentance till it's too late?[15]

Ranting through this, at first a standing locomotive building up steam and finally a great iron monolith speeding down its single-minded track, Lancaster mounts on his face every fierce and tender expression in the book, ranges his voice as though he were a tenor singing "Mi chiamano Mimì," and himself appears, as we would observe, hurled into raptures of heavenly peace by the very thought of what earnest prayer can do. Can do, might have done, could perhaps do some day . . .

The continuing plot of the story and the film, Elmer's involvement with Sharon Falconer, her disillusionment with him and his with her, the entanglements of purpose and feeling that tear them asunder like a Flood and finally send the revival tent up in (holy) flames, are not of further interest to me here. There is something else that demands attention and that shows another way in which principles of adaptation roil at the center of the project. The actor Lancaster must adapt himself so as to become the evangelist Gantry. Burt transmogrified into Elmer. So that we can believe. So that as we are transfixed by him on the screen, he can heal us.

Once we believe in Elmer we will believe whatever he urges us to believe in, though all along we know how false his urging, how hollow his fanaticism, how craven his faith. We must believe, so that the film can both exist in its own form and continue forward each moment into the next, as films are meant to do.

## BURT'S GANTRY

Let us acknowledge that for the cinematic reproduction of the revival meeting—the hordes of spasmodically barking, babbling, kneeling souls—no astonishing talent is required in the actors given the roles. They can, each, be told to go wild, and their personal way of doing this can be observed, given small correction and shaping, and approved. The trick, and it is one of the true mysteries of the filming process, lies in arranging all these people in the screen rectangle, choreographing them into a coherent shot that, when the eye of the beholder is fixed upon it from a particular angle of view, seems to reveal not a section but a world. We need to see the floppy walls of the canvas forming a boundary (of divine flesh) inside the tent, and the frayed banners—"The Light of the Body is the EYE . . ."—drooping haphazardly enough to convince the viewer such decorations get strung up lackadaisically every night and taken down in the raw damp of morning. We need to see the flimsy chairs—no one really wants the worshipers sitting; the worshipers are only awaiting a cue to rise up. We must be given leave to see not only individual, tortured, and overstressed faces and bodies but whole masses of changing arm-raisers: farmers and businesspeople from the nearby town and dutiful wives and desirous adolescents, all these as a throbbing mass not only self-directed toward the apotheotic revelation promised by Elmer and Sharon but at the same time madly and incoherently ignorant, uncomprehending, blind followers of the resonating voice. For emphasis, a sycophant or two will be seen advancing with desperation toward Sharon's pulpit, straight out of Dostoyevsky—

> He saw many who came with sick children or grown-up relatives and besought the elder to lay his hands upon them and offer up a prayer over them, return very soon afterwards, and some even the next day, and fall

weeping on their knees before the elder, thanking him for healing their sick. Whether they had actually been healed or whether it was only a natural improvement in their health was a question that did not exist for Alyosha, for he fully believed in the spiritual powers of his teacher, whose fame he considered almost his own triumph.[16]

—but Brooks's camera is by the pulpit so that the figure is advancing toward us.

An important technical matter inflected the filmmaker's use of Lancaster. By the late 1950s this star was firmly established and broadly recognized. As well, he had emerged from a background in gymnastics at which he excelled. Being a man with a well-tuned athletic frame, he had posed before the camera not only in heightened dramatic moments but also in complex action scenes. He was a mover and shaker in Hollywood, having formed, with Harold Hecht and James Hill, the production company Hecht-Hill-Lancaster. Before Elmer prodded him he was a mover and shaker *already*. To see his fluency and expressivity, watch *Separate Tables* (1958), *Sweet Smell of Success* (1957), *The Rainmaker* (1956), *The Rose Tattoo* (1955), and *His Majesty O'Keefe* (1954), to choose only films recent to *Gantry*; and for action exertions *The Unforgiven* (1960), *Run Silent, Run Deep* (1958), *Gunfight at the O.K. Corral* (1957), *Trapeze* (1956), *Vera Cruz* and *Apache* (both 1954). In John Frankenheimer's physically demanding *The Train* (1964) and *The Gypsy Moths* (1969), Lancaster would do all his own stunts, including engine driving and sky diving. If Elmer was going to be a creature astoundingly magnetic here, now, and always, what could be done with the established astounding magnetism of Lancaster to bring it out with special flair? The answer was a pair of tactics. First, John Alton's wide-angle lens, in this case roughly 40mm, to produce a broadening spread of the facial features whenever the performer came close to it. Secondly, a blocking scheme that would repeatedly have the camera begin at a distance from Elmer and have him walk, stumble, or race toward it in an expanding zoom. One of Lancaster's brilliant achievements in this film is his control and regulation of facial and bodily expression *given that he knows himself to be performing to a wide-angle lens.* Less is more.

Lancaster manages to aggregate a group of symptoms into what we might call an evangelical syndrome:

[1] *Futurism.* A man hopes for, anticipates, plans for, then counts on tomorrow. "Tomorrow, and tomorrow, and tomorrow,/Creeps in this petty pace from day to day,/To the last syllable of recorded time;/And all our yesterdays have lighted fools/The way to dusty death." The past is but prologue. The American Way. On a very personal level, from one's foibles one gains strength. The Lord will help those who help themselves. And to embody this conviction and sensibility, to bring it to *present* life, because onscreen each instant is *present life*, Lancaster uses his posture, his gaze, the openness of his mouth in eagerness to find words, the persuasive cant of his shoulders—the whole expressive regime—to give the

effect of continually *leaning forward* into what is to come. He greets the future. This leaning forward can easily seem nothing more than an ecstasy of delight in promise, but with Elmer it is a hard-won striving for accomplishments that are never quite fully found. Thus the continuity of the striving, the everlastingness of the *vis a tergo* that is pushing him. Leaning into the lens is one way of showing this, but even when Elmer stands still we have a sense of his mind racing to the next spot on the game board, pre-calculating his interlocutor's moves. His pressing forward to make the acquaintance, then the intimacy of Sharon Falconer could make him seem aggressive, even, by today's remoter standards, a stalker. Not only does Elmer not give up the challenge, he openly shows his hunger, his feeling of obligation to work hard for what he most definitely wants, and what he wants is Sharon, not only her self, not only her ministry, not only her direct line to the Almighty, but her soul. For all the financial chicanery in the Falconer Revival operation, Elmer Gantry is the hardest-working individual we meet, the only one who doesn't take a break.

And because our Elmer doesn't take a break, we can esteem him as a personage with boundless, inexhaustible energy reserves, a man who even in deflation is thinking of what comes next. That he will be obstructed, waylaid, put a stop to, are all unimaginable in the face of his personality, and it is his personality that shines from the screen before any dictum or observation or exhortation. The personality triumphs over even the spirit, over the conditions, over the dangers of the moment, over even love. One of Henry Clay's self-made men, modeled after Benjamin Franklin, Frederick Douglass, Pierpont Morgan, yet born to low circumstances and therefore as he climbs through life making his progress through dirt, not gardens. Yet, as we see him, even more than success—with Falconer, with his flock, or with God—Elmer wants to be loved, loved for everything he is. "The principal imperialism the American exercises," writes Lerner, "is the imperialism of attraction. If he is not admired, he is envied; and even his enemies and rivals pay him the homage of imitation."[17] Elmer leans forward to the warm bonfire of other people's admiration and affection, perennially chilled to the bone and requiring some flood of warmth so he can keep going. Going and going and going.

In the sense of his bent for non-stop achievement, Elmer is an archetype of John Maynard Keynes's "purposive man":

> Purposiveness means that we are more concerned with the remote future results of our actions than with their own quality or their immediate effects on our own environment. The "purposive" man is always trying to secure a spurious and delusive immortality for his acts by pushing his interest in them forward into time. He does not love his cat, but his cat's kittens; nor, in truth, the kittens, but only the kittens' kittens, and so on forward for ever to the end of cat-dom.[18]

So, with Lancaster, the glow of Elmer's features is an advance reflection of tomorrow's shining sun, not today's; and what he aims for is what he prays for, a glittering success (sanctified or not) that is somehow, at each breath, just out of reach. This is a marvelous strategy for cinematic performance, of course, since it accompanies the unfurling of film itself by continually—key word, *continually*—urging us to feel, think, presume, and estimate *forward* to a terminus purely arbitrary that, if all conditions are right, will provoke us to pay at the box office tomorrow and tomorrow and tomorrow to see it again. Not a one of Elmer's evangelical triumphs, no twitching, foaming, barking, shrieking moment, could be as rich as the next one.

[2] *The Teeth of the Matter.* Early in the film, Elmer is in a bar when some waiflike canvassers for the Salvation Army come begging for Christmas donations. He finagles his drunken companions to cough up money, against their wishes even, but in doing this his triumphant maneuver, the spring that releases the catch, is a powerfully acrobatic approach to their faces (the camera) and, while leaning in and mouthing the key word "Love" (as only Burt Lancaster can say it), baring his pearly teeth. It is a smile of persuasion, the salesman's Great Trick, but also a smile of the most quintessential genuineness, so shapely are the stretched lips, so blinding are the teeth. The genuineness is both pure Lancaster (even in *Sweet Smell of Success*, one of his great triumphs, J. J. Hunsecker's malevolent narcissism is genuine) and pure Gantry, Gantry gazing out at the glowing river and *crooning*, "Shen-an-doah!"[19] In the book he is Sharon's humble (if hungry) disciple:

"You smoke, don't you?"
   "Why, yes."
"I smelled it. I hate it. Will you stop it? Entirely? And drinking?
"Yes. I will."
   And he did. It was an agony of restlessness and craving, but he never touched alcohol or tobacco again, and he really regretted that in evenings thus made vacuous he could not keep from an interest in waitresses.[20]

Much later in the film he meditates with a conviction born of whole self-sacrificing love (edged by whole self-concealing chicanery) on Sharon's everlasting blessing: "She don't hate ya, she love's ya. And what is love? Love is the mornin' and the evenin' star . . ." There is starlight in his gaze and his smile is as broad as heaven.

The Lancaster smile is a repetitive element in his screen performances, but it is nowhere used to more calculating effect than here, when he transmutes it into Elmer's smile. Elmer, the grinning monkey; but at the same time Elmer, the man whose smile is truth. Smile of understanding. Smile of optimism. Smile of forgiveness. Smile of hesitation, because he never does or can know what his urging will bring forth and so he is always riding the wave, perched on the blade of the knife, and always praying that success will come his way, here, now. The smile is at one time a token of the man's enormous expressive power, then—Joe E. Brown, Jerry Lewis, Martha Raye could all get the mouth *very* wide open, but not with this kind of a smile—and of his own dubiousness and self-doubt. Elmer is always praying. Elmer never stops praying. But until he falls under Sharon's odd spell, he is praying for himself.

For a movie star of the 1950s, as for those of the previous decades since the sound revolution, it was a commonplace that one could be known by their declarative power. The lungs, the trained articulation, the syllables correctly bitten off—in short, when a character spoke, one could understand what was being said and know the form of the sayer with a kind of intimacy. But Lancaster took verbal expressiveness to a new height, bolstering his diction with an athletically developed breathing that made it possible for him to produce sound in an extraordinary range from the whisper to the cry to heaven. He was a stage performer, now onscreen, now embodying a man who was a stage performer. Elmer Gantry had no truck with movies, he worked on a platform, and his audience was alive before him. When we see Elmer in full blaze we are hearing a voice, albeit a stage voice, shot up to heaven, directly addressing (as he would have his listeners believe, as he believed himself so far as we can see) the Ear of God. This is, of course, the voice that entranced me as a child when it came out of Oral Roberts's mouth. A conviction so shockingly loud it had to be true. But beyond the musical shaping Elmer was also producing—thanks to Lancaster alone—a chain of untouchable symbols woven into words, a language. He was speaking the language of redemption.

As to teeth and language, here is Marshall McLuhan (known in the period shortly after the release of *Elmer Gantry* as *the* media prophet):

> The Greek myth about the alphabet was that Cadmus, reputedly the king who introduced the phonetic letters into Greece, sowed the dragon's teeth, and they sprang up armed men. Like any other myth, this one capsulates a prolonged process into a flashing insight. The alphabet meant power and authority and control of military structures at a distance.[21]

McLuhan writes this in the context of noting how, "Because of its action in extending our central nervous system, electric technology seems to favor the inclusive and participational spoken word over the specialist written word."[22] Because of the way Lancaster's bright eyes beam at his listeners while he addresses them, because of his inclusive gesturing, because of those dental weapons he flashes, his invocations could not be more participational, as we see evidenced by the congregation's shrieking, trembling responses. It is as though Elmer's nervous system is extended by way of his voice into the nervous systems of his self-denigrating listeners. But the language, the clipping of sound, the articulation, the assemblage of meaningful glyphs into a vocative chain: all this is in those sparkling teeth. Lancaster demonstrates in character not only *what Elmer is preaching*, because the soundtrack nicely enough conveys the content of his sermons, but *that he is mouthing his exhortations*, that from a distance he is singing the army of his flock into the service of God.

Lancaster's notably crisp articulations are what Harold Innis would have referred to as marginally Semitic in origin:

> The Egyptians with an abundance of papyrus and the use of the brush had worked out an elaborate system of writing and the Babylonians with dependence on clay and the stylus had developed an economical system of writing. Semitic peoples borrowed the Sumerian system of writing but retained their language and in turn improved the system of writing through contacts with the Egyptians. The Phoenicians as a marginal Semitic people with an interest in communication and trade on the Mediterranean improved the alphabet to the point that separate consonants were isolated in relation to sounds.[23]

There is no way to hear the depths of Elmer's rants, to hear them all the way to his core, without recognizing the interest that was his supreme passion: communication and trade.

[3] *Cajolery*. Lancaster's Elmer, like so many other Lancaster characters in and around the 1960s, was a hunk (see Frank Perry's *The Swimmer* [1968]), one of those congregants who took to heart the sermon of Lewis's Eddie Fislinger (the hero's chum):

> A preacher has got to be just as husky and pack just as good a wallop as a prize-fighter. He ought to be able to throw out any roughneck that tries to interrupt his meetings, and still more, strength makes such a hit with the women in his congregation.[24]

With the congregants he is in fact tender and restrained, using the muscles of his voice to extend his declarative gaze as a fist. There is no mistaking that he is the sort of (special) man willing to fight for God's attention, on his own and on his listeners' behalf. A pugnacious preacher who scraps with argument. A warrior for Jesus who sees his way to the temple—the tent of Sharon's sovereignty—and will be tangled by no vines, affronted by no phalanx of fiduciary shields in getting there. Her manager/escort Cecil (Dean Jagger at his best) is smarmy and sophisticated, a weak, too self-assured winner, until Elmer converts him to stone and topples him.

As a preacher, the cinematic Elmer's main technique is the same as the salesman's in executing persuasion. You take somebody who doesn't want to go your way, you show them how they are essentially wrong in this refusal, you urge them with a promise and a smile to change direction, and you offer them a warm berth on your schooner. "Nobody dast blame this man," we hear of Willy Loman in the finale of Arthur Miller's immediately postwar *Death of a Salesman*:

> You don't understand; Willy was a salesman; and for a salesman, there is no rock bottom to the life. He don't put a bolt to a nut, he don't tell you the law, or give you medicine. He's a man way out there in the blue, riding on a smile and a shoeshine; and when they start not smiling back—boy, that's an earthquake. And then you get yourself a couple of spots on your hat, and you're finished. Nobody dast blame this man. A salesman is got to dream, boy; it comes with the territory.[25]

Elmer is a salesman, too, one of the vast American multitude who traffic in the Age of the Pitch. Lancaster goes beyond showing us Elmer's spiel *as* a spiel, even to the extent of hinting at the backstage behind the wings to which he ducks his consciousness once in a while. And the actor uses a spiel of his own to sell us Elmer Gantry. The point Brooks's film needs to establish involves our own credulousness, after all; our own savvy x-ray vision that always assuredly detects the sewer beneath the spiel. Recognizing the famous star Burt Lancaster (in 1960 he was one of the titans of Hollywood), can we manage to dissolve him into the river of blissful forgetfulness and see in his stead only a desperado hawker turned to God's tent? Can we believe in Elmer, in the way that any accomplished salesman would have us believe in his product? Because if the coins in the hat are Elmer's product, the produce that he harvests from the dry fields he must roam, Lancaster's Elmer himself is largely Brooks's goods. Brooks can fashion his film out of Lewis because he recognizes the salesman in himself.

[4] *Fox*. You cannot sell a stranger without dancing. Or without breathing, either. And for creatures like Elmer Gantry, it is the body breath enters and exits, not the spirit. He is finally a man of the body, a detail the casting of Burt Lancaster makes manifest. The blood of desire courses in him as much as the blood of principle (to be heeded or skirted). A woman named Lulu Bains (Shirley Jones) has alleged to the press that Gantry took advantage of her. This trope is inflected by Lewis with a sneering edge that is missing in the film, where finally the touting headline "ELMER GANTRY CLEARED OF MORALS CHARGE" lifts the pall. But in the novel, back in the bedroom of Mizpah Theological Seminary, Brother Gantry is confronted by his roommate Frank Shallard about it:

> "You look here, Shallard! I'm not going to have you poking your long nose into my business, and that's all there is to it, see?"

"Yes, it would be if you were a layman and I had no official connection with this outfit. I don't believe too much in going around being moral for other people. But you're the preacher here—you're an ordained minister—and I'm responsible with you for the welfare of this church, and I'm damned if I'm going to watch you seducing the first girl you get your big sweaty hands on—Oh, don't go doubling up your fists. Of course you could lick me. But you won't . . .

"Now, by God, if you think I'm going to stand—Let me tell you right now, you've got the filthiest mind I ever heard of, Shallard! Why you should think I intend for one single second to be anything but friendly and open and aboveboard with Lulu—with Miss Bains— . . .[26]

With the Elmer on the page and the Elmer on the screen, one so fleshed out and with such a quickness (since in adapting a text to film one always knows that strung out on the page however deftly the cold letters of an ancient alphabet will in the fire of transposition warm the skin), with both these Elmers, the one on the page and the one on his feet, we have not the smallest doubt of the man's pugnacious sophistry. Lancaster's Elmer would use fewer words, more teeth. Yet Shallard is right, of course (but not in the script). He has teased out Elmer's hidden motives (that Lancaster gives over in mime). The pretender is always caching a motive, and Lancaster's Elmer is a vibrant pretender, but also, crucially, thoroughgoing as a performer. He makes himself a character (a character behind the character), showing flaws through which underlying intent glows. Of course, in the real Burt Lancaster's veneer, so beautifully and invisibly laid on, there are no such flaws. The undetectable Lancaster is giving us the adamant but so very detectable Gantry.

Elmer's balance, a matter of keen importance to him, is that of a tightrope walker (again, courtesy of the actor's expertise). He must always be poised between an ambitious move ahead and a darting retrenchment should anyone spot him, and this equivocal stance hands over to the viewer a tension-filled entertainment in which we can never be certain whether the hero—for all his gaffes and forwardness, we cannot cease loving Elmer—will succeed. And he himself has no certainty, of course; he is no Tom Jones redux. It is his urgent struggle toward the light, the same light that makes the teeth shine and the heavens illuminate, that endears him, that makes us see how vital, how alive is the character's quest and how vital, how almost alive is the film for bringing us close. The Lewis novel was a rational recounting of the conversion—or semi-conversion—of a confidence man, a poseur who finally comes to pray, "Dear Lord, thy work is but begun! We shall yet make these United States a moral nation!" An entire nation to be healed!—a sound and investible sentiment, to be sure, in light of the perils of agriculture and the potholes of commerce. But with Lancaster in its wheelhouse, the film never steers a course toward rational development. There is always a sunset to squint at desirously, always footholds to secure for a new tomorrow.

Finally, however, the new tomorrow shows a somber, tragic gray morning with the wind gone from the sails. The previous night a conflagration devoured the revival tent like a fiery mouth from heaven, ate it up whole, and pretty Sister Sharon with it. She had been in process of mouthing a flaming invocation: "At this very moment the power of the holy ghost has descended on this tabernacle. He is here—here right now. Just now I saw an omen, a fiery line written by the hand of god and a glorious shooting star. Have we not faith? Because without faith we are morally sick." In the book, she has been exhorting the frantic, milling crowd: "Who will trust the Lord God of Hosts? Now we'll try our faith!" And Elmer, falling into a black cloud of retreat,

> grasped Sharon's arm again. In a voice abject with fear he shouted, "For God's sake, beat it! We can't wait!"
> She had an insane strength; she thrust him away so sharply that he fell against a chair, bruising his knee. Furious with pain, senseless with fear, he raged, "You can go to hell!" and galloped off, pushing aside the last of the hysterical choir.[27]

Lewis has the life of Elmer Gantry march on for almost another two hundred pages, as he puts the Falconer revival into the past. But it is 1960, still the age of movie stars, and Brooks needs a conventional dyadic coupling to fuel the motor. With Sharon dead, the film must take its final breath (one the Catholic Legion of Decency didn't like),[28] with chastened, depleted Elmer picking up his little suitcase and walking away.

## NOTES

1. See further my *A Dream of Hitchcock* (Albany: SUNY Press, 2019), p. 201 ff.
2. Kate Buford, *Burt Lancaster: An American Life* (New York: Da Capo Press, 2001), p. 201.
3. Max Lerner, *America as a Civilization* (New York: Simon & Schuster, 1957), p. 107.
4. Ibid. p. 141.
5. Quoted in Lerner, *America as a Civilization*, p. 143.
6. Ibid. p. 147.
7. Sinclair Lewis confided to Pat McGilligan that he and Mencken were in an everlasting fight (59). See Pat[rick]McGilligan, "Richard Brooks: The Professional," interview with Richard Brooks, in *Backstory 2: Interviews with Screenwriters of the 1940s and 1950s* (Berkeley: University of California Press, 1991), pp. 27–72.
8. Lerner, *America as a Civilization*, p. 707.
9. Sinclair Lewis, *Elmer Gantry* (New York: New American Library, 1970 [1927]), p. 156.
10. Ibid. p. 197.
11. Fyodor Dostoyevsky, *The Brothers Karamazov*, trans. David Magarshack (London: Penguin, 1958), p. 31.
12. Lewis, *Elmer Gantry*, pp. 51–3.
13. McGilligan, "Richard Brooks," p. 58.
14. Ibid. p. 59.

15. Lewis, *Elmer Gantry*, p. 172.
16. Dostoyevsky, *The Brothers Karamazov*, p. 31.
17. Lerner, *America as a Civilization*, p. 61.
18. John Maynard Keynes, *Essays in Persuasion* (New York: W. W. Norton, 1963), p. 200, as quoted in Norman O. Brown, *Life Against Death: The Psychoanalytical Meaning of History* (Middletown, CT: Wesleyan University Press, 1959), pp. 107–8.
19. Lewis, *Elmer Gantry*, p. 179.
20. Ibid. p. 175.
21. Marshall McLuhan, *Understanding Media: The Extensions of Man* (New York: Signet, 1964), p. 82.
22. Ibid.
23. Harold Adams Innis, *The Bias of Communication* (Toronto: University of Toronto Press, 1952), p. 7.
24. Lewis, *Elmer Gantry*, p. 86.
25. Arthur Miller, *Death of a Salesman* (New York: Dramatists Play Service, Inc., 1980 [1948]), p. 101.
26. Lewis, *Elmer Gantry*, p. 107.
27. Ibid. p. 220.
28. McGilligan, "Richard Brooks," p. 59.

CHAPTER 13

# "Monstrous Cinemascope": Richard Brooks Adapts *Sweet Bird of Youth* (1962)

*William H. Epstein*

> As soon as I saw that first big close-up of myself on that monstrous Cinemascope, I tell you, I ran right out of there! I screamed for a taxi, and I haven't stopped running since.
> —Alexandra Del Lago, in Brooks's film, remembering the terrifying preview of her comeback movie

Richard Brooks's wide-screen adaptation (1962)[1] of Tennessee Williams's *Sweet Bird of Youth* (1959) is shadowed by and projected onto the metaphorics of the monstrous. The trope appears frequently in both the play and the film, the essential conflict of which is neatly summarized in Alexandra Del Lago's famous formulation—"When monster meets monster, one monster must give way, AND IT WILL NEVER BE ME"[2]—and self-loathingly elaborated and confessed in the flashbacked memory of her comeback preview, words and images that writer-director Brooks (trying to resuture the Broadway play's meta-theatrically modernist, subversively estranged dramatic language and design into a more or less familiar Hollywood commercial product) slyly and reflexively added to a film he was forced, against his artistic judgment and hard-won professional experience, to shoot in Cinemascope.

The *locus classicus* for the conceptual practice of "monstrous Cinemascope" is probably Richard Fleischer's *20,000 Leagues Under the Sea* (1954), based on Jules Verne's classic novel, one of Hollywood's earliest Cinemascope films and the Disney Studio's very first. As J. P. Telotte has convincingly argued, virtually everything about this movie is monstrous (in various senses of the term: enormous, hideous, terrifying, unnatural, malformed, repellent, evil, abject): the wide-screen process itself, of course, as well as the budget, the hype, the risk, the special effects, the language, the visual style, and, most tellingly perhaps, the narrative. The story is driven by an expeditionary quest for a mysterious, ship-sinking, South-Sea monster, which turns out to be the prototype submarine, *Nautilus*, created by its mad-scientist Captain Nemo (James Mason), a "self-professed 'avenger' against humanity's own monstrous nature," a human "monster" himself, whose "facial features" in "extreme [Cinemascope-distorting] close-ups . . . as he plays his organ" "evok[e] a cinematic tradition of monstrous madmen, specifically recalling" here Lon Chaney in *The Phantom of the Opera* (1925).[3] Nemo is rehumanized and redeemed in the battle against the giant squid, a "more traditional cinematic monster," and in his decision to blow up his nuclear-powered home-island base, "produc[ing] a familiar mushroom cloud" that "marks the final monster of the film."[4] These and other "shifting notions of the monstrous" in the film[5] indicate as well a "narrative instability . . . that betokens an effort, both within the culture and the Disney studio at this time," as well as within the general Hollywood community, "to negotiate different points of view on" paradigm-shifting "technological" innovation.[6]

One of that community's most established movie-makers (the 1960 Academy Award winner for Best Adapted Screenplay), Brooks was especially conflicted by its emergent wide-screen technology and the consequent narrative instability and cinematographic redesigning it induced—hence, as we shall see, his seizing this opportunity to become a kind of blasphemous mad scientist, who, cleverly redeploying the monstrous language of Williams's play and the implicitly monstrous praxis of adaptation itself, deviously subverted as he was re-enacting Hollywood's exploitation and disfigurement, celebration and abjection of the splendors and horrors of modern American life.

\*

But, first, let's establish the trope. Brooks introduces the monstrous in a scene that isn't in the play, the *Citizen-Kane*-like newsreel[7] about Boss Finley (Ed Begley)'s career, in which his political opponent, Professor Smith (James Chandler), displays the gnarly rubber monster masks worn by the Finley Youth Club "hoodlums" who "invaded his home" and "burned books and paintings on his lawn." Later, in a bedroom-scene moment preserved from the play, Chance Wayne (Paul Newman)—placing Alexandra (Geraldine Page)'s oxygen mask (she gets panic attacks)[8] on his own face, a bit of business almost certainly imported from the Elia Kazan-directed Broadway production in which both Newman and Page appeared—reassures the Princess Kosmonopolis (the alias the actress has adopted in her flight into "oblivion")[9] that she doesn't, as she fears, "look hideous in it": "You just look exotic. Like a Princess from Mars or a big magnified insect," a likely reference to 1950s sci-fi monster flicks like

*Them* (1954) and *Tarantula* (1955), to which we shall return. A little later in this bedroom scene, after she seems disappointed that he didn't "molest" her while she was passed out in a drunken stupor, Chance qualifies his earlier characterization: "I like you. You are a nice monster," to which, with a line Brooks adds, she replies, "Well, I was born a monster."

Alexandra's first recalled memory of her comeback, most of the language (and some of the imagery) of which is in Williams's play-script, is presented, in part, as if she were in a horror film.[10] "The screen is a very clear mirror. There is a thing, God help us, called a close-up," she begins, staring into a mirror, triggering a flashback to a voice yelling "Playback!" and a huge camera lens filling up and jutting out of Brooks's Cinemascope screen. Next, as the lens moves menacingly forward, we hear Alexandra's voiceover: "The camera dollies in . . . and you are caught in the frame with the lights blazing . . . and all your terrible history screams while you smile."

Then, after Brooks cuts to the premiere, we hear the audience muttering and tittering at this same close-up moment, and a teenage girl saying (a Brooks addition), "I thought she was dead and buried," a vampiric allusion that sends Alexandra running out of the theater, panicky, pitching forward onto the pavement outside, as the crowd, which has fawned over her on her glamorous way in, now ridicules her. Back in the bedroom, still staring into the mirror, Alexandra closes the memory, once again echoing Williams's horror-film language: "After that . . . flight. Running away from that frightful comeback. And I've never stopped running, until now."

Later in this extended bedroom scene comes the most quoted line from the play. After Chance tapes her talking about smuggling hashish into the country and tries to blackmail her, Alexandra dismisses his clumsy criminality: "When monster meets monster, one monster has to give way and it will never be

Figure 13.1 Alexandra Del Lago's (Geraldine Page) monstrous close-up.

me"[11]—not exactly the original *King Kong vs. Godzilla*, also released in 1962, but a familiar enough monster-movie plot-point that Williams, an avid moviegoer from his adolescence on,[12] was probably invoking and to which we shall return. The play continues to develop this trope at great length, in scene after scene (for example: "I wasn't always this monster"; "I'm not that kind of monster"; "the country of the flesh-hungry, blood-thirsty ogre"; "Don't leave me. If you do I'll turn into the monster again"; "Monsters don't die early. They hang on long"; "Face it—pitiful monster . . . We are two monsters, but with this difference between us"),[13] but Brooks deploys it only three more times, each time in a piece of dialogue he invents for the screenplay. After Alexandra finally offers him a screen test, Chance starts a sentence, "Oh, Princess, you are a glorious, beautiful, lovely—" that Alexandra finishes, "—monster!" Then the passage with which this chapter began, and to which we shall be returning later, when Alexandra, on the phone with Walter Winchell, recalls the memory of the premiere for a second time with the phrase "monstrous Cinemascope." And finally—with a spoken line and another mirrored, framed, monstrous close-up that recapitulates the trope's first appearance in the monster masks and its subsequent deployment as a reflection of the way that the movies exploit and disfigure, celebrate and abject, beauty, youth, heteronormative romance, and the American dream—comes this moment of horror. After Tom Junior (Rip Torn) has spreadeagled Chance on the hood of a car and battered in his face, he drags him to the driver's side-mirror and, showing him the bloody, mutilated result, spits out, "No woman will ever again pay to love that face."

\*

For Williams, "monstrosity" was habitually inflected by his tortured sense of himself as, to employ diverse senses of the term and its cognates, "an imaginary creature, part animal, part human"[14] or, by extension, "something repulsively unnatural, an abomination; a thing which is outrageously or offensively wrong,"[15] that is, as a gay artist "malformed"[16] (a Kristevan queer theorist might say "abjected") by a strict religious upbringing against which he struggled to rebel, a late-arriving (homo)sexuality obsessively and at times dangerously pursued, and a poetic sensibility striving to express "wicked or depraved"[17] personal longings in commercial entertainment venues (Broadway and Hollywood) dominated by (as D. H. Lawrence, one of Williams's favorite writers, would have it) "the bitch-goddess Success."[18] Indeed, Williams characteristically thought, spoke, and wrote of himself and his autobiographical fictional and dramatic personae in this way: "as if I were an uncaged monster which perhaps I was";[19] "How on earth did I explain to myself, at that time, the fascination of his physical being without, at the same time, confessing to myself that I was a little monster of sensuality?";[20] reassuring the actress Anna Magnani that she was *his* kind of monster, because "all good artists [are] monsters . . . in the sense of departing extravagantly from the norm";[21] "Who am I/A wounded man, badly bandaged,/A monster among angels or angel among monsters";[22] "'I'm a peculiar blend of the pragmatist and the Romanticist and the crocodile. The monster,' he told *The Miami Herald* in the [19]70s."[23] "By 1958," his most recent biographer, John Lahr, observes, "the term 'monster' was one that he regularly applied to himself, a defining descriptor in the idiom of his 'out-crying heart.' 'I am a monster, but I don't hurt anybody by plan or intention,' he wrote to Kazan as they were reworking *Sweet Bird of Youth*" for its Broadway premiere.[24] Edmund White waggishly reticulates the confluence of monstrosity, sexuality, artistry, and commercial success we have been tracing here. "I mean he [Williams] loved Broadway, and he loved having a hit. I heard him say towards the end of his life, 'If I had one more hit I would fuck a monkey.'"[25]

\*

For Brooks, "monstrosity" was associated with Hollywood, with the money, power, fame, and success induced by movie-making, as well as with ethnic and religious assimilation and deracination. Brooks was a notoriously difficult director who terrorized casts and (especially) crews—angry, demanding, "tough as nails" (the title of Douglass K. Daniel's biography), to the extent that his second wife, the actress Jean Simmons, felt she had to defend him from "the talk that her husband was a monster, and an eccentric, their marriage a variation of the fabled Beauty and the Beast."[26] Brooks himself associated movie-making, at least the Hollywood-studio version of it through which he had risen to prominence, with monstrosity: "'You know, these were pretty monstrous bastards who were running the studios at that time. But they gave me a chance . . . And I learned from some great people. The Mayers, the Warners, the Cohns— they did terrible things, but they *loved* movies!'"[27] Moreover, from a certain mid-twentieth-century high-art perspective, the movies themselves (as both a cultural artifact and an industry) could be considered monstrous, an "unnaturally large"[28] and "congenitally malformed"[29] phenomenon: as "a middle-aged New York actor with a fake British accent" puts it in *The Producer* (1951), Brooks's Hollywood-insider novel, "'Movies are a curiosity like a giant idiot.'"[30]

Indeed, *The Producer* insinuates the ironically inflected ambivalence, tough-minded but guilt-ridden, with which Brooks interpolated his immersion in Hollywood movie-making as well as his own and his Jewish-dominated industry's liminal status in American society.[31] Born Reuben Sax in Philadelphia in 1912 to Russian-Jewish immigrants, he was known professionally as Richard Brooks from 1936 and legally changed his name in 1943.[32] As Mr. Flax (note the resemblance to "Sax"), the studio head in the novel, says to Matt Gibbons (né Grubow), the title-character: "'Never trust a Jew who changes his name or smokes a pipe.'"[33]

Brooks himself, of course, did both. In the novel, Matt goes home to Philadelphia to see his estranged father, to whom he confesses his own malformation, the deracination and self-loathing induced by the financially expedient compromises of post-WWII American capitalist triumphalism (of which Hollywood is the quintessential instance and reflection). "'I was ashamed of you. You are my father, and I was ashamed of you.'" "'You know what I wanted, Papa? I wanted success. That's the only thing that mattered to me: success. Not the work I do, only the success from it . . . I don't believe in myself, Papa. I'm a fake.'"[34]

\*

Brooks's interpolation of "monstrous Cinemascope" into the screenplay of *Sweet Bird of Youth* is an excellent example of how he struggled for (what he consistently called) "control"[35] in his career-long guerrilla warfare with the monstrous bastards running the studios. Although he had managed to resist filming in Cinemascope for *Elmer Gantry* (1960), M-G-M, shooting more and more movies in a wide-screen format it hoped would draw customers away from their TV screens, was now insisting on it. As Brooks said in a 1965 *Movie* interview, when asked if he had wanted to make an intimate picture like *Sweet Bird* in Cinemascope: "I never want to make anything in CinemaScope, but it's no use any more. I've given up the battle . . . You can't beat the rap . . . I don't find it conducive to compose the scene well, unless you have a mass scene."[36] Thus "monstrous Cinemascope": a phrase which expresses not only Alexandra's self-loathing terror of her own "unnaturally large" and "hideously frightening" screen image but also Brooks's slyly reflexive disdain for the "deviating from the conventional" (non-Academy ratio), "extraordinarily large dimensions" of the wide-screen format itself.[37]

"But," as he acknowledged in the same interview, "when it came to those scenes in *Sweet Bird* with dual images, I had no problems. I felt thankful for the process."[38] Brooks is referring here to the many flashback scenes, triggered by Chance's or Alexandra's remembering, with which he opened up the play, bridged the narrative gaps in Williams's fragmented plot lines, and cinematically reconceptualized the Broadway production's rather experimental, meta-theatrical, minimalist "stage language" (design elements dominated by projections and filmic lighting effects).[39] The sheer breadth of the wide screen enabled Brooks to enlarge and transform the familiar practice of the flashback lap dissolve into, as he put it, lingering side-by-side "dual images" in which present and past narrative lines momentarily share visual space—another kind of monster, if you will, an unconventionally hybridized narrative device which disgusted some reviewers ("Screen elephantiasis . . . with irrelevant iris-flashbacks") and thrilled others ("ingenious flashbacks that skillfully blend the past with the present").[40]

The visual and (for Brooks and other 1950s directors still clinging to the Academy ratio)[41] professional monstrosity of Cinemascope is also, of course, entangled in the fraught relationship between the rise of television ("the small screen") and the decline of the studio system and the mass-cultural prominence of the movies, a relationship that, perhaps a little surprisingly, informs *Sweet Bird* as both play and film.[42] For the Broadway premiere, "to help carry off" what he saw as a "weak second act" he couldn't get Williams to improve, Kazan "introduced"—"for the projection of Boss Finley's [violently racist, nationally televised] speech"—what one reviewer called "an overwhelming theatrical *tour de force*":[43] "a huge television screen" (actually, a back-projected film simulating a live television program, "in creating the effect" of which the great set and lighting designer Jo Mielziner sought "the advice of experts from MGM," which had already bought the film rights) that occupied most of the cyclorama at the back of the stage.[44] Thus Kazan and Mielziner merged two monstrosities, the brutally overwhelming terror of Boss Finley's political machine (paralleling his abusive, patriarchal dominance of his family) with the explosive growth and pervasive impact of this new technology which, seemingly, has expanded out of all proportion to the (accustomed) size of its image.

Brooks's film reorders the size and prominence of these two emerging and competing visual technologies. Cinemascope, as we have seen, is now monstrous, the innovative industrial process and business strategy terrorizing its own practitioners as it tries to lure customers out of their living rooms and back into the theaters.[45] Television, in a new scene suggested by an incident Miss Lucy narrates in the play, is minimized and debased, associated with personal betrayal and sexual inadequacy, reduced to two aggravating sets in her room, violent scenes of gunplay blaring away unwatched on both.

Figure 13.2 Boss Finley (Ed Begley) in Miss Lucy's (Madeleine Sherwood) room before a television showing a scene of violence.

As Boss Finley, intent on punishing her for writing on a ladies' room mirror that he "is too old to cut the mustard," comes in the room, he angrily turns off the TVs before he smashes her finger in the jewel box he is pretending to give her. The actual televising of his speech, which demanded an enormous production enterprise on Broadway but would have been a simple enough thing to reproduce on film, is never shown in the movie, suggested only by the presence of a comparatively small, unintimidating TV camera at the rally.

\*

In the play, Chance and Heavenly are never on stage together. Their romance is all in the past, ruined, irrecoverable, something she can acknowledge even if he can't. She appears in only one scene, in which she asks her father, "Papa, you married for love, why wouldn't you let me do it, while I was alive inside and the boy still clean, still decent?" The scene ends with Boss Finley threatening to mutilate, if not kill, Chance, unless she will "stand there beside me" as he gives his television speech. "I'm going to remove him, he's going to be removed from St. Cloud. How do you want him to leave, in that white Cadillac he's riding around in, or in that scow that totes the garbage out to the dumping place in the Gulf?" Chance, of course, doesn't leave town, and, as "*The curtain closes*," he is waiting alone on "the forestage" for Tom Junior and his henchmen to come in and castrate him.[46] In this and so many other ways (the venereal disease Chance gives Heavenly, the hysterectomy she endures as a result, Boss Finley's brutal treatment of his wife and Miss Lucy, Chance's gigolo career, his and Alexandra's "monstrous" relationship), Williams's *Sweet Bird of Youth* is a travesty of the heterosexual-romance plot of traditional commercial theater—a familiar contention about many of Williams's plays that has characteristically been associated, by contemporaneous reviewers and retrospective scholars and critics, with his queerness in both sexual practice and artistic vision.

In the film, Heavenly (Shirley Knight) is in nine scenes, in three of which she and Chance are together: two flashbacks (a montage of her dancing with him and watching him dive; the long, intimate lighthouse scene) and the final scene, in front of her home, when, telling her father, "Papa, I'm never coming into that house again," she drives away, reunited at last with Chance, bloody and mutilated but finally off the "merry-go-round" to "Successville" he has been futilely riding. As R. Barton Palmer and William Robert Bray's essential study of the films made from Williams's work reminds us, heterosexual "romantic fulfillment (the 'constitution of the couple,' as academic theory terms it)" was perhaps the most deeply engrained narrative plot in "the classic Hollywood film,"[47] a hegemony already being challenged in the forties and fifties by an array of sensationalized family melodramas (the new woman's pictures, small adult pictures, and European imports) that explored the boundaries of what could be shown and said by a film industry in transition. "Williams' dramatic texts ['providing shock and sensation in carefully calibrated doses'] played a key role as source material in this profitable development of adult films in crisis-ridden Hollywood, beginning a trend that would culminate during the late sixties in the institutionalization of the adult film and the ratings system that now defines it."[48] "A kind of sequel in the traditional Hollywood sense"[49] to M-G-M's very successful *Cat on a Hot Tin Roof*, also adapted and directed by Brooks and starring Paul Newman,[50] *Sweet Bird* similarly reconstitutes the couple and reinstitutes heterosexual romantic fulfillment as, yet again, Brooks "brilliant[ly]" reconfigures a bifurcated dramatic narrative Williams and Kazan barely managed to reconcile.[51] And yet, as we have seen, the language and imagery of monstrosity, already permeating Williams's *Sweet Bird* and, to a certain extent, already influenced by Williams's own inveterate movie-going and cinematically inflected theatrical imagination, also gave Brooks a way to subtly and reflexively undermine this industrial imperative to un-queer his movie's source, and thus to reinstantiate its shocking sensationalism.

Harry Benshoff's groundbreaking *Monsters in the Closet: Homosexuality and the Horror Film* (1997) helps us understand the cultural attitudes, financial exigencies, and generic conventions underpinning this persistence. Building on the work of Michel Foucault and Robin Woods, Benshoff connects "the horror film" and the monsters that inhabit them to queerness and industrial filmmaking: "Since the demands of the classical Hollywood narrative system usually insist on a heterosexual romance within the stories they construct, the monster is traditionally figured as a force that attempts to block that romance," and thus "many monster movies (and the source material they draw upon) might be understood as being 'about' the eruption of some form of queer sexuality into the midst of a resolutely heterosexual milieu."[52] Benshoff provides numerous instructive instances of this monstrous queering from the early thirties (most famously, the "queer 'domestic' couple[s]"[53] in James Whale's *Frankenstein* movies and Todd Browning's *Dracula* and *Freaks*) through the forties (most notoriously, Val Lewton's noirish Satanists and lesbian cat people), but more directly pertinent here are the queer monsters and monster movies alluded to or suggested by the play and the film. "[T]he sado-masochistic monstrous couple so often played by [Boris] Karloff and [Bela] Lugosi"[54] in the late thirties and forties recalls the "when monster meets monster" power dynamics of Chance and Alexandra's relationship. The "actively heterosexual couple" of the 1950s monster-invasion movies—"menaced by something unknown, something queer," like "the giant, irradiated egg-laying ants of *Them* (1954)," thus "blurring or 'queering' the usual explanatory binaries (technology/nature, male/female, science/religion)"[55]—invokes not only Chance's "Like a Princess from Mars or a big magnified insect" remark but also the various ways in which Boss Finley's "Voice of God" boundary-crossing manipulations destroy his marriage and Heavenly and Chance's "clean" and "decent" love. Yet other 1950s sci-fi monster movies, in which alien invaders insinuate themselves into the bodies and homes of small-town American couples (*Invasion of the Body Snatchers* [1956], *I Married a Monster from Outer Space* [1958], *Attack of the 50 Foot Woman* [1958]), reveal the terrifying mutability of gender and gender relations, as they remind us that Alexandra Del Lago is not only, like Williams's other "hothouse hot-blooded 'earth mothers' and drag queens[,] . . . unmistakably a product of the fifties" and "of his own baroquely transvestized homosexual fantasies,"[56] but also yet another kind of monster, a movie star, a larger-than-life screen persona, commercial product, and performative identity—the profane "legend that I was and the ruin of that legend" (as the self-loathing Alexandra would have it), a metaphorical fifty-foot woman who has outgrown Cold War American domesticity, "an ontological oddity, a being whose membership in categories like biological sex [as well as cultural gender and social role] is often unstable and a sham."[57]

The extent to which Brooks was willing to pursue this monstrously cunning deconstruction of the heterosexual romance-fulfillment plot that he had been hired to reintroduce into this very valuable property upon which M-G-M was lavishing wide-screen production values can be measured by a new final scene he wrote and which, he claimed in a story he told often and well, the studio thwarted:[58]

> I had a different ending for Sweet Bird, but they wouldn't let me use it . . . You dissolve, in my other ending, straight to the ferry. At the beginning of the picture you saw the ferry as they arrive. They have to leave by the same ferry. The Princess and Lucy are leaving in the car and they stop for a moment. Once they're on the ferry boat, they're out of that town. They're very relieved, and they light cigarettes. The boat slows down, toots its horn, pulls away a little bit to cross over, because passing is a garbage scow. On that scow is Chance Wayne. That's all. Not another word is said, because at the beginning of the picture, the old man said to his daughter—You want him to leave this town on a garbage scow? But M.G.M. said—Hey! You can't do that. He came for the girl. He doesn't get the girl. So they said—We'll let you shoot it after we've had the preview, and, of course, they never did.

This is precisely the kind of grotesque, disgusting image of human waste invoked by Julia Kristeva's theory of abjection, which underlies much recent horror-film academic criticism (as, for instance, in this summary by Jay McRoy): "For Kristeva, abject materials like semen, blood, feces, severed limbs, and corpses externalize the repressed understanding of our own physical corruptibility; they trouble the tenuous distinctions between interior and exterior, as well as self and other, that we invent to create the illusion of ourselves as discrete and coherent beings."[59] As Steffen Hankte has demonstrated, a 1950s sci-fi monster movie like *Tarantula* (1955) conjoins "horror and science fiction: abjection and technoscience." The horror of monstrous abjection arises not only "from the massive spider's body" but also from "the grotesquely disfigured body of its [contaminated] scientist creator"—an "abject spectacle" but also a "physical transformation mark[ing] a significant psychological shift that, in effect, humanizes him."[60] The ending to *Sweet Bird of Youth* that Brooks didn't shoot—Paul Newman's beautiful movie-star face and body, disfigured and discarded, lying in a pile of garbage—is just this kind of horrific abject spectacle: itself a kind of grotesque monster of filmmaking that threatens the destabilizing but humanizing "eruption of some form of queer sexuality into the midst of a resolutely heterosexual milieu"[61] and thus cannot, must not, be shown.

\*

The morning after Alexandra agrees to sign over some Travelers Checks to Chance and they finally have sex, she awakes to the sound of church bells. "What are those lovely bells?" she asks him, in an exchange Brooks adds to the screenplay. "Why, madam, it is Easter Sunday." "How fitting," she responds, "I feel positively reborn." Williams's tragic vision would never have accommodated this profanely narcissistic identification with the Risen Christ of Easter Sunday: in the play, Alexandra is not reborn to divine apotheosis, and enjoys only "*a little, very temporary, return to . . . spurious glory.*"[62] Indeed, after the revelatory phone call with the (fictional) gossip columnist Sally Powers, during which Alexandra learns that her comeback has in fact been a success, Williams inserts an unusual interpretive "Note" into the play-script: "*The report from Sally Powers may be and probably is accurate; but to indicate she is going on to further triumph would be to falsify her future.*" She too is "*faced with castration, and she knows it.*"[63] But the movie doubles down on the Christ imagery. On the phone now with (the real-life) Walter Winchell, Alexandra is being distracted, as in the play, by Chance, who wants her to tell the columnist about him. "Oh, go into the bathroom," she hisses at Chance, twisting around on the bed away from the phone in her hand and the camera (placed, unusually, in a wide and low "theatrical" Cinemascope position),[64] "and stick your head under cold," a brief pause while she turns back to the phone and the camera, "water. Walter, now tell me." By using Winchell's first name, by eliminating the pauses before and after the name ("Sally" in the play), and by adding a pause before "water" and then immediately voicing its near homonym after it, Brooks's screenplay effectively changes "water" into "Walter," an equally profane and trivializing echo of what is generally considered Christ's first miracle, changing water into wine during the wedding at Cana.[65]

Brooks's "monstrous Cinemascope" interpolation, which comes a little earlier in this phone call, as Alexandra offers Winchell a short version of her horror-film experience of the premiere, prepares the way for and comments upon these Christological figurations. Advertently or inadvertently, Brooks is invoking what the radical philosopher Slovoj Žižek, discussing "the paradox" of Resurrection Sunday, terms "the monstrosity of Christ," the "contingent singularity" upon which "human freedom is grounded."[66] In his vampiric rising from the grave and then his divine apotheosis, Christ is, after Hegel, a "monstrosity," "the first figure of Reconciliation, the appearance of God in the finite flesh of a human individual," "a grotesque 'inappropriateness as such.'"[67] "This blasphemous God," for whom "there is nothing normal in our universe" and for whom "every normal thing is a monstrosity," is, in fact, "the God of modern science, since modern science is sustained precisely by such an attitude of wondering at the most obvious."[68] Citing (as does Žižek) Mary Shelley's *Frankenstein*, both Julie Grossman and Dennis Perry link the Promethean monstrosity of modern science to adaptation. Grossman argues "that *any* adaptation might be considered 'monstrous,' that is, isolated from its predecessors because it is born of new concerns, new desires to express ideas in a different medium" and to ask "new questions about fundamental issues of human and textual identities." Perry claims that the Frankenstein films are "implicitly about adaptation" because "the patchwork creation of Frankenstein's monster . . . is a perfect analogy for the underlying intertextual processes of artistic creation itself," as it is for the suturing process of editing (the quintessential cinematic conceptual practice), and thus film adaptation in general as inherently and unavoidably monstrous.[69]

*

So there you have it: Richard Brooks, screenwriter/film director as blasphemous mad scientist, a rebellious Promethean creator fighting throughout his career for control of his artistic output in a workplace full of monstrous bastards who loved movies. Resistant to and constrained by the conceptual practices of adaptation itself and by the way the movie industry defamiliarizes "every normal thing," he slyly repurposes the trope of the monstrous in Tennessee Williams's *Sweet Bird of Youth* into a commentary on Hollywood's exploitation and disfigurement, celebration, and abjection, of beauty, youth, heteronormative romance, and the American dream's grotesque coupling of material success and spiritual fulfillment.[70] Let's close with two characteristic Brooksian moments of abjection and resistance, one from the film, one from his public life, both canine analogies. In a scene Brooks added to the movie, another monstrous bastard, Boss Finley, warns Chance on the church threshold Easter morning: "I had to butcher [my dog Prince] to keep all the bitches in town from being violated." When Chance nevertheless asks if he can see Heavenly, Finley responds, "Sure, Prince, when I've had you taken care of like my dog." This, of course, is what happens to Chance in Williams's play but not, crucially, in Brooks's film, where Brooks grants him the agency to resist abjection and the death of hope—as Brooks also did in a celebrated, fiery 1988 speech to the striking Writers Guild. Urging his fellow, increasingly desperate, writers to continue supporting the union, Brooks spoke of going to find his star on the Hollywood Walk of Fame and watching "a small dog pee on it." Remembering "all the other [Hollywood] dogs who have pissed on me," he admonished his audience: "You can always find some mangy cur who will piss on a writer, but don't piss on yourselves."[71] Words to live by.

## NOTES

1. The film is dated 1961 but was not released until Spring 1962.
2. Quoted here as it appears in the play: Tennessee Williams, *Sweet Bird of Youth*, intro. Lanford Wilson (1959; pb. New York: New Directions, 2008), p. 39.
3. J. P. Telotte, *The Mouse Machine: Disney and Technology* (Urbana and Chicago: University of Illinois Press, 2008), pp. 88–9.
4. Ibid. p. 90.
5. Including, somewhat incongruously, a musical number, Ned Land (Kirk Douglas)'s sea shanty, "A Whale of a Tale," with its comically monstrous, commingled combinations of humans and sea creatures.
6. Telotte, *The Mouse Machine*, p. 93.
7. This allusion is also noted by Gene D. Phillips, *The Films of Tennessee Williams* (East Brunswick, NJ, London, Toronto: Associated University Press, 1980), p. 169.
8. Perhaps she is also using oxygen as a hangover cure.
9. In the film, there is no pre-history to the name Princess Kosmonopolis—it is merely an alias under which Alexandra seeks to disappear.
10. This resemblance is also noted by Phillips, *The Films of Tennessee Williams*, p. 169.
11. Although the play-script's capitalizing of these last six words suggests an emphatic performance of them, I am lower-casing them here because Page understates them in the film.
12. "Go[ing] to a film" was "for him a lifelong escape": Lyle Leverich, *Tom: The Unknown Tennessee Williams* (New York: Crown, 1995), p. xx, who observes, as do many other Williams scholars and critics, that the playwright "was in fact deeply impressed with the wide-ranging, often poetic freedom of film itself," which would become a major "influence" on his work (p. 530).
13. Williams, *Sweet Bird of Youth*, pp. 75, 89, 93.
14. *OED*, "monster" 1a.
15. *OED*, "monstrosity" 2b.
16. *OED*, "monstrosity" 1a.
17. *OED*, "monstrous" 5a.
18. D[avid] H[erbert] Lawrence, *Lady Chatterley's Lover* (1928; "The Samuel Roth Edition," 1930; New York: William Faro, 1931), p. 21; in various iterations, see also pp. 28, 64, 113–14.
19. Tennessee Williams, *Tennessee Williams' Letters to Donald Windham*, ed. Windham (New York: Holt, Rinehart, and Winston, 1977), p. 170, June 6, 1945.

20. Tennessee Williams, "The Resemblance Between a Coffin and A Violin Case" (1949), *Collected Stories*, intro. Gore Vidal (New York: New Directions, 1985), p. 277.
21. John Lahr, *Tennessee Williams: Mad Pilgrimage of the Flesh* (New York and London: W. W. Norton, 2014), p. 376.
22. The 1968 poem "You and I," as in Lahr, *Tennessee Williams*, p. 346.
23. John Lahr, "A Monster Among Angels," *Airmail* (August 24, 2019), np (online).
24. Lahr, *Tennessee Williams*, pp. 376–7.
25. Michael Ehrhardt, "Of Monsters and Mad Love: Edmund White," *The Gay and Lesbian Review Worldwide* 19:1 (2012): p. 30. "If I had" here should be understood as "If I could have." See also Edmund White, *Sacred Monsters* (New York: Magnus, 2011), pp. xi–xiii, for Williams as "sacred monster."
26. Douglass K. Daniel, *Tough as Nails: The Life and Films of Richard Brooks* (Madison: University of Wisconsin Press, 2011), p. 186.
27. Ibid. p. 142.
28. *OED*, "monstrous" 3a.
29. *OED*, "monstrous" 4a.
30. Richard Brooks, *The Producer* (New York: Simon and Schuster, 1951; pb. New York: Pocket Books, 1953), p. 190.
31. Brooks also seizes on Williams's fascination in *Sweet Bird* and elsewhere with the trope of success: his added scenes often use it, especially the lighthouse scene, where Heavenly challenges Chance's quest for "Successville," his "Hollywood merry-go-round," as a "ride . . . that's going nowhere."
32. Daniel, *Tough as Nails*, p. 12.
33. Brooks, *The Producer*, p. 215.
34. Daniel, *Tough as Nails*, p. 241.
35. See Francis Patrick Frost, "A Historical-Critical Study of the Films of Richard Brooks with Special Attention to his Problems of Achieving and Maintaining Final Decision-Control," USC Diss. (1976), passim. Based, in part, on a series of interviews with Brooks, Frost's dissertation is more or less devoted, as its title indicates, to Brooks's struggle for "control" of his work. See also Brooks's 1985 two-part interview with French television, https://www.youtube.com/watch?v= 7HTngdwbljw and https://www.youtube.com/watch?v=FYc3rVglMpU, accessed July 26, 2021, in which, discussing his career-long battles with the studios, he uses the word "control" repeatedly.
36. Richard Brooks, "Interview," *Movie*, 12 (Spring 1965): p. 8. Nevertheless, by the time he made *The Professionals* (1966), Brooks's use of Panavision, the wide-screen process that was coming to dominate the market, was masterful.
37. *OED*, "monstrous," 1a, 2a, 3a.
38. Brooks, "Interview," p. 8.
39. Brenda Murphy, *Tennessee Williams and Elia Kazan: A Collaboration in the Theatre* (Cambridge: Cambridge University Press, 1992), pp. 144–9; Jo Mielziner, *Designing for the Theatre: A Memoir and a Portfolio* (New York: Bramhall House, 1965), p. 202; Mary C. Henderson, *Mielziner: Master of Modern Stage Design* (New York: Watson-Guptill, 2001), p. 224; Richard Allen Duprey, "Mass Media and the Theatre," N.Y.U. Diss. (1969), pp. 148–9.
40. Colin Bennett, "At the Cinema," *The Age* (Melbourne, Australia), July 7, 1962: p. 19; R. W. Gardner, "'Sweet Bird of Youth' Strictly For Laughs," *Baltimore Sun*, April 1, 1962, p. 52. See also Brenda Murphy, "How to Fix a Second Act: The Film and Television Adaptations of *Sweet Bird of Youth*," *Tennessee Williams Annual Review* 15 (2016), np (online): "this series of flashbacks carries the tragic subtext of the play within the movie's melodrama."

41. For example, see Charles Barr, "Cinemascope: Before and After," *Film Quarterly* 16:4 (Summer 1963): pp. 17–18, 20, for similar and contemporaneous objections by Howard Hawks and Sidney Lumet.
42. For an overview of the contentious yet "symbiotic relationship" between "Hollywood and Television in the 1950s," see Janet Wasko's chapter in Peter Lev, *Transforming the Screen: 1950–1959*, Vol. 7 in *History of the American Cinema*, gen. ed. Charles Harpole (Berkeley, Los Angeles, London: University of California Press, 2003), pp. 127–46.
43. Tom F. Driver, "Tennessee Williams' Best," *The New Republic* 140 (April 20, 1962): p. 21.
44. Murphy, *Tennessee Williams*, pp. 139–40; see also Harry W. Smith, "Performative Devices and Rhetorical Desires: Ritual and Rhetoric in the Work of Jo Mielziner and Tennessee Williams, 1955–1964," *Theatre History Studies* 15 (June 1995): p. 193, and Brian Parker, "Elia Kazan and *Sweet Bird of Youth*," *Tennessee Williams Annual Review* 7 (2005), np (online).
45. The standard text on the development and marketing of wide-screen cinema is John Belton, *Widescreen Cinema* (Cambridge, MA, and London: Harvard University Press, 1992); for Cinemascope's introduction in the 1950s and the disruptions it caused in moviemaking and spectatorship, see pp. 113–57 and 183–210. The classic early studies, which chronologically surround *Sweet Bird*, are by André Bazin (1953, 1954, 1955), as in Bazin, "Three Essays on Widescreen," trans. Catherine Jones and Richard Neupert, *Velvet Light Trap* 21 (Summer 1985): pp. 8–16, and Charles Barr, "Cinemascope: Before and After," *Film Quarterly* 16:4 (Summer 1963): pp. 4–24. For wide-screen modalities amid the technological spectacle of 1950s cinema, see Peter Lev, "Technology and Spectacle," in Lev, *Transforming the Screen*, pp. 115–25.
46. Williams, *Sweet Bird of Youth*, pp. 51, 54, 96.
47. R. Barton Palmer and William Robert Bray, *Hollywood's Tennessee: The Williams Films and Postwar America* (Austin: University of Texas Press, 2009), p. 38.
48. Ibid. p. 162.
49. Ibid. p. 185.
50. And also featuring monsters: the phrase "no-neck monsters," with which Maggie habitually characterizes her nieces and nephews, and their mother, "that monster of fertility, Mae." Moreover, in the play's "Notes for the Designer," Williams describes the bedroom's "*huge* console combination" radio, hi-fi, tv, and liquor cabinet as "a monumental monstrosity peculiar to our times," *Cat on a Hot Tin Roof* (pb. New York: New Directions, 1955), pp. xiii–xiv. See also R. Barton Palmer, "Chance's Main Chance: Richard Brooks's *Sweet Bird of Youth*," *Tennessee Williams Annual Review* 3 (2000), np (online), for a discussion of how the two films depict "masculinity in a crisis of desire and purpose."
51. Both Daniel (p. 148) and Phillips (p. 165) quote Williams as using the word "brilliant" to describe Brooks's writing and direction, although I could not verify their nebulous sourcing. Cf. Williams and Albert J. Devlin, *Conversations with Tennessee Williams* (Jackson: University of Mississippi Press, 1986), where Williams says "Richard Brooks wrote a *fabulous* screenplay of *Sweet Bird of Youth*" (emphasis added) except for the "happy end," "which is a contradiction to the meaning of the play" (p. 275).
52. Harry M. Benshoff, *Monsters in the Closet: Homosexuality and the Horror Film* (pb. Manchester and New York: Manchester University Press, 1997), p. 4.
53. Ibid. p. 49.
54. Ibid. p. 91.
55. Ibid. pp. 128–9.
56. Molly Haskell, *From Reverence to Rape: The Treatment of Women in the Movies*, 2nd edn (1974; Chicago, IL, and London: University of Chicago Press, 1987), p. 249.
57. Rhonda J. Berenstein, *Attack of the Leading Ladies: Gender, Sexuality, and Spectatorship in Classic Horror Cinema* (New York: Columbia University Press, 1996), p. 4. Another

terrorizing fifty-foot woman in contemporaneous film culture was Anita Ekberg's giant billboard ad come to life in "Le Tentazioni Del Dottor Antonio," Federico Fellini's contribution to *Boccaccio 70*, also released in 1962.
58. Brooks, "Interview," p. 8; see also Phillips, *The Films of Tennessee Williams*, p. 164; Palmer and Bray are somewhat skeptical: "Brooks surely protests too much" (p. 186).
59. Jay McRoy, "Recent Trends in Japanese Horror Cinema," in Richard J. Hand and McRoy, eds., *Monstrous Adaptations: Generic and Thematic Mutations in Horror Film* (pb. Manchester: Manchester University Press, 2007), p. 420, summarizing Kristeva's *The Powers of Horror: An Essay on Abjection* (1982).
60. Steffen Hantke, "Science Fiction and Horror in the 1950s," in *A Companion to the Horror Film*, ed. Harry M. Benshoff (Chichester: John Wiley and Sons, 2014), pp. 257, 259.
61. Benshoff, *Companion to the Horror Film*, p. 4.
62. Williams, *Sweet Bird of Youth*, p. 94.
63. Ibid.
64. For "Emerging Stylistic Norms in Cinemascope," exploring the kind of camera placements and compositional techniques Brooks was resisting, see Harper Cossar, *Letterboxed: The Evolution of Widescreen Cinema* (Lexington: University of Kentucky Press, 2010), pp. 95–184. As Murphy, "How to Fix," notes, "the only part of the film that makes much [stylistic] use of the Cinemascope [Brooks] hated" is "the opening sequence."
65. An even more explicitly blasphemous "line by Alexandra Del Lago saying this would be her resurrection day," also not in Williams's play-script, was cut from the finished film under pressure from the Legion of Decency. See Frost, "A Historical-Critical Study," p. 206.
66. Slavoj Žižek, "The Fear of Four Words: A Modest Plea for the Hegelian Reading of Christianity," in Slavoj Žižek and John Milbank, *The Monstrosity of Christ: Paradox or Dialectic?*, ed. Creston Davis (Cambridge, MA, and London: MIT Press, 2009), pp. 89, 91.
67. Ibid. p. 74.
68. Ibid. p. 88.
69. Julie Grossman, *Literature, Film, and Their Hideous Progeny: Adaptation and ElasTEXTity* (New York: Palgrave Macmillan, 2015), pp. 2–4, and Dennis Perry, "The Recombinant Mystery of Frankenstein: Experiments in Film Adaptation," in *Oxford Handbook of Adaptation Studies*, ed. Thomas Leitch (New York: Oxford University Press, 2017), np (online). See also Glenn Jellenik, "A Frankensteinian Model for Adaptation Studies, or 'It Lives!': Adaptive Symbiosis and Peake's Presumption, or the Fate of Frankenstein," in *Adapting Frankenstein: The Monster's Eternal Lives in Popular Culture*, ed. Dennis R. Cutchins and Dennis R. Perry (Manchester: Manchester University Press, 2018), p. 82, who makes a similar argument. As Hand and McRoy's collection, *Monstrous Adaptations: Generic and Thematic Mutations in Horror Film*, also indicates, the reciprocal interplay between monstrosity and adaptation has become a significant theoretico-critical trope in both horror-film studies and adaptation studies.
70. Obituaries of Brooks in the *New York Times* (William Grimes, "Richard Brooks, 79, Screenwriter and Director of Dramas, is Dead," March 13, 1992, B:6), *Washington Post* (Bart Barnes, "Film Director, Writer Richard Brooks Dies," March 13, 1992, np [online]), *Los Angeles Times* (Edward J. Boyer, "Director-Writer Richard Brooks Dies," March 12, 1992, np [online]), and *Variety* all remark on how he channeled his legendary anger into social commentary. See, for example, Todd McCarthy, "Obituaries: Richard Brooks," *Variety*: March 16, 1992: p. 75: "Called 'God's angry man' by fellow writer Fay Kanin, Brooks frequently made films exposing social and moral conditions he deplored." See also Pat McGilligan, "Richard Brooks: The Professional," in *Backstory 2: Interviews*

*with Screenwriters of the 1940s and 1950s*, ed. McGilligan (Berkeley, Los Angeles, Oxford: University of California Press, 1997), pp. 27–72, passim, but esp. p. 63 for Brooks's professional "code of honor," and Daniel, *Tough as Nails*, passim, but esp. p. 63 for Brooks as "an angry progressive who loudly bristled at any injustice."

71. Richard Brooks, "WGA 1989," https://www.youtube.com/watch?v=GIQsTW9UB_4, accessed May 9, 2021. The strike and the speech were actually in 1988.

CHAPTER 14

# Adapting the Unadaptables: *Lord Jim* (1965)

*Thomas Leitch*

Soon after *Lord Jim* premiered in the United Kingdom on February 16, 1965, a day after its screening for a select audience that included Queen Elizabeth II and co-star James Mason's aging parents, who so disliked the film that they "left the theater during the break"[1] and missed their son's entire performance, the verdict was in. Despite the London *Daily Mail*'s enthusiastic claim that "LORD JIM has just about everything!",[2] the film was an extravagant failure, Richard Brooks's "brave but exhausting attempt," as *New York Times* reviewer Bosley Crowther put it, "to run with the subtle Conrad character and hunt with the gross big-picture hounds."[3] Calling the film "a debacle of such awesome dimensions that I shrink from the demands of detailed analysis," Andrew Sarris concluded: "The most depressing aspect of all this is that Brooks had absolute freedom to do whatever he wanted, and demonstrated conclusively that he carried all the studio compromises inside him. Brooks wanted to film Conrad all his life, but when the chips were down, he simply couldn't believe that the mass audience could possibly understand Conrad without visual aids on the kindergarten level."[4]

The critics whose verdicts foretold the film's colossal financial failure agreed on two points. In attempting to make an action film that was also a psychological study of his neurotic, guilt-ridden hero's quest for redemption, Brooks had succeeded in doing neither, betraying the classic modernist novel Joseph Conrad had published in 1900. More fundamentally, the paramount aim of Brooks, a writer-director who had not made a film from an original screenplay since at least *The Last Time I Saw Paris*, loosely based on F. Scott Fitzgerald's story "Babylon Revisited," in 1954, had been to adapt Conrad's novel, as he had had the audacity to adapt works as challenging as *Something of Value*, *The Brothers Karamazov*, and *Cat on a Hot Tin Roof* in the intervening years.

It would surely be charitable to forgive Brooks on the grounds that Conrad's novel is unadaptable. And indeed many of Conrad's trademark narrative techniques make *Lord Jim* highly resistant to film adaptation. These begin with the casual introduction at the beginning of Chapter Five of Marlow, the seaman first introduced in the 1898 story "Youth" who had also narrated "Heart of Darkness," as a first-person narrator whose narrative is casually introduced, "'Oh, yes, I attended the inquiry,' he would say,"[5] *he* establishing Marlow as a pre-existing character who can be summoned at will, *would* implying that Marlow has already told this story many times. Although first-person narratives are widely believed to be more difficult than third-person narratives to adapt to the cinema, *Lord Jim*'s challenges only begin with its first-person narrative. As the story unfolds, it presents events from the perspectives of several subsidiary storytellers: Captain Montague Brierly, one of two assessors at the board of inquiry that cancels the hero's professional certification after he abandons the *Patna*, to which he has signed on as first mate; Jones, the friend of the benevolent merchant Stein, who reports on Jim's wanderings after he loses his livelihood; the Frenchman who contributes his own sense of Jim's state of mind; and the anonymous friend of Marlow who provides a home to Jim until he leaves to avoid "that little second engineer of the *Patna*" (230) whose arrival has provoked intolerable memories of the fatal moment when Jim leaped from the deck of the foundering ship, abandoning the eight hundred Muslim pilgrims traveling below decks, into a lifeboat from which he would ultimately be rescued along with the captain and the two engineers.

Figure 14.1 Jim (Peter O'Toole) agonizes over the decision that will haunt him for the rest of his life.

Instead of bringing Jim's trials and adventures into sharper relief, all these narrators, especially the discursive, oracular, endlessly analytical Marlow, obscure them beneath their own preoccupations, which lead Brierly, who sees Jim's failure as an indictment of the system Brierly himself represents, to commit suicide shortly after delivering his verdict and Marlow to return repeatedly to the conclusion that Jim is both vivid and ineffable in his quixotic attempt to redeem himself from his failure. Their individual narratives, and the novel as a whole, play havoc with linear time, jumping forward and backward with such abandon that Marlow waits over fifty pages after Jim abandons the *Patna* to reveal that the ship, like the *Jeddah*, the real-life counterpart on which Conrad had based the unfinished short story that eventually grew into the novel, did not sink after all but was "towed successfully to Aden" (165) without loss of life, making Jim's leap ironically unnecessary. Marlow recounts the deaths of both Brierly and Gentleman Brown, the pirate who sets himself against Jim upon Brown's arrival in Patusan, before he allows them to speak, as they both do at considerable length. More generally, Conrad seems bent on keeping not only his enigmatic leading character but all the dramatic incidents that define that character at a distance, using these incidents largely as motives for the moral and psychological developments on which Marlow expatiates. The accident aboard the *Patna*, Jim's involuntary decision to jump, the decision by the board of inquiry to cancel his professional certification, his final move to Patusan, the sudden act of courage that makes him "the virtual ruler of the land" (337)—these all emerge through a dense fog of cerebration that makes it necessary to take an active role in reconstructing the story and impossible for anyone, even Jim himself, to understand the hero. After Jim tells Marlow, "I would like to explain—I would like somebody to understand—somebody—one person at least! You! Why not you?" (98), Marlow realizes, "He was not speaking to me, he was only speaking before me" (112), in a tortured attempt to explain himself to himself. No wonder Marlow concludes that "of all mankind Jim had no dealings but with himself" (420).

As many college students could presumably attest, Conrad seems determined to swath a large-scale tale of adventure in the exotic tropics in so many generalizations about its reclusive, ungraspable hero and his crucial failures to live up to his own impossibly heroic standards that the only reasonable way to adapt it to the cinema would be to extricate the story from the layers of narrative obscurantism in which its author had enshrined it, just as Victor Fleming's 1925 silent adaptation had sought to do. To be content with extracting the story behind the novel, however, would amount to betraying the novel itself.

More important, the novel is only one of many scripts that prescribe directions for the film. All films, as I have argued elsewhere,[6] are produced not only by a team of collaborators often at odds with each other, but under the influence of a wide range of imperatives, some of them written (e.g. the screenplay and nominal source material behind the screenplay, contracts that specify budgets, deadlines, and salaries for the participants, memos from David O. Selznick), some of them unwritten (e.g. the established reputation of its director, the image of stars the film hopes will lure audiences into movie theaters, the popular genres whose audiences it seeks to attract, the aura of literary prestige that it hopes will establish its own cachet). What is most remarkable in the case of *Lord Jim* is that so many of these scripts resist adaptation as staunchly as Conrad's novel, either in themselves or in combination with each other. For this reason, *Lord Jim* offers a fruitful case study, not simply of the challenges of adapting an unadaptable novel, but of the paradoxically more frequent challenge of adapting multiple scripts that are unadaptable either on their own or together.

Brooks's adaptation of Conrad, which has been condemned as both too faithful and too free, is much more attentive to some aspects of Conrad's novel than others. Brooks wants so much to retain Marlow in the film that he gives him a diegetic role in the story as the captain of his title character's training ship, although the film's Marlow disappears from both the visuals and the soundtrack during the inquiry after Jim abandons the *Patna*, just at the moment the novel's Marlow had first begun to speak. It is not surprising, therefore, that Wallace S. Watson is disappointed in the film's adaptation of Conrad's narrator: "Jack Hawkins combines the role of Jim's training ship instructor with that of the narrator Marlow, but his voice-over comments on the action and on Jim's character remain introductory and perfunctory".[7] By contrast, Brooks makes no attempt to recreate Conrad's ambiguity or suspense concerning the fate of the *Patna*, which provokes Jim's helpless laughter when he recognizes it in the Aden port as soon as his own lifeboat arrives. Unlike Conrad, who pointedly declines to give Jim a last name—"He had, of course, another name, but he was anxious that it should not be pronounced" (3), he writes early on, and adverts to the court of inquiry's verdict laconically after the fact: "James so-and-so . . . mate . . . certificates cancelled" (196)—the film identifies Jim late in the story as "James Burke" and gives the pirate Gentleman Brown (James Mason) a speech in which he identifies himself as "Gentleman Duncan Malcolm Brown, at your service." Instead of following Conrad in calling the European-Malay woman Jim falls in love with (Daliah Levi) "Jewel" (343), a name the 1925 film adaptation had retained, Brooks's film refers to her only as "The Girl." Although he gestures toward the novel's most memorable speech, Stein's injunction, "in the destructive element immerse" (262), he rewords it, relocates it to the film's closing movement, and has Stein (Paul Lukas) direct his advice to Jim rather than Marlow. More generally, Brooks is less interested in reproducing the cadences of either Marlow's monologue or the other characters' dialogue than in recreating Jim's pervasive silence. Like Conrad's hero, who barely says a word before he is questioned by the court of inquiry in Chapter Four, Brooks's hero says nothing in the first six minutes of the film and speaks fewer than a hundred words in its first half-hour. When Stein, who has watched Jim's heroic refusal to abandon Stein's boat carrying gunpowder and his success in dousing the fire that has been set by a treacherous helper, opines to Jim, "Some men can never become heroes, and some heroes never become men," and Jim replies, "Some are lucky enough to be both," it is the first time in the movie that Jim volunteers an opinion or makes a gratuitous speech.

Brooks's adaptation of Conrad's novel follows a playbook long familiar to Hollywood adapters. He recasts many of his tormented hero's internal conflicts as external conflicts with other characters. He invents expository or dramatic dialogue to crystallize (and often clarify or simplify) these conflicts. He inflates action set pieces like the attack in which Jim leads the Patusan natives against the stockade of the oppressive European warlord the General (Eli Wallach), which, as Catherine Dawson and Gene M. Moore point out, "is described briefly in the novel" but "takes up fully one-fourth of the film,"[8] in order to establish Jim more firmly, at least for a time, as an action hero. He provides intermittent visual flashbacks literalizing Jim's guilt over abandoning the *Patna*. Brooks frequently invents new dialogue scenes, like the one in which Stein, who has conveniently traveled to Patusan for the film's closing movement, begs Du-Ramin (Tatsuo Saitô), the leader of the Patusan community, whose son Dain Waris (Ichizo Itami), Jim's closest friend, has been killed by Gentleman Brown and his confederates, to spare Jim's life instead of executing him, in accordance with Jim's own pledge in accepting the word of Gentleman Brown. He provides another dialogue scene that explicitly grounds Jim's decision to stay in Patusan in interpersonal romance along with his quest for self-redemption through his value to, and his idolatry by, his new community. He gives Jim a climactic speech that explains and crystallizes the rationale behind his decision to sacrifice his life in expiation of his calamitous error in judgment and shows Jim offering his own rifle to Du-Ramin as a weapon of execution. On balance, the film charts its hero's journey from indecisively abstracted to conventionally, albeit incompletely, worthy of trust, actively seeking expiation through his own death, earning The Girl's last sad smile of acceptance, and confirming the film's credentials as an action film featuring a fatally flawed hero rather than a more faithful adaptation of Conrad's novel, which is better described as an anatomy of action than an Aristotelian imitation of an action.

In addition to the challenges of adapting Conrad's novel, Brooks faced **the impossibility of adapting its locations**. Determined to shoot in the Far East but uninterested in scouting locations in northwest Sumatra, the most likely location for Patusan, Brooks and his crew spent five weeks in Hong Kong and then moved to a site near the Angkor Wat ruins in Cambodia. This decision replaced "the Muslim world of the novel with more vivid Buddhist costumes, ceremonies, and music."[9] At this second location, where one condition of filming was that Brooks's crew would be responsible for adding a new wing containing forty-five rooms to enlarge a local hotel, at a cost of over half a million dollars,[10] the crew were forced to contend with widespread dysentery, heat rash, snakes, and local officials constantly pressing them for bribes.[11] Rising political tensions concerning the shoot, inflamed by the festering Vietnam conflict, came to a head when Prince Sihanouk, Cambodia's pro-Chinese leader, visited the set and unleashed a barrage of anti-British sentiments, leading Brooks's star, Peter O'Toole, to reply: "I couldn't agree with you more. I'm Irish meself [sic]."[12] The climax came with Conradian suddenness: "One day a stranger appeared on the location and advised Brooks to get his company out of Cambodia by 12 March 1964. Deciding to take no chances, Brooks ordered the work schedule to be doubled. Shooting went on for seven days a week and from noon until nearly dawn in order for everyone to be safely out of the country. One week later the US and British embassies were attacked by mobs."[13]

O'Toole's insouciant reply to Prince Sihanouk was only the most publicized of many incidents that indicated **the impossibility of adapting the star**. He was cast in the film's title role on the strength of his two most recent leading roles: Lawrence of Arabia, and King Henry II in *Becket*. The public perception of O'Toole as an outsized heroic figure led to the expectation that the new film would be "a mammoth, *Lawrence*-like epic."[14] As an action star, however, O'Toole, whose wife, actress Siân Phillips, described him as a "dangerous, disruptive human being,"[15] came with heavy baggage. During the location shooting in Hong Kong, where he was repeatedly and violently seasick during six weeks of shooting in and off the coast, he had ended take after take by vomiting offscreen. As Brooks recalled: "He'd rush to the side of the ship and heave, and then go before the camera as if nothing had happened."[16] O'Toole, who dismissed the cosmopolitan city as "Manchester with slanted eyes," capped his well-known habit of carousing by "personally pulling a rickshaw and its driver into the main lobby [of the posh Peninsula Hotel] at 2am and buying the fellow a drink."[17] When Prince Sihanouk "denounced the movie company as 'Western imperialist invaders' on national radio, O'Toole took revenge by telling a reporter from *Life* magazine: 'If I live to be a thousand, I want nothing like Cambodia again. It was a bloody nightmare.' [. . .] When word of the interview reached the Prince, Peter O'Toole was persona non grata."[18] The single most important way in which Brooks's screenplay follows Conrad's novel was to make the hero a sporadically volcanic but largely reclusive man, a loner whose intermittent public actions never came close to expressing his deepest self. O'Toole, a flamboyant performer never noted for understatement, eventually decided that he had been miscast, admitting that "he suited neither the film nor the role and that it had been an error of judgement: 'I was in danger of becoming known as a tall, blond, thin dramatic actor, always self-tortured and in doubt and looking off painfully into the horizon. *Lord Jim* was my comeuppance.'"[19]

Closely related to the challenges of adapting the film's star was **the impossibility of adapting Conrad's hero**. Wallace S. Watson, speaking for many commentators in saying that the film "takes the protagonist largely at his own self-indulgent valuation as the hero of a simple romantic-heroic epic, offering no hint of the complexity with which he is presented in the novel,"[20] observes that the film, like similar adaptations of Conrad's novels *Under Western Eyes* and *Victory*, makes no attempt to provide "adequate cinematic analogues of the complex narrative screens through which the reader experiences the events of the novel," producing a "deeply ambiguous account of Jim, balancing the sympathetic view that he is 'one of us,' unfairly victimized by the circumstances of his life, with the recurrent intimation that his romantic self-absorption verges on the ridiculous"[21]—a judgment that implies that the older, more self-consciously ironic and self-deprecating O'Toole might have played the reticently performative hero better. The film's setting, scope, and budget demanded that it be headlined by a marketable star. But just as O'Toole came to believe that he had been wrong for the leading role, it might have been wrong for any marketable star, because for most of the film's running time the role is anti-heroic, even anti-agentive—a hero, in both Conrad and Brooks, whose most significant actions are reactions to circumstances beyond his control. Stars reading Brooks's screenplay might well have wondered what is so compelling about Jim that he deserves his own film. It is certainly not his conventionally assertive heroism, for it is hard to think of a more recessive action hero. Nor is it his gift with language, since he remains silent for much of the film and the novel, and when he does speak, he is never nearly as eloquent as Marlow, Stein, or even Brierly, or the

Figure 14.2 At the most suspenseful moment in the attack on the General's stockade, Dain Waris (Ichizo Itami) and The Girl (Daliah Levi) find Jim looking away from them into the distance.

gorgeously deceptive Gentleman Brown. Repeatedly framed in the novel by Marlow as "one of us" (x, 113, 409, 448, 577)—a label the film extends to a Patusan woman who confirms Jim's leadership of the community by telling him, "Now you are one of us"—the film's hero has instead of a signature line of his own a signature gesture: looking off abstractedly into the distance, often away from other characters framed together with him but otherwise not able to maintain a connection to him.

Brooks's hero follows a narrative arc quite distinct from Conrad's. Upon his arrival alone in Patusan after one of his crew, intent on sabotaging the shipment of guns and gunpowder, throws a knife at the other one and jumps overboard, Jim, accepting the advice of a young boy, drags his crates and barrels of cargo across the beach, carries them through the jungle, and hides them overhead in a series of animal traps. The General tortures Jim in an attempt to make him reveal where he has hidden the armaments, but Jim, very much in the spirit of Conrad's hero, refuses to break. Only when the chained captive meets The Girl, who is set before him as relief and temptation before his next round of torture, does his arc begin to depart from that of his literary counterpart. As she stands facing him, her breasts bared by the General, Jim asks, "Do you believe that death is the end of everything?"—the first conversational exchange he has initiated in the film. After she frees him so that he can deliver the weapons to her people (an act that already gives her a great deal more agency than the novel's Jewel), Jim unfolds a plan to the insurgents: "If we can keep them locked in their own stockade . . . if we can destroy their munition dump, if we can attack them on their own grounds, if we can keep them inside, on the defensive, if we can be ready by tomorrow sunrise, then perhaps we might win," a telling use of "we" that eventually leads Du-Ramin to say, "I know not why you have made our cause yours, but—" "Does it matter?" replies Jim, crystallizing his turn from acting, or not acting, alone toward acting in concert with others. His plan for the attack, which depends on precise coordination among all the participants—"All the fuses must be lighted at the same time. All the spears must be thrown at the same time"—confirms his new communal ethos. Even though Gentleman Brown appeals to Jim's racial solidarity with him, as he does in the novel when he says, "You have been white once, for all your tall talk of this being your own people and you being one with them" (473), Brooks's Jim is now both one of us and one of them, a status he announces when he improbably resumes the maritime uniform he had set aside on coming to Patusan for the last scene in which he offers himself to Du-Ramin for execution, still looking off into the distance.

Alongside all these difficulties was a challenge peculiar to Brooks: **the impossibility of adapting the screenwriter/director himself.** His entire professional life before *Lord Jim* can be seen as a series of exercises in successful self-adaptation. Born Ruben Sax to Russian-Jewish immigrant parents, he dropped out of Temple University to work as a sports reporter and journalist and writer for NBC Radio, first identifying himself professionally as "Richard Brooks" in 1930 and changing his name legally in 1943, three years after becoming director of the New York City's Mill Pond Theatre and just around the time he began to receive credit for writing or co-writing *Cobra Woman* (1943), *Brute Force* (1947), *Key Largo* (1948)—though neither he nor John Huston was credited for the screenplay to the 1946 Hemingway adaptation *The Killers*—and the novel *The Brick Foxhole*, which served as the basis for the 1947 film *Crossfire*. On the strength of his writing credits, he talked Cary Grant into letting him direct *Crisis* in 1950 and two years later wrote and directed *Deadline—U.S.A.*, the first film on which he received what was to become his trademark double credit. Having first established himself in his double role with adaptations based on the bestselling novels *The Blackboard Jungle* and *Something of Value*, Brooks shifted gears again to the more culturally ambitious adaptations of *The Brothers Karamazov*, *Cat on a Hot Tin Roof*, *Elmer Gantry*, and *Sweet Bird of Youth*, all of them yoking controversial characters and literary cachet.

This string of successful adaptations ended with *Lord Jim*, which marked still another deliberate shift for Brooks. Chafing under the compromises required by the Hollywood studio system, which was taking its last breaths, he had produced *Elmer Gantry* independently for United Artists, and the film had received three Academy Awards: one for Burt Lancaster as Best Actor, one for Shirley Jones as Best Supporting Actress, and one for Brooks himself for Best Adapted Screenplay. After collaborating with producer Pandro S. Berman on *Sweet Bird of Youth*, Brooks was determined to break decisively with the studio system in *Lord Jim*, an oversized epic over which he would have complete control: "In December 1961, shortly after completing *Sweet Bird of Youth*, he signed an agreement with Columbia Pictures that promised him a percentage of the profits and, more important to him, complete autonomy. He was not even required to tell the studio what movie he would undertake, which the *New York Times* called unprecedented in Hollywood deal-making."[22] Brooks, who had dreamed of adapting *Lord Jim* for years and had purchased the adaptation rights from Paramount for $25,000 in 1958, saw the film, whose $9 million budget made it by far his most expensive, as both a deeply personal project about the importance of "a second chance" as "the story of mankind. [. . .] the story of me and everybody else"[23] and his crowning professional achievement to date. He arranged for the film to be shot in Super Panavision 70 to make the most of its foreign locations and hired production designer Geoffrey Drake, who had worked on *The Bridge on the River Kwai*, and cinematographer Freddie Francis, who had shot *Lawrence of Arabia*. The film's failure at the box office cast a long shadow over Brooks's career. He responded to the widespread verdict that his adaptation had been a failure by adapting still again, taking on smaller projects and forgoing a high up-front salary in exchange for a guarantee of the artistic control to which he had become addicted as a filmmaker determined "to use film as a medium for self-expression" even as he demanded "a degree of autonomy that was impractical in an art form requiring millions of dollars."[24]

Brooks was not the only auteur *Lord Jim* sought to adapt. An even more obvious auteur was Joseph Conrad himself. Like so many other Conrad adaptations before and since, the film attests to **the impossibility of adapting the author**. The very first words spoken in the film—Jack Hawkins's voiceover as Marlowe saying, "Joseph Conrad wrote, 'If you want to know the age of the earth, look upon the sea in a storm'" over the opening montage—stamp it with Conrad's brand. But that brand would have been much more equivocal than this appeal to Conrad the sage implies. Of the seventeen Conrad films that had preceded *Lord Jim*, fully eight of them were based on *Victory*, the author's most conventionally romantic novel, which in the space of a single year, 1931, spawned adaptations in France, Poland, Germany, Italy, and Sweden, in addition to a pair of American adaptations in 1919, only four years after the novel's publication, and 1940. When Brooks began dreaming of adapting *Lord Jim*, Conrad was best known in Hollywood as the author of exotic romances. Only three British films had been adapted from his fiction: *Sabotage*, the 1936 Alfred Hitchcock thriller based on *The Secret Agent*; Herbert Wilcox's *Laughing Anne* (1953), based on the story "Because of the Dollars"; and Carol Reed's *An Outcast of the Islands* (1951), still the most highly regarded of all Conrad adaptations. Brooks's film, the first feature-length adaptation of Conrad since *Laughing Anne*, returns to the tradition of exotic romance within which most of these adaptations found their place, departing from a twelve-year period of decidedly unspectacular television adaptations. Brooks's determination to produce a faithful adaptation of Conrad that would also satisfy the appetites of contemporary reviewers and the demands of the box office heightened the tension between fidelity and adaptability already implicit in every act of adaptation.

The stakes were raised still further by **the impossibility of adapting *Lord Jim*'s genre**. Whatever first attracted Brooks to the project—the novel's Englishness, its exoticism, its adventure, its literariness, its potential for generating a big-budget, wide-screen spectacular like *Lawrence of Arabia*—he must have recognized that those generic scripts were already at odds with each other in Conrad's novel. The imposing model that David Lean's film provided could not readily be duplicated, for few filmgoers would have read *Seven Pillars of Wisdom*, on which it was nominally based, and even fewer of them would have been troubled by the freedom with which Robert Bolt's screenplay adapted T. E. Lawrence's memoir, often using it as a window through which to view an episode in history the film felt free to dramatize directly. But the historical reality behind Conrad's novel, the premature abandonment of the *Jeddah* in 1880, was nothing more than anecdote that led to the creation of the story. Conrad's hero was based on an actual person,

*Jeddah* first mate Augustine Podmore Williams, who survived his disgrace to become first mate of the *Vidar* in 1882, a post in which he was succeeded five years later by Conrad, who "may then have heard accounts of Williams from the other officers."[25] But Williams provides nothing like an heroic counterpart to Lawrence, who can be directly invoked as a heroic figure, and the window Marlow provides through which to view Conrad's hero is so ornately inscribed that it is by design nearly impossible to see through.

This generic challenge indicates a weightier challenge that confronts any number of prestige adaptations: **the impossibility of adapting a canonical work of literature**. Brooks conceived *Lord Jim* specifically as a serious attempt to adapt a classic novel dear to his heart, an English novel that rivaled *The Brothers Karamazov* in its psychological insight and moral power. Whether or not they approved Brooks's work, reviewers recognized it as an example of literary cinema, a movie that frankly aimed to bring a great novel and its author to a wider public. Even more than film versions of plays by Shakespeare, Chekhov, and Tennessee Williams, however, literary cinema is itself an irreducibly self-contradictory term, since, as Brooks himself acknowledged in a widely quoted remark, "If you're going to make a book just as a book, then there's no need to make it as a film at all."[26] Sometimes the characteristics that make a classic novel a classic, like Jane Austen's witty dialogue or Charles Dickens's evocative descriptions of Victorian London, are readily transferable to the screen; more often, as George Bluestone points out in *Novels into Film*, the modernist movement in fiction from Conrad to Woolf, which "tended to retreat more and more from internal action to internal thought, from plot to character,"[27] often seems to have set itself deliberately against cinema, generating a series of decidedly unadaptable monuments as if to refute the upstart medium's aspiration to serious artistic status. Filming a masterpiece not only fails to guarantee that a masterpiece will result; it incurs judgment by the impossibly high standard set by the masterpiece.

Even filmgoers who did not find this standard oppressively exacting because they knew nothing about *Lord Jim* or Joseph Conrad would have recognized one last daunting challenge: **the impossibility of adapting the story's cultural project**. The film at once invokes, celebrates, and criticizes the values of a specific culture, the British Empire, at a specific moment in time, the dawn of the twentieth century. As Allan H. Simmons has pointed out, Conrad's novel already includes an international cast: "Europe is represented by characters from England, Scotland, Germany, France, Scandinavia, Italy, Switzerland, Denmark and Portugal in a Far East of Chinese, Javanese, Arabs, Malays and Bugis. The novel's international scope is everywhere—often present in the hybrid form of the half-caste, such as the brigantine captain—resulting in complex cultural configurations." For Simmons, "*Lord Jim* transcends the specific context of Eurocentric values during the Age of Empire to engage with the wider cultural dialogues from which they emerged."[28] The film is equally international in its setting and casting. Yet in seeking to replicate Conrad's cultural sweep, the film inevitably replicates his novel's colonialism, for "the making of colonial films is also a colonial endeavor, and one that requires an ethnic and cultural sensitivity of which all professional 'armies' are incapable, whether they are shooting with cameras or with guns."[29] The critique of Eurocentrism that had crested in Conrad's novella "Heart of Darkness" (1898) and his novels *Nostromo* (1904) and *Under Western Eyes* (1911) was already inseparable from a cultural tourism broadly implied by the latter novel's title. The implication of the phrase "under Western eyes," so pointedly ironic in Conrad's novel, is threatened with being emptied of all irony in a wide-screen Technicolor adaptation of his novel released to a world in which the British Empire has shrunk to a ghost of itself. Dawson and Moore note that "in the history of Conrad films, all too often the colonial world has been reduced to a common repository of cultural tokens in which human values are seen only in terms of their power to reinforce traditional Western stereotypes about meek civil servants, evil savages in the bush, or ceremonial dances and sacrifices."[30] On the one hand, they argue, "it is both a sign of the times and a credit to Brooks that references to white supremacy in Conrad's novel are addressed explicitly in the film,"[31] most notably in Gentleman Brown's racist appeal to Jim's whiteness as a basis for a trust that proves disastrously misplaced: "Yet even though racial issues are thematized more prominently in Brooks's film than was possible in films of the early fifties, stereotypical class differences still prevail."[32] So the film, produced sixty-five years after the novel, is caught in a double bind, measured against both its perceived need to remain faithful to the novel and its equally exigent need to correct the novel's colonialism and racism. Does changing the billing of the European-Malay woman Jim calls "Jewel," a name that appears in only a few places in the novel, to "The Girl" make Brooks's film more or less colonialist? Brooks's decision to drop the name Jim had given his multiracial love may seem just as enlightened as the prominent credit "The Girl" seems depersonalizing. Yet this particular dilemma was unavoidable, since Brooks's choices were limited to calling the character by a name her English lover had chosen for her, imposing a new name himself, or leaving her with no name at all.

More generally, Brooks's film raises two questions: whether every adaptation is willy-nilly an act of cultural tourism, and whether this tourism is already implicit in Conrad's novel. Stephen Donovan observes that "there is something incongruously touristic about the self-imposed nomadism which makes Jim into a 'rolling stone' (*LJ* 197) in the novel's middle section, moving continually from one port to the next in a melancholy parody of 'independent' travel. In turn, Marlow's attempt to break this pattern and 'get him out of the way' (221) involves finding him employment with Stein, who, as the former assistant of 'a

Dutch traveler—a rather famous man' (205), embodies a bygone era of heroic travel. From this perspective, Jim's voluntary exile to Patusan, an idealized space of romance out of the sight of tourists and sailors alike, represents his return to what John Urry defines as the 'romantic' gaze of middle-class tourists for whom the 'collective' gaze is a disconcerting and even repulsive experience."[33] Two of the tag lines used to market the film make this invitation to cultural tourism explicit: "Between Suez and the China Sea . . . many nameless men live and die unknown!" and "Filmed in the far corners of the Far East . . . High Adventure that reaches across the world!"

Shortly after the film opened, Orson Welles, in conversation with Peter Bogdanovich, delivered what has frequently been regarded as its epitaph. Recalling his own unproduced first project, *Heart of Darkness*, he said: "My script was terribly loyal to Conrad. And I think that, the minute anybody does that, they're going to have a smash on their hands. Any of them. Think what *Lord Jim* could have been, if some attention had been paid to the original book."[34] Brooks's film, widely dismissed as a failed compromise between aggressively competing scripts, would have been saved, Welles opines, if only it had stuck closer to Conrad's novel. Yet the novel itself is already riven by many of these competing loyalties and contradictions, as even its most sympathetic contemporaneous reviewers recognized. The anonymous reviewer for the *Pall Mall Gazette*, complaining of the novel's "formlessness," which "is vastly augmented" by its division into two unequal parts presented from several points of view, announced that "*Lord Jim* is tedious, over-elaborated, and more than a little difficult to read."[35] The reviewer for the *Daily News* called the novel "really more of an epic than of a story. It is grandiose, it is poetic, it is thoughtful; in a word, it is masterly, yet it is hardly the sort of thing that will tend much to the butterflies of fiction. The obstructions set in the way of the reader are many, and, moreover, are mainly owing to Mr. Conrad's idiosyncrasies."[36] The reviewer for *Sketch*, calling it "an impossible book—impossible in scheme, impossible in style," conceded that "it is undeniably the work of a man of genius, of one who, wrongly I think, despises every popular and accepted method."[37]

It would be foolish to conclude that all attempts to adapt unadaptable scripts are doomed to failure. The paths of all movies, and most other texts as well, are set by multiple authors who often prescribe competing, often blankly contradictory scripts, as Conrad's novel already does by offering a portrait of a hero who is repeatedly invoked as "one of us" even though his features are discernible only by steadily gazing through a fog of narration. Brooks's film, a project whose creator spent years struggling to adapt and then more years struggling to recover from, is most illuminating not as a story of success or a failure but as a case study showing the results of the need adaptations take upon themselves to serve more masters than one.

## NOTES

1. Douglass K. Daniel, *Tough as Nails: The Life and Films of Richard Brooks* (Madison: University of Wisconsin Press, 2011), p. 159.
2. Quoted in the full-page advertisement for *Lord Jim* in *Billboard* (March 27, 1965): p. 13.
3. Bosley Crowther, "Conrad's 'Lord Jim' Arrives: Peter O'Toole Stars in Brooks Version," *New York Times*, February 26, 1965: p. 18.
4. Andrew Sarris, Review of *Lord Jim*, *Village Voice*, April 29, 1965: p. 12.
5. Joseph Conrad, *The Works of Joseph Conrad: Vol. 4: Lord Jim* (London: William Heinemann, 1921), p. 40. All otherwise unidentified parenthetical references are to this text.
6. See Thomas Leitch, "The Texts Behind *The Killers*," in *Twentieth-Century American Literature and Film*, ed. R. Barton Palmer (New York: Cambridge University Press, 2007), pp. 26–44; "Scripting the Saints," *Studia Filmoznawcze* 40 (2019): pp. 113–32; and *The History of American Literature on Film* (New York: Bloomsbury Academic, 2019), pp. 16–18.
7. Wallace S. Watson, "Conradian Ironies and the Conrad Films," in *Conrad on Film*, ed. Gene M. Moore (Cambridge: Cambridge University Press, 1997), p. 23.
8. Catherine Dawson and Gene M. Moore, "Colonialism and Local Color in *An Outcast of the Islands* and *Lord Jim*," in *Conrad on Film*, ed. Moore (Cambridge: Cambridge University Press, 1997), p. 114.
9. Ibid. p. 115.
10. Daniel, *Tough as Nails*, p. 155.
11. Robert Sellers, *Peter O'Toole: The Definitive Biography* (London: Sidgwick and Jackson, 2015), p. 141.
12. Ibid. p. 142.
13. Ibid.
14. Ibid. p. 140.
15. Ibid. p. 228.
16. Ibid. p. 141.
17. Ibid. p. 140.
18. Ibid. p. 142.
19. Ibid. p. 143.
20. Watson, "Conradian Ironies and the Conrad Films," p. 21.
21. Ibid. p. 22.
22. Daniel, *Tough as Nails*, p. 152.
23. Ibid. pp. 154, 155.
24. Ibid. p. 219.
25. Ian Watt, *Conrad and the Nineteenth Century* (Berkeley: University of California Press, 1979), p. 266.
26. Daniel, *Tough as Nails*, p. 146.
27. George Bluestone, *Novels into Film* (Baltimore, MD: Johns Hopkins University Press, 1957), p. 46.
28. Allan H. Simmons, "Nationalism and Empire," in *Joseph Conrad in Context*, ed. Simmons (Cambridge: Cambridge University Press, 2009), pp. 191–2.
29. Dawson and Moore, "Colonialism and Local Color," p. 117.
30. Ibid. pp. 104–5.
31. Ibid. p. 115.
32. Ibid. p. 116.

33. Stephen Donovan, *Joseph Conrad and Popular Culture* (Houndmills: Palgrave Macmillan, 2005), p. 89. See John Urry, *The Tourist Gaze: Leisure and Travel in Contemporary Societies* (London: Sage, 1990), pp. 46–7.
34. Peter Bogdanovich, *This Is Orson Welles*, ed. Jonathan Rosenbaum (New York: HarperCollins, 1992), p. 32.
35. Anon., Review of *Lord Jim*, *Pall Mall Gazette*, December 5, 1900, p. 4; reprinted in Norman Sherry (ed.), *Joseph Conrad: The Critical Heritage* (London: Routledge & Kegan Paul, 1973), p. 123.
36. Anon., Review of *Lord Jim*, *Daily News*, December 14, 1900, p. 9; reprinted in Sherry, *Joseph Conrad*, p. 124.
37. Anon., Review of *Lord Jim*, *Sketch*, November 14, 1900, p. 142; reprinted in Sherry, *Joseph Conrad*, p. 118.

## FILMOGRAPHY

*Lord Jim* (Columbia, 1965). Directed by Richard Brooks.

CHAPTER 15

# Adaptation as Mutation: *In Cold Blood* (1967)

*Jennifer L. Jenkins*

When *In Cold Blood* appeared in four successive issues of *The New Yorker* magazine in September and October 1965, Truman Capote proposed a new literary form: the "nonfiction novel." Both its provenance and status as form or genre are contested: Norman Mailer claimed invention of the form,[1] and naturalist genre fiction had probed the lethal aspects of American consciousness since at least the turn of the century.[2] Echoing in tone the stark realism of Steinbeck's fictionalized depiction of Oklahoma in *Grapes of Wrath* (1939), Capote proffered an equally raw and purportedly nonfiction portrayal of events[3] that occurred in neighboring Kansas exactly twenty years later, replacing Steinbeck's omniscient narrator with a framing literary consciousness, his own. In January 1966, *LIFE* magazine presented a kind of visual intertext, bridging Capote's novel and the film to come.[4] Featuring photographs by Richard Avedon of the crime location and the killers as they awaited execution in April, the photo-story was the first narrative and visual adaptation of Capote's account of the 1959 murders of the Clutter family of Holcomb, Kansas. Just as Capote adapted prior novelistic tropes, so Richard Brooks's 1967 film of *In Cold Blood* similarly draws upon visual antecedents, notably the work of Farm Security Administration (FSA) documentarians. Brooks seemed the natural choice for a cinematic realization of Capote's tour de force: a veteran journalist, oft-nominated adapter of literary texts, mercurial director of celebrated *films noirs*, and a seasoned negotiator of the liminal ground of nonfiction narrative. Both the film and its source text reveal a process of borrowing, including, and excluding—that is, of adaptation—that marked the lives of the protagonists. Brooks's black-and-white wide-screen film blends the FSA visual aesthetic, filtered through Avedon's images, with Capote's text into a cinematic hybrid, a mutation of visual and narrative realism.

The Farm Security Administration/Office of War Information (FSA-OWI) Collection at the Library of Congress contains images captured from 1935 to 1944 by staff who would become some of the most famous mid-century documentary photographers, among them Walker Evans and Dorothea Lange. With a mandate to capture the work and impact of Depression-era federal agencies, camera artists were deployed across the country with special attention to rural and economically isolated areas. Kansas images by Russell Lee, Jack Delano, and John Vachon show beneficiaries of FSA funding as well as the impact of the railroad on the rural farmbelt. The work of Lee, Delano, and Vachon shares a FSA 'house style' of sorts with the more famous Evans and Lange images of the period: individuals are framed in low-angle shots against prairie land or prairie skies; structures and towns appear in vanishing-point composition along roadways or railroad tracks.[5] With the exception of Delano's night shots of the Santa Fe Rail Road's Argentine shops in Kansas City, the majority of images are well-lit, medium-contrast, daylight images of Americana, captured in an objective but not unkind manner. For example, Russell Lee's 35mm nitrate black-and-white image of *Mr. Germeroth, Sheridan County, KS* (1939) places the subject in profile and above the camera, with what appears to be a tractor smokestack behind him for scale.[6] The monumentalizing effect of the low-angle shot confers dignity and solidity. While similar in composition to a profile mugshot, this outdoor portrait conveys the opposite effect to an indoor identification image made for juridical purposes.

The Library of Congress describes the FSA process of documentation as research-based:

> Staff photographers were given specific subjects and/or geographic areas to cover. These field assignments often lasted several months. Before beginning their assignments, photographers read relevant reports, local newspapers, and books in order to become familiar with their subject. A basic shooting script or outline was often prepared. Photographers were encouraged to record anything that might shed additional light on the topic that they were photographing, and they received training in making personal contacts and interviewing people.[7]

Capote's own literary process was quite similar, from his first scan of the *New York Times* next-day story of the Clutter murders to extensive site visits and interviews:

> The book wasn't something reconstructed from some great distance. I did it right along as it was happening. [. . .] But there was a tremendous amount of research. All those endless interviews with all of those people, and I traveled all over the country and to all of the places that appear in

the book, all those motels where the boys stayed, all those sordid motels and hotels in Acapulco and Miami. And I wrote 6,000 pages of notes before I ever sat down to write the book.[8]

Both Capote's novel and the FSA images are grounded in the reality of the place and events being recorded. Neither process is objective, of course. What the camera records, just as how one interviews, recalls, and retells a subject, depends upon placement and position of the observer. Capote did not use a tape recorder and claimed perfect recall of conversations which he later typed up. Just as camera angle and photo finishing can change the depiction of a subject, so Capote's process could (and did) condense and displace details. The Clutter family and subsequent journalists and scholars have disputed Capote's method and accuracy, suggesting that his approach was more mutation of facts than simple recording of objective details.[9]

For *LIFE* magazine's January 1966 teaser story announcing "a Book-of-the-Month Club selection, a paperback and a movie," Richard Avedon was dispatched to Garden City, Kansas for the photo spread.[10] The stark, large-format images in the 22-page story mimic the style and content of the FSA photos: Capote, foregrounded in a two-page eye-level close-up head-and-shoulder shot on a dirt road that recedes to a vanishing point in the far distance;[11] Susan Kidwell[12] and Bobby Rupp[13] in slightly low-angle three-quarter shots against a backdrop of receding prairie horizon; the Clutter home in a wide shot taken from across a span of lawn, as though to document the architectural structure and its site.[14] (Indeed, this shot is precisely replicated in the opening sequence of the film, which was largely shot on location.) Holcomb Postmistress Myrtle Clare stands in front of the one-room post office in a head-on full-length image, indistinguishable from a Depression-era WPA rural location shot but for her trousers and the fifty-star American flag.[15] Avedon's spread also includes cyc-level head-and-shoulder portraits of Hickock and Smith, both looking directly into the camera and displaying their tattoos against a white background, presumably a prison wall.[16] Only these images of the killers stray from the FSA aesthetic into Diane Arbus territory. Only Truman's face occupies more frame-space than those of the killers. One month later, perhaps motivated by the need to steal some of Avedon's publicity, Capote published a short photo-story in *Vogue* with three photos:

> The two faces belong to Perry Edward Smith and Richard Eugene Hickock. These portraits, the work of a local photographer more accustomed to taking high school graduation pictures, were made in the Garden City jailhouse the morning after their return and incarceration—a snowy morning in January, 1960. The landscape, a desolate sand road winding across the western Kansas prairies, was photographed by me one afternoon

last October, almost exactly six months after the two murderers were hanged for their crime in a cold warehouse at Kansas State Penitentiary in Lansing, Kansas.[17]

While certainly read by the glitterati of Capote's world, the *Vogue* piece would have had far less influence on the image of Kansas or the murderers in the minds of movie-going Americans than the spread in *LIFE*.

Arguably, the *LIFE* feature defines the visual aesthetic of the film almost two years before its December 1967 premiere. Avedon and Brooks seemed to self-consciously mirror the familiar Depression-era photographic image of Kansas and the western Midwest that was well established in the public imagination by the FSA project. In invoking images of thirty years before, Avedon's photos function as nostalgia, preview, and screen test. Avedon's images, widely seen by *LIFE*'s readership of as many as 5.6 million people weekly,[18] revived the FSA aesthetic, and thus allowed Brooks to adapt a familiar image of Kansas within the visual vernacular of Americana. As Douglass K. Daniel explains in his appreciative biography,

> [Brooks] chose to mimic the style of the book by taking a semi-documentary approach. Instead of working on a back lot at the studio, the production would visit as many of the actual locations as possible. Black-and-white film, the traditional stock of the documentary, would be shot, instead of color. Those choices and others would support his efforts as a writer to mirror the reality of the book.
> [. . .] "To me, the story deals to a great degree with fear," Richard said. "To me, fear is best exemplified in black and white." By shooting in Kansas, the entire look of the picture would carry the reality he sought.[19]

Location shooting in black and white would implicitly convey the documentary aesthetic and its grounding in truth. Such visual truth had been established by documentary photography from the Farm Security Administration, recorder of both model farms and less than ideal living conditions in rural America a generation before. Capote's novel drew upon such tropes for verisimilitude, and Brooks's adaptation of that text into his own screenplay and screen narrative further reified the presumed veracity of stark, high-contrast monochrome images.

Since Brooks was determined to cast as realistically as possible, even using Holcomb and Garden City locals to play themselves or composite types, Avedon's images serve as character profiles for casting the leads. In concurrence with Capote's wishes, Brooks committed to hiring unknowns to play the murderers, allowing for physical type rather than movie-star typecasting and further establishing the vernacular of the film. Avedon's portraits of the murderers participate in the popular imaginary of Americana, a point both Capote and Brooks stress in their respective media narratives. Composed as portraits of working- or lower-class young men, the images are quite aesthetically distinct from mugshots in size, lighting, and background. The very fact of their publication in *LIFE* magazine would seem to confer a kind of normalization. Avedon's subjects are not visibly evil. Capote's text predicted as much in the reception the killers received in Garden City: "But when the crowd caught sight of the murderers, with their escort of blue-coated highways patrolmen, it fell silent, as though amazed to find them humanly shaped."[20]

Mediation of reality into image—that is, *adaptation*—fuels the fraught issue of Capote's veracity and ethics. Any fact-based narrative must negotiate not only facts but the degree to which literary style embellishes, de-emphasizes, or changes those facts. Ever confident of his own genius and acuity, Capote crafted a work of impressive literary elegance that was vivid and evocative, all while trumpeting the birth of a new genre, the nonfiction novel. His descriptions fixed places and people in his readers' imaginations. When Avedon's photos reached the public eye, Capote's brainchild became something of a changeling, as George Garrett explains:

> When pictures of the people involved appeared in the magazines, it was clear how much of Capote's descriptions and judgments was subjective, literary. The people did not look much like the people he described. Later it turned out that they did not do or say all the things he attributed to them; and some things neither he nor anyone else could have known . . . There is also the slightly more disturbing fact that neither the Clutters nor the killers were fictional constructs. They were real people.[21]

This indictment might be extended to Richard Avedon and Richard Brooks, as well. Conscious invocation of the tropes of pictorial or filmic documentary style inevitably involves mutation, as it is a kind of quoting of an earlier visual text, repositioned in a new context and format. As such, Brooks's film participates in what Thomas Leitch terms "intertext," that is, the variety of interrelated textual forms, broadly linked by similar or overlapping narratives.[22]

Truman Capote's holographic notebook about the cinema adaptation, held in the New York Public Library archives, explains his own goals in choosing Brooks for the adaptation and contains notes about everything from visual style to casting. Written in longhand, the notebook is a narrative "making-of" account of the film, recorded retrospectively.

> I'd long made up my mind that if a picture was to be made, then I wanted the writer-director Richard Brooks to be the intermediary between and book and screen. Why? Because, aside from long personal acquaintance and respect for his no-nonsense, yet imaginative professionalism, he

was the only director who understood and agreed with my own concept of how the book should be transformed to film. Brooks was the one person who entirely agreed with and would commit himself on the important points, and they were that I wanted [the] film made in black and white, and played by a cast of "unknown" actors—that is, without 'public' faces."

[. . .] We both wanted the film to duplicate reality—to have the actors resemble their prototypes as much as possible, and have every scene filmed in its real locale: the Clutter house in Holcomb, Kansas; stores in Kansas City; certain hotel rooms, highways, Las Vegas streets, particular stretches of the Mojave desert, courthouses, prisons, filling stations—a complicated process but the only one in which most elements of fantasy could be removed and reality achieve its proper reflection.[23]

Realism is in the eye of the beholder, of course, but exacting visual detail was clearly an aesthetic and narrative priority for both the writer of the source text and the adapter-director. Brooks's commitment to realism was a selling point, although ultimately the director's understanding of realism and the novelist's diverged significantly. The reflected reality referenced in the notebook's title was held up to different mirrors by Brooks and Capote.

While not a literary focus of the film adaptation, the visual vernacular does provide the background to the true-crime genre being developed in both text and film. Moreover, photo-realism is embedded in the text of the novel, evidence of the adaptation and mutation of a visual vocabulary into the text and subsequently into the film. Capote clearly wrote the narrative with filmic conventions in mind, pre-screening the movie (at least in his head) as he developed the narrative. He contended to George Plimpton that he used film techniques, "Consciously, not at all. Subconsciously, who knows?"[24] The opening of the first of four sections that follow the four installments in *The New Yorker* magazine, September 17–October 16, 1965, functions as an establishing shot for the entire textual narrative to follow:

The village of Holcomb stands on the high wheat plains of western Kansas, a lonesome area that other Kansans call "out there." Some seventy miles east of the Colorado border, the countryside, with its hard blue skies and desert-clear air, has an atmosphere that is rather more Far West than Middle West. The local accent is barbed with a prairie twang, a ranch-hand nasalness, and the men, many of them, wear narrow frontier trousers, Stetsons, and high-heeled boots with pointed toes. The land is flat, and the views are awesomely extensive; horses, herds of cattle, a white cluster of grain elevators rising as gracefully as Greek temples are visible long before a traveller reaches them.

Holcomb, too, can be seen from great distances. Not that there is much to see—simply an aimless congregation of buildings divided in the center by the main-line tracks of the Santa Fe Railway, a haphazard hamlet bounded on the south by a brown stretch of the Arkansas (pronounced "Ar-kan-sas") River, on the north by a highway, Route 50, and on the east and west by prairie lands and wheat fields.[25]

Setting, ambience, diction registers, costuming, and mise en scène: all shape this passage. It establishes not only the visual language of the novel, but the structural conventions of the true-crime screen narrative for six decades to follow. The formula begins with an environmental scan of the region or locale, followed by a description of the crime scene prior to violation, an introduction to the victims, and a parallel introduction to the perpetrators, if known. This Act I information is followed in Act II by the crime, and in Act III by the detection process, apprehension, trial, and, in Act IV or an epilogue, the disposition of the malefactors. Capote's text employs this structure, presciently distributing information in narrative units that translate naturally to the sequence and pacing of a film.

While the novel is not overtly prescriptive in terms of being laid out as a screenplay, it is very much pre-scripted in terms of scene-setting and narrative juxtaposition. Framed by a visual imagination from the opening sequence, the story of the Clutters and their killers detailed in "Part One: The Last to See Them Alive" proceeds in a sequence of alternating vignettes. As the killers draw closer to the River Valley Farm, Capote constructs a pattern of cross-cutting scenes of decreasing length, drawing the six people together across 369 miles of Kansas to an inevitable collision. In the aftermath of the crime, the description of the murderers' honeymoon trip to Mexico and the U.S. West, and their pursuit by Kansas Bureau of Investigation (KBI) officers alternate similarly. Donald Pizer viewed this structure as "achiev[ing] narrative suspense as well as documentary authenticity" without connecting it to film form.[26] Brooks hews closer to Sergei Eisenstein's principles of intellectual montage than D. W. Griffith's (and Capote's) parallel editing, using matchcuts and contrasting movement in frame to narrow the space and time between the principals on November 15, 1959.

Brooks eschews Capote's establishing shot, rejecting the plains panorama to begin his 1967 adaptation with a sequence from *film noir*: a Greyhound bus advancing head-on toward the camera. Brooks sets the shot at night, and opts to shift camera position and track the passing bus right at the last instant of its approach. The left-to-right diagonal bus trajectory match-cuts to the bus interior corridor as Quincy Jones's jazz score fades to a minor drum beat under low and simple guitar strumming. A child approaches the sound of the music coming from the rear seat, and the only lighted element is the sole of the guitarist's Cat's Paw boot.[27] Conrad Hall's black-velvet cinematography here establishes not only anonymity but intimacy within the bus interior. As the child moves away along the corridor to rear frame, the full-black reverse shot is pierced by a sound of a match strike and then a flame illuminates Perry Smith (Robert Blake) in extreme close-up as he lights a cigarette and the Jones score returns, matching a trumpet blare to the sulphur flare. Cinematographer Conrad Hall's extreme chiaroscuro appears twice more in the film: during Perry's telling of the murder sequence in flashbacks during the cross-country overnight drive; and in the penultimate and final scenes of the killers in their holding cells and then at the gallows. The three dark moments all focus on Perry Smith, and all use Robert Blake's physicality and dark coloring to foreshadow or underscore the moral limbo Smith occupies.

Like Capote's plains panorama, Brooks's 54-second opening sequence fully establishes setting, ambiance, and mise en scène, culminating in a character reveal. But Brooks trades Capote's "hard blue skies and desert-clear air" for the rootless world of the overnight Greyhound, making the narrative more about person than place. This dark introduction to Perry is matched immediately by a daytime introduction to Dick in extreme close-up, filling left frame and looking frame right. As he examines a shotgun newly unwrapped from burlap, his eyes and the gun barrels lit by an indirect source, the sound of coughing draws him out the door of a shack to his father's side. The long shot that captures their interaction evokes the FSA photos: a horizontal composition of sky, land, and built environment trisected by vertical elements of (L to R) an outhouse, the shack, and a sedan. The effect is a triptych of rural desolation. Desolation, but not poverty: the Hickocks have land and a car, if not indoor plumbing. Here Brooks downgrades Capote's description of "the pleasant kitchen of a modest farmhouse" where Dick returned for Sunday dinner after the killings and stayed to watch basketball in a "parlor" that contained a television set.[28] By recasting the Hickock farm through familiar visuals of Depression-era rural life, Brooks signals the normality that produced the killer, Dick Hickock (Scott Wilson). This 58-second sequence balances the 54-second sequence introducing Perry. Brooks links the two men through editing, again adapting Eisenstein's intellectual montage: Dick's p.o.v. sightline focuses away across winter fields toward the horizon, met in a match-cut by Perry's Kansas City-bound bus closing from left distance into center frame as the actor-credits for these two principal characters appear onscreen. The corrugated side of the passing bus match-cuts to the corrugated side of a Santa Fe train, moving past the Holcomb depot and on into the horizon, reversing that most iconic of diagonal perspective cinema shots: the train arriving at the station. The fast pass of the train by the Holcomb depot indicates isolation and initiates a pair of local reference establishing shots: the tree-lined River Valley Farm road; pan left to the Clutter house in an exact match to Avedon's *LIFE* magazine image; jump cut to a closer shot of the house; pan right, back to the tree-lined road and, in the distance, the highway that passes at a 90-degree angle and that will bring the six principals together. All of these moving images closely resemble the FSA documentation stills from the Kansas of twenty years before. They establish the locale—the actual locale—as consistent with "rural America" in the public imagination, and underscore the implicit message that the American pastoral is a mere image: it *can* happen here.

The Holcomb depot seems incidental in the shot of the bypassing train, a mere vertical element to balance the horizontal composition of the shot. Capote opens a new section of the first chapter, following hard upon the townsfolk's descriptions of the murder scene, with a narrative cutaway: "Eight non-stop passenger trains hurry through Holcomb every twenty-four hours. Of these, two pick up and deposit mail . . ."[29] Jack Delano's 1943 rail images of Emporia and Argonis, Kansas affirm the centrality of rail lines to the geography and identity of this region. Brooks mirrors Capote's juxtaposition of crime scene and context: the depot-and-tracks shot returns as a familiar image in the sequence following the discovery of the bodies at River Valley Farm. From the offscreen scream that signals Susan Kidwell's gruesome discovery, the visual cuts to a police car speeding into center frame, only to turn right onto a Holcomb street; the sound bridges from the scream into the wail of a police siren. Cut to the depot shot as before, now with the train approaching the camera position, moving into and out of center frame as mail bags hurtle from the passing train; the sound bridges here to the train whistle. A hard cut to the tree-lined River Valley Farm driveway captures a police car racing from the center distance toward the camera position, turning into the Clutters's driveway as a cacophonous, nearly buzzing trumpet replaces the siren on the soundtrack. Holcomb depot also serves as the fulcrum of a nearly 70-degree pan shot that tracks the ambulance and additional police vehicles as they race to the crime scene. Ubiquitous in U.S. farm country, the railroad serves in both Capote's narrative and in Brooks's film as a vernacular anchor of location and underscores the nascent ways in which isolation will become connection through this crime.

One of the most literary passages of this nonfiction novel frames the return of the killers to Garden City after their arrest in Las Vegas. The penultimate section of the "Answer" chapter takes place inside a KBI police car during the overnight drive across the mountain states to Kansas, and contains Perry Smith's long description of the night in the Clutter house. The narrative concludes with Perry's statement that the killers only got "between forty and fifty dollars" from the crime.[30] The successive and final section begins with what can only be termed a cinematic cutaway, a necessary refocusing after the shock of the senseless waste of life for such meager yield:

> Among Garden City's animals are two gray tomcats who are always together—thin, dirty strays with strange and clever habits. The chief ceremony of their day is performed at twilight. First they trot the length

of Main Street, stopping to scrutinize the engine grilles of parked automobiles, particularly those stationed in front of the two hotels, the Windsor and Warren, for these cars, usually the property of travelers from afar, often yield what the bony, methodical creatures are hunting: slaughtered birds—crows, chickadees, and sparrows foolhardy enough to have flown into the path of oncoming motorists. Using their paws as though they are surgical instruments, the cats extract from the grilles every feathery particle.[31]

By moving from night-time automobile interior to daylight public square, from moving vehicle to static environment, Capote is able to turn attention from the killers and at the same time draw an analogy to the opportunistic feline predators that haunt Main Street. This scene is prelude to the arrival of the KBI cars carrying Hickock and Smith to the Finney County jailhouse in Garden City; in the film, that sequence occurs not at twilight but in broad daylight. When they arrive, a crowd of locals surges forward, only to be checked by a phalanx of journalists. As the killers are marched up the steps from the cars, a gantlet of newsreel and still photographers sets flashbulbs ablaze. The killers' entrance is shot in low-angle medium close-up with shaky pans that lose focus as the killers pass by. The perspective shifts to a camera position at the bottom of the courthouse steps, facing the approaching men, as though newsreel footage from different cameras were being spliced together. As the KBI agents lead Smith and Hickock inside and up the stairs to the third-floor jail, a camera positioned on the floor above captures their ascent in a series of simple pans left and right. The slight judder suggests a handheld camera, exacerbated by jostling from the crowd eager to see these monsters. The final shot of the sequence centers on the steep and narrow third-floor staircase, signaling the thirteen steps to the gallows that await them. With his *film noir* roots and sensibility, Brooks here employs classic noir elements of realist shot selection, interior labyrinthine staircases, chiaroscuro lighting in law enforcement settings. Capote scripts the scene to end dramatically: "The cameramen, pursuing the prisoners and the police into the courthouse and up three flights of stairs, photographed the door of the county jail slamming shut."[32] Brooks pans from the staircase to the courtroom door, then cross-fades into the trial on the rap of the gavel. Capote adds a final paragraph in which humans exit the scene, "leaving the cold square to the two gray cats, [and] the miraculous autumn departed too; the year's first snow began to fall."[33] This closing is more cinematic than Brooks's documentary and realistic transition to the trial. Clearly there is no way to verify the presence of the furtive cats, nor the realism of the birds caught in car grilles. Capote adapts a dramatic moment to narrative embellishment, while Brooks forces it back to the real locations, lighting, and context, de-poeticizing what is actually an extremely mundane occurrence: the intake of suspects to the criminal justice system.

Figure 15.1  Dick Hickock (Scott Wilson) being led up the courthouse steps.

One of Brooks's notable changes from Capote's text is the insertion of a journalist figure meant to stand in for Capote himself. Particularly in the fourth section of the novel, "The Corner," this observing presence emerges as a fly on the wall to convey details that in the text come from letters and first-hand visits. As Jensen, Brooks cast the esteemed character actor Paul Stewart, who had played a similar role more than twenty-five years earlier as the knowing, all-seeing butler Raymond in *Citizen Kane* (1941). In this film, Jensen also stands in for Brooks, voicing a moral stance against capital punishment at various key points in the killers' legal trajectory to the gallows. By including an embodiment of the authorial persona, Brooks strays from Capote's putative pose of objectivity. On the one hand, this choice might be seen as an acknowledgment of Capote's slanted truth-claims; on the other, it simply might be Brooks's intent to include an author-director stand-in as a gesture of objectivity and a voice against the death penalty.[34]

Despite Jensen's authorial-observer presence, he is absent from the most notable subjective sequence in the film: an intimate reflection that occurs in the last moments before Perry's execution. Capote himself omits a penultimate jailhouse scene. The majority of Capote's closing movement of the novel occurs in the "cold warehouse" that housed the "platform at the top of the wooden instrument's thirteen steps."[35] Although much has been made of and written about Capote's fascination with Smith, the novel moves briskly through the executions, with more attention to the observers than to the condemned men. It is Brooks who foregrounds the arguably worse of the two killers, choosing to end his film with the actual murderer of the Clutters presented as a pitiable figure. Brooks adds a scene after Hickock has already left the holding cells, while Smith stays behind with a minister. This speech is drawn from a passage that Capote places much earlier in the novel, in "Persons Unknown," during the so-called Mexican honeymoon sequence before the killers are even identified. While going through his personal papers, Perry's reminiscence is triggered by his rereading of a biographical summary his father wrote to the Kansas parole board during his previous sentence. Brooks lifts from this passage, in which Perry recites his father's abuses and recalls a physical fight during which the father holds a gun on the boy: "He said, 'Look at me, Perry. I'm the last thing living you're ever gonna see.' I just stood my ground. But then he realized the gun wasn't even loaded, and he started to cry."[36] In the film, the speech ends with Perry stating that the only thing he'll miss in life is "that poor old man and his hopeless dreams," a statement that does not appear in Capote's text.

Brooks repositions and repurposes the speech to the film's final moments, perhaps making a case against execution of such a damaged individual. Conrad Hall again lights Perry as a creature of darkness as his world shrinks to the space of a cell and the gallows. The complete sequence lasts almost exactly four minutes, starting at the cutaway from Dick climbing the gallows steps over in the warehouse. Back in the holding cell, the first minute establishes the scene with ambient lighting and a practical desk lamp to enhance chiaroscuro in this anything but black-and-white moment of reckoning. Robert Blake moves around the space as though blocked on a grid, crossing wall to wall right to left, and door to window, foreground to background. He does not pace like the clichéd caged animal, but changes direction as though seeking an answer when a new thought or action strikes him in the short time he has left. Wide shots of the room reveal the backlit rain-soaked window, with lit water drops running down the darker panes; the wall opposite carries the shadow of the window, with dark raindrops running down the white wall. This ambient reverse image nicely underscores the ambiguity of the rain as symbolic backdrop to the speech.

Then, in a three-minute take interrupted only by one two-second reaction shot of the minister, Perry talks about his father in the waning moments of his own life. This sequence has been lauded as a master stroke of cinematography, and doubtless clinched Hall's Academy Award nomination. Prompted by the minister's offer to write to his father, Perry shakes his head and crosses into a shadowy corner. With a smirk, he says, "Send him my treasure maps. Maybe he'll get lucky. The Lone Wolf." On that ironic note, Perry steps toward the window and begins the recitation that Brooks culled and expanded from an earlier position in Capote's narrative. The change of context changes meaning, of course. In the novel Perry's memory of his father is somewhat nostalgic and, as told to Capote, merely one episode in a biography that leads to killing. Brooks might well say that its repositioning just prior to Perry's execution also constructs a narrative that leads to killing, but there are other embedded meanings, among them the pathos (or bathos) of Perry's treatment by his father and the generational parallel of luck running out for both father and son. During this speech, Perry appears in three-quarter face, lit from the right by the exterior lighting from the prison yard which also backlight raindrops on the window. This mise en scène, discovered during tech rehearsal, became an iconic moment in the film and in Hall's career:

> "While I was lighting the scene, I noticed that the light from outside was shining through the water sliding down the window pane and projecting a pattern resembling tears on the face of Robert Blake's stand-in. I brought it to Richard's attention. In the finished scene, the acting, cinematography, direction and writing all come together to create a very memorable moment. People think you're a genius for planning something like that, when in reality you were just smart enough to notice it and exploit it."[37]

The visual impact of this effect cannot be overstated. The shadows of tears on Perry's face are mesmerizing, as though he is producing the patterns from within.

This is an unexpected and poetic instance of pathetic fallacy. Capote's novel did not contain and could not have predicted this finishing touch on the adaptation of the mid-novel speech to a farewell moment in the film. In this sequence, Brooks—and Hall—fully move the narrative from the realm of adaptation to mutation, creating a new coalescence of filmic, narrative, and visual elements.

In the next four minutes, a duration equal to that of the preceding scene, Perry arrives at the warehouse, is read his sentence, speaks last words, ascends the scaffold, and drops to his death. As slowly as his penultimate scene unfolds, this final scene moves briskly. The nearly static penultimate scene is

Figure 15.2  Rain shadows from the cell window produce tear images on Perry (Robert Blake)'s face moments before he is removed to face execution.

answered in counterpoint by the swift machinery of justice, slowing only after the drop as Perry's body swings in backlit chiaroscuro to the decelerating beat of a dying heart.

The process of Capote's research becoming text, becoming a "nonfiction novel," then becoming photo-stories in *LIFE* and *Vogue*, and then a film, charts a series of mutations of genre, character, point of view, authorial presence, style, and structure, among other elements. A subsequent miniseries, two feature films, and a documentary have further transfigured the events of November 15, 1959 and April 14, 1966.[38] Capote was clear from the beginning that this project was the result of his desire to further develop the concept of the nonfiction novel that he had first attempted with *The Muses Are Heard*. He even referred to the idea as "my big experiment."[39] The replication and mutation of his results affirm Leitch's contention that adaptation is not merely a matter of fidelity. For this narrative, text and intertext have merged, replicated, and mutated through collateral print, visual, and filmic forms, and will most likely continue to do so.

## NOTES

1. Although Mailer's first truly nonfiction novel, *Armies of the Night* (1968), succeeded *In Cold Blood* by two years, *The Naked and the Dead* (1948) made significant strides toward creative nonfiction. For an appraisal, see Michiko Kakutani, "A Novelist's Spirit Captured the American Spirit," *New York Times*, November 11, 2007, https://www.nytimes.com/2007/11/11/books/11appraisal.html. This view counters David Carr, who argues for the priority of Capote's aesthetic. See David Carr, "In Cold Print: The Genre Capote Started," *New York Times*, July 13, 2005.
2. See, for example, Frank Norris's *McTeague* (1901) and Theodore Dreiser's *An American Tragedy* (1925).
3. Capote's truth-claims are highly contested and were so from the beginning, thanks in no small part to his own explanations of his documentation method and his narrative affectations. See, for example, Ralph F. Voss, *Truman Capote and the Legacy of* In Cold Blood (Tuscaloosa: University of Alabama Press, 2011), p. 80.
4. Jane Howard, "Horror Spawns a Masterpiece," photographs by Richard Avedon, *LIFE Magazine*, January 7, 1966: pp. 59–76.
5. For a collection overview, see the digital resource, *Farm Security Administration/Office of War Information Black-and-White Negatives*, Library of Congress at https://www.loc.gov/pictures/collection/fsa/. For representative Kansas images, see Russell Lee's portrait, "Mrs. Shoenfeldt, wife of FSA (Farm Security Administration) client, Sheridan County, Kansas," Farm Security Administration (August 1939) https://www.loc.gov/pictures/item/2017740688/; Jack Delano's *noir*-lit night shot, "Santa Fe R.R. yards, Argentine, Kansas. Argentine yard is at Kansas City, Kansas," Farm Security Administration (March 1943) https://www.loc.gov/pictures/item/2017878097/; and John Vachon's evocative Main Street shot, "Centralia, Kansas," Farm Security Administration (October 1938) https://www.loc.gov/pictures/item/2017717444/.
6. Russell Lee, "Mr. Germeroth, Sheridan County, KS," Farm Security Administration (August 1939) https://www.loc.gov/pictures/resource/fsa.8a26907/.

7. Farm Security Administration, *How the Photographs Were Produced*, collection description, Library of Congress, https://www.loc.gov/collections/fsa-owi-black-and-white-negatives/about-this-collection/
8. Haskell Frankel, "The Author," *Truman Capote: Conversations*, ed. M. Thomas Inge (Jackson: University Press of Mississippi, 1987), pp. 70–1.
9. For scholarly analyses, see Kelly A. Marsh, "Empathy, Authority, and the Narrative Ethics of Truman Capote's 'La Côte Basque, 1965,'" *Journal of Narrative Theory* 43. 2 (2013): pp. 218–44, and Donald Pizer, "Documentary Narrative as Art: William Manchester and Truman Capote," *Journal of Modern Literature* 2.1 (1971): pp. 105–18; for a popular reassessment and Clutter family perspectives, see *Cold Blooded: The Clutter Family Murders*, directed and produced by Joe Berlinger, Allison Berg, and Kahane Cooperman (2017, Sundance).
10. Howard, "Horror Spawns a Masterpiece," p. 58.
11. Ibid. pp. 58–9.
12. Ibid. p. 62.
13. Ibid. p. 63.
14. Ibid. pp. 60–1.
15. Ibid. p. 62.
16. Ibid. pp. 64–5.
17. Truman Capote, "Two Faces and a Landscape," *Vogue*, February 1, 1966: p. 148.
18. Loudon Wainwright, *The Great American Magazine: an Inside History of* Life (New York: Knopf, 1986), p. 280.
19. Douglass K. Daniel, *Tough as Nails: The Life and Films of Richard Brooks* (Madison: University of Wisconsin Press, 2011), pp. 174–5.
20. Truman Capote, *In Cold Blood* (New York: Random House, 1965), p. 248.
21. George Garrett, "Then and Now: *In Cold Blood* Revisited," *The Virginia Quarterly Review* 72.3 (Summer 1996): p. 473.
22. Thomas Leitch, "Twelve Fallacies in Contemporary Adaptation Theory," *Criticism* 45.2 (Spring 2003): p. 168.
23. Truman Capote, "Reality's Reflections: Concerning the Filming of *In Cold Blood*," Holographic Notebook (Regarding: Movie Filming), Truman Capote Papers, Manuscripts, and Archives Division, The New York Public Library: Box 11, folder 1 (undated): pp. 9–10 [unnumbered pages].
24. George Plimpton, "The Story Behind a Nonfiction Novel," in *Truman Capote: Conversations*, ed. M. Thomas Inge (Jackson: University Press of Mississippi, 1987), p. 63.
25. Capote, *In Cold Blood*, p. 3.
26. Pizer, "Documentary Narrative as Art," p. 113.
27. Capote, *In Cold Blood*, p. 83.
28. Ibid. p. 73.
29. Ibid. p. 66.
30. Ibid. p. 246.
31. Ibid.
32. Ibid. p. 248.
33. Ibid.
34. Daniel, *Tough as Nails*, p. 174.
35. Capote, *In Cold Blood*, p. 337.
36. Ibid. p. 136.
37. Stephen Pizello, "Wrap Shot: *In Cold Blood*," *American Cinematographer*, March 22, 2019: n.p. https://ascmag.com/articles/wrap-shot-in-cold-blood

38. See the miniseries *In Cold Blood*, directed by Jonathan Kaplan (2016, Hallmark); the feature films *Capote*, directed by Benedict Miller (2005, United Artists), and *Infamous*, directed by Douglas McGrath (2006, Warner); and the documentary *Cold Blooded: The Clutter Family Murders*, directed by Berlinger, Berg, and Kahane (Sundance, 2017).
39. Frankel, "The Author," p. 70.

CHAPTER 16

# Looking for Mr. Good Guy: Anatomizing '70s Fracture and Fragmentation

*Julie Grossman*

According to Paramount's Press Notes, six filmmakers said no to directing *Looking for Mr. Goodbar* (1977). Intrigued by the sociological and documentary potential of the project, however, Richard Brooks wanted to present Theresa Dunn (Diane Keaton) as a "product of her times," imagining that numerous contexts were in play:

> Of her fantasies, of television commercials, beauty products continually being hawked, sex magazines displayed openly on newsstands, her religious upbringing, her parental guidance or lack of it, her schooling, how she looks physically, what opinion she has of herself emotionally and psychologically. These are factors which play a part in her development. I thought if those things could be utilized without making a documentary, it might be an interesting film.[1]

Brooks's comment on trying to locate a form of social documentary within the storytelling is especially noteworthy given that the source of the film, Judith Rossner's bestselling 1975 novel by the same name, was based on the actual murder of Roseann Quinn, a teacher of deaf children in New York City, in 1973 (itself also the source for *Closing Time: The True Story of the "Goodbar" Murder* by Lacey Fosburgh [1977]). Having written and directed *Looking for Mr. Goodbar*, Brooks sets the film's opening credits to a montage approximating a documentary tone, with black-and-white stills featuring the characters in the film, as well as random denizens at crowded bars and on the city streets; at the same time, a splintered musical soundtrack suggests a theme of fragmentation and marks a cultural shift in urban nightlife from singles bars to disco clubs. In 1970, NYC mayor John Lindsay signed a bill prohibiting male-only bars in the city; the

Figure 16.1 Diane Keaton, luminously shot, while Brooks also opts for a documentary style in the film's opening sequence.

famed McSorleys was obliged to admit women; and Chicago (where *Goodbar* was filmed some years later) lifted a ban on female bartenders.[2]

In the same year that the film *Looking for Mr. Goodbar* was released, Lacey Fosburgh published what she would call an "interpretive biography" of Roseann Quinn and John Wayne Wilson, the real victim and murderer in the 1973 crime.[3] A journalist who wrote about the case after the killing, Fosburgh speculates on the characters of Katherine Cleary and Joe Willie Simpson (as *Closing Time* renames Quinn and Wilson), toggling back and forth between their stories and backgrounds, establishing a symmetry between them. As the story develops, the chapters become shorter and shorter, creating a hurried tone and generating suspense in increasingly staccato accounts of their days and hours leading up to Katherine's murder. The form seems part of Fosburgh's effort to posit this chance meeting between Katherine and Joe Willie as fated. In contrast to Fosburgh's "interpretive biography," the film *Looking for Mr. Goodbar* doesn't sensationalize the story but renders it cinematically as an artistic reflection on trauma and the brutality of overbearing social roles, and sex, gender, and religious conventions.

The film, as an adaptation of Rossner's novel inspired by Quinn's death, takes artistic liberties that also suggest a parallel between Theresa and Gary (the murderer, played by Tom Berenger), though as Robin Wood has suggested, this link is based on both characters struggling with predetermined sex and gender roles, floundering amid uncertain or unsatisfying social conventions.[4] For Wood, in its ambiguous tone, *Goodbar* is one of a number of

1970s films whose ideological and aesthetic properties constitute an "incoherent" text riven with contradictions in representation.[5] Wood suggests that among *Goodbar*, *Taxi Driver*, and *Cruising*, *Goodbar* is the most "unreadable."[6] Brooks's effort to document the challenges facing a vibrant woman craving independence—suggesting, as the filmmaker said, that Theresa "mistakes sexual freedom for women's liberation"[7]—created a contradictory text that bemoans some of Theresa's choices while still illuminating the female protagonist's vitality, desire for independence, and humor. While some critics and viewers responded to the film with revulsion, others appreciated Keaton's performance and observed the film's devastating emotional impact. This chapter locates the impact of the film in its fusion of a critique of fixed social roles and Keaton's embodiment of Theresa Dunn. Such a focus may yield more clarity, hopefully, than incoherence, despite the film's difficulty and its indefinite tone with regard to Theresa's sexual life.

Admittedly, *Looking for Mr. Goodbar* is something of a critical crux, with questions circulating about Theresa's complicated life and how the film's characterization of its female protagonist relates to its tragic ending. By day, Theresa is an empathic teacher of deaf children; by night, she bar-hops, engaging in casual sex with strangers. When the film was released in 1977, scholars writing for *Cineaste* and *Film Quarterly* saw it as "reactionary and unoriginal," hawking a "petrified ideology" and "celebrating the kind of sexist wooden morality that is, in part, responsible for the very issue it attempts to illuminate."[8] In this view, the film's tone is allied with its plot, *Goodbar* punishing its female protagonist for claiming her independence and expressing that desire for freedom through sex. The appraisal of Theresa's life through her death was moralistic, though as later critics have pointed out, such imposition of a moral framework to make sense of the trajectory of the narrative is a critical act, a choice on the part of viewers that carries its own burdens and problems. The awfulness of what happens to Theresa is not free of context—Brooks's intent to document a social moment, for example; the writer-director's focus on Theresa's fantasies and pleasure; and Keaton's uncanny performance, all of which this chapter seeks to emphasize. Such contexts complicate the binary good/bad model that informed much contemporary reception of the film.

Seeing the film as a counter to positive feminist expressions of female independence, some of the film's first critics and a number of film scholars insisted on its badness. As R. Barton Palmer observes about the later controversial film *Cruising*, however, *Goodbar* also reminds us that the aesthetics of "badness, like goodness, is a relational term usually connecting to instrumentality in some sense."[9] If the "instrumentality" Palmer references finds "goodness" in an affirmative representation of female liberation, *Goodbar* could never gratify audiences. It might, however, *interest* viewers in its goodness in another sense: its anatomizing of social conventions that, even amid the rise of popular feminisms, remained harmful to women. Fathers, priests, doctors, and male professors seek to control Theresa and other vulnerable figures in her world, such as the young Black student Amy, in need of a hearing aid and whose single mother has taken a lover to find some pleasure in her difficult life ("I got a right to something," she says). In an early scene in the film, social worker James (William Atherton) tells Amy's fed-up mother that her welfare check will be denied if she continues a relationship with her lover. She tells Theresa about James, "he pulls the plug, no welfare, no school, nothing." "Him?" Theresa responds, offended by James's power in his job to determine another's life and well-being. It is this painful social environment in which individuals are dictated to without being helped or nurtured by their supposed support systems that Theresa's character rebels against in her battle for self-determination. Consequently, the teacher by day/sexual adventurer by night framework for understanding Brooks's story is not a sufficient account of the film's complexity, despite popular language (even used by the writer/director himself) focused on doubleness, as in Betsy Erkkila's review of the film for *Cinéaste*: "However good Theresa may be as a teacher, her professionalism is ultimately undermined by her evening escapades."[10] While Theresa's casual sexual encounters later in the film are meant to be painful to watch and are also absurdist in their representation of unfulfillment for the woman, the language of "evening escapades" suggests a condemnation of the character for being sexual, exactly what some critics accused the film of doing. Trying to figure out how the duality of Theresa resolves, or doesn't resolve, in her murder, misses the film's participation in a noir tradition of breaking down cultural categories, binary ways of understanding experience, and dichotomous expressions of virtue and unworthiness. The murkiness of Theresa's experience places the film in a line of bleak or bracing neo-noir texts such as *Klute* (1971) (on which more later), *Chinatown* (1974), *Blade Runner* (1982), and *Blue Velvet* (1986), where female characters systematically blur distinctions between the conventionally good and bad.

When *Goodbar* was released, some critics objected not only to its depiction of a brutally reprimanded female sexuality but also to the film's homophobia in its representation of the killer Gary, a self-loathing gay man goaded into anger, who murders Theresa after he isn't able to perform sexually. Derek Nystrom cites Geoffrey Nowell-Smith's discussion of "hysterical texts" to argue that the excess in the representation of Gary's character is an example of how "repressed energies, produced by contradictions they cannot resolve, return as textual excesses and incoherencies. In this sense, Gary can be seen as the textual excess generated by the film's failure to resolve its contradictory attitude to Theresa's two selves."[11] Notwithstanding my own rejection of the "two selves of Theresa" approach to the film, later in the essay Nystrom writes that "Gary's sudden and seemingly unmotivated arrival at the end of *Goodbar* signals the film's panic at its own inability to represent the unreadable world suggested by Theresa's new, protofeminist sexuality."[12] Though Nystrom is most interested in the film's representation of class and *Goodbar*'s portrayal of violent men and their "extra masculinity" (focused on Richard Gere's tour de force portrayal of Tony), his reading of the film focuses usefully on its "subtle indictment of male violence and domination"[13] and on the by-products of a failed era of liberation, "in which there are no mutually understood signals or codes."[14] Going back to Brooks's stated intention to "document" a woman's experience without making a documentary, and despite Henry A. Giroux's claim in *Film Quarterly* that Brooks's characters are "ahistorical,"[15] as Caetlin Benson-Allott argues, "Male and female, straight and gay, African American and Caucasian, these heterogeneous bar patrons represent the social experiment of the singles bar and the sexual revolution: Crucially, their images historicize rather than localize Theresa's story."[16] Part of the incoherence of Theresa's story may be explained by the film's insistence on trial and error, characters bouncing among different experiences in a concerted effort to reject the past in a cultural present defined by contradictory messages about empowerment and desire. At this time of flux, where long-established cultural rules were breaking down, there was difficulty knowing what to replace the outmoded social practices with; this explains the haphazard quality of lived experience, as well as the stress of liminal interests, pastimes, and endeavors. Such messiness relates interestingly to Brooks's interviews with "hundreds of women" about their experience of Rossner's novel: "They all read into it something very personal, having little to do with the book and much more to do with feelings the book has triggered."[17] I wasn't interviewed by Brooks but might have been a worthy source. I read avidly and was preoccupied with Rossner's novel when I was an older teenager, and I frequented discotheques in New York City in the late '70s. I witnessed and participated in the excitement and confusion of urban dance and music club culture during that time, which may explain why I was, with much equivocation and a strong investment in women's independence, drawn to the novel in the first place. I think it quite inevitable in retrospect that this exhilarating and somewhat disorienting setting would inspire a representation defined by contradiction.

Aesthetically, the fragmented sampling of disco music in the film represents this cultural ambiguity and disjunction. *Goodbar* shows personal freedom to be difficult to obtain and even obscure or unintelligible within a culture labeled and marketed as uninhibited, while also being still very bound to patriarchal religious and moral conventions. Such contradiction causes a bewilderment expressed aptly in Theresa's exchanges with her sister Katherine (Tuesday Weld), whose "masquerade parties," tangled relationships, and chaotic life belie these women's "enlightened" social moment. Katherine tells Theresa her husband Barney "doesn't even know me," and later reveals that she has given up drugs and alcohol in favor of analysis and group therapy. Theresa says,

"Everybody's taking something, or they'd never make it to morning," to which Katherine says, "We all hurt someplace and we're all looking for a pain killer." The film is unequivocal about the traps laid for Theresa, but like the society it seeks to "document" has trouble articulating what the advertised freedom for women means for those struggling with intransigent social institutions and the oppressive men who surround them. No doubt the diminishment of 1950s and early '60s puritanism was a welcome change, but the film depicts the problems with implementing such transformation, tamped down or appropriated by patriarchy and masculine sexual fantasy.

In *Goodbar*, Theresa's authoritarian father (played by Richard Kiley) engineers her repressive Catholic upbringing, a form of entrapment Brooks shows by focusing in a flashback on Theresa's body cast, in which the girl lay fixed for a full year, following surgery for scoliosis. An apt metaphor for Theresa's confinement, the body cast is a predicate for Theresa's desire to break out ("So much of her life," Rossner writes in the novel, "she had felt strapped down"[18]). Brooks shows imagistically the oppressiveness of Catholic guilt as a defining feature of her rebellion: After having sex with a married professor, she stands on the subway platform. Greeted as the doors of the train open with a censorious nun staring at her, the doors shut without the nun exiting the train. In a shot echoing a European art film, Brooks shows the external world giving Theresa signs that she has sinned.

But the film insists all the same on her resistance, which is largely figured through fantasy sequences that accentuate Theresa's affinity for pleasure. Rather than depicting Theresa as unhappy, oppressed by multiple forces, the film instead emphasizes her resilience and vitality. Even in increasingly degraded encounters or environments, Keaton's protagonist shows a striking joie de vivre. Molly Haskell described this as "a life force . . . an inner light"[19] (in one scene, that light is figured literally as that of film projection, as Theresa watches a pornographic film for the first time and the film valorizes her desire and erotic curiosity). When Theresa introduces herself to Tony (Richard Gere) as "Sonia Katrina Raskolnikov," Brooks telegraphs Theresa's sense of humor about guilt and religion (while channeling the writer/director's own fascination with the novelist—he had helmed an M-G-M adaptation of Dostoevsky's *The Brothers Karamazov* in 1958). But her reference to Sonia also indicates Theresa's Dostoevskyan spirit and innocence, exemplified, for example, when her sister Katherine disappoints their father by bringing her new Jewish husband home for Easter dinner. Theresa breaks through a chilly reception by running to embrace Barney with warmth and openness, saying "Happy Passover."

Keaton's appearance in the film flummoxed some viewers, who saw her quirky "Annie Hall" persona (*Annie Hall* was also released in 1977) as an obstacle to reading her as an erotic protagonist; others found Keaton's performance astonishing, like Haskell, whose positive review of the film in 1977 stood out from others castigating *Goodbar* as anti-feminist and abject. Before getting back to Haskell, I would note the scenes in the film in which Keaton's sly humor and "Annie Hall" charm add layers to Theresa's character, distinguishing her from the more grim and self-hating figure in Rossner's novel (a point Haskell makes with which I agree—Brooks's Theresa, as Haskell argues, is "a brilliant improvement on the novel"[20]). Most striking about *Looking for Mr. Goodbar* is Keaton's embodiment of delight, standing in stark contrast to the desolation wrought on her character in the novel. Such a contrast may contribute to audiences' perplexity in watching the film, but there is also a way to read Theresa's "inner light," externalized by Brooks's camerawork and Keaton's performance, as a clear rebellion against the violence characterizing the social world that surrounds the character. The film is buoyed by Keaton's charm, the camerawork emphasizing frequently how enchanted Theresa is by certain moments of fantasy or in her encounters with others.

Theresa's fantasy of her first meeting with Tony (Richard Gere) trying to pick her up in a bar is a good example. Theresa is reading *The Godfather*, whose film adaptation, of course, featured Keaton in 1972 (followed by *The Godfather 2* in 1974). Tony says, "I seen the movie. That Pacino is something." "Uh huh," she responds slyly, to which Tony returns, "I'm gonna make you an offer you can't refuse."

Part of the charm in Theresa's smiles is based on her previous observation within the fantasy of Tony about to steal a wallet from another woman at the bar. Realized in Keaton's performance, Theresa's subjectivity is comprised of

Figure 16.2 Diane Keaton and Richard Gere playfully discuss Mario Puzo's *The Godfather* and Coppola's film adaptation, in which Keaton had appeared in 1972 (and again in the sequels).

a scrutiny of what's happening around her, a sense of humor, a desire to experience the unknown, and a genuine pleasure in indulging her daydreams and expressing her desires. Arguing that Keaton "gives the performance of a lifetime,"[21] Haskell focuses on the productive collaboration between Brooks's style and Keaton's vitality: "The tension between Brooks's bluntness and Keaton's distinctive delicacy has produced the ideal chemistry."[22] Keaton's Academy Award for *Annie Hall* was likely for both performances—if not a covert way of awarding Keaton for a film in the same year that was so controversial, then certainly, as *Goodbar* co-star William Atherton observed, a recognition of her range as an actor.[23]

In 2015, Caetlin Benson-Allott published a superb essay on *Looking for Mr. Goodbar* in *Feminist Media Studies*, tracking the parallel disappearance of the material film—out of circulation since 1997—with the death of Theresa within the story. Reception of the film has turned it into part of the "abject archive," in Nathan Carroll's terms;[24] unavailable on DVD or via streaming, the film exists for now as a difficult-to-find blurry text; the film is not in circulation except via bad transfers from VHS copies. Given the insights perhaps generated by a retrospective view of the film's intensity and its controversy, the extras a Blu-ray edition would proffer are a real loss.

Benson-Allott reminds us of the deprivation that follows a film's negative reception, with *Goodbar* thrust into oblivion as a result of anxieties about it being a "'feel-bad' movie":[25] "dark forces," says Benson-Allott, "are erasing all traces of Theresa Dunn."[26] Benson-Allott links the trauma besetting the character to the loss of the film itself, which stages a "figural encounter with loss."[27] Wanting to participate in a "reparative reading" of the film (citing Eve Kosofsky Sedgwick in this regard), Benson-Allott writes movingly about the film's traumatic trajectory, wondering if there are "other ways it might have ended,"[28] suggesting that the film invites empathic attentiveness. I would contrast Benson-Allott's understanding of the film with my earlier references to Fosburgh's journalism as "interpretive biography," a sensationalist retelling of the Quinn murder. Brooks's film not only emphasizes Theresa's fantasies and imagination; it invites our own. I am reminded here of Davinia Thornley's introduction in her 2018 book *True Event Adaptation: Scripting Real Lives*, in which Thornley says, "Speaking for myself through my work on *Out of the Blue* [the 2006 New Zealand film based on the 1990 Aramoana massacre], the film looks hard into the face of the unthinkable—and then it lays that burden down and turns toward what is still possible, what remains, what is worth saving."[29] Does the film *Goodbar* represent "the unthinkable" and beckon to us forty-five years later to see "what is still possible, what remains"?

I have been reviewing three major shortcomings of viewings of *Looking for Mr. Goodbar* that are centered on the brutality of the killing of Theresa as a reflection of moral logic. One, they eclipse the film's critique of the failure of conventionally organized liberatory movements of the 1960s and '70s, which much of the film takes pains to enact. Mainly, Brooks's film suggests, it is nearly impossible to gain a freedom of choice when individuals are bombarded with images that conflate desire with consumption (as in the first scene of the film, when Theresa stands in a subway car next to a passenger reading *Hustler* magazine, or when the TV game show *The Price is Right* is notably in the background of a family gathering at the Dunns's house). In Brooks's words, society told women, "If you use this toothpaste, that fellow will kiss you. That is a *violent* lie."[30]

Two, in a notably long film whose violent ending comprises a small part, focusing on the film's conclusion endorses a plot-centered reading of the film that ignores the dynamism of the film's art and Diane Keaton's striking presence throughout. More than simply complicating a univocal view of the film, Wood's, Haskell's, and Benson-Allott's readings of *Goodbar* suggest its radical denunciation of social roles and systemic bias, underscoring in their emphases the errors that are often made in mistaking a narrative trajectory for a film's tone. It is no more appropriate to read *Goodbar* as endorsing the horror that ultimately befalls Theresa Dunn than it is to imagine Alexander Payne's *Election* celebrating the resilience and good fortune of Mr. McCallister's "landing on his feet" at the end of that film.

Three, perhaps a consequence of the first two pitfalls, the trauma of the film's final scene—including the "fractured shot" of Theresa,[31] her face floating into the darkness at the end of the film—produces an emotional jolt on the part of the viewer. How we characterize that jolt is important to understanding the film's significance and its power. If *Goodbar* wishes to depict social failures that puncture an illusion of freedom, does the tragic conclusion of the film, as Benson-Allott suggests, invite us to wonder about how the story might otherwise have ended? Does it remind us of the stakes of gender violence, the brutally inauthentic masks of normalcy, and the consequences of the culture's suppression of desire? In Benson-Allott's words,

> The elegiac rhythm with which the film alternates between image and blackness gives the spectator time to experience the loss of this young woman. It invites less defensive, more open-minded viewers to reconsider Theresa's narrative and imagine other ways it might have ended. Such viewers might fill in the darkness by envisioning other futures for Brooks's heroine—or simply refuse to revile the film that tells this tragic story. They might choose to embrace the film instead, to love the bittersweetness of this catalyzing art experience. Through its beauty, Brooks's final shot can provoke viewers to see more than violence in Theresa's death, to dream of change rather than accepting the status quo. Such ideations amount to a viewerly gesture of home, which is no less painful than wallowing in fatalism, but it does offer the viewer an alternative way to sustain herself in the face of trauma and loss.[32]

If some critics and viewers have found the film *Looking for Mr. Goodbar* too appalling to bear, one wonders forty-five years later if such dread has changed shape. In reflecting on the reception of Brooks's *Goodbar*, one is reminded of Vincent Canby's scathing review of another film about trauma and the death of a vibrant female character, David Lynch's *Twin Peaks: Fire Walk with Me*, when it premiered in Cannes in 1992, Canby saying, "It's not the worst movie ever made; it just seems to be."[33] By 2013, however, *The Village Voice* called *Fire Walk with Me* "David Lynch's masterpiece,"[34] suggesting the contingency of reception in valuing a text. Indeed, *Fire Walk with Me* shares characteristics with *Looking for Mr. Goodbar* worth considering: directed by established auteurs, both films focus on powerful and passionate women who are victims of trauma and brutal male violence. Laura Palmer (played by Sheryl Lee) and Theresa Dunn aspire to more fulfillment than what is on offer in their small towns or imprisoning settings; they rebel against parochial upbringings that come to be experienced, because of other factors still, as traumatic. Theresa's "inner light"[35] prefigures the same in Laura Palmer in *Twin Peaks: Fire Walk with Me*. Violated, traumatized, Laura is the "strongest of them all," as Lindsay Hallam says of her.[36]

Haskell's description of Keaton's Theresa is similar, focusing on how the character may "seek out degradation, while her spirit remains magically inviolate."[37] Such representation of power and vulnerability owes a lot to the work of actors Diane Keaton and Sheryl Lee, whose stunning performance achievements were in both cases veiled by the blunt and quite visceral reactions to difficult material.

Figure 16.3 Laura Parker (Sheryl Lee) and Theresa Dunn (Diane Keaton), radiant embodiments of traumatized female characters.

As the Paramount press material I cited earlier demonstrates, *Goodbar* blames Theresa's trials with romance and sex on superficially gendered mass marketing and media messaging: Theresa does bust exercises as she listens to a news report on TV about how the '70s were supposed to be the "decade of the dame," the use of such diction belying the feminist movement ostensibly referenced in the news story.

Brooks is intent on exposing such pat popular rhetoric as vulgar and deceitful, and he is also wanting to unmask superficially good guys to reveal their toxicity. As Haskell saw distinctly in 1977, the men in the film "are all part of a social nightmare in which there are no mutually understood signals, no rituals, no codes for deciphering the intentions of another individual."[38] Theresa's father is a perfect example of the failures of a patriarchy militarized by religious fervor. From early on in the film, Brooks portrays Mr. Dunn as a threatening force—in a flashback to Theresa's childhood medical traumas, the young girl looks up at her father while undergoing a procedure: "Papa?" she calls out. The dramatic low-angle camera shot of Dunn emphasizes his menacing authority and judgmental rejection of her for failing to be perfect (as her sister Katherine is presumed to be). After Theresa breaks with James later in the film, her father excoriates her for rejecting a good Catholic boy:

> Not man enough for our gimpy Miss America?! I don't understand you. I don't understand your crazy world, I don't understand your crazy talk! Freedom this, and freedom that! Free to leave your family. Free to quit the church. Free love. Free to abort your own kids. Free to go to hell.

As his sickly cough is interjected in this caustic speech, the film shows him to be a dying breed, more desperate for being on the wrong side of history.

In my work on the *femme fatale* in *film noir*,[39] I've suggested that a more nuanced representation of female power and sexuality is embedded in the *femme fatale*'s transgressions and rejoinder to a sexist society that not only boxes women into narrow gender types but also that doesn't hold men responsible for the rage they act on as a result of feeling like the culture has given them the "go-by." Theresa's insistence that Gary leave, an assault to his masculinity, makes him feel justified in becoming ferocious. But perversely, Gary may, as Robin Wood suggests, be the least toxic male in the film, only in the sense that like Theresa, he is traumatized by fixed sex and gender roles that make him feel like an outcast for not being heteronormative. Instead, what stands out in the film is the creepy James, an unambiguously good guy in Rossner's novel whom Brooks changes in the film, absorbing him into a landscape of savage men who are only on the very surface of things part of a stable patriarchy.

This final part of my chapter takes up explicitly the chapter's title, "Looking for Mr. Good Guy," adding a further subtitle, "John, James, Mike, and Ryan."

I take my lead from Haskell, who observes in 1977 that *Goodbar* is "*Klute* ten years later."⁴⁰ Both films are certainly interested in what it means to be an independent woman during an era labeled as liberatory. Both films explore society's confused gender messaging, but both also sneakily suggest that dangerously controlling men exist outside of the realm of the psychotic murderer. Demonstrating *film noir*'s habit of breaking down binaries, private detective John Klute (Donald Sutherland) himself shadows Bree Daniels (Jane Fonda) and has an air of threat about him. A later example of the same blurring of good and bad guys appears in the neo-noir *The Last Seduction* (1994), in which Bridget Gregory (Linda Fiorentino) goads Mike Swale (Peter Berg) into raping her to set him up for her ex-husband Clay's murder. Desperate to prove his hetero-masculinity, Mike removes his cloak of amiability and opts for violent sexual assault.

Similar gender patterns are in Brooks's film. While Tony seems the most obvious threat to Theresa, with his sudden appearances and dangerous play with neon-lit knives and kung fu antics seducing her with manic displays, significantly, he doesn't appear dominating; instead, he seems like a frenzied lost boy, drumming restlessly on tabletops. While more clever than Travis Bickle, Tony shares his and Jake LaMotta's habit of pumping himself up in front of mirrors, a gesture signaling a basic insecurity underlying the performance of masculinity. When Theresa calls the police on Tony as he tries to break into her apartment, Brooks makes him the MacGuffin: "that does it," he yells through the door. "You are dead!"

But it is the good Catholic father, the college English professor, and the mild-mannered social worker who are most damaging to Theresa. I've already discussed Theresa's tyrannical and belligerent father. Her first lover is smarmy English professor Martin Engle, a smug and moody misogynist who tells Theresa that right after sex, "I just can't stand a woman's company." When Theresa calls Martin over the holidays, and his wife answers the phone, he righteously screams at her later, "I will not be compromised, not here on campus, not in my home, not at work!" The gap between the reality of the narcissistic and exploitative teacher and Theresa's fantasies that he is a loving partner (in one of these, Theresa wins an Olympic medal for ice skating, and Martin embraces her, lauding her achievement as "poetry in motion") underscore the disconnect between cultural stereotypes of romance and the real challenges of sexism and rampant exploitation as independent women seek suitable mates. While alone in one scene, Theresa energetically parodies Tony's tough-guy air-boxing moves, cigarette hanging from her mouth, her imitation exposing the dearth and insufficiency of role models for female empowerment and pleasure.

The most compelling instance of malice disguised as benevolent masculinity or patriarchy appears in the film as Theresa's suitor James. Robin Wood rightly notes the significance in *Goodbar* of Brooks's changed portrayal of

James, Theresa's "nice-guy" suitor, whom she is deeply ambivalent about, at least in the novel, because he is interested in her. That is, Rossner presents Theresa's rejection of James as masochism, as a sign of Theresa's low self-esteem. He is good to her and unconditionally loving, and she finds this attention unbearable ("*I despise you for loving me*," Theresa reflects, in the novel[41]). Wood emphasizes the significance of the film's James, changed from the novel, in which he is "safe, reliable, and loving, everything a good girl is supposed to need. The film makes him just as neurotic and potentially dangerous as everyone else."[42] As Nystrom observes, this point is reinforced by montage, the film cutting from James's violently angry outburst to Theresa's father chasing her in an apoplectic fit.[43] Ripping off the costumes of normalcy, the portrayal of James is quite terrifying.

This would-be priest who becomes a social worker wheedles his way into the Dunn family, showing up inappropriately at the hospital when Theresa's father is admitted, ingratiating himself with her family generally, and eventually stalking her and turning to domestic abuse. In one scene, James appears at Theresa's school to show off that he has learned sign language so that he can communicate with her students and impress her. In another scene, he tells Theresa that she is only frustrated with his unwelcome insinuations into her life because she is lonely. She responds, "I am alone, not lonely, and depressed, and you're depressing me," an apt expression of Theresa's efforts to evade men trying to take control of her life. James doesn't like the way she has decorated her apartment, having appropriated from her sister's apartment a set of glass chimes engraved with erotic imagery, telling her "this place isn't like you at all." Men repeatedly seek to define Theresa. A manipulative liar who tells Theresa fake stories about how his mother sexually shamed his father, who then left home, James carries a repressed rage that is eventually unleashed. For Christmas, James gives Theresa the strobe light that serves as the setting for her murder. The disco light ball reminded him of her—"light and dark, on and off, now I see you, now I don't"—implicating James in the binary view of Theresa that doesn't allow for complex and sometimes contradictory selfhood. I would also note that despite the suddenness of Gary's appearance at the end of the film, it is telling that Theresa turns to him as he plays pinball at the bar as a direct result of trying to escape the stalking presence of James, who is also at the club. In other words, in the film, the logic of Gary's appearance is part of a chain of violent men, whose various surprises to Theresa and the viewer reinforce the omnipresence of the threat of predation.

*Goodbar* appears in a sequence of noir-inflected films that posit patriarchy as psychosis, analyzing its extreme effects on women. A recent example of how strong women may stoke male insecurity to reveal a shocking toxicity beneath a veneer of normal gender roles appears in Emerald Fennell's *Promising Young Woman* (2020). The film's devastating ending—the victim/victimizer *femme fatale* Cassie

(Carey Mulligan) calling the rapist to account—stands alongside an equally chilling denouement in an earlier scene with Cassie and Ryan (played by Bo Burnham). Cassie and Ryan have fallen in love in romcom fashion, a ploy the film uses to make viewers feel safe within the warm glow of genre conventions. When, later in the film, *Promising Young Woman* picks up its feminist rape-revenge story threads, we understand that the romcom trick on viewers has cleverly replicated the nice-guy male ruse depicted in the film. Eventually, mild-mannered, charming good-guy pediatric surgeon Ryan is stoked to anger when reminded of his own complicity in the rape then suicide of Cassie's best friend, whose death she seeks to avenge. Exposed as a collaborator in the violence against the absent woman who haunts our protagonist, Ryan puts his self-preservation ahead of doing what's right and appears defensively and angrily justified in so doing.

Brooks's change to the character of James is much more coherent in the context of the film's critique of patriarchy. Casting good-guy social worker James as one in a series of psychotic men, the film emphasizes the inauthenticity of sex and gender costumes, which, when unveiled, reveal deep wells of rage and dissatisfaction.

Such destabilization of these films' purpose, meaning, and representational strategies reinforces *Goodbar*'s productively ambiguous genre identity as a noir-inflected thriller that focuses on a would-be *femme fatale*. The figure's classic unknowability—suspended as Theresa is in Brooks's last shots—the film's "incoherence," is, on the one hand, a consequence of Brooks's attempts to anatomize philosophical and modern cultural/psychological experiences of desire and trauma within shifting social forms, but on the other hand belied by a thoroughly vital and expressive performance by the lead female actor.

## NOTES

1. *Looking for Mr. Goodbar* Press Notes, Author's Collection.
2. See Caetlin Benson-Allott, "Looking for *Looking for Mr. Goodbar*: Or, Strategies for Sitting with the Abject Archive," *Feminist Media Histories* 1, No. 3 (2015): p. 134.
3. Lacey Fosburgh, *Closing Time: The True Story of the "Looking for Mr. Goodbar" Murder* (New York: Open Road Integrated Media, 1975), p. 7.
4. See Robin Wood, *Hollywood from Vietnam to Reagan* (New York: Columbia University Press, 1986).
5. Ibid. pp. 55–8.
6. Ibid. p. 58.
7. See Douglass K. Daniel, *Tough as Nails: The Life and Films of Richard Brooks* (Madison: University of Wisconsin Press, 2011), p. 204.
8. Henry A. Giroux, "Review of *Looking for Mr. Goodbar*," *Film Quarterly* 31, No. 4 (1978): pp. 52–4.
9. R. Barton Palmer, "Redeeming *Cruising*: Tendentiously Offensive, Coherently Incoherent, Strangely Pleasurable," in *B is for Bad Cinema: Aesthetics, Politics, and Cultural Value*, eds. Claire Perkins and Constantine Verevis (Albany: SUNY Press, 2015), p. 86.

10. Betsy Erkkila, "Review of *Looking for Mr. Goodbar*," *Cinéaste* 8, No. 3 (1978): p. 43.
11. Derek Nystrom, *Hard Hats, Rednecks, and Macho Men: Class in 1970s American Cinema* (Oxford: Oxford University Press, 2009), p. 137.
12. Ibid. p. 138.
13. Ibid. p. 131.
14. Ibid. p. 137.
15. See Giroux, "Review of *Looking for Mr. Goodbar*," p. 53.
16. See Benson-Allott, "Looking for *Looking for Mr. Goodbar*," pp. 134–5.
17. Brooks, quoted in Daniel, *Tough as Nails*, p. 203.
18. Judith Rossner, *Looking for Mr. Goodbar* (New York: Simon and Schuster, 1975), p. 261.
19. Molly Haskell, "Exposing a Nerve," *New York Magazine* (October 31, 1977): p. 116.
20. Ibid.
21. Ibid.
22. Ibid.
23. Actor William Atherton, quoted in Daniel, *Tough as Nails*, p. 209.
24. See Benson-Allott, "Looking for *Looking for Mr. Goodbar*," p. 143.
25. Ibid.
26. Ibid. p. 142.
27. Ibid. p. 129.
28. Ibid. p. 128.
29. Davinia Thornley (ed.), *True Event Adaptation: Scripting Real Lives* (London: Palgrave Macmillan, 2018), p. 9.
30. Brooks, quoted in Daniel, *Tough as Nails*, p. 204.
31. See Benson-Allott, "Looking for *Looking for Mr. Goodbar*," p. 128.
32. Ibid. pp. 128–9.
33. Vincent Canby, "One Long Last Gasp for Laura Palmer," *New York Times*, August 29, 1992: p. 11.
34. See Calum Marsh, "*Twin Peaks: Fire Walk with Me* Is David Lynch's Masterpiece," *Village Voice*, May 17, 2013.
35. Molly Haskell's phrase (note 19) works for both female characters, as embodied by the two performers.
36. See Lindsay Hallam, *Twin Peaks: Fire Walk with Me* (Liverpool: Auteur Press, 2018), p. 21.
37. Haskell, "Exposing a Nerve," p. 116.
38. Ibid. p. 119.
39. See Julie Grossman, *Rethinking the Femme Fatale: Ready for Her Close-Up* (Basingstoke: Palgrave Macmillan, 2009) and *The Femme Fatale* (New Brunswick, NJ: Rutgers University Press, 2020).
40. Haskell, "Exposing a Nerve," p. 119.
41. Rossner, *Looking for Mr. Goodbar*, p. 269.
42. Wood, *Hollywood from Vietnam to Reagan*, p. 56.
43. See Nystrom, p. 132.

CHAPTER 17

# Failing to Locate *Wrong is Right* (1982) and What that Reveals about Cinematic Reality

*Allen H. Redmon*

By most every account, Richard Brooks's penultimate project, *Wrong is Right* (1982), is not a very good movie. Brooks's biographer, Douglass K. Daniel, determines that "by nearly every measure, *Wrong is Right* should have ended Richard's career."[1] Daniel notes that even Brooks refers to the film as "the biggest disaster of his career," although he does refuse to dismiss it entirely.[2] Brooks suggests the film has some merit for its prophetic ability. In very short order, the very dangers *Wrong is Right* shows developing had occurred in lived reality, including suicide bombers throwing themselves into crowds and significant landmarks.[3] Brooks suggests that such confirmation confirms that his film was too honest to gain the audience it deserved, even if the film was woefully underfunded, as he was also fond of saying.

Critics have been less forgiving. Vincent Canby refers to the film as a "wholehearted mess."[4] Canby lodges two primary complaints. The film fails to offer a clear point of entry since the main character, Patrick Hale (Sean Connery), is something of an intertextual mess caught between Edward R. Murrow and James Bond. Even more confusing for Canby is the site of action for the film. Canby writes that the movie moves across the globe at such a pace that "the audience often can't be sure where things are taking place."[5] Opinion of the film hardly changes over the two-plus decades that pass between its theatrical release and its release on DVD. Stuart Galbraith's 2004 reassessment of the movie refers to *Wrong is Right* as a cinematic "bomb."[6] For Galbraith, the movie spins in the "air of a [poorly produced] TV movie [with too much] stock footage [and] lousy (even for 1982) special effects." Galbraith reserves his sharpest criticism for the film's agonizing humor. Beyond the one-liners that often fall flat, Galbraith also protests Brooks's decision to pretend to film *Wrong is Right* on location in "Hagreb," a made-up country in North Africa.

One might rightly attribute this choice to Brooks's source-text for his script, Charles McCarry's *The Better Angels*, which also occurs in "Hagreb." But Galbraith is right to imply that describing a made-up location in a novel and filming a movie in a made-up location has a different effect. The image on the movie screen is often thought to have some basis in the actual world that a novel's setting need not have. In fact, the actual location *is* on the screen regardless of whether it is described as such or not, and this certainly impacts what one sees and how one sees it.[7] This chapter takes particular interest in this impact, particularly as it relates to the various ways Brooks and others achieve (or fail to achieve) a sense of cinematic reality, either in a film that means to be realistic, or, in the case of *Wrong is Right*, that means to be more stylized.

To appreciate the particular style Brooks seems to desire for *Wrong is Right*, one does well to account for some of the ways that Brooks adjusts McCarry's novel. In some fundamental ways, Brooks's story is akin to McCarry's. Various agencies including the President of the United States, his chief political rival, two different terrorist groups, and Patrick Hale's own news channel race to find two suitcases packed with atom bombs. The suitcases themselves, as they exist in the film, certainly mean to provide the filmic narrative something of a focal point. Unfortunately, they fail to do that, in part, because they never establish the narrative tension one would expect from such a plot device. Brooks does his best to create moments where some tension might arise. One such moment arises through a scene that Brooks almost certainly wants to appear as a hard-hitting television exposé that brings to the public in the film (and the audience) a recap of action that occurs earlier in the movie. Hale exposes United States President Lockwood (George Gizzard) for approving a C.I.A. assassination of King Awad (Ron Moody), the ruler of Hagreb. The reporter reveals that Rafeeq (Henry Silva), the head of an international terrorist group, sought the suitcases to carry out a plot against the United States.

The report creates a block of action that could produce some tension if it were more properly executed. The competing groups in the film each try their best to secure the bombs, each for their own reasons. Rafeeq needs the suitcases to prevent the world from seeing that Hale's story is true. A second terrorist group needs the bombs to execute the plans Rafeeq is no longer willing to perform. President Lockwood needs the bombs to validate his decision to assassinate King Awad. Lockwood's political opponent, Mallory (Leslie Nielsen), needs the bombs to keep Lockwood from having that validation. Hale and his television studio need the bombs to secure an exclusive story. So, each party descends on the bunkhouse of the film's arms dealer, Helmut Unger (Hardy Krüger). The plot seems to be working toward an open contest, only to avoid showing it. The various rivals encounter each other, but not in plain sight on the screen. Brooks suggests more than he shows to create some sense of suspense, it would seem. If that was the intention, the choice does not work terribly well, and even minimizes the tension that might otherwise emerge from such a contest.

The same sort of effect occurs during what should be one of the most tension-filled scenes in the film. Members of the President's Cabinet and Hale race against a clock to discover and deactivate the bombs that have been placed in New York City. Brooks places that clock on the screen in several key points of what begins to work as a deadline plot. The race never realizes the tension it might, if only because the outcome is never in doubt. In the final moments of the chase to find the suitcases, Hale and C.I.A. head Philindros (G. A. Spradlin) race across the top of the World Trade Center—the actual World Trade Center—to retrieve the suitcases from a flagpole. The moment has the sort of shots one would expect in such a scene, men running to their target before standing over a bomb as it is slowly and carefully disarmed. But the images do not generate tension. The tight shots, which remove the World Trade Center from the frame more than recover it as some choices for framing might do, even strip the screen of the chilling effect contemporary audiences might feel seeing the World Trade Center as the site of a terrorist attack in 1982. As the scene comes to exist in the film, the moment is reduced to little more than its narrative function and as a bridge to a series of final jokes the film wants to register. Congress and the President use the presence of the suitcases on American soil as a reason to declare war. A newspaper headline reads "War at Last," as a graphic scrolls across the bottom of the screen: "President Assured Re-election." The images resolve various narrative threads. They also sharpen the implicit condemnation of political duplicity the film seems resolved to pronounce. They do not leave audiences imaging a clear cinematic reality.

The film misses a clear sense of cinematic reality, in part because Brooks never decides the distance his story or his camera will have from some literal reality. Will it be one step removed, in the way the most realistic depictions are? Will it be mediated by television, stock images, and special effects, as it is at so many different points of the plot? Brooks never settles into one strategy. He adopts them all, even at the end of his film, a point captured most succinctly in an image that shows the film's two political rivals, Lockwood and Mallory, enjoying a phone conversation together as wartime images surround them. Mallory tells the newly re-elected President to "hit 'em with everything you got" before joking, "Just don't hit those oil wells." Both men laugh. More stock images follow the would-be joke as the plot works toward one last punch-line. General Wombat (Robert Conrad) and Hale ready themselves to jump from what is clearly meant to suggest rather than represent an airplane high above some target. The final set is like so many other set pieces in the film, an open artifice. In a more developed film, the artificial sets might smartly match the duplicity of the dialogue. Brooks's preference for tight shots in *Wrong is Right* keeps that from happening. As such, the audience can only focus on the

Figure 17.1 Mallory (Leslie Nielsen) on the phone congratulating the newly re-elected President Lockwood (George Gizzard).

dialogue. Wombat reminds Hale of his orders: "Now you're here for one reason: no matter what happens nothing happens until it happens on television." Hale shows that he understands before offering his own reminder: "Before you take the oil wells, remember, we're taking a three-minute commercial break." Both men jump the plane. Another stock image fills the screen. Stop action.

Brooks's story stops, but it does not reach a terribly satisfying ending. Audiences almost assuredly leave a viewing of the film unsure of what they have just witnessed. They are never provided a way to watch what Brooks asks them to see. In other words, Brooks does not provide enough clear criterial prefocusing, to use Noël Carroll's term, to establish a meaningful cinematic reality.[8] The failure is surprising if only because Brooks so regularly delivers a clear and coherent cinematic reality across an impressive career. Brooks demonstrates clear ability in earlier films to reimagine literary works and actual locations for the screen. *Wrong is Right* becomes something of an outlier, then, which makes the movie noteworthy not only for those interested in Brooks, specifically, but for those interested in exploring the reasons the qualities most marking that film succeed or fail. This chapter is most interested in the various ways Brooks could have achieved a meaningful sense of cinematic reality. The fact that the film is an open adaptation provides one path toward a cinematic reality. The fact that Brooks injects so many different filmic genres in *Wrong is Right* offers another. The satirical persona adopted by Brooks offers the promise of a third path to a cinematic reality. The parts of the film that start to operate like cinematic camp hint at a fourth path. To be blunt, *Wrong is Right* misses on each of these fronts, but a discussion of how it misses does reveal some interesting insights into the various kinds of cinematic reality Brooks helps establish over his career.

Before discussing the above four secondary senses of cinematic reality, it is worth admitting the most fundamental sense of reality that awaits movies shot with a lens-based camera. There is, of course, the reality that exists in front of the camera. This possibility stood for many years as film's great achievement, a point film theorists tend to find celebrated most succinctly in André Bazin's essay, "Ontology of the Photographic Image." Peter Wollen recounts using a review Bazin wrote of Vittorio de Sica's *Bicycle Thieves* (1948), what is often taken as Bazin's primary perspective in that essay: de Sica's film, Wollen writes, serves as the "first example of pure cinema [as Bazin would have it . . .] no more actors, no more plot, no more *mise en scene* [. . .] no more cinema."[9] From Bazin's perspective, de Sica provides audiences the highest form of cinematic reality, a reality that extends from a world that exists before the camera.[10] Interestingly, this is a sense of reality that Brooks regularly brought to his films by virtue of his willingness to shoot on location.

*In Cold Blood* (1967) might be the most significant example of Brooks shooting on location. Brooks moves his film crew to Kansas in order "to capture the reality [of the horrible crimes that film details] with absolute honesty," to quote the film's original trailer. By being in Kansas, Brooks and crew can bring to the screen images of *the* phone, *the* gas station, *the* store, *the* farmhouse, and *the* courtroom where the original events being "re-enacted" in the film took place. The result, to return to the declarations of the trailer, is "a terrifyingly *true* story." The concluding remark captures an assumption that certainly marks many of the films in Brooks's oeuvre. Most of the twenty-six films directed by Brooks were shot on location and were shot there to lay bare some form of authenticity.[11] Brooks, in fact, realized an exceptionally diverse record for on-location filmmaking. Two early films, *The Light Touch* (1951) and *Flame and the Flesh* (1954), took Brooks to Italy. *The Last Time I Saw Paris* (1954) and *$* (1971) took him to France and Germany, respectively. *Something of Value* (1957) took Brooks to Kenya, while *Lord Jim* (1965) took him to Cambodia. In addition to these international locales, Brooks also shot films in New York City; Blackstone, Virginia; El Paso, Texas; Malibu, California; Overton, Nevada; Denver, Colorado; Chicago, Illinois; Las Vegas, Nevada; and the already mentioned location of River Valley Farm in Holcomb, Kansas. One can reasonably refer to Brooks as one of the most prolific on-location directors in the history of cinema.

Brooks's opportunity to develop as an on-location director certainly connects to industry practices in play when he began directing films. Daniel Steinhart describes the Hollywood that exists when Brooks begins directing to be something of "an international production operation."[12] Steinhart uses the pretense of a film released at the tail-end of this practice to parody this practice, Vincent Minnelli's *Two Weeks in Another Town* (1962). Minnelli's film is shot in an M-G-M studio, but it moves on a stage meant to replicate Rome and Cinecittà Studios in Italy. The resulting scenario very nearly recreates what would have been the conditions of Brooks's first film directed abroad, *The Light Touch*, which moves along the very streets of Rome and in the very same Cinecittà Studios. Following Steinhart, during the early 1950s, M-G-M would have preferred Italy to Hollywood to spare costs. The principal members of the film's crew, Brooks, the two leading actors, Stewart Granger and George Sanders, the cinematographer, Robert Surtees, and one of the art directors, Cedric Gibbons, could be prominent entities, while the rest of the crew would consist of local talent willing to work at a much cheaper rate than would need to be paid if the film were shot in Southern California.

Steinhart lists another advantage to foreign shooting locations, namely, cinema's chance to do what its biggest competitor, television, could not: deliver audiences in the United States images of Europe after WWII. Films set in Italy, to stay with the conditions of *The Light Touch*, could provide U.S. audiences the chance to see the cities U.S. soldiers saw during the war. Steinhart quotes a 1949 comment from cinematographer John Alton to explain the appeal of such a sight: "During the war, millions of soldiers were sent to various locations to shoot, but not motion pictures. These men know a real London fog, were disappointed in the women of the jungle, and recognize Rio, Budapest, or Cairo [. . .] no more will they buy Hollywood-made Africa," or, by extension, any other locale.[13] The films *had* to be on location to deliver an authentic encounter with Western Europe.

R. Barton Palmer provides a more essential reason for on-location shooting. Palmer uses *The Big Lift* (1950) to describe the way a film shot on location can include "dramatic encounters [that] draw out and express the meanings of the *real place* in which they are set."[14] Palmer asserts that *The Big Lift* can be regarded as a film that is "every bit as much a documentary as a fiction film."[15] Palmer's proposal is exciting for the way it places attention on a setting that is more "than a backdrop or frame" as it exists in film.[16] The actual location becomes a "dwelling [that] configures, or makes manifest, the interrelationship of the characters who inhabit it."[17] *The Big Lift* offers one example of this. *The Remains of the Day* (1993) offers another. James Ivory's film chooses the place it does, Palmer reasons, because Ivory needs a sense of place in the film to be more than a site of action; place needs to become "a function of narrative."[18] Palmer's proposal makes an interesting distinction between cinematic sets and cinematic setting. The former provides a scene. The latter provides a sense of place. A film shot on location can lean into that sense of place to create a sense of cinematic reality that differs even from that space as it exists in the world. The place on the screen helps establish a meaningful sense of cinematic reality.

This sense of place does not need a literal reality to emerge. The images just need to achieve a sense of place. Some of the most successful films of all time, in fact, do not depend on a literal reality. They prefer a more constructed cinematic reality, one that opens through the portal things like cinematic adaptations, genre films, filmic satire, or camp provide. These types of realities present themselves even when a film also promises to deliver some literal reality—something a return to *In Cold Blood* can illustrate. Brooks's *In Cold Blood* means to be read alongside Truman Capote's *In Cold Blood*. The cinematic adaptation means, in other words, to stand alongside rather than replace its literary inspiration. The marketing campaign around Brooks's film encourages audiences to keep the two texts together rather than to draw them into competition with one another at least as much as it encourages audiences to see the action on the screen occurring in some real Kansas. The cinematic reality of *In Cold Blood* depends on both realities.

Brooks's reliance on Capote's novel does not require Brooks to preserve Capote's novel. In fact, audiences will expect—if not require—some departure from the admitted source if the film is to be successful. Deborah Cartmell and Imelda Whelehan explain the reason for this in their work on "impure cinema."[19] For Cartmell and Whelehan, as for other scholars working from a process-rather-than-product-minded perspective of cinematic adaptations, a film must do more than recreate the novel it adapts. It must also intermix the original with the conventions of the cinematic medium. In other words, the cinematic adaptation must be *cinematic* if it is to achieve a clear sense of cinematic reality. Cartmell and Whelehan offer Peter Jackson's *Lord of the Rings: The Fellowship of the Ring* (2001) as an example of such a film. Cartmell and Whelehan argue Jackson's film received the positive reception it does, in part, "because it adapted the novel to Hollywood conventions."[20] One might make a similar argument for Brooks's *In Cold Blood*. Brooks's adaptation is clearly marked by the cinematic conventions at play when it was released. As such, *In Cold Blood* realizes a sense of place, and it does so through a doubly framed sense of cinematic reality, one that depends on *the* actual places in Kansas and the pages of Capote's novel.

It is worth reiterating the extent to which *In Cold Blood* remains in contact with Capote's novel. A cinematic adaptation does well to remain in sufficient contact with its source text if it intends to establish its cinematic reality through some juxtaposition with the literary source it reproduces in one way or another. *Wrong is Right* fails on this point. Brooks seems a little too ready to abandon the particulars of his source, Charles McCarry's novel, *The Better Angels*. The two texts share some commonalities, but their similarities seem trivial and coincidental rather than significant or constructive. Brooks makes two shifts that distance his story from McCarry's novel. The first is that Brooks injects the film with a sense of humor, which changes the tone of every detail in the film, even those he carries forward from *The Better Angels*. For example, Brooks focuses just as McCarry did on a President intent on doing whatever he must do to secure a second term, up to and including having a foreign king assassinated. Brooks's President is more of a Richard Simmons exercise nut, parading through the White House in a sweatsuit and working out than he is ever presidential. The truth is that none of the details in Brooks's story play as straight as they do in McCarry's novel, which keeps the film at some distance from the novel.

Brooks also removes the one plot-point from the novel that gave McCarry's story a short-lived second life after the terrorist attacks of 9/11. McCarry's story includes a passage involving terrorists flying passenger airplanes into buildings. Brooks removed that detail presumably, in keeping with Daniel's assumption, for the same reason the director passed on the "Thomas Harris novel *Black Sunday* [. Brooks] doubted he would be able to obtain the permissions necessary for a movie about terrorists using the Goodyear blimp for an attack on Miami's Orange Bowl during the Super Bowl."[21] So, rather than have airplanes hit buildings, Brooks stages suicide bombers jumping into crowds or from planes. The two events are hardly the same thing. They are made even more different by how poorly the effect is realized. Perhaps due to a woeful budget, or perhaps because he wanted the moment to appear comedic rather than realistic, Brooks creates what Galbraith describes as a series of "inept" special effects that has a "spate of suicide bombers [. . .] light up like giant Fourth-of-July sparklers [. . .] instead of exploding into nothingness [. . .] as they leap like acrobats into crowds of passerby[s]." Regardless of what accounts for the effect, Brooks's choice to remove the terrorist plot involving passenger airplanes keeps his film from grabbing the post-9/11 attention McCarry's novel did. The two texts come to exist in two different universes.

This is not to say that Brooks's film refuses all intertextual relationships. Forty years removed from the release of *Wrong is Right*, one finds some interesting connections between Brooks's film and other films that do some of the same things Brooks's film does. Critics routinely name two of those. *Wrong is Right* is often mentioned as a less successful *Dr. Strangelove* (1964), which is a similarly carnivalesque Cold War satire targeting the military-industrial complex. *Wrong is Right* is also mentioned alongside *Network* (1976), which dramatizes the then contemporary mainstream media's willingness to adopt an "if it bleeds it leads" yellow journalism attitude. Audiences might also relate Brooks's film as something of a follow-up to Barry Shear's *Wild in the Streets* (1968), or a precursor to Menahem Golan's *Delta Force* (1986) or Barry Levinson's *Wag the Dog* (1997). *Wrong is Right* certainly shares some commonalities with those films. It is just often regarded as a less accomplished example of what those films are doing.

One of the reasons *Wrong is Right* misses a mark some of these other films are thought to hit is that Brooks never develops a meaningful sense of genre in his film. *Wrong is Right* alludes to several different genres. It is something of a thriller and a melodrama and a dark comedy, but it is just as well none of these film types. Brooks never keeps his script or his direction to the rules or iconography for these filmic genres, which means that spectators are never able to use the conventions these genres provide to negotiate what they see. This shortcoming is interesting for several reasons, but it is most especially interesting for the way it reminds scholars of how the notion of genre changes during Brooks's career. His earliest films would still mostly fit within the more traditional genre discussions and understandings that emerge during the studio days when a genre existed as an organizing principle for a film's production and reception. In keeping with Thomas Schatz, a genre film provides audiences with characters, a setting, a plot, and techniques that possess "prior significance as elements of some generic formula."[22] Part of the pleasure of seeing these sorts of elements extends from the opportunity they provide the audience to reflect on departures from the "preordained, value-laden narrative system."[23] This possibility becomes especially important as genres become more self-conscious. Following Steve Neale, once genres become more aware of themselves, they become a "multi-faceted phenomenon [meant to] be approached from the point of view of the industry and its infrastructure, from the point of view of their aesthetic traditions, from the point of view of broader socio-cultural environment upon which they draw and into which they feed, and from the point of view [of] audience understanding and response."[24] Genre becomes, in short, a site of negotiation. When a film tolerates more than one generic sensibility, as *Wrong is Right* certainly tries to do, it can even tolerate a variety of ways to read the one film.

Redmon considers how Coen brother films like *The Big Lebowski* (1998) or *O Brother, Where Art Thou?* (2000) invite more than one way to read their action. Following Redmon, *The Big Lebowski* provides sustained attention to the characteristics of the detective genre, the war genre, or the queer genre; *O Brother* engages notions of the cinematic adaptation, the classical Hollywood musical, and the social problem film.[25] One can read either of these films from start to finish as an instance of the genres they use or even as some mix of those genres. The result is a polysemous film that possesses an initial rather than a final form. A kind of incessant play opens around each element of the film that encourages spectators to enter a process of ongoing construction and reconstruction of the film in front of them. This invitation can only be extended, though, when the filmmakers establish an ongoing relationship with the genres being employed. Unfortunately, Brooks never establishes the consistent connections with any of the genres he uses, which means his film cannot invite the same type of spectatorial play, nor can it rely on generic sensibility to achieve a meaningful sense of cinematic reality.

To be fair, Brooks was almost certainly never intending to make a straight adaptation nor a genre film. Brooks chooses to frame *Wrong is Right* as something of a prophetic satire in the tradition of Swift and Juvenal. Brooks attempts to follow these satirists by offering an all-out assault on the social evils of his day, employing moral indignation, ridicule, irony, hyperbole, sarcasm, allegory, and politically partisan ad hominem attacks. *Wrong is Right* even conveys the sense of outrage, a desperate need to see transformative social reform, and a pessimism that such reform will ever occur that most especially marks Juvenalian satire. Somewhat ironically, the presence of these traits might frustrate Brooks's film as much as they shape it. This is, in part, because the film adopts these more caustic traits without providing sufficient humor or a satisfying ending. The Marx Brothers's *Duck Soup* (1933) stands as an interesting contrast to *Wrong is Right*. The Marx Brothers's film is every bit the same Juvenalian satire, but it also balances its social criticism with other important qualities that *Wrong is Right* misses. *Duck Soup* employs the vaudevillian artistry of the Marx Brothers to savage the rise of global fascism in the 1930s. Its pace and ending provide it a tone that proves pleasant to watch. Without a proper ending, pace, and sense of humor, Juvenalian just threatens to isolate audiences. That might have been what happened with Terry Gilliam's dystopian comedy *Brazil* (1985), had U.S. distributors not reduced Gilliam's 142-minute director's cut with a downbeat ending to a more manageable 94-minute studio version complete with a happier ending. Unfortunately, the distributors did not "save" *Wrong is Right* in a similar way. The film is released in all its outrage, desperation, and pessimism.

The above three-part problem might not sink *Wrong is Right* on its own. Some films filled with outrage, desperation, and pessimism find success. They just require an audience that needs the protest the film provides. Brooks was fond of making this point. He claims that his film depends on a smart audience that knows how to respond to the insights he provides. Unfortunately, *Wrong is Right* has yet to find such an audience. The final form of the film might be responsible for that, too. *Wrong is Right* might very well overplay its hand, playing with too much cynicism and thinly veiled characterization to find a thinking audience. What *Wrong is Right* is most missing is some moment that empathetically portrays either the human suffering in the film or the environmental devastation experienced in what amounts to a dystopian world. In other words, Brooks fails to set within this dystopian world any character who can articulate an alternative worldview or who will fight for such a world. Hale is the closest thing to such a character; regrettably, Brooks dresses Hale in too much cynicism and duplicity to carry that torch. Hale becomes something of a trap for audiences, as they have no place to exist save beneath the deep-seated cynicism of a failed idealist, who begins to replicate the very behaviors he presumably began his journalistic career to expose. In this respect, Brooks favors a cinematic perspective, one limited to Hale, rather than to developing a true cinematic world around a character that has a broader perspective or a set of characters that represent a range of equally valid perspectives. In short, Hale's perspective is not an effective satirical voice because it participates too much in the business-as-usual of Brooks's fallen society. *Wrong is Right* becomes a collection of grotesque characters and scenes marked with emotional inauthenticity that its expressions of moral outrage gesture more toward camp than incisive cultural critique.

Had Brooks pushed these more exaggerated perspectives farther than he did, *Wrong is Right* might exist as a form of cinematic camp that might have also redeemed what otherwise look like flaws. One sees in Susan Sontag's "Notes on Camp" how camp can redeem such weaknesses. Sontag cites an array of defining features of the camp, all of which could have helped *Wrong is Right*: the promotion of artifice over authenticity, grandeur and extravagance over subtlety, unconvincing special effects, transgressive androgynous figures, and inadvertently achieving bathos while striving for pathos.[26] One sees aspects of each of these traits in *Wrong is Right*, just as the above discussion makes plain. Sontag makes an important distinction, though, between two types of camp: unintentional camp, which seems to arise by accident and comes to exist as something of a guilty pleasure to watch, and intentional camp, which seems forced and artificial. *Wrong is Right* certainly falls into the latter category. Nothing in the film seems coincidental. Every detail seems contrived. The combination strips the picture of the senses of contingency a more established sense of cinematic reality can provide.[27] Without any meaningful sense of contingency, some outside perspective, one cannot have a significant cinematic reality.

There are two moments in *Wrong is Right* where the potential for some outsider perspective begins to emerge. These moments, brief as they may be, are important to *Wrong is Right*, not only for the film, but to those who want to see some evidence of the qualities that mark Brooks's most successful films. One such moment arises during a speech Rafeeq gives when he is referred to as a reprehensible murderer and terrorist. Rafeeq recoils at the suggestion and replies with the righteous anger of a Muslim living in a Middle East governed by oppressively anti-democratic American oil interests and their political allies. Rafeeq rattles off a list of state-sponsored terrorist initiatives that took place around the world throughout history, citing the genocide of indigenous peoples, the subjugation of Irish Catholics, the Holocaust, and other atrocities. For Rafeeq, these evils are infinitely more despicable than anything he would do because they were perpetrated by the powerful and corrupt, rather than the disenfranchised. Worse, the perpetrators of these human rights violations would largely escape widespread moral condemnation. It is significant that Hale—and, by extension, the film—does not laugh at Rafeeq or condemn him in this moment, especially since *Wrong is Right* is a broad comedy that, at some point, laughs at each of its characters. Here, Rafeeq is taken seriously. Brooks's script gives Rafeeq space to condemn western imperial subjugation of the Middle East, which distances his film from the one-note depiction of the

Muslim villain found in other 1980s films, including *Raiders of the Lost Ark* (1981) and Connery's own *Never Say Never Again* (1983).

Brooks does something similar in a key scene with Vice President Ford (Rosalind Cash). President Lockwood tells the Vice President that he feels like he has been backed into a political corner and will probably need to resign. The Vice President asks him if he is ready to relinquish power to her, thereby making her both the first female and the first African American president. The question is one that rings nearly as clearly today as it would have rung in 1982. Was America ready for a president who broke those barriers? Ford asks the question archly, but not so disdainfully that the seriousness of it is washed away. Her appointment would be made precarious because of her president's political situation, but even more so by the responsibility she would face as a Black woman president.

Ford's face shows humor, but humor leavened with sobriety. It's a sobriety that extends from the subversive power of Cash's very presence in *Wrong is Right*, which can be always felt, but that rises to the surface in this key moment. The surface quickly fades though, and so too does the weight *Wrong is Right* could have mustered were it more committed to such moments. Brooks's script shows signs of wanting to stay in this moment a little longer, but it can only do so through a joke. The President half-jokingly agrees with his Vice President's hesitation, offering that stepping down and allowing Ford to replace him would be akin to putting a member of the Black Panthers in the White House. The moments leading up to and even including this particular joke reward those

Figure 17.2 Vice President Ford (Rosalind Cash) responding to the political dilemma with her party face.

that stay in them. There is an intimacy in this scene that would be refreshing to see in any film, but that is particularly welcome in this one. The most artistically successful and ideologically effective social satires include moments like these, moments that reveal a strong counterculture or "outsider" perspective that challenges the evils of the established order. *Wrong is Right* is just too quick to leave such moments.

*Wrong is Right* creates space for the types of countercultural or "outsider" moments that brings contingency back into the story, but it does not build on them. Viewers of *Wrong is Right* are not privy to the backgrounds of Rafeeq or Ford. Brooks refrains from giving the backgrounds for any of the elements brought into his drama. Each detail becomes a feature in search of a context. The film as a whole constructs a platform where a cinematic reality might more properly be. Brooks had several avenues to a meaningful cinematic reality. He could have leaned into the moral authority that arises through the outsider perspective Rafeeq or Ford bring to the film and realized the cinematic reality that awaits camp. He could have found a more satisfying humor, consistency, or ending to achieve a more effective satirical cinematic reality. He could have relied more heavily on the genres he uses. He could have created a more satisfying partnership with his source text. More generally, Brooks could have realized a more convincing cinematic reality by creating some unexpected moment of empathy in the film. Without any one of these qualities to buttress his world, Brooks leaves his viewers without the well-established and rewarding cinematic reality he so often provided throughout his career.

## NOTES

1. Daniel K. Douglas, *Tough as Nails: The Life and Films of Richard Brooks* (Madison: University of Wisconsin Press, 2011), p. 212.
2. Ibid.
3. Daniel quotes Brooks saying, "Everything that happened in that movie has since happened in real life [. . .] including people who crash into an embassy on a suicide mission" (ibid.).
4. Vincent Canby, "'Wrong is Right,' Globe Hopping Thriller." *New York Times*, April 16, 1982. https://www.nytimes.com/1982/04/16/movies/wrong-is-right-globe-hopping-thriller.html
5. Ibid.
6. Stuart Galbraith, "Wrong is Right," *DVDtalk*, March 16, 2004. https://www.dvdtalk.com/reviews/review/10379
7. In the case of *Wrong is Right*, much of the action set in "Hagreb" was actually shot in White Sands National Monument, New Mexico. Interestingly enough, White Sands was also the location for much of the filming for Brooks's *Bite the Bullet*, a film released seven years earlier.
8. Noël Carroll, *The Philosophy of Motion Pictures* (Hoboken, NJ: Blackwell Publishing, 2008).
9. Peter Wollen, *Signs and Meanings in the Cinema* (Bloomington, IN: Indiana University Press, 1969), p. 131.

10. I do mean to suggest both senses of *before* in this phrasing, as both senses inform the concept of cinematic reality Bazin describes, which is a sense of being *in front of* and of occurring *earlier in time*.
11. Notable exceptions to Brooks's practice of shooting on location include *Crisis* (1950), *Blackboard Jungle* (1955), *The Brothers Karamazov* (1958), *Cat on a Hot Tin Roof* (1958), *Elmer Gantry* (1960), *Sweet Bird of Youth* (1962), *The Professionals* (1966), *Bite the Bullet* (1975), and *Looking for Mr. Goodbar* (1977).
12. Daniel Steinhart, *Runaway Hollywood: Internationalizing Postwar Production and Location Shooting* (Oakland: University of California Press, 2019), p. 3.
13. Ibid. p. 8.
14. R. Barton Palmer, *Shot on Location: Postwar American Cinema and the Exploration of Real Place* (New Brunswick, NJ: Rutgers University Press, 2016), p. 22.
15. Ibid. p. 23.
16. Ibid. p. 24.
17. Ibid. p. 30.
18. Ibid. p. 31.
19. Deborah Cartmell and Imelda Whelehan, *Screen Adaptation: Impure Cinema* (London: Macmillan International Higher Education, 2010), p. 2.
20. Ibid. p. 76.
21. Daniel, *Tough as Nails*, p. 201.
22. Thomas Schatz, *Hollywood Genres: Formulas, Filmmaking, and The Studio System* (New York: McGraw-Hill, 1981), p. 10.
23. Ibid.
24. Steve Neale, *Genre and Contemporary Hollywood* (London: British Film Institute, 2019), p. 2.
25. Allen Redmon, *Constructing the Coens: From* Blood Simple *to* Inside Llewyn Davis (New York: Rowman & Littlefield Publishers, 2015), pp. 81–95.
26. Susan Sontag, *Notes on Camp* (London: Penguin Classics, 2018).
27. One sees this sense of contingency detailed most fully in Mary Ann Doane's *The Emergence of Cinematic Time: Modernity, Contingency, the Archive* (Boston, MA: Harvard University Press, 2002).

# FILMOGRAPHY

Directed by Richard Brooks:
*$* (Columbia Pictures, 1971)
*Bite the Bullet* (Columbia Pictures, 1975)
*Blackboard Jungle* (M-G-M, 1955)
*The Brothers Karamazov* (M-G-M, 1955)
*Cat on a Hot Tin Roof* (M-G-M, 1958)
*Crisis* (M-G-M, 1950)
*Deadline—U.S.A.* (Twentieth Century-Fox, 1952)
*Elmer Gantry* (United Artists, 1960)
*Flame and Flesh* (M-G-M, 1954)
*The Happy Ending* (United Artists, 1969)
*In Cold Blood* (Columbia Pictures, 1967)
*The Last Time I Saw Paris* (M-G-M, 1954)
*The Light Touch* (M-G-M, 1951)
*Looking for Mr. Goodbar* (Paramount Pictures, 1977)

*Lord Jim* (Columbia Pictures, 1965)
*The Professionals* (Columbia Pictures, 1966)
*Something of Value* (M-G-M, 1957)
*Sweet Bird of Youth* (M-G-M, 1962)
*Wrong is Right*. 1982. Columbia Pictures
Coen, Joel and Ethan, dirs. *The Big Lebowski* (Polygram Filmed Entertainment, 1998)
Coen, Joel and Ethan, dirs. *O Brother, Where Art Thou?* (Touchstone Pictures, 2000)
de Sica, Vittorio, dir. *Bicycle Thieves* (Produzioni de Sica, 1948)
Gilliam, Terry, dir. *Brazil* (Criterion Collection, 2006)
Golan, Menahem, dir. *The Delta Force* (M-G-M, 1986)
Ivory, James, dir. *The Remains of the Day* (Columbia Pictures, 1993)
Jackson, Peter, dir. *The Lord of the Rings: The Fellowship of the Ring* (New Line Cinema, 2001)
Kershner, Irvin, dir. *Never Say Never Again* (Twentieth Century-Fox, 1983)
Kubrick, Stanley, dir. *Dr. Strangelove or: How I Learned to Stop Worrying and Love the Bomb* (Columbia Pictures, 1964)
Levinson, Barry, dir. *Wag the Dog* (New Line Cinema, 1997)
Lumet, Sidney, dir. *Network* (United Artists, 1976)
McCarey, Leo, dir. *Duck Soup* (Paramount, 1933)
Minnelli, Vincent, dir. *Two Weeks in Another Town* (M-G-M, 1962)
Seaton, George, dir. *The Big Lift* (Twentieth Century-Fox, 1950)
Shear, Barry, dir. *Wild in the Streets* (American International Pictures, 1968)
Spielberg, Steven, dir. *Raiders of the Lost Ark* (Paramount Pictures, 1981)

# Bibliography

Academy Film Archive. "The Last Time I Saw Paris, 1954." Accessed September 17, 2021. http://collections.new.oscars.org/Details/Archive/70077669
Advertisement for *Lord Jim* (1965), *Billboard*, March 27: p. 13.
Advertisement [*The Professionals*], *Variety*, November 2, 1966: p. 18.
Anderson, Maxwell. *Key Largo—A Play In a Prologue and Two Acts*. Washington, D.C.: Anderson House 1939.
Anon. (1900a). Review of *Lord Jim*, *Sketch*, November 14: p. 142.
— (1900b). Review of *Lord Jim*, *Pall Mall Gazette*, December 5: p. 4.
— (1900c). Review of *Lord Jim*, *Daily News*, December 14: p. 9.
Arendt, Hannah. *On Revolution* (New York: The Viking Press, 1965).
Baker, Peter. "Cat on a Hot Tin Roof," *Films and Filming* (November 1958): p. 21.
Barnes, Bart. "Film Director, Writer Richard Brooks Dies," *Washington Post*, March 13, 1992.
Barr, Charles. "Cinemascope: Before and After," *Film Quarterly* 16:4 (Summer 1963), pp. 4–24.
Basso, Hamilton. "Notes from Purgatory," *The New Yorker*, June 2, 1945: p. 68.
Bazin, André. "Three Essays on Widescreen." Trans. Catherine Jones and Richard Neupert. *Velvet Light Trap* 21 (Summer 1985): pp. 8–16.
Bazin, André and Hugh Gray. "Ontology of the Photographic Image," *Film Quarterly* 13:4 (Summer 1960): pp. 4–9.
Behlmer, Rudy. *Memo from Darryl F. Zanuck: The Golden Years at Twentieth Century Fox* (New York: Grover Press, 1993).
Belton, John. *Widescreen Cinema* (Cambridge, MA, and London: Harvard University Press, 1992).
Bennett, Colin. "At the Cinema," *The Age* (Melbourne, Australia), July 7, 1962: p. 19.
Benshoff, Harry M. *Monsters in the Closet: Homosexuality and the Horror Film* (Manchester and New York: Manchester University Press), 1997.
Benson-Allott, Caetlin. "Looking for *Looking for Mr. Goodbar:* Or, Strategies for Sitting with the Abject Archive," *Feminist Media Histories* Vol. 1 No. 3 (2015): pp. 127–62.
Berenstein, Rhona J. *Attack of the Leading Ladies: Gender, Sexuality, and Spectatorship in Classic Horror Cinema* (New York: Columbia University Press, 1996).
Bernstein, Sergeant Walter. "Stateside Army," *The New Republic* 113:4 (July 23, 1945): p. 10.
Billington, Michael. "*Cat on a Hot Tin Roof*: Tennessee Williams's southern discomfort," *The Guardian*, September 30, 2012. Accessed July 4, 2021. https://www.theguardian.com/stage/2012/sep/30/cat-on-a-hot-tin-roof

Bluestone, George. *Novels into Film* (Baltimore, MD: Johns Hopkins University Press, 1957).
Bodnar, John. *The Good War in American Memory* (Baltimore, MD: Johns Hopkins University Press, 2010).
Bogdanovich, Peter. *This Is Orson Welles*, ed. Jonathan Rosenbaum (New York: HarperCollins, 1992).
Boggs, Johnny D. *The American West on Film* (Santa Barbara, CA: ABC-CLIO, 2020).
Boozer, Jack (ed.). "Introduction," in *Authorship and Film Adaptation* (Austin: University of Texas Press, 2008).
Boyer, Edward J. "Director Writer Richard Brooks Dies," *Los Angeles Times*, March 12, 1992.
Brill, Lesley. *Crowds, Power, and Transformation in Cinema* (Detroit, MI: Wayne State University Press, 2006).
Brooks, Richard. *The Brick Foxhole* (New York: Harper & Brothers, 1945).
Brooks, Richard. "Interview," *Movie*.12 (Spring 1965): pp. 2–9.
—. "Interview 1985." 2 parts.
—. "A Novel Isn't a Movie," *Films in Review* Vol. 3 (1952): pp. 55–9.
—. *The Producer* (New York: Simon and Schuster, 1951; Pb. New York: Pocket Books, 1953).
—. "WGA1989." https://www.youtube.com/watch?v=GIQsTW9UB_4. Accessed May 9, 2021.
Brown, Norman O. *Life Against Death: The Psychoanalytical Meaning of History* (Middletown, CT: Wesleyan University Press, 1959).
Buchsbaum, Jonathan. "Richard Brooks," *Dictionary of Literary Biography: American Screen Writers Second Series*, ed. Randall Clark (Detroit: Gale 1986), pp. 52–62.
Buford, Kate. *Burt Lancaster: An American Life* (New York: Da Capo Press, 2001).
Busch, Niven. "A Yell of Pain in War," *The Saturday Review of Literature* 28:22 (June 2, 1945): p. 12.
"B'way Helped by Voting Day Holiday; 'Professionals' Giant 86G, 'My Wife' Big $43,000, 'Liquidator' Lusty 31G," *Variety*, November 9, 1966: p. 9.
Cagle, Chris. *Sociology on Film: Postwar Hollywood's Prestige Commodity* (New Brunswick, NJ: Rutgers University Press, 2016).
Cain, James M. *Double Indemnity* (1936; New York: Vintage Crime, 1992), pp. 114–15.
Calendo, John. "New Again: Tennessee Williams," *Interview* (April 1973). Reprinted in interviewmagazine.com (June 4, 2014). Retrieved August 9, 2021. https://www.interviewmagazine.com/culture/new-again-tennessee-williams
Canby, Vincent. "One Long Last Gasp for Laura Palmer," *New York Times*, August 29, 1992: p. 11.
—. "'Wrong is Right,' Globe Hopping Thriller," *New York Times*, April 16, 1982. https://www.nytimes.com/1982/04/16/movies/wrong-is-right-globe-hopping-thriller.html
Canetti, Elias. *Crowds and Power*, trans. Carol Stewart (New York: Farrar Strauss Giroux, 1984).
Capote, Truman. *In Cold Blood* (New York: Random House, 1966).
—. "Two Faces and a Landscape," *Vogue*, February 1, 1966: pp. 144–9.
—. "Reality's Reflections: Concerning the Filming of *In Cold Blood*," Holographic Notebook (Regarding: Movie Filming), Truman Capote Papers, Manuscripts and Archives Division, The New York Public Library, Box 11, folder 1 (n.d.).
"Cardinal Scores *Baby Doll* Film," *New York Times*, December 17, 1956: p. 28.
Carr, David. "In Cold Print: The Genre Capote Started," *New York Times*, July 13, 2005.
Carroll, Noël. *The Philosophy of Motion Pictures* (Hoboken, NJ: Blackwell Publishing, 2008).
—. "The Professional Western: South of the Border," in *Back in the Saddle Again—New Essays on the Western*, eds. Edward Buscombe and Roberta E. Pearson (London: The British Film Institute, 1998).
Cartmell, Deborah and Imelda Whelehan. *Screen Adaptation: Impure Cinema* (London: Macmillan International Higher Education, 2010).

"*Cat on a Hot Tin Roof.*" *AFI Catalog of Feature Films* (n.d.). Retrieved November 12, 2021. https://catalog.afi.com/Catalog/moviedetails/52496

"*Cat on a Hot Tin Roof* with Elizabeth Taylor, Paul Newman and Burl Ives," *Harrison's Reports* Vol. 40 No. 33 (August 16, 1958): p. 130.

Cavell, Stanley. *Pursuits of Happiness. The Hollywood Comedy of Remarriage* (Cambridge, MA: Harvard University Press, 1981).

—. "The Uncanniness of the Ordinary," in *In Quest of the Ordinary. Lines of Skepticism and Romanticism* (1988; Chicago: University of Chicago Press, 1994), pp. 153–78.

—. *Contesting Tears. The Hollywood Melodrama of the Unknown Woman* (Chicago: University of Chicago Press, 1996).

"Col. Officials to Hollywood To View 'Professionals,'" *Boxoffice*, June 13, 1966: p. 10.

Colpitts, George. "A Métis View of the Summer Market Hunt on the Northern Plains," in *Bison and People on the North American Great Plains—a deep environmental history*, eds. Geoff Cunfer and Bill Waiser (College Station, TX: Texas A & M University Press, 2016).

Conrad, Joseph. *Lord Jim*, with a general Introduction by Albert J. Guerard (New York: Dell Publishing Company, c. 1961).

Conrad, Joseph. *The Works of Joseph Conrad: Vol. 4: Lord Jim* (London: William Heinemann, 1921).

Corber, Robert. *Homosexuality in Cold War America: Resistance and the Crisis of Masculinity* (Durham, NC: Duke University Press, 1997), pp. 79–103.

Cossar, Harper. *Letterboxed: The Evolution of Widescreen Cinema* (Lexington: University of Kentucky Press, 2010).

Crowther, Bosley. "Capitol's Film Inspired by Fitzgerald Story," *New York Times*, November 19, 1954. Digitized version. Accessed January 10, 2022. https://www.nytimes.com/1954/11/19/archives/capitols-film-inspired-by-fitzgerald-story.html

—. "Conrad's 'Lord Jim' Arrives: Peter O'Toole Stars in Brooks Version," *New York Times*, 26 February 26, 1965: p. 18.

—. "Review of *Ace in the Hole*," *New York Times*, June 30, 1951.

—. "Screen: Out Where the Buffalo Roam; 'The Last Hunt' Has Premiere at State," *New York Times*, March 1, 1956: p. 37. https://www.nytimes.com/1951/06/30/archives/the-screen-in-review-ace-in-the-hole-billy-wilder-special-with-kirk.html

—. "Review of *Deadline—U.S.A.*," *New York Times*, March 15, 1952. https://www.nytimes.com/1952/03/15/archives/deadline-u-s-a-humphrey-bogart-as-crusading-editor-opens-at-roxy.html

Cullen, Jim. *Sensing the Past: Hollywood Stars and Historical Visions* (Oxford: Oxford University Press, 2013).

Cumings, Bruce. *The Korean War: A History* (New York: Modern Library, 2011).

Daniel, Douglass K. *Tough as Nails: The Life and Films of Richard Brooks* (Madison: University of Wisconsin Press, 2011).

Davis, Colin. "Hauntology, Specters and Phantoms," *French Studies* Vol. 59 No. 3 (2005): pp. 373–9.

Dawson, Catherine and Gene M. Moore. "Colonialism and Local Color in *An Outcast of the Islands* and *Lord Jim*," in Moore (ed.), *Conrad on Film* (Cambridge: Cambridge University Press, 1997), pp. 104–19.

*Deadline—U.S.A.* film trailer. https://www.youtube.com/watch?v=CniKtNOzzuE

De Bellis, Jack. "Visions and Revisions: Truman Capote's *In Cold Blood*," *Journal of Modern Literature* Vol. 7 No. 3 (1979): pp. 519–36.

Delano, Jack. [Untitled photo, possibly related to: Emporia, Kansas. An Atchison, Topeka, and Santa Fe train between Argentine and Emporia, Kansas passing an eastbound freight train], March 1943. Library of Congress Prints and Photographs Division. LC-USW3- 019806-E. https://www.loc.gov/pictures/item/2017847680/

—. [Untitled photo, possibly related to: Argonis, Kansas. Wheat storage bins on the Atchison, Topeka and Santa Fe Railroad between Wellington, Kansas, and Waynoka, Oklahoma], March 1943. Library of Congress Prints and Photographs Division. LC-USW3- 019842-E. https://www.loc.gov/pictures/item/2017847711/resource/
Dent, Sara. *Losing Eden—An Environment History of the American West* (Chichester: Wiley Blackwell, 2017).
DeStefano, Anthony M. *Top Hoodlum: Frank Costello, Prime Minister of the MAFIA* (New York: Citadel Press, 2018).
"Director Richard Brooks Demands Authenticity," *Boxoffice* Vol. 105 Issue 9 (June 10, 1974): W8.
Doane, Mary Ann. *The Emergence of Cinematic Time: Modernity, Contingency, the Archive* (Boston, MA: Harvard University Press, 2002).
Doherty, Thomas. *Cold War, Cool Medium: Television, McCarthyism, and American Culture* (New York: Columbia University Press, 2003).
—. "Frank Costello's Hands: Film, Television, and the Kefauver Crime Hearings," *Film History* 10 (1998): pp. 359–74.
Donovan, Stephen. *Joseph Conrad and Popular Culture* (Houndmills: Palgrave Macmillan, 2005).
Dostoevsky, Fyodor. *The Brothers Karamazov*. Trans. Richard Pevear and Larissa Volokhonsky (New York: Farrar, Straus, and Giroux, 2002).
—. *The Brothers Karamazov*. Trans. David Magarshack (London: Penguin, 1958).
Driver, Tom F. "Tennessee Williams' Best," *The New Republic* 140 (April 20, 1962): pp. 21–2.
Duprey, Richard Allen. "Mass Media and the Theatre," NYU Diss., 1969.
Ebert, Roger. "A Searing Portrait of the human condition," *Chicago Sun-Times*, October 12, 2007: p. B6.
Eberwein, Robert T. "'As a Mother Cuddles a Child': Sexuality and Masculinity in World War II Combat Films," in Krin Gabbard and William H. Luhr (eds.), *Screening Genders*. (New Brunswick, NJ: Rutgers University Press, 2008), pp. 111–22.
Ehrhardt, Michael. "Of Monsters and Mad Love: Edmund White," *The Gay and Lesbian Review Worldwide* 19.1 (2012): pp. 30–2.
Elliott, Kamilla. "Unfilmable Books," *South Atlantic Review* 80 No. 3–4 (2015): pp. 79–95.
Erickson, Glenn. "*Deadline—U.S.A.*," September 2, 2016. https://trailersfromhell.com/deadline-u-s-a/
Erkkila, Betsy. "Review of *Looking for Mr. Goodbar*," *Cinéaste* Vol. 8 No. 3 (1978): pp. 43–5.
Farm Security Administration. *How the Photographs Were Produced*. Collection description, Library of Congress. https://www.loc.gov/collections/fsa-owi-black-and-white-negatives/about-this-collection/
Finler, Joel W. "Box Office Hits 1914–2002," *The Hollywood Story* (London and New York: Wallflower Press, 2003).
Fitzgerald, F. Scott. "Babylon Revisited," in *Babylon Revisited and Other Stories* (Richmond: Alma Classics, 2014), pp. 3–26.
—. "The Crack-Up," in *The Crack-Up*, ed. Edmund Wilson (New York: New Directions, 1993), pp. 69–84.
Fitzpatrick, John. "Richard Brooks (1912–)," in *American Directors, Volume* II, eds. Jean-Pierre Coursodon with Pierre Savage (New York: McGraw-Hill, 1983), pp. 55–9.
Fosburgh, Lacey. *Closing Time: The True Story of the "Looking for Mr. Goodbar" Murder* (New York: Open Road Integrated Media, 1975).
Frank, Joseph. *Dostoevsky: A Writer in His Time* (Princeton, NJ: Princeton University Press, 2010).
Frankel, Haskell. "The Author," in *Truman Capote: Conversations*, ed. M. Thomas Inge (Jackson: University Press of Mississippi, 1987), pp. 69–72.
Freud, Sigmund. "Extracts from the Fliess Papers," in *The Standard Edition*, Vol. I, London: Hogarth Press, 1892–9).

—. "The Uncanny," in *The Standard Edition*, Vol. XVII (London: Hogarth Press, 1919).
—. "Fetishism," in *The Standard Edition*, Vol. XXI (London: Hogarth Press, 1927).
Frost, Francis Patrick. "A Historical-Critical Study of the Films of Richard Brooks with Special Attention to his Problems of Achieving and Maintaining Final Decision-Control," USC Diss., 1976.
Fulkerson, Randal. "Leisure in the West," in *The World of the American West*, ed. Gordon Morris Bakken (New York: Routledge, 2010).
Galbraith, Stuart. "Wrong is Right," DVDtalk.Com, March 16, 2004. https://www.dvdtalk.com/reviews/review/10379
Gardner, R. W. "'Sweet Bird of Youth' Strictly For Laughs," *Baltimore Sun*, April 1, 1962: p. 52.
Garrett, George. "Then and Now: *In Cold Blood* Revisited," *The Virginia Quarterly Review* Vol. 72 No. 3 (Summer 1996): pp. 467–74.
Giglio, Ernest. *Here's Looking at You: Hollywood, Film, and Politics* (New York: Peter Lang, 2003).
Girard, René. *Deceit, Desire and the Novel*. Trans. Yvonne Freccero (Baltimore, MD: Johns Hopkins University Press, 1965).
Giroux, Henry A. (1978), "Review of *Looking for Mr. Goodbar*," *Film Quarterly* Vol. 31 No. 4 (1978): pp. 52–4.
Golub, Adam. "They Turned a School into a Jungle! How *The Blackboard Jungle* Redefined the Education Crisis in Postwar America," *Film & History* 39:1 (2009): pp. 21–30.
Goudsouzian, Aram. *Sidney Poitier: Man, Actor, Icon* (Chapel Hill: The University of North Carolina Press, 2015).
"Granger, Brooks, Tamblyn To 'Last Hunt' Opening," *The Hollywood Reporter* (February 15, 1956): p. 2.
Grimes, William. "Richard Brooks, 79, Screenwriter and Director of Dramas, is Dead," *New York Times*, March 13, 1992: B:6.
Grossman, Julie. *The Femme Fatale* (New Brunswick, NJ: Rutgers University Press, 2020).
—. *Rethinking the Femme Fatale: Ready for Her Close-Up* (Basingstoke: Palgrave Macmillan, 2009).
Grossman, Julie. *Literature, Film, and Their Hideous Progeny: Adaptation and ElasTEXTity* (New York: Palgrave Macmillan, 2015).
Hallam, Lindsay. *Twin Peaks: Fire Walk with Me* (Liverpool: Auteur Press, 2018).
Hand, Richard J. and Jay McRoy (eds.). *Monstrous Adaptations: Generic and Thematic Mutations in Horror Film*. Pb. (Manchester: Manchester University Press, 2007).
Hanner, John. "Government Response to the Buffalo Hide Trade, 1871–1883," *Journal of Law and Economics* XXIV (October 1981): pp. 239–71.
Hantke, Steffen. "Science Fiction and Horror in the 1950s," in *A Companion to the Horror Film*, ed. Harry M. Benshoff (Chichester: John Wiley and Sons, 2014), pp. 255–72.
Haskell, Molly. *From Reverence to Rape: The Treatment of Women in the Movies* (1974; Chicago and London: University of Chicago Press, 1987).
—. "Exposing a Nerve," *New York Magazine*, 1977: pp. 116, 118–19.
Henderson, Mary C. *Mielziner: Master of Modern Stage Design* (New York: Watson-Guptill, 2001).
Hiney, Tom and Frank MacShane (eds.). *The Raymond Chandler Papers—Selected Letters and Nonfiction, 1909–1959* (New York: Grove Press, 2000).
Hoberman, J. *An Army of Phantoms: American Movies and the Making of the Cold War* (New York: The New Press, 2011).
Hoffman, Irving. "'Key Largo' Greeted With Good Reviews in Gotham," *The Hollywood Reporter*, July 20, 1948: p. 6.
Horne, Gerald. *Black and Brown—African Americans and the Mexican Revolution, 1910–1920* (New York: New York University Press, 2005).
Howard, Jane. "Horror Spawns a Masterpiece," photographs by Richard Avedon, *LIFE Magazine*, January 7, 1966: pp. 59–76.

"'Hunt' Paces New Cincy Pix, $11,000; 'Brooks' 81/2G, 'Cry' Hot 12G, 2d," *Variety*, March 28, 1956): p. 8.
"'Hunt' Smash 24G, Mpls; 'Darling' 8G," *Variety*, February 22, 1956: p. 8.
Hunter, Evan. *The Blackboard Jungle* (1954; New York: Open Road, 1999).
Inge, M. Thomas (ed.). *Truman Capote: Conversations* (Jackson: University Press of Mississippi, 1987).
Innis, Harold Adams. *The Bias of Communication* (Toronto: University of Toronto Press, 1952).
Isenberg, Andrew C. "Environment and the Nineteenth-Century West: Or, Process Encounters Place," in *A Companion to the American West*, ed. William Deverell (Oxford: Blackwell Publishing, 2004).
Jameson, Frederic. "Marx's Purloined Letter," in *Ghostly Demarcations: A Symposium on Jacques Derrida's "Spectres de Marx"*, ed. Michael Sprinker (Paris: Galilée, 1993), pp. 26–67.
Jellenik, Glenn. "A Frankensteinian Model for Adaptation Studies, or 'It Lives!': Adaptive Symbiosis and Peake's Presumption, or the Fate of Frankenstein," in *Adapting Frankenstein: The Monster's Eternal Lives in Popular Culture*, eds. Dennis R. Cutchins and Dennis R. Perry (Manchester: Manchester University Press, 2018), pp. 80–103.
Juergens, George. *Pulitzer and the New York World* (Princeton, NJ: Princeton University Press, 1966).
Kael, Pauline. *5001 Nights at the Movies: A Guide from A to Z* (New York: Holt, Rinehart, and Winston, 1982).
Kakutani, Michiko, "A Novelist's Spirit Captured the American Spirit," *New York Times*, November 11, 2007. https://www.nytimes.com/2007/11/11/books/11appraisal.html
Keats, John. *Complete Poems and Selected Letters of John Keats*, Introduction by Edward Hirsch, Notes by Jim Pollock (New York: The Modern Library, 2001).
Kefauver, Estes. Kefauver Committee Report. https://www.senate.gov/about/powers-procedures/investigations/kefauver.htm
—. *Crime in America* (New York: Doubleday, 1951).
Kelley, Beverly Merrill. "Isolationism in *The Steel Helmet*," in *Reelpolitik II* (Oxford: Rowman & Littlefield, 2004).
*Key Largo (1948): SHOOTING SCRIPT, Screenplay by Richard Brooks and John Huston.*
"Key Largo," *Variety*, Wednesday, July 7, 1948: p. 6.
Keynes, John Maynard. *Essays in Persuasion* (New York: W. W. Norton, 1963).
Kierkegaard, Søren. "Repetition," in *The Essential Kierkegaard*, eds. Howard V. Hong and Edna H. Hong (Princeton, NJ: Princeton University Press, 2000), pp. 102–15.
Koresky, Michael. "Queer & Now & Then: 1947," May 9, 2018, accessed March 3, 2022. https://www.filmcomment.com/blog/queer-now-1947/
Krutnik, Frank. *In a Lonely Street: film noir, genre, masculinity* (New York: Routledge, 1991).
"Lack of PCA 'Adult' Rating for 'Professionals' Flayed," *Boxoffice*, November 28, 1966: p. 10.
Lahr, John. *Tennessee Williams: Mad Pilgrimage of the Flesh* (New York: W. W. Norton, 2014).
—. "A Monster Among Angels," *Airmail*, August 24, 2019.
Langdon, Jennifer E. *Caught In the Crossfire: Adrian Scott and the Politics of Americanism in 1940s Hollywood* (New York: Columbia University Press, 2008). https://hdl-handle-net.proxy.library.emory.edu/2027/heb.99024
"'Last Hunt' Premieres," *The Hollywood Reporter*, February 9, 1956: p. 3.
"The Last Hunt (C'Scope—Color)," *Variety*, February 15, 1956: p. 6.
"The Last Hunt," *Picturegoer*, May 19, 1956: p. 18.
Lawrence, D[avid]. H[erbert]. *Lady Chatterley's Lover* (1928; The Samuel Roth Edition, 1930; New York: William Faro, 1931).
Lee, Russell. *Mr Germeroth, Sheridan County, KS*, Farm Security Administration, August 1939. https://www.loc.gov/pictures/resource/fsa.8a26907/

Leitch, Thomas (ed.). *The Oxford Handbook of Adaptation Studies* (Oxford: Oxford University Press, 2017).
—. *The History of American Literature on Film* (New York: Bloomsbury Academic, 2019).
—. "Scripting the Saints," *Studia Filmoznawcze* 40 (2019): pp. 113–32.
—. "The Texts Behind *The Killers*," *Twentieth-Century American Literature and Film*, ed. R. Barton Palmer (New York: Cambridge University Press, 2007), pp. 26–44.
—. "Twelve Fallacies in Contemporary Adaptation Theory," *Criticism* Vol. 45 No. 2 (Spring 2003): pp. 149–71.
Lenihan, John H. *Showdown—Confronting Modern America in the Western Era* (Urbana and Chicago: University of Illinois Press, 1980).
Lerner, Max. *America as a Civilization* (New York: Simon & Schuster, 1957).
Lev, Peter. "Westerns," in "Genres and Production Trends, 1950–1954," *The Fifties—Transforming The Screen, 1950–1959* (Berkeley and Los Angeles: University of California Press, 2003).
—. *Transforming the Screen: 1950–1959*. Vol. 7 in *History of the American Cinema*, gen. ed. Charles Harpole (Berkeley, Los Angeles, and London: University of California Press, 2003).
Leverich, Lyle. *Tom: The Unknown Tennessee Williams* (New York: Crown, 1995).
Lewis, Sinclair. *Elmer Gantry* (1927; New York: New American Library, 1970).
—. "Obscenity and Obscurity," *Esquire* (June 1945): p. 51.
*Looking for Mr. Goodbar* Press Notes, Author's Collection.
Lucia, Cynthia. "The Last Time He Saw Paris: An Interview with Cédric Klapisch," *Cineaste* Vol. 23 (1), January 1, 1997: pp. 10–14.
Marsh, Calum. "*Twin Peaks: Fire Walk with Me* Is David Lynch's Masterpiece," *Village Voice*, May 17, 2013.
Marsh, Kelly A. "Empathy, Authority, and the Narrative Ethics of Truman Capote's 'La Côte Basque, 1965,'" *Journal of Narrative Theory* Vol. 43 No. 2 (2013): pp. 218–44. http://www.jstor.org/stable/24484803
Masaryk, T. G. *Masaryk on Marx*, ed. and trans. Erazim V. Kohák (Lewisburg, PA: Bucknell University Press, 1972).
McCarry, Charles. *The Better Angels* (New York: E. P. Dutton, 1979).
McCarthy, Todd. "Obituaries: Richard Brooks," *Variety*, March 16, 1992: p. 75.
McCoy, Beth. "Manager, Buddy, Delinquent: *Blackboard Jungle*'s Desegregating Triangle," *Cinema Journal* 38:1 (1998): pp. 25–39.
McFarland, Douglas and Wesley King (eds.). *John Huston as Adaptor* (Albany: SUNY Press, 2018).
McGilligan, Pat[rick]. "Richard Brooks: The Professional," interview with Richard Brooks, in *Backstory 2: Interviews with Screenwriters of the 1940s and 1950s* (Berkeley: University of California Press, 1991), pp. 27–72.
McLuhan, Marshall. *Understanding Media: The Extensions of Man* (New York: Signet, 1964).
Merleau-Ponty, Maurice. "The Visible and the Invisible," in *Basic Writings*, ed. Thomas Baldwin (London and New York: Routledge, 2004), pp. 247–71.
"Metro Fights Atlanta Lady Censor Who Banned *Blackboard Jungle* Outright," *Variety* Vol. 199 No. 1 (June 8, 1955): p. 5.
Meyers, Jeffrey. Introduction to *Double Indemnity—the complete screenplay* (Berkeley: University of California Press, 2000).
Mielziner, Jo. *Designing for the Theatre: A Memoir and a Portfolio* (New York: Bramhall House, 1965).
Miklitsch, Richard. *Siren City—Sound and Source Music in Classic American Noir* (New Brunswick, NJ: Rutgers University Press, 2011).
Miller, Arthur. *Death of a Salesman* (1948; New York: Dramatists Play Service, Inc., 1980).
Mitchell, Lee Clark. *Westerns—Making the Man in Fiction and Film* (Chicago: University of Chicago Press, 1996).

Monaco, Paul. "Appendix 1—Number of Feature Films Released by the Seven Major Distribution Companies, 1960–1968, 1970," *The Sixties—1960–1969* (New York: Charles Scribner's Sons, 2001).
Moore, Gene M. (ed.). *Conrad on Film* (Cambridge: Cambridge University Press, 1997).
Moore, William Howard. *The Kefauver Commission and the Politics of Crime, 1950–52* (Columbia: University of Missouri Press, 1974).
Murphy, Brenda. "How to Fix a Second Act: The Film and Television Adaptations of *Sweet Bird of Youth*," *Tennessee Williams Annual Review* 15 (2016).
—. *Tennessee Williams and Elia Kazan: A Collaboration in the Theatre* (Cambridge: Cambridge University Press, 1992).
Nabokov, Vladimir. *Lectures on Russian Literature* (New York: Harcourt Inc., 1981).
Naipaul, V. S. *The Return of Eva Perón with the Killings in Trinidad* (New York: Alfred A. Knopf, 1980).
Naremore, James. *More Than Night: Film Noir in its Contexts, Updated and Expanded* (Berkeley: University of California Press, 2008).
"National Boxoffice Survey," *Variety* Vol. 212 No. 6 (October 8, 1958): p. 4.
Neale, Steve. *Genre and Contemporary Hollywood* (London: British Film Institute, 2019).
Niebuhr, Reinhold. *Moral Man and Immoral Society: A Study in Ethics and Politics* (New York: Charles Scribner's Sons, 1960).
Niemi, Robert. *The Cinema of Robert Altman: Hollywood Maverick* (New York: Columbia University Press, 2016).
Norton, Dan. "'The Brick Foxhole,'" *New York Times*, June 3, 1945: BR 9.
Nystrom, Derek. *Hard Hats, Rednecks, and Macho Men: Class in 1970s American Cinema* (Oxford: Oxford University Press, 2009).
"The Ordeal of Middlebrow Culture," *Transition* 67 (1995): p. 87.
O'Rourke, Frank. *The Professionals* (New York: Avon Books, 1966).
Palmer, R. Barton and William Robert Bray. *Hollywood's Tennessee: The Williams Films and Postwar America* (Austin: University of Texas Press, 2009).
—. *Shot on Location: Postwar American Cinema and the Exploration of Real Place* (New Brunswick, NJ: Rutgers University Press. 2016).
—. "Redeeming Cruising: Tendentiously Offensive, Coherently Incoherent, Strangely Pleasurable," in *B is for Bad Cinema: Aesthetics, Politics, and Cultural Value*, eds. Claire Perkins and Constantine Verevis (Albany: SUNY Press 2015, pp. 85–104).
—. "Chance's Main Chance: Richard Brooks's *Sweet Bird of Youth*," *Tennessee Williams Annual Review* 3 (2000).
—. "The Small Adult Film: A Prestige Form of Cold War Filmmaking," in *Cold War Film Genres*, ed. Homer Pettey (Edinburgh: Edinburgh University Press, 2019), pp. 62–78.
Parker, Brian. "A Preliminary Stemma for Drafts and Revisions of Tennessee Williams's *Cat on a Hot Tin Roof*," *The Papers of the Bibliographical Society of America* Vol. 90 No. 4 (December 1996): pp. 475–96.
Parker, Brian. "Elia Kazan and *Sweet Bird of Youth*," *Tennessee Williams Annual Review* 7 (2005).
—. "Swinging a Cat," in Tennessee Williams, *Cat on a Hot Tin Roof* (New York: New Directions, 2004), pp. 175–92.
Parker, Richard. "F. Scott Fitzgerald," in F. Scott Fitzgerald, *Babylon Revisited*, op cit., pp. 263–78.
Pastoureau, Michel. *Red: The History of a Color*, trans. Jody Gladding (Princeton, NJ and Oxford: Princeton University Press, 2017).
—. *Yellow: The History of a Color*, trans. Jody Gladding (Princeton, NJ and Oxford: Princeton University Press, 2019).

Perlstein, Daniel. "Imagined Authority: *Blackboard Jungle* and the Project of Educational Liberalism," *International Journal on the History of Education* 36:1 (2000): pp. 407–24.
Perry, Dennis. "The Recombinant Mystery of Frankenstein: Experiments in Film Adaptation," in *Oxford Handbook of Adaptation Studies*, ed. Thomas Leitch (New York: Oxford University Press, 2017).
Pettey, Homer B. "*Crossfire* and Homeland Insecurity," in *Film Noir: Light and Shadow*, eds. Alain Silver and James Ursini (Milwaukee, WI: Applause Theatre and Centerna Books, 2017), pp. 256–71.
Phillips, Adam. *Promises, Promises: Essays on Psychoanalysis and Literature* (New York: Basic Books, 2001).
Phillips, Gene D. *The Films of Tennessee Williams* (Philadelphia: Art Alliance Press, 1980).
Pizello, Stephen. "Wrap Shot: *In Cold Blood*," *American Cinematographer* (March 22, 2019): n.p. https://ascmag.com/articles/wrap-shot-in-cold-blood
Pizer, Donald. "Documentary Narrative as Art: William Manchester and Truman Capote," *Journal of Modern Literature* Vol. 2 No. 1 (1971): pp. 105–18. http://www.jstor.org/stable/30053177.
Plimpton, George, "The Story Behind a Nonfiction Novel," *Truman Capote: Conversations*, ed. M. Thomas Inge (Jackson: University Press of Mississippi, 1987), pp. 47–68.
Pomerance, Murray. *A Dream of Hitchcock* (Albany: SUNY Press, 2019).
Prescott, Orville. "Books of the Times: Unsuited to a Military Life," *New York Times*, May 28, 1945: p. 17.
"'Professionals' Theft," *Boxoffice*, December 19, 1966: ME-1.
"'Professionals' Shown For Mountain Showmen," *Boxoffice*, September 26, 1966: W-8.
"'The Professionals' 250 in Minneapolis," *Boxoffice*, December 5, 1966: NC-1.
"'The Professionals (Color-Panavision)," *Variety*, November 2, 1966: p. 6.
"'Professionals' Biz Wins Brooks A Nod," *Variety*, January 18, 1967: p. 13.
"'Professionals' Smash $527,000 in Tokyo Run," *Variety International*, March 22, 1967: p. 27.
Pryor, Thomas M. "Hollywood *Cat*," *The New York Times*, January 5, 1958: section X: p. 7.
Punke, Michael. *Last Stand—George Bird Grinnell, The Battle to Save the Buffalo, and the Birth of the New West* (2007; New York: HarperCollins, 2020).
Rauschenbusch, Walter. *A Theology for the Social Gospel* (New York: Macmillan, 1917).
Redmon, Allen. *Constructing the Coens: From* Blood Simple *to* Inside Llewyn Davis (New York: Rowman & Littlefield Publishers, 2015).
Reinsch, Paul N. "Music over Words and Sound over Image: 'Rock Around the Clock' and the Centrality of Music in Post-Classical Film Narration," *Music and the Moving Image* 6:3 (Fall 2013): pp. 3–22.
Robb, David. "'Angry' Richard Brooks is honored by guilds," *Variety, Los Angeles*, Vol. 341 Issue 3 (October 29, 1990): pp. 8, 75.
"Robinson Is No Bathing Beauty But He Draws in Lobby Bathtub Scene," *Boxoffice*, September 25, 1948: p. 46.
Rossner, Judith. *Looking for Mr. Goodbar* (New York: Simon and Schuster, 1975).
Russo, Kurt. "The Flora and Fauna," in *The World of the American West*, ed. Gordon Morris Bakken (New York: Routledge, 2010), pp. 20–49.
Sante, Luc. *The Other Paris* (London: Faber and Faber, 2017).
Sarris Andrew. *The American Cinema: Directors and Directions, 1929–1968* (New York: Da Capo, 1996).
—. Review of *Lord Jim*, *Village Voice*, April 29, 1965: p. 12.
Schatz, Thomas. *Hollywood Genres: Formulas, Filmmaking, and The Studio System* (New York: McGraw-Hill, 1981).

Sedgwick, Eve Kosofsky. "Paranoid Reading and Reparative Reading, or, You're So Paranoid, You Probably Think This Essay Is About You," in Sedgwick, *Touching Feeling* (Durham, NC: Duke University Press, 2003), pp. 123–54.

Sellers, Robert. *Peter O'Toole: The Definitive Biography* (London: Sidgwick and Jackson, 2015).

Sherry, Norman (ed.). *Conrad: The Critical Heritage* (London: Routledge & Kegan Paul, 1973).

Simmons, Allan H. "Nationalism and Empire," in *Joseph Conrad in Context*, ed. Allan H. Simmons (Cambridge: Cambridge University Press, 2009), pp. 187–94.

Sklar, Robert. *City Boys: Cagney, Bogart, Garfield* (Princeton, NJ: Princeton University Press, 1992).

—. *Movie-Made America: A Cultural History of American Movies* (New York: Vintage, 1994).

Smith, Harry W. "Performative Devices and Rhetorical Desires: Ritual and Rhetoric in the Work of Jo Mielziner and Tennessee Williams, 1955–1964," *Theatre History Studies*, June 15, 1995: pp. 183–98.

Smith, Judith E. *Visions of Belonging: Family Stories, Popular Culture, and Postwar Democracy, 1940–1960* (New York: Columbia University Press, 2004).

Sontag, Susan. *Notes on Camp* (London: Penguin Classics, 2018).

Steinhart, Daniel. *Runaway Hollywood: Internationalizing Postwar Production and Location Shooting* (Oakland: University of California Press, 2019).

Stevens Jr., George. "Richard Brooks," in *Conversations with the Great Moviemakers of Hollywood's Golden Age* (New York: Vintage Books, 2007), pp. 532–57.

Stoever-Ackerman, Jennifer. "Reproducing U.S. Citizenship in *Blackboard Jungle*: Race, Cold War Liberalism, and the Tape Recorder," *American Quarterly* 63:23 (2011): pp. 781–806.

Taylor, M. Scott. "Buffalo Hunt: International Trade and the Virtual Extinction of the North American Bison," *The American Economic Review* 101.7 (December 2011): pp. 3162–95.

Telotte, J. P. *The Mouse Machine: Disney and Technology* (Urbana and Chicago: University of Illinois Press, 2008).

Thomas, Dylan. *In Country Sleep, and Other Poems* (New York: New Directions, 1952).

Thornley, Davinia (ed.). *True Event Adaptation: Scripting Real Lives* (London: Palgrave Macmillan, 2018).

*Time Magazine*. "The Last Time I Saw Paris," December 23, 1940. Digitized version. Accessed January 10, 2022. https://web.archive.org/web/20090201051156/http://www.time.com/time/magazine/article/0,9171,765092,00.html

"Top Film Grossers for 1956," *Variety*, January 2, 1957: p. 4.

United States Senate Special Committee on Organized Crime in Interstate Commerce. https://www.senate.gov/about/powers-procedures/investigations/kefauver.htm

Urry, John. *The Tourist Gaze: Leisure and Travel in Contemporary Societies* (London: Sage, 1990).

Voss, Ralph F. *Truman Capote and the Legacy of* In Cold Blood (Tuscaloosa: University of Alabama Press, 2011).

Wainwright, Loudon. *The Great American Magazine: an Inside History of* Life (New York: Knopf, 1986).

Wallmann, Jeffrey, *The Western—Parables of the American Dream* (Lubbock: Texas Tech University Press, 1999).

Walsh, Margaret. *The American West. Visions and Revisions* (Cambridge: Cambridge University Press, 2005).

Watson, Wallace S. "Conradian Ironies and the Conrad Films," in *Conrad on Film*, ed. Gene M. Moore (Cambridge: Cambridge University Press, 1997), pp. 16–30.

Watt, Ian. *Conrad and the Nineteenth Century* (Berkeley: University of California Press, 1979).

Wear, Mike. "'Hawaii,' 'Professionals' as December Pace Setters; 'Alfie' & 'The Bible' Zingy; 'Paris Burning' Ranks 7," *Variety*, January 11, 1967: p. 20.

Weber, Max. *From Max Weber: Essays in Sociology*, trans., ed., and with an Introduction by H. H. Gerth and C. Wright Mills (New York: Oxford University Press, 1958).

White, Edmund. *Sacred Monsters* (New York: Magnus, 2011).
Whyte, Kenneth. *The Uncrowned King: The Sensational Rise of William Randolph Hearst* (Berkeley, CA: Counterpoint, 2009).
Williams, Tennessee. *Cat on a Hot Tin Roof* (New York: New Directions, 1955).
—. *Cat on a Hot Tin Roof* (New York: New Directions, 2004).
—. *Collected Stories*. Intro. Gore Vidal (New York: New Directions, 1985).
—. Letter to Elia Kazan (November 30, 1954). Elia Kazan Collection, Cinema Archives, Wesleyan University.
—. *Tennessee Williams' Letters to Donald Windham*, ed. Windham (New York: Holt, Rinehart, and Winston, 1977).
—. *Memoirs* (New York: New Directions, 2006).
—. *The Selected Letters of Tennessee Williams, Volume II: 1945–1957*, ed. Albert J. Devlin (New York: New Directions, 2004).
—. "Three Players of a Summer Game," *The New Yorker* Vol. 28 No. 37 (November 1, 1952): pp. 27–36.
—. *Sweet Bird of Youth*. Intro. Lanford Wilson (1959; New York: New Directions, 2008).
—, and Albert J. Devlin. *Conversations with Tennessee Williams* (Jackson: University Press of Mississippi, 1986).
Williams, Tony. "Beyond Fuller and *M.A.S.H.*: Korean War Representations in Film, Genre, and Comic Strip," *Asian Cinema*, Spring/Summer 2009: p. 3.
Willis, Sharon. *The Poitier Effect: Racial Melodrama and Fantasies of Reconciliation* (Minneapolis: University of Minnesota Press, 2016).
Wiseman, John B. "Darryl F. Zanuck and the Failure of *One World*: 1943–45," *Historical Journal of Film, Radio, and Television* Vol. 7 No. 3 (1987): pp. 279–87. https://www.tandfonline.com/doi/abs/10.1080/01439688700260351?journalCode=chjf20
Wollen, Peter. *Signs and Meanings in the Cinema* (Bloomington: Indiana University Press, 1969).
Wood, Robin. *Hollywood from Vietnam to Reagan* (New York: Columbia University Press, 1986).
Wright, Richard. "A Non-Combat Soldier Strips Words for Action," *PM* Sunday Magazine Section, June 24, 1945: p. 16.
Wright, Will. *Sixguns and Society: A Structural Study of the Western* (Berkeley: University of California Press, 1975).
Yacowar, Maurice. *Tennessee Williams and Film* (New York: Frederick Ungar, 1977).
Yeats, William Butler. "To a Friend Whose Work Has Come to Nothing," in *Responsibilities and Other Poems* (New York: The Macmillan Company, 1916), p. 34.
Žižek, Slavoj. "The Fear of Four Words: A Modest Plea for the Hegelian Reading of Christianity," in Slavoj Žižek and John Milbank, *The Monstrosity of Christ: Paradox or Dialectic?*, ed. Creston Davis (Cambridge, MA, and London: MIT Press, 2009), pp. 24–109.

# Index

1.85:1 (aspect ratio), 158
*8 ½* (1963, film) 166
20th Century Fox, 4, 46, 61, 63, 69, 259–61
307th Bomb Group, 64
8666th M.A.S.H. Unit, 67
*20,000 Leagues Under the Sea* (1954, film), 183

*Abandoned* (1949, film), 62
Abraham, Nicolas, 163
Academy Awards, 51, 64, 89, 139, 153–4, 184, 208, 226, 238
Acapulco (Mexico), 217
*Ace in the Hole* (1951, film), 57, 61, 263
Africa, 247, 251
*African Queen, The* (1951, film), 51
*Air Force* (1943, film), 16
Albee, Edward, 152
Aldrich, Robert, 157, 165
*Alfie* (1966, film), 118, 122, 270
Alighieri, Dante, 139, 150
*All About Eve* (1950, film), 130
Allyson, June, 67
Altman, Robert, 63–4, 67, 71, 74, 268

Alton, John, 174, 251
American Legion, 72
American Municipal Association, 48
American Overseas Press Club, 60
Ames, Leon, 35
Anderson, Judith, 155
Anderson, Maxwell, 2, 5, 7, 9–11, 13, 261
Angeli, Pier, 44
*Annie Hall* (1977, film), 236–8
Anti-Semitism, 15, 18, 21, 24–5, 36, 48, 56
Arabia, 210
Arbus, Diane, 217
Argentina, 31, 39
Argentine Shops, 216, 228, 263
Argonis (Kansas), 223, 264
Arkansas, 221
Aronson, Boris, 156
*Asphalt Jungle, The* (1950, film), 3
*Attack of the 50 Foot Woman* (1958, film), 192
Austen, Jane, 210
Avedon, Richard, 215–19, 223, 228, 266

INDEX     273

*Baby Doll* (1956, film), 115, 157, 164–5, 262
"Babylon Revisited" (1931, short story), 76–8, 88, 200, 264, 268
Bacall, Lauren, 7
Backus, Jim, 51
*Bad Day at Black Rock* (1955, film), 65
*Bad Seed, The* (1956, film), 115
BAFTA Awards, 63, 153–4, 163
Balin, Mireille, 80
*Bamboo Prison, The* (1954, film), 70
Barbados, 48
Barrymore, Ethyl, 51
Barrymore, Lionel, 7, 26
Basehart, Richard, 144
Basso, Hamilton, 24, 29, 261
*Battle Circus* (1953, film), 14, 63–74
*Battle Cry* (1953, novel), 1, 215, 228
Battle of San Pietro (1943), 9
Bazin, André, 108, 197, 250, 259, 261
*Becket* (1964, film), 205
Begley, Ed, 184, 189
Bellamy, Ralph, 109–11
Benshoff, Harry, 191, 197–8, 261, 265
Benson-Allott, Caetlin, 235, 238–9, 244–5, 261
Berenger, Tom, 232
Berg, Peter, 242
Bergman, Alan & Marilyn, 89
Berman, Pandro S., 157–9, 208
Berneis, Peter, 156, 165
Bernstein, Matthew H., 12, 14–30, 56, 60
Bernstein, Walter, 24, 29, 261
Best Screenplay (Oscar), 63
*Best Years of Our Lives, The* (1946, film), 16
*Better Angels, The* (1979, novel), 247, 252–3, 267
*Beyond a Reasonable Doubt* (1956, film), 62

*Bhowani Junction* (1956, film), 116
*Bicycle Thieves* (1948, film), 250, 260
*Big Knife, The* (1955, film), 157, 165
*Big Lebowski, The* (1998, film), 254, 260
*Big Lift, The* (1950, film), 251, 260
*Big Tip Off, The* (1955, film), 62
*Big Town After Dark* (1947, film), 62
*Bite the Bullet* (1975, film), 3, 258–9
*Blackboard Jungle, The*
  (1954, novel), 90–1, 102, 105–6, 138, 208, 266
  (1955, film), 3–4, 36, 41–3, 46, 72, 90–107, 138, 158–9, 164–5, 259, 265–7, 269–70
Black Panthers (party), 257
Blackstone (Virginia), 250
*Black Sunday* (1975, novel), 253
*Blade Runner* (1982, film), 234
Blake, Robert, 222, 226–8
*Blonde Ice* (1948, film), 62
Bloom, Claire, 143
*Blue Dahlia, The* (1946, film), 16
*Blue Gardenia, The* (1953, film), 62
Bluestone, George, 210, 213, 262
*Blue Velvet* (1986, film), 234
"B" Movies/Noir, 45, 49
Bodnar, John, 72, 74, 262
Bogart, Humphrey, 2, 7, 14, 26, 46, 51–3, 55–7, 61, 67–8, 71, 74, 80, 86, 263, 270
Bogdanovich, Peter, 212, 214, 262
Boggs, Johnny D., 121, 262
Bolt, Robert, 209
*Bonjour, Tristesse* (1958, film), 45
*Boomerang!* (1947, film), 57
Boozer, Jack, 5, 12, 262
Borgnine, Ernest, 124, 131–2
Borneo (Island), 64
*Boxoffice* (Publication), 13, 74, 122, 263–4, 266, 269
Brando, Marlon, 101

274 INDEX

Bray, William Robert, 155, 163, 190, 197–8, 268
*Brazil* (1985, film), 255, 260
Breen Office (Censors), 18, 29, 69, 158
*Brick Foxhole, The* (1945, book), 1, 7, 14–30, 35, 43, 56, 64–5, 208, 262, 268
*Bridge on the River Kwai, The* (1957, film), 208
*Bridges at Toko-Ri, The* (1955, film), 7
Bridges, Lloyd, 86
Brill, Lesley, 119, 122, 262
British Empire, 210–11
British New Wave, 4
British West Indies, 48
Brodie, Steve, 19
Bronfen, Elisabeth, 123–37
Brontë, Emily, 2
*Brothers Karamazov, The* (1958, film), 4, 107, 116, 138–52, 163, 165, 181–2, 200, 208, 210, 236, 259, 264
Browning, Todd, 191
*Brown v. Board of Education* (1954, Supreme Court case), 108
*Brute Force* (1947, film), 2, 14, 27, 52, 208
Brynner, Yul, 143
Budapest (Hungary), 251
Buford, Kate, 167, 181, 262
Bugis (People), 210
Burnett, W. R., 2
Burnham, Bo, 244

Cagle, Chris, 3, 12, 61, 262
Cain, James M., 6–7, 12, 21, 262
Cairo (Egypt), 251
*Call Northside 777* (1947, film), 56
Cambodia, 204–5, 250
Canada, 118

Canby, Vincent, 240, 245–6, 258, 262
Canetti, Elias, 119–20, 122, 262
Cannes Film Festival, 63, 240
Capote, Truman, 2, 138, 165, 215–30, 252, 262–4, 266–7, 269–70
*Captive City* (1952, film), 49
Cardinale, Claudia, 109–10, 117
Carroll, Nathan, 238
Carroll, Noël, 108, 121, 249, 258, 262
Carson, Jack, 154
Cartmell, Deborah, 252, 259, 262–3
*Casablanca* (1942, film), 80, 86
Cash, Rosalind, 257–8
*Cat Ballou* (1965, film), 117
*Catered Affair, The* (1965, film), 4, 115, 123–37
*Cat on a Hot Tin Roof* (1958, film), 2, 4, 41, 43, 72, 116, 139, 152–65, 191, 197, 200, 208, 259, 261, 263, 268, 271
Cavell, Stanley, 127–30, 135, 137, 263
Celli, Teresa, 36
*Certain Smile, A* (1958, film), 45
Champlin, Charles, 84
Chandler, James, 184
Chandler, Raymond, 5–7, 12, 56, 184, 265
Chaney, Lon, 184
Charisse, Cyd, 115
Chayefsky, Paddy, 2, 131
Chekhov, Anton, 210
Chicago (Illinois), 18, 131, 137, 195, 197, 232, 250, 263–5, 267–8, 270
*Chicago Deadline* (1949, film), 62
China, 69, 205, 210
*Chinatown* (1974, film), 234
Christ, Jesus, 139–42, 145–6, 150–1, 172, 193–4, 198, 271
Christie, Audrey, 51
*Cineaste* (Publication), 89, 233–4, 245, 264, 267

INDEX   275

Cinecittà Studios, 251
CinemaScope (Process), 116, 183–6, 188–9, 193–4, 197–8, 261
*Citizen Kane* (1941, film), 49, 60, 155, 165, 184, 225
Clare, Myrtle, 217
Clayton, Jack, 4
Clift, Montgomery, 156
*Closing Time: The True Story of the "Goodbar" Murder* (1977, book), 231–2, 244, 264
Clutter Family (Murders), 215–17, 220, 222–3, 229–30
Cobb, Lee J., 142
*Cobra Woman* (1943, film), 208
Cockburn, Claude, 2
Cody, William "Buffalo Bill," 114
Coen, Joel & Ethan, 254, 260
Cold War, 60–1, 65–7, 69, 72–4, 105, 192, 218, 225, 253, 263–5, 268, 270
Colombia (Country), 32
Colpitts, George, 113, 121, 263
Columbia Pictures, 117–18, 122, 171, 208, 214, 259–61
Committee on Organized Crime (US Senate), 47, 270
Commodore (New York Hotel), 167
Concourse Plaza Hotel (New York), 131–2
Condon, Richard, 2
Connery, Sean, 246, 257
Conrad, Joseph, 2, 41, 43, 138, 165, 200–7, 209–14, 263–4, 268, 270
Conrad, Robert, 248
Cook, Willis, 118
Cooper, George, 17, 22
Cornell University, 139
Costello, Frank, 46–7, 49–50, 52, 54, 61, 264
Cotton, Joseph, 79

"Crack-Up, The" (1936, essay), 86–7, 89, 264
Crane, Stephen, 2
*Crisis* (1950, film), 1, 27, 31–45, 61, 66, 208, 259
*Crossfire* (1947, film), 14–20, 22–30, 36, 43, 64, 208, 266, 269
*Crowds and Power* (1984, book), 119, 122, 262
Crowther, Bosley, 44, 55, 57, 61, 78–9, 83, 88, 116, 122, 200, 213, 263
*Cruising* (1980, film), 233, 244, 268
Cuba, 7–8, 11
Cullen, Jim, 67, 71, 74, 263
Cumings, Bruce, 65, 74, 263
Custer State Park (South Dakota), 116

*Daily Mail* (publication), 200
*Daily News* (publication), 212
Dakota, North and South, 113–14, 116
Daniel, Douglass K., 12, 27, 42–3, 61, 65, 73–4, 77, 88–90, 97, 105–6, 137, 151, 157–8, 161, 163–4, 187, 196–7, 199, 213, 218, 229, 244–6, 250, 253, 258–9, 263, 269
Darin, Bobby, 86
Davis, Bette, 26, 123, 126, 130–1, 136–7
Dawson, Catherine, 204, 211, 213, 263
*Deadline—U.S.A.* (1952, film), 3–4, 14, 44–62, 66, 208, 259, 263–4
*Dead Reckoning* (1947, film), 53
Dean, James, 101
*Death of a Salesman* (1949, play), 179, 182, 267
*Deceit, Desire and the Novel* (1965, book), 140, 151, 265
de Cordoba, Pedro, 37
Dees, Michael, 87
Defense Department (U.S.), 69
Delano, Jack, 216, 223, 228, 263

*Delta Force* (1986, film), 253, 260
DeMille, Cecil B., 166, 171
Denmark, 210
Dent, Sara, 121, 264
Denver (Colorado), 118, 250
de Rochemont, Louis, 52, 56–7
Derrida, Jacques, 163, 165, 266
Descher, Sandy, 82
De Sica, Vittorio, 250, 260
de Stefano, Anthony M., 49, 61
Dickens, Charles, 210
Director's Guild of America, 64
Dmytryk, Edward, 14–15, 24, 28, 36, 43, 64
*Doctrine and Discipline of Divorce* (1643, book), 128
Doherty, Thomas, 61, 264
Dolenz, George, 81
*Dollars$* (1971, film), 45
*Doll's House, A* (1879, play), 128
"Do Not Go Gentle Into That Good Night" (1951, poem), 162
Donovan, Stephen, 211, 214, 264
Dostoevsky, Fyodor, 2, 138–40, 143, 146–7, 149–51, 165, 236, 264
*Double Indemnity*
  (1943, novel), 6, 262
  (1944, film), 5–6, 12, 267
*Dracula* (1931, film), 191
Drake, Geoffrey, 208
Dreiser, Theodore, 2, 228
*Dr. No* (1962, film), 117
*Dr. Strangelove* (1964, film), 253, 260
*Dr. Zhivago* (1965, film), 118, 142
Duchamp, Marcel, 6
*Duck Soup* (1933, film), 255, 260
Dunning, John D., 79
Dutch East Indies, 64

Eastman Tri-X Panchromatic Negative (film stock), 95–6
Ebert, Roger, 161, 164, 264

Eiffel Tower, 79–80
Eisenhower, Dwight, 73
Eisenstein, Sergei, 221–2
*Election* (1999, film), 239
Elliott, Kamilla, 12, 264
Elizabeth II, 200
*Elmer Gantry* (1960, film), 4, 29, 41–3, 107, 163, 165, 167, 171, 175, 177, 179, 181–2, 188, 208, 259, 267
El Paso (Texas), 250
Emery, Gilbert, 2
Emporia (Kansas), 223, 263
England, 114, 210
Epstein, Julius J. and Philip G., 78, 89, 165
Epstein, William H., 183–99
Erickson, Glenn, 54, 61, 264
Erkkila, Betsy, 234, 245, 264
Ermey, R. Lee, 66
Europe, 7, 9, 11, 27, 45, 69, 77, 79, 84, 114, 190, 203–4, 210–11, 236, 251
Evans, Gene, 69
Evans, Walter, 216

Fairfield County (Ohio), 48
Farm Security Administration (FSA), 215–18, 222–3, 228–9, 264, 267
Farrow, John, 157, 165
*Fastest Gun Alive* (1956, film), 116
*Fat City* (1972, film), 3
*Father of the Bride* (1950, film), 85
Feist, Felix E., 60
Fellini, Federico, 166, 198
*Feminine Mystique, The* (1963, book), 75
*Feminist Media Studies* (publication), 238
Femme Fatale (trope), 10, 241, 243–5, 265

Fennell, Emerald, 243
Ferguson, Robert S., 118
Ferrer, José, 31, 34, 44, 61, 66
*Fever Pitch* (1986, film), 3
Fields, Kathy, 85
*film noir* (genre), 7, 10–11, 15, 28, 53, 58, 221, 224, 241–2, 266, 268–9
*Film Quarterly* (publication), 197, 233, 235, 244, 261, 265
Finney County (Kansas), 224
Fiorentino, Linda, 242
*Fistful of Dollars, A* (1964, film), 117
Fitzgerald, F Scott, 2, 75–9, 81–4, 86–9, 166, 200, 263–4, 268
*Five Fingers* (1952, film), 48, 52–3
*Fixed Bayonets!* (1951, film), 69–70
*Flame and the Flesh* (1954, film), 250
Fleischer, Richard, 183
Fleming, Ian, 117
Fonda, Jane, 242
Forbes, Bryan, 4
*Forbidden Planet* (1956, film), 116
Ford, Glenn, 41, 93–7, 100, 102–5
Forester, C. S., 2
*Forever Darling* (1956, film), 116
Forsythe, John, 85, 89
*Fort Massacre* (1958, film), 108
Fosburgh, Lacey, 231–2, 238, 244, 264
Foucault, Marcel, 191
Fowles, John, 2
France, 77, 209–10, 250
Francis, Freddie, 208
Frank, Joseph, 139–40, 146, 151, 264
Frankenheimer, John, 3, 174
*Frankenstein*
 (1818, novel), 194, 198, 266, 269
 (1931, film), 191, 194, 198
*Freaks* (1932, film), 191
Freed, Arthur, 1
Freud, Sigmund, 77–8, 137, 146, 155, 264

Friedan, Betty, 75
*Friendly Persuasion* (1956, film), 115–16
*From Here to Eternity* (1951, novel), 1, 17
*From Russia With Love* (1963, film), 117
Fulkerson, Randal, 121, 265
Fuller, Samuel, 69–70, 74, 271
*Full Metal Jacket* (1987, film), 66, 74

Gabel, Martin, 46–7, 49–50
Gabin, Jean, 80
Gabor, Eva, 82
Galbraith, Stuart, 246–7, 253, 258, 265
Garden City (Kansas), 217–19, 223–4
Gardner, Leonard, 2
Garfield, John, 51, 270
Garrett, George, 219, 229, 265
Gary (Indiana), 47
Gary, Romain, 2
*Gentleman's Agreement* (1947, film), 15, 48
Gere, Richard, 235–8
Germany, 14, 209–10, 250
*Giant* (1956, film), 115
Gibbons, Cedric, 251
Giglio, Ernest, 69, 74, 265
Gilliam, Terry, 255, 260
Girard, René, 140, 144–6, 148, 151, 265
Giroux, Henry A., 235, 244–5, 265
Gizzard, George, 247, 249
Glasgow, Ellen, 2
*Glass Alibi, The* (1946, film), 62
*Glass Menagerie, The* (1944, play), 156, 165
Glenville, Peter, 157, 165
*Godfather, The* (1972, film), 237–8
*Godfather Part II, The* (1974, film), 237

Goethe, Johann Wolfgang von, 20, 139
Golan, Menahem, 253, 260
Golden Globes, 63, 163
*Goldfinger* (1964, film), 117
Golub, Adam, 105, 265
Gómez, Vicente, 36
Goodman, Milt, 118
*Good War in American Memory, The* (2010, book), 72, 74, 262
Goudsouzian, Aram, 101, 105–6, 265
Graham, Billy, 167–9
Granger, Stewart, 44, 109, 116, 251, 265
Grant, Cary, 1, 31–2, 34, 44–5, 61, 66, 208
*Grapes of Wrath, The* (1939, novel), 215
Great Depression, 127, 130, 216–18, 222
*Great Escape, The* (1963, film), 117
*Greatest Show on Earth, The* (1952, film), 166
Greene, Graham, 44
Grenville, George, 85
Griffith, D. W., 221
Grimes, William, 27, 198, 265
Grossman, Julie, 194, 198, 231–45, 265
Guillory, John, 4
*Guilty of Treason* (1950, film), 60
*Guns of Navarone, The* (1961, film), 117
*Guy Named Joe, A* (1943, film), 26

Haley, Bill & the Comets, 91
Hall, Conrad, 118, 222, 226–7
Hallam, Lindsay, 240, 245, 265
Hammett, Dashiell, 2, 21
Hankte, Steffen, 193
Hanner, John, 113, 121, 265
*Happy Ending, The* (1969, film), 75–89, 259

Harlan, Russell, 95
Harris, Thomas, 253
*Harrison's Reports* (publication), 161, 164, 263
Haskell, Molly, 197, 229, 236–42, 245, 264–5
Hasso, Signe, 33
Hathaway, Henry, 56, 58
Hawkins, Jack, 203, 209
Hawks, Howard, 16, 197, 62
Hearst, William Randolph, 49, 58, 60, 271
*Heart of Darkness* (1898, novella), 201, 211–12
Hellinger, Mark, 2, 14, 52–3
Hellman, Lillian, 2
Hemingway, Ernest, 21, 208
*Henry V* (1599, play), 92–4
*High Society* (1956, film), 115
Hiney, Tom, 12, 265
Hippocratic Oath, 34, 37
Hitchcock, Alfred, 3, 44, 83, 119, 181, 209, 269
Hoberman, J., 69, 74, 265
Hoffman, Irving, 13, 265
Holcomb (Kansas), 215, 217–18, 220, 222–3, 250
Holiday, Billie, 10
*Hollywood Reporter, The* (publication), 7, 13, 122, 265–6
Holocaust, The, 256
Horning, William A., 158
*Hot Summer Night* (1957, film), 62
House Committee on Un-American Activities (H.U.A.C.), 65, 69, 167
*House on 92nd Street, The* (1945, film), 51
Howard, Leslie, 85
Howard, Roy, 59
Hoyt, John, 93
Hunter, Evan, 2, 90–106, 138, 165, 266

Hunter, Kim, 51–2
*Hustler* (publication), 239
Huston, John, 2–4, 7–8, 12–14, 66, 208, 266–7

Ibsen, Henrik, 128
*I'll Cry Tomorrow* (1956, film), 115–16
*I Married a Monster from Outer Space* (1958, film), 192
*In Cold Blood* (1967, film), 4, 27, 72, 152, 165, 215–30, 250, 252, 259, 262–3, 265, 269–70
*Invasion of the Body Snatchers* (1956, film), 192
*Invitation to the Dance* (1956, film), 115
Irish Catholics, 256
Isenberg, Andrew C., 121, 266
*Island in the Sun* (1957, film), 48
Italy, 209–10, 250–1
Itami, Ichizo, 204, 207
Ives, Burl, 152, 154–5, 164, 263
Ivory, James, 251, 260

"Jack and the Beanstalk" (1734, story), 99–100
Jackson, Peter, 252, 260
Jackter, Rube & Norman, 118
James Bond (franchise), 117–18, 246
Japan, 118, 210
Japanese Americans, 65
Jarre, Maurice, 118
*Jaws* (1975, film), 64
Jenkins, Jennifer L., 215–30
Johns Hopkins University, 33, 74, 151, 213, 262, 265
Jones, James, 1, 17
Jones, Quincy, 221–2
Jones, Shirley, 86, 179, 208
Jones, Tom, 180
Joyce, James, 2
Juergens, George, 57, 59, 61–2, 266

Kael, Pauline, 4, 161, 164, 266
Kahn, Richard, 118
Kandinsky, Wassily, 83
Kansas, 215–18, 220–3, 226, 228, 250, 252, 263–4
Kansas Bureau of Investigation (KBI), 221, 223–4
Kansas City (Missouri), 47, 118, 216, 220, 222, 228
Kansas State Penitentiary, 218
Karloff, Boris, 191
Karlson, Phil, 49
Kaszner, Kurt, 79
Kaufman, Irving, 65
Kaufman, Millard, 65–6
Kazan, Elia, 3, 48, 51, 57, 154, 156–7, 159, 164–5, 184, 187, 189, 191, 196–7, 268, 271
Keaton, Diane, 75, 231–3, 236–41
Keats, John, 41–2, 266
Kefauver, Estes, 47, 49, 51–2, 61, 264, 266, 268, 270
Keith, Robert, 68
Kelly, Gene, 115
Kelly, Grace, 83, 156
Kennedy, John F., 72
Kenya, 250
*Key Largo*
  (1939, play), 5, 7, 261
  (1948, film), 2, 5, 7–10, 13–14, 27, 45, 51, 65, 208, 265–6
Kidwell, Susan, 217, 223
Kierkegaard, Søren., 75, 86–9, 266
Kiley, Richard, 51, 91, 236
*Killers, The* (1946, film), 2, 14, 45, 52–3, 208, 213, 267
King, Wesley, 12, 267
*King Kong vs. Godzilla* (1962, film), 186
Kipling, Rudyard, 2
Klapisch, Cédric, 80, 89, 267
*Klute* (1971, film), 234, 242
Knight, Shirley, 190

280   INDEX

*Knock on any Door* (1949, film), 53
Kolker, Robert, 71
Korean War, 63, 66
Krasner, Milton, 55
*Kremlin Letter, The* (1973, film), 3
Krüger, Hardy, 247
Kubrick, Stanley, 66–7, 74, 110, 260

Lahr, John, 153, 163–4, 187, 196, 266
LaMotta, Jake, 242
Lancaster, Burt, 109, 111, 117, 167–8, 170, 172–4, 176–81, 208, 262
Langdon, Jennifer, 19, 21, 26–30, 266
Lange, Dorothea, 216
Lansing (Kansas), 218
Lardner, Ring Jr., 63
*Last Hunt, The*
  (1954, novel), 107, 111, 115, 121
  (1956, film), 3, 107–22, 263, 265–6
*Last Seduction, The* (1994, film), 242
*Last Time I Saw Paris, The* (1954, film), 4, 75–89, 200, 250, 259, 261, 270
Las Vegas (Nevada), 115, 220, 223, 250
Latin America, 39, 44, 66–7, 69–70, 72–4, 263, 271
Lawrence, D. H., 186, 195, 266
*Lawrence of Arabia* (1962, film), 117–18, 205, 208–9
Lawrence, T. E., 209–10
League of Nations, 56
Lean, David, 142, 209
Lee, Russell, 216, 228–9, 267
Lee, Sheryl, 240–1
Legion of Decency, 164, 181, 198
Legrand, Michel, 89
Leitch, Thomas, 12, 198, 200–14, 219, 228–9, 267, 269
Le May, Alan, 2
Le Mure, Pierre, 2

Lenihan, John H., 108, 121, 267
Lester, Richard, 4
Lev, Peter, 108, 120, 197, 267
Levene, Sam, 17–18
Levi, Dahlia, 203, 206
Levinson, Barry, 253, 260
Lewis, Sinclair, 2, 21, 138, 165, 167–72, 177–82, 267
Lewton, Val, 191
L.H.O.O.Q. (1919, postcard), 6
Library of Congress, 216, 228–9, 263–4
*LIFE* (Publication), 205, 215, 217–19, 223, 228–9, 266, 270
*Life and Times of Judge Roy Bean, The* (1972, film), 3
*Light in the Piazza* (1962, film), 45
*Light Touch, The* (1951, film), 3, 44, 250–1, 259
Lindsay, John, 231
Little, Thomas, 55
Logan, Joshua, 156
*Lone Ranger, The* (TV series), 115, 166
*Looking for Mr. Goodbar* (1977, film), 75, 88, 138, 231–45, 259, 261, 264–5, 267, 269
*Lord Jim* (1965, film), 4, 27, 41–3, 108, 163, 165, 200–14, 250, 260–1, 263, 269
*Lord of the Rings: The Fellowship of the Ring* (2001, film), 252, 260
Los Angeles, 8, 120, 165, 197, 199, 267
*Lost Boundaries* (1949, film), 52
Lott, Milton, 107, 111, 115, 121
Louisville (Kentucky), 118
Love, A. C., 5
Lowry, Malcolm, 2
Luciano, Lucky, 49
Lugosi, Bela, 191
Lumet, Sidney, 3–4, 197, 260

*Lust for Life* (1956, film), 115
Lynch, David, 240, 245, 267

MacArthur, Douglas, 73
MacMurray, Fred, 6
McCarry, Charles, 247, 252–3, 267
McCarthy, Joseph, 61, 65, 264
McCleary, Urie, 158
McCoy, Bath, 105, 267
McFarland, Douglas, 12, 138–51, 267
McGilligan, Patrick, 28–9, 171, 181–2, 198–9, 267
MacGuffin (trope), 242
McKenzie, Joyce, 51
*Mackintosh Man, The* (1973, film), 3
McPherson, Aimee Semple, 167, 169
McRoy, Jay, 192, 198, 265
MacShane, Frank, 12, 265
McSorleys Club (New York), 232
Mahler, Gustav, 142
Mailer, Norman, 1, 215, 228
Malaysia, 210
Malibu (California), 250
*Maltese Falcon, The* (1941, film), 3
*Manchurian Candidate, The* (1962, film), 70
*Man for All Seasons, A* (1966, film), 117
Mankiewicz, Joseph L., 45, 48, 156–7
*Man Who Shot Liberty Valance, The* (1962, film), 110
Marine Corps (USA), 15
*Marty* (1955, film), 131–2
Marvin, Lee, 109, 111, 117
Marx Brothers, The, 255
*M\*A\*S\*H* (1970, film), 63–4, 67, 71, 74
"MASH 66" (story), 66
Mason, James, 52, 184, 200, 203
Mayer, Louis B., 1, 44–6, 187
*Meet Me in Las Vegas* (1956, film), 115

Melville, Herman, 2
Merleau-Ponty, Maurice, 84, 89, 267
Metrocolor (Process), 158
Mexico, 111, 221
Meyers, Jeffrey, 12, 267
M-G-M (Metro-Goldwyn-Mayer), 1, 14, 32, 43–4, 46, 51, 66, 78, 89, 115–16, 122, 138, 141, 156–8, 161, 164, 188, 191–2, 236, 251, 259–60, 267
Miami (Florida), 217, 253
*Miami Herald* (publication), 187
Middle East, 256–7
Mielziner, Jo, 189, 196–7, 265, 267, 270
Miklitsch, Robert, 10, 13, 267
Milestone, Lewis, 70
Miller, Arthur, 2, 179, 182, 267
Mill Pond Theatre (New York), 208
Milton, John, 128–9, 139
Mindszenty, József, 60
Minnelli, Vincente, 251, 260
Mitchell, Lee Clark, 109, 121, 267
"Moanin' Low" (song), 10
*Monsters in the Closet: Homosexuality and the Horror Film* (1997, book), 191, 197, 261
Moody, Ron, 247
Moore, Gene M., 204, 211, 213, 263, 268, 270
Moore, Roger, 82
Moore, William Howard, 47, 61, 268
Moran, Erin, 86
Moreno, Antonio, 37
Morrow, Vic, 96
*Movie* (Publication), 188, 196, 262
*Mr. Germeroth, Sheridan County, KS* (1939, image), 216, 229
*Mule for the Marquesa, A* (1964, novel), 107, 109
Mulligan, Carey, 244

Murrow, Edward R., 246
*Muses Are Heard, The* (1956, book), 228
Myrtil, Odette, 79

Nabokov, Vladimir, 139, 143, 151, 268
Naipaul, V. S., 39, 42, 268
*Naked and the Dead, The* (1948, novel), 1, 228
*Naked City, The* (1948, film), 53
Naremore, James, 18, 20, 28, 268
*Nassau Literary Magazine* (publication), 76
National Catholic Office for Motion Pictures, The, 117
National League of Cities, 48
NBC (radio network), 5, 76–7, 208
Neale, Steve, 254, 259, 268
Neimi, Robert, 63–4
*Network* (1976, film), 253, 260
*Never Say Never Again* (1983, film), 257, 260
Newman, Paul, 152–6, 158, 163–4, 184, 191, 193, 263
*New Republic, The* (publication), 29, 197, 261, 264
"Newspaper Story" (provisional Title), 51
New York City, 46–7, 58, 208, 231, 235, 248, 250
*New York Daily News, The* (Publication), 54
*New Yorker, The* (publication), 24, 29, 153, 161, 163, 215, 220, 261, 271
*New York Journal* (publication), 60
New York Public Library, 219, 229, 262
*New York Times* (publication), 16, 21, 27, 29, 61, 88, 116, 122, 158–9, 164, 198, 200, 208, 213, 216, 228, 245, 258, 262–3, 265–6, 268–9
*New York World* (publication), 56, 59, 61, 266

Niebuhr, Reinhold, 31, 40, 42, 268
Nielsen, Leslie, 247, 249
*Night of the Iguana* (1964, film), 2
Nixon, Richard, 63, 72, 85
Nolan, Lloyd, 109
Normandy (France), 69
North Africa, 246
*North by Northwest* (1959, film), 119
North Manual Trades High School (Bronx), 92
Norton, Dan, 21, 29, 268
*Nostromo* (1904, novel), 211
*Notes from Underground* (1864, novella), 139
"Notes on Camp" (1964, essay), 256, 259, 270
Novarro, Ramon, 32
*Novels into Film* (1956, book), 210, 213, 262
Nowell-Smith, Geoffrey, 234
*Now, Voyager* (1942, film), 130
Nystrom, Derek, 234–5, 243, 245, 268

*O Brother, Where Art Thou?* (2000, film), 254, 260
O'Connor, Flannery, 2
Odets, Clifford, 14, 157, 165
Office of War Information (OWI), 216, 228–9, 264
Okinawa (Japan), 18
Old Testament (Bible), 2
*One Minute to Zero* (1952, film), 70
*One World* (1943, book), 56, 61, 271
"Ontology of the Photographic Image" (1967, essay), 250, 261
*Operation Cicero* (1969, book), 48
Orange Bowl (Miami), 253
O'Rourke, Frank, 2, 107, 121, 268
*Other Paris, The* (2017, book), 80, 89, 269
O'Toole, Peter, 41, 202, 205–6, 213, 263, 270

## INDEX

*Our Miss Brooks* (TV series), 115–16
*Outcast of the Islands, An* (1951, film), 209, 213, 263
*Out of the Blue* (2006, film), 238
Overton (Nevada), 250

Page, Geraldine, 184–5, 195
Paget, Debra, 110
Palance, Jack, 109
Pall, Gloria, 142
*Pall Mall Gazette* (publication), 212, 214, 261
Palmer, R. Barton, 1–13, 27, 44–62, 155, 163, 190, 197–8, 213, 233, 244, 251, 259, 267–8
Paramount Pictures, 171, 200, 208, 231, 241, 259–60
Parker, Brian, 156, 162–5, 197, 268
Pastoureau, Michel, 83–4, 89, 268
*Paths of Glory* (1957, film), 74
Patrick, George, 55
*Patton* (1970, film), 63
Payne, Alexander, 239
Paxton, John 14–15, 23–4, 29, 43
Peck, Gregory, 48, 51
Peckinpah, Sam, 3, 108
Pentecostal Ministry, 167, 170
*Pépé le Moko* (1937, film), 80
Perelman, S. J., 157, 165
Perlstein, Daniel, 105, 269
Perón, Juan and Eva, 31, 39, 42, 268
Perry, Dennis, 194, 198, 266, 269
*Petrified Forest, The* (1935, play), 95
Pettey, Homer B., 1–13, 17, 25, 27–8, 30, 45, 61, 107–22, 268–9
*Phantom of the Opera, The* (1925, film), 184
*Phenix City Story, The* (1955, film), 49, 62
*Philadelphia Story, The* (1940, film), 115
Phillips, Adam, 88–9, 269

Phillips, Gene D., 154, 157, 163–5, 195, 197–8, 269
Phillips, Siân, 205
Phipps, William, 19, 23
*Picturegoer* (publication), 116, 122, 266
Pidgeon, Walter, 81
Pizer, Donald, 221, 229, 269
Poe, James, 43, 157–8, 163, 165
Poitier, Sidney, 101–6, 265, 271
"Politics as a Vocation" (1919, essay), 37, 42
Pomerance, Murray, 166–82, 269
*Pork Chop Hill* (1959, film), 70
Portugal, 210
Postwar Crime Scare, 47
Prescott, Orville, 16, 20–1, 27, 29–30, 269
*Price is Right, The* (TV series), 239
Princeton University, 61, 76, 88–9, 151, 264, 266, 268, 270
*Prisoner of War* (1954, film), 70
*Producer, The* (1951, book), 187, 196, 262
Production Code Administration (PCA), 17, 20, 28, 39, 69, 117, 122, 158, 266
*Professionals, The* (1966, film), 3 4, 107–22, 259–63, 266, 268–70
Prohibition, 7, 46
*Promising Young Woman* (2020, film), 243–4
Pulitzer, Joseph, 49, 56–62, 115, 266
Punke, Michael, 113, 121, 269

Quantico (Virginia), 15, 64
Quinn, Roseann, 231–2, 238

Race Relations, 19, 48, 101–2
*Raiders of the Lost Ark* (1981, film), 257, 260
Rapper, Irving, 156, 165
Rauschenbusch, Walter, 51, 269

Raymond, Paula, 31, 45
RD-DR (film company), 52
*Reader's Digest* (publication), 52, 56
*Rear Window* (1954, film), 83
Redmon, Allen H., 246–60, 269
Reed, Carol, 209
Reed, Donna, 81
Reed, Rex, 84
Reinsch, Paul N., 90, 105, 269
Reisz, Karel, 4
*Remains of the Day* (1993, film), 251, 260
Reynolds, Debbie, 123, 130, 132–3
Richardson, Tony, 4
Rio (Brazil), 251
Ritt, Martin, 3
River Valley Farm (Kansas), 221–3, 250
Roberts, Oral, 166–7, 169, 177
Robinson, Edward G., 6–8, 13, 269
Robson, Mark, 70
"Rock Around the Clock" (1955, song), 91, 98, 105, 269
Roland, Gilbert, 36, 40
*Roman Holiday* (1953, film), 45
Rome (Italy), 251
Rosenberg, Julius & Ethel, 65
*Rose Tattoo, The*
  (1950, play), 156
  (1955, film), 174
Rossen, Robert, 3, 48
Rossner, Judith, 231–2, 235–7, 241, 243, 245, 269
Rothman, Mo, 118
Rouault, Georges, 141
Ruark, Robert, 2, 138
Rupp, Bobby, 217
Russo, Kurt, 121, 269
Ryan, Robert, 15, 18, 109, 111, 117
Rybin, Steven, 90–106

*Sabotage* (1936, film), 209
Sade, Marquise de, 145
Saitō, Tatsuo, 294
Salmi, Albert, 144
Sanders, George, 44, 251
Santa Fe (railroad), 216, 221–2, 228, 263–4
Sante, Luc, 80, 89, 269
Sarris, Andrew, 4, 12, 200, 213, 269
*Scandal Sheet* (1952, film), 62
Scandinavia, 210
*Scarface* (1983, film), 8
Schary, Dory, 15, 46, 66
Schatz, Thomas, 254, 259, 270
Schell, Maria, 144
Schlesinger, John, 4
Scotland, 210
Scott, Ian, 63–74
Scott, Walter M., 55
Scripps-Howard (newspaper chain), 59
*Searchers, The* (1956, film), 108, 115
*Secret Agent, The*
  (1907, novel), 209
  (1953, film), 209
Sedgwick, Eve Kosofsky, 238, 270
Selznick, David O., 203
Senate (U.S.), 47, 49, 61, 266, 270
Senate Resolution 202, 47
Senate Special Committee on Interstate Organized Crime, 47, 270
*Sergeant Rutledge* (1960, film), 110
*Seven Pillars of Wisdom* (1926, book), 209
*Shakedown* (1950, film), 62
Shakespeare, William, 93–4, 139, 147, 149, 172, 210
Shatner, William, 142
Shaw, Irwin, 1
Shear, Barry, 253, 260
Shearer, Norma, 85
Shelley, Mary, 194
Sherwood, Madeleine, 154, 189
Showalter, Max, 167

Show-A-Rama (Kansas City), 118
Shurlock, Geoffrey, 159
Sicily (Italy), 45, 69
*Sidestreet Vignettes* (radio show), 76–7, 88
Sihanouk, Prince Norodom, 205
Silva, Henry, 247
Silverheels, Jay, 166
Simmons, Alan H., 210, 213, 270
Simmons, Jean, 75, 84–5, 167, 170, 187
Simmons, Richard, 253
*Singin' in the Rain* (1952, film), 130
Sioux (Tribe), 110–11, 113–14
Sioux Falls (South Dakota), 116
*Sketch* (Publication), 212, 214, 262
Sklar, Robert, 63, 74, 270
*Smilin' Through* (1931, film), 85
Smith, Judith E., 18, 26, 28–30, 270
Sobchack, Vivian, 26
Social Justice, 32, 35
*Somebody Up There Likes Me* (1956, film), 116
*Something of Value* (1957, film), 116, 138, 200, 208, 250, 260
Sontag, Susan, 256, 259, 270
South America, 31–2, 39, 52
Southern California, 16, 251
*Spartacus* (1960, film), 110
Spradlin, G. D., 248
Stanwyck, Barbara, 6
Stapleton, Maureen, 156
*Star Wars* (1977, film), 64
*Steel Helmet, The* (1951, film), 69–70, 74, 266
Steinbeck, John, 215
Steinhart, Daniel, 250–1, 259, 270
Sterritt, David, 152–65
Stevens, George Jr., 76, 78, 88, 270
Stevens, Warren, 51
Stewart, James, 56, 83
Stewart, Paul, 51, 225
Stoever-Ackerman, Jennifer, 105, 270

*Stranger on the Third Floor* (1940, film), 62
*Streetcar Named Desire, A* (1951, film), 51, 156, 165
Strode, Woody, 108–11, 117
Sturges, John, 65
*Summer and Smoke* (1948, play), 156–7, 165
Sunday, Billy, 167, 169
Super Bowl, 253
Super Panavision 70, 208
Surrender of Germany (1945), 15
Surtees, Robert, 251
Sutherland, Donald, 242
*Sweet Bird of Youth* (1962, film), 2, 183–99, 208, 259–60, 265, 268, 271
*Sweet Smell of Success* (1957, film), 62, 174, 176
*Swell Guy* (1946, film), 2
Switzerland, 210

Tabori, George, 31
*Take the High Ground!* (1953, film), 66–7
Tamblyn, Russ, 109, 116, 122, 265
*Taps at Reveille* (1935, book), 76
*Tarantula* (1955, film), 185, 193
*Taxi Driver* (1976, film), 233
Taylor, Elizabeth, 75, 81, 84–5, 152, 154, 156–7, 160–1, 163–4, 263
Taylor, M. Scott, 114, 121, 270
Taylor, Robert, 109, 112
Taylor, Rod, 123
*Tea and Sympathy* (1956, film), 116
Telotte, J. P., 183, 195, 270
Temple University, 206
Terranova, Dan, 96
Thanksgiving-Christmas Season, 118, 176, 243
*Them* (1954, film), 185, 191
*Theology for the Social Gospel, A* (1917, book), 51, 269

*Third Man, The* (1949, film), 79
Thomas, Dylan, 162, 165, 270
"Three Against Grenada" (unpublished short story), 153
*Three Coins in the Fountain* (1954, film), 45
*Three Judges* (1936, Painting), 141
"Three Players of a Summer Game" (1952, short story), 153, 163, 271
*Thunderball* (1965, film), 117
"To a Friend Whose Work Has Come to Nothing" (1914, poem), 162, 164, 271
*To Catch a Thief* (1955, film), 45
Todd, Mike, 157–8, 164
Tony Awards, 156
Torok, Maria, 163
Tracy, Spencer, 26, 65, 85
Traven, B., 2
*Treasure of the Sierra Madre, The* (1948, film), 3
Trevor, Claire, 10
Trotti, Lamar, 69
Truman, Harry, 73
*Twin Peaks: Fire Walk with Me* (1992, film), 240, 245, 265, 267
*Two Weeks in Another Town* (1962, film), 251, 260

"Uncanny, The" (1919, article), 137, 265
*Under Western Eyes* (1911, novel), 206, 211
United Artists Theatre (Louisville), 118
United Kingdom, 88, 198, 200
Universal Pictures, 1, 64
Uris, Leon, 1
Urry, John, 212, 214, 270
U.S. Air Force, 16, 64

Vachon, John, 216, 228
"Vale of Soul-making" (1819, letter), 41
Van Gogh, Vincent, 83, 115
*Variety* (Publication), 7, 13, 61, 64, 74, 116–18, 122, 164, 198, 261–2, 266–70
Varndell, Daniel, 75–89
*Victory* (1915, novel), 206, 209
Vienna (Austria), 79
Vietnam War, 63, 67, 205, 244–5, 271
*Village Voice* (publication), 213, 240, 245, 267, 269
*Vogue* (publication), 83, 217–18, 228–9, 262
Voltaire (François-Marie Arouet), 145

*Wag the Dog* (1997, film), 253, 260
Wallace, DeWitt, 56
Wallace, Lew, 2
Wallach, Eli, 156, 204
Wallis, Hal, 159
Wallmann, Jeffrey, 108, 120, 270
Warner Bros., 1, 115, 187, 230
Washington D.C., 13, 16–17, 19–21, 24, 30, 73, 261
Watson, Wallace S., 203, 206, 213, 270
Waugh, Alec, 48
Wear, Mike, 118, 122, 270
Weber, Max, 37, 42, 270
Weld, Tuesday, 233
Welles, Orson, 49, 60, 155, 165, 212, 214, 260
Whale, James, 191
"What are You Doing the Rest of Your Life" (song), 87
Wheeler, Lyle, 55
Whelehan, Imelda, 252, 259, 263
*Whistle at Eaton Falls, The* (1951, film), 52
White, Edmund, 187, 196, 264, 271

Widmark, Richard, 51, 66
Wilcox, Herbert, 209
*Wild Bunch, The* (1969, film), 108
Wilder, Billy, 4, 6, 57–8, 61, 263
*Wild in the Streets* (1968, film), 253, 260
Wilkie, Wendell, 56
Williams, Tennessee, 2, 138–9, 149, 151–65, 183–99, 210, 261–2, 264, 266–71
Williams, Tony, 69, 74, 271
Willis, Sharon, 101–2, 105–6, 271
*Wilson* (1944, film), 56, 61
Wilson, Scott, 222, 225
Wilson, Woodrow, 56
Wise, Robert, 3, 49
Wolfe, Thomas, 82
*Woman of the Year* (1942, film), 135
*Woman on the Run* (1950, film), 62
Wood, Robin, 191, 232–3, 239, 241–5, 271
Woolfolk, Alan, 31–43, 45

*World-Telegram* (Publication), 59
World Trade Center (New York), 248
World War II (WWII), 1, 7, 9, 17–18, 22, 27, 29, 31, 41, 56, 64, 68–70, 72–4, 80, 130, 188, 251, 264
WPIX 11 (TV station), 47
Wright, Richard, 21, 29, 271
*Wrong is Right* (1982, film), 3, 246–60, 262, 265
Wyler, William, 2, 4
Wynn, Keenan, 70

Yacowar, Maurice, 160, 164, 271
Yeats, William Butler, 162, 164, 271
*You Can't Go Home Again* (1940, novel), 82
Young, Robert, 15, 23
*Young Lions, The* (1948, novel), 1

Zinnemann, Fred, 4
Žižek, Slavoj, 194, 198, 271